SWORD OF SAN JACINTO

Sam Houston

SWORD
OF
SAN JACINTO

A Life of
Sam Houston

MARSHALL DE BRUHL

RANDOM HOUSE
NEW YORK

*Frontispiece drawing by Tom Lea. Collection of Mrs. Joyce
Pate-Capper, Fort Worth, Texas.
Photographic credits appear on page 425.*

Library of Congress Cataloging-in-Publication Data

De Bruhl, Marshall.
Sword of San Jacinto: a life of Sam Houston / Marshall De Bruhl.
p.   cm.
ISBN 0-394-57623-3
1. Houston, Sam, 1793–1863. 2. Governors—Texas—Biography.
3. Legislators—United States—Biography. 4. United States.
Congress. Senate—Biography. I. Title.
F390.H84D4 1993
976.4′04′092—dc20   92-50513

Manufactured in the United States of America

24689753

First Edition

Book design by Carole Lowenstein

For

Gloria Jones

Deane De Bruhl Blankenship

Liz Carpenter

I have sought not to live in vain.
SAM HOUSTON

Contents

Author's Note

"MY LIFE AND HISTORY are public property," said Sam Houston in his sixty-eighth year, "and it is the historian's privilege to record the good as well as the evil I have done." My own study of the man has revealed quite a bit of good but no evil, at least by the standards of the twentieth century, a time that has produced some truly wicked men.

There was some bad, of course. After all, Houston lived through the most tumultuous time in the nation's history and in some of the most dangerous places in America. So early on he had to learn to defend himself. But chiefly he was a defender of others, in the great populist tradition of his cherished idol and mentor, Andrew Jackson.

Houston was an authentic American hero. Wounded in the War of 1812 and the Texas revolution. Congressman. Governor of two states, Tennessee and Texas. Ambassador from the Cherokee Nation. United States senator. Commander-in-chief of the Texan army. Twice president of the Republic of Texas.

And his great victory at the Battle of San Jacinto not only freed Texas from Mexico but added all or part of six states to the United States.

He was one of the first truly public figures in America. From his first term as a congressman from Tennessee, beginning in 1823, until he was deposed from the governorship of Texas in 1861, he was constantly in the news. His protestations to the contrary, he clearly enjoyed the attention.

An admirer remarked that two types of people were drawn to Sam Houston—artists and women. She might also have added biographers, who, in dozens of books, beginning in the 1840s, have captured him with varying degrees of success and honesty.

"As I have been of the millions, and am yet one of them, a biography will be regarded by me with particular interest," said Sam Houston, in a remark that could be seen as either a threat or as encouragement to a biographer. I chose the latter interpretation and embarked on a five-year journey of exploration into the life and mind of another person.

"If my history is read, posterity will judge of my actions fairly, I have no doubt," he also said. He might just as well have said, "fairly—and with admiration." The hero, the legend, and the man have survived.

Any biographer of Sam Houston owes a very large debt to those who have gone before—in particular, Llerena B. Friend, Amelia W. Williams, and Eugene C. Barker. These are giants on whose shoulders I have stood for a very long time.

These years of biographical research also brought me into direct contact with many people and many places. Happily, all of them were welcoming and all of them were helpful. First in my heart are the Texans, who opened their libraries, archives, collections, museums, and homes to me.

Michael Green, Donaly Brice, Jean Carefoot, and David Richards at the Texas State Archives, Austin, guided me through the nearly five thousand items in the unexplored Andrew Jackson Houston Collection, the primary resource for this book.

Ralph Eldridge and the staff of the Barker Texas History Center in Austin, Robert Schaadt and the staff at the Sam Houston Regional Library and Research Center in Liberty, and Lois Pierce and Richard Rice and the staff at the Sam Houston Memorial Museum at Huntsville were equally generous with their time.

I am also indebted to the public librarians at Lexington, Virginia; Nachitoches, Louisiana; Nacogdoches, Texas; Marion, Alabama; Asheville, North Carolina; and East Hampton, New York; and the staffs at the University of North Carolina at Asheville, Washington and Lee University, the University of Texas at Austin, the New York Public

Library, and the Library of Congress for steering me to the right sources and people.

Visiting the museums, forts, houses, churches, and battle sites associated with Sam Houston made me appreciate anew the many Americans charged with preserving our country's heritage—in particular, The Hermitage, San Jacinto, Horseshoe Bend, Sequoyah Birthplace, Washington on the Brazos, Fort Towson, Fort Gibson, Fort Loudoun, Presidio La Bahia at Goliad, and Fort Jesup.

Especially valuable information was provided by the Reverend Al Hamman of Timber Ridge Presbyterian Church and Terri Gordon of New Providence Presbyterian Church, Virginia; Joseph Benthall, Fort Loudoun, Tennessee; Inez Burns, the Sam Houston Schoolhouse, Maryville, Tennessee; Roy Crawford, Jr., Blount County Courthouse, Tennessee; Chris Morgan and Richard Ryan, Fort Gibson Military Park, Oklahoma; Sam Malone, San Augustine, Texas; Bob William, Jonesborough, Texas; Lee Cage, Nacogdoches, Texas; Sarah C. Spruill, Cheraw, South Carolina; Linda Edwards, the Alamo, San Antonio, Texas; Newton Warzecha, Presidio La Bahia, Goliad, Texas; Larry Spasik, J. R. Martin, and T. J. Zalar, San Jacinto Museum of History; Jim McLaughlin, Muskogee, Oklahoma; and Astrid Knudsen and Allison Scruggs, Marion, Alabama.

Texas hospitality and generosity were exemplifed by Lady Bird Johnson, Governor Ann Richards, Jacqueline Goettsche, Deedie and Rusty Rose, Patsy and Marshall Steves, H. C. Carter, Richard and Colleen Hardin, Elizabeth Crook, Harry Middleton, William and Eleanor Crook, D. J. and Jane Sibley, and the G-BATTS.

Among the many others to whom I am personally grateful are Shana Alexander, Dr. Martin J. Anisman, Jim and P. J. Barrett, Carolyn Blakemore, Loy Blanton, Gregg Cantrell, John Cantrell, Sue Chapasian, Betty Comden, Betty Cox, Mike Cox, Ann Fears Crawford, Jean Houston Daniel, Lamont De Bruhl, Paul Drymalski, Philip Earnshaw, John Ehle, Frank Fritts, John A. Garraty, John Gary, Marilyn Gary, Rachel Ginzburg, Sherri Goodman, Enid Hardwicke, Stephen Harrigan, John and Barbara Hearst, David Huson, Ruben Johnson, Tom Keener, David King, Twyla Kirkpatrick, Adolph Kremel, Tom Lea, Thomas Ricks Lindley, William Marshall, Douglass Y. Nichols, Cody Norman, Jo Parker, James Patton, Billy Porterfield, Jim and Ellen Quackenbush,

George Russell, Desi von Saher, Elaine Smith, Dorle Soria, Elsie Stern, Charles Sullinger, Charles Thompson, Jacqueline Thompson, John Thornton, James A. Williams, Don Zornow. And, of course, Sadie Wright Ingle, without whom nothing.

David Phillips, in North Carolina, was unfailingly helpful and supportive throughout. And Sabra Moore and Nancy Inglis consistently displayed that good judgment, good sense, and unfailing good humor that are characteristic of true daughters of Texas.

My agent, Doe Coover, is firmly in the tradition of the great agent and even greater friend. I owe her much.

Robert Loomis of Random House shares an even greater tradition— the selfless man of letters, the distinguished editor and publisher, who is dedicated to making it right.

Budd Levinson believed in me as a writer and in this book, and his support enabled me to put aside other things and press on. I shall always be grateful.

MARSHALL DE BRUHL
Lake Lure, North Carolina
November 3, 1992

SWORD OF SAN JACINTO

1

The Houstons
of Virginia

O N A CLEAR SPRING MORNING in 1808, at the crossroads hamlet of
Timber Ridge, in the Shenandoah Valley of western Virginia, a
tall, gray-haired woman in her early middle age directed the final preparations for a great journey. The possessions of a lifetime had been gone
through carefully and only the essentials had been loaded on the two
wagons that stood in the yard.

Featherbeds and bedclothes but no bedsteads. A few books but no
bookcase. Iron pots and pans and an oven were loaded on with pewter
knives, forks, and spoons. Heavy but utilitarian plates and bowls and a
few good pieces of china were carefully stowed away, with enough close
to hand for use on the road. Tables and chairs were left behind.

Flour, cornmeal, beans, potatoes, dried fruit, and smoke-cured meat,
enough to last over a dozen people for weeks, had to be made room for,
along with clothing for everyone. Seeds for planting next year's crops.
Axes, saws, and a few tools to repair broken bridles, chains, and wagon
wheels. Guns, powder, and shot. A tinder box and a supply of tobacco.
Needles, thread, scissors. And, of course, the family Bible.

When measured against the available space, even essential items had
seemed frivolous, unnecessary. Mementos, keepsakes, souvenirs had had
to give way. There was little room in the confines of two small covered

wagons for sentiment. But now it was finished. They were ready to go.

When the woman was satisfied that everything was in order, she nodded to a tall, fifteen-year-old boy, who was standing beside the lead wagon. Young Sam Houston put out his hand and helped his mother up the single step onto the wagon. He then jumped up and joined her on the driver's seat. With a snap of the reins and a sharp command to his five-horse team, Sam moved the little wagon train onto the drive leading out of the plantation.

In the wagon bed behind Elizabeth Houston rode her four youngest children, a boy and three girls, crammed in among pots, pans, bed-clothes, and food. Two female slaves and their children and the remain-der of the household goods were aboard the other wagon, which was driven by one of the older boys. The three other sons would alternate driving the wagons and riding alongside on the good saddle horses.

The little caravan descended a gentle slope and passed by the fifty-year-old stone Timber Ridge Presbyterian Church where the family had spent so many Sunday mornings. A few yards farther on was the little school where the boys had learned to read and write. Just past the school they turned left and onto the main road south, toward Lexington.

Elizabeth Houston looked back up the road for the last time at the two-story, white-columned house on the hill. She had lived in that house, which had been built by her husband's grandfather, for twenty-five years. All of her children had been born there. It had been the only home that any of them had known.

Since the 1740s Houstons had worked this land, three generations of them, and she had expected that it would be passed on to her sons. However, carelessness and bad management had robbed them of their patrimony.

Their mother, however, was determined to keep her large family intact and to make new lives for them. So, with her husband dead this past year and the plantation sold, Elizabeth Houston was setting out for Tennessee.

The great valley that runs from north to south down the length of western Virginia remained unknown territory for more than a century after the founding of Jamestown in 1607. The early British colonists and their descendants preferred to remain in the enclaves lying along the Chesapeake Bay and the James, Rappahannock, York, and Potomac rivers. Life was easier there and guaranteed a more direct connection with England.

Another reason for the late movement to the west was the slow pace of immigration from the mother country. There was no need for new land since there were not enough new settlers to force movement away from the coast. Seventeenth-century Englishmen preferred to stay at home. England might have been rife with religious, political, social, and economic problems, but a life abroad in an untamed and savage wilderness was not an attractive alternative.

In addition, the rugged western mountain barrier and the hostile Indian tribes were major deterrents to westward migration in Virginia. Few people were willing to risk violent death to settle beyond the Blue Ridge.

And there was yet another, more subtle barrier—the snobbery of the eastern planter class. They had established their feudal baronies in the Tidewater, and they considered the rest of the colony a barbarous place, not even worth visiting, much less colonizing. Their attitude created sectional rivalries and political enmities that lasted for centuries.

By 1700 Virginia was the most populous of the colonies. This growth was stimulated largely by the cultivation of tobacco, which was made possible by great numbers of slaves and indentured servants. It is estimated that half of all whites who came to colonial America were indentured. They were bound to their masters for periods as long as seven years.

The system of indenture furnished ample cheap labor, but the practice created an abiding social problem—the class conflict between poor whites and the upper classes and poor whites and the blacks. The great landholders, whose empires were based on servitude—for the most part slavery—either ignored the issue or were oblivious to it. Here was born the southern slaveocracy.

Eventually a few farsighted Easterners began to realize the importance of expanding to the west, and the chief advocate was the acting royal governor himself, Alexander Spotswood. In 1716, Spotswood led an entourage—dubbed the Knights of the Golden Horseshoe—westward from Williamsburg. None of the knights was a member of the old landed aristocracy. Spotswood loathed the old guard and during his tenure was involved in endless rows with them.

Ostensibly the journey was to reinforce the British claim to the Northwest Territory and expand the fur trade, which was dominated by the French. The repeated incursions by the French into British territory threatened the British claims to the area. Spotswood supposedly thought that the Great Lakes, on which he hoped to found trading stations, were just on the other side of the Blue Ridge.

An equally important but unstated purpose of the expedition was to survey the area and through the introduction of thousands of new settlers create a buffer between the hostile French and Indians to the west and the eastern settlements. A human shield would be put in place. Whether this was official policy or not, it was perceived to be so by those people who finally settled the frontier and it created a host of new problems.

Spotswood and his train crossed the Blue Ridge at Swift Run Gap and descended into a beautiful valley, the Shenandoah, from the Indian "Daughter of the Stars." Carried away by its beauty, the governor called this fertile and well-watered place the Euphrates. Almost three hundred years later, the Shenandoah Valley retains much of the great beauty that so entranced those early visitors.

After the party returned to Williamsburg, the governor had a small golden horseshoe made for each of the thirteen companions. He had them inscribed with the motto *Sic juvat transcendere montes* ("Thus it is a pleasure to cross the mountains").

In spite of the enthusiasm of Spotswood and the Knights, it was still several years before settlement of the valley began. The Indian troubles continued for decades, but by the late 1720s and early 1730s the tribes were sufficiently pacified for whites to begin to move into the area. Land developers and speculators began campaigns for large land grants and then greater campaigns to entice settlers.

The lure of cheap land has ever proved irresistible and immigrants by the thousands began to move into the valley. The nomadic Indians and the virgin forests gave way to permanent settlers, traders, soldiers, and farms. Forts, trading posts, and villages grew slowly; but within less than fifty years Virginia was settled from the Atlantic to the Alleghenys.

Germans from Pennsylvania arrived in the valley first. They settled chiefly in the northern areas near Harrisonburg and Winchester and kept to themselves. And, as they had in William Penn's colony, they set up their tidy villages and neat farmsteads and got along with the Indians.

Next came the Scotch-Irish, among whom was a John Houston, Gentleman. He was descended from those Scottish Presbyterians who had immigrated from the Scottish lowlands to Northern Ireland, or Ulster, in the early 1600s, during the reign of James I. The Protestant king had confiscated the estates of Roman Catholics in Ulster and had given them to his fellow English Protestants. These new Anglican landlords imported thousands of Scottish Protestants to work on their Ulster estates and in the woolen trade. This was James I's "Great Plantation" of Northern Ireland, an attempt to make it permanently English and permanently Protestant.

Anglicans, Catholics, and Puritans, all had a go at being the only true religion in England in the seventeenth century. Scottish Presbyterians were at first the beneficiaries of the Anglican persecution of Roman Catholics. But they soon became the victims of religious intolerance themselves at the hands of the Church of England.

All ministers were required to use the Anglican Book of Common Prayer. It was a crime for more than four persons to assemble for worship unless they were Anglican. Presbyterian ministers could not go within five miles of a town where they had previously served, and all Presbyterians were forced to pay taxes to support the Church of England. Presbyterians were excluded from military or civil office, and they were forbidden to build churches and their ministers could not perform marriage ceremonies.

However, the economic persecution was probably the most compelling reason for leaving Ulster. The Scotch-Irish Nonconformists managed to keep their religion in spite of the laws. One can, after all, worship privately and secretly. Food and shelter require more public exertions.

An English ban against Irish wool caused widespread unemployment among the Scotch-Irish, but it was the ever-higher rents demanded by British landlords that finally provided the major impetus for wholesale immigration.

Some ten thousand Scotch-Irish arrived in American ports in a single year. At one point ten ships, loaded with immigrants for America, lay at anchor in Belfast harbor waiting for clearance to sail.

John Houston, the great-grandfather of Sam Houston, joined with a group to leave Ulster in 1735. He traced his Scottish ancestry back to the Middle Ages, and Houstons had become followers of John Knox in the late sixteenth century. Family tradition says that Houstons were at Derry when it was besieged by the Catholic forces of James II in 1689. John Houston was born the following year.

No records exist of the Houstons' departure from Ulster, probably from Belfast, or their arrival in America, very likely in Philadelphia. The typical voyage took at least eight weeks and the only certainty is that it could not have been easy, even though the Houstons traveled with friends and fellow members of their Presbyterian congregation in Northern Ireland. It was common for entire church bodies to immigrate together.

John Houston arrived in Pennsylvania with his widowed mother, his wife, Margaret, and six of their seven children. Their eldest son, James, had remained behind in Northern Ireland, where he was studying for the ministry.

Philadelphia was the most cosmopolitan of the British colonial cities and was, after London, the largest English-speaking city in the world. But the Houstons were not city dwellers. They were people of the soil, and land was cheap in William Penn's colony. John Houston's subsequent success as a planter supports the idea that he had had considerable previous experience on the land and that farming was his vocation. So John Houston, like most of the Presbyterians who had been farmers in Scotland and Ulster, did not stay long in Philadelphia but headed for one of the many Scotch-Irish settlements in the countryside.

Houston remained in Pennsylvania until at least 1742. He married off his two daughters, Isabella and Esther, and his son John during the family's stay there. But like many Presbyterians he found the Quakers no more hospitable to their fellow Nonconformists than the Anglicans had been. As one historian observed, "Had the Quakers been more inclined to observe the spirit of their institutions, they would have retained most of this immigration."

Pennsylvania coldness, in particular Quaker standoffishness, no doubt was unpleasant, but it was the promise of even cheaper land farther south that was the major impetus for the Houstons and their fellow Scotch-Irish to move on.

They were particularly attracted to the Borden Grant in Virginia. In

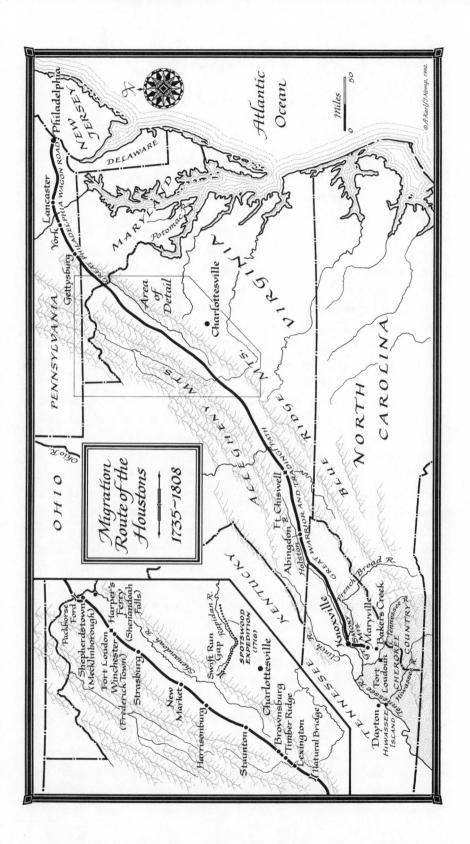

Atlantic Ocean

Miles
0   50

© A. Karl/J. Kemp, 1992.

NEW JERSEY

Philadelphia

DELAWARE

Lancaster

York

MARYLAND

Gettysburg

Potomac

GREAT PHILADELPHIA WAGON ROAD

Charlottesville

PENNSYLVANIA

Area of Detail

VIRGINIA

ALLEGHENY MTS

BLUE RIDGE MTS

NORTH CAROLINA

OHIO R.

OHIO

Migration
Route of the
Houstons

1735–1808

Ft. Chiswell

Abingdon R.

HOLSTON AND TRADING PATH

GREAT WARRIOR AND TRADING PATH

French Broad R.

KENTUCKY

Knoxville

GT. SMOKY MTS

Maryville

Baker's Creek

Packhorse Ford

Shepherdstown (Mecklinborough)

Harper's Ferry (Shenandoah Falls)

Fort Loudon Winchester (Frederick Town)

Strasburg

Shenandoah R.

Swift Run Gap Rapidan R.

SPOTSWOOD EXPEDITION (1716)

Charlottesville

New Market

Harrisonburg

Staunton

Brownsburg

Timber Ridge

Lexington

Natural Bridge

TENNESSEE R.

Clinch R.

Dayton

Fort Loudoun

HIWASSEE ISLAND

Tennessee R.

Hiwassee R.

CHEROKEE COUNTRY

N

1739, Governor William Gooch of Virginia, on behalf of the Crown, granted 92,100 acres of land in Augusta County to Benjamin Borden. The grant was in some ways a hunting license. Borden had no exact idea where his new land was, so the first order of business was to find it and survey it. He could then set about attracting settlers.

Entire congregations of Presbyterians, who had left Northern Ireland together, now packed up and left for the South, where they would be in the majority. Along with hundreds of other Scotch-Irish, John Houston happily left Pennsylvania for Virginia. In 1742, he bought 228 acres from Borden, near present-day Brownsburg.

The Houstons traveled west on the Great Philadelphia Wagon Road, a route as important to American history as the Rhine and the Danube are to European history. It was the primary route to the South and the old Northwest for a century. The great road went first to York, then on to Gettysburg, and then south into Maryland, Virginia, and the Carolinas.

Big game was still common in the lush meadows of the Great Valley of Virginia, and the sight of buffalo or elk astounded these natives of Ulster. But another sight was even more astounding and unsettling—the appearance of Indians on the trail.

The first settlers had arrived in Augusta County only ten years before, in 1732, when homesteads were established two miles south of Staunton. The country was still wild, although most of the valley land was clear. At the close of the hunting season, the Indians, in order to create more grazing land for elk, buffalo, and deer, set fire to the meadows, which ensured a better growth of grass the next year. The trees bordering the great meadows were also burned and thus the forest was pushed back a bit farther each year, until by the 1700s it was confined to the hills and mountains.

The standard portrait of the native Americans as benign ecologists is somewhat marred by this practice. One forester observed that had this seasonal burning continued, in a few centuries Virginia would have become either a prairie or a desert.

Mountain lions, bears, and wolves were common. Travelers complained of being unable to sleep at night because of the howling of the wolves. In fact, the area was so overrun with them that a bounty was offered. In November 1753, 225 wolf heads were brought into the courthouse at Staunton for payment of the bounty. Deer were protected by law.

The Indians themselves were by no means pacified. Not until 1744, under the Treaty of Lancaster, did they agree to move farther west, which presumably made the valley safe for settlement. But Indian grievances were exploited by French provocateurs, and they joined with the French to war against the British and Americans.

Bloody incidents kept the frontier aroused until after the American Revolution and colored the settlers' perceptions of their Indian neighbors for generations. The hostile Indians were fearsome, but the Scotch-Irish were a match for anyone. They had been fighting for a century and a half against the Catholics, the Anglicans, and sometimes even against other Dissenters, Nonconformists, and Puritans.

Henry Adams observed that as "fighters—wherever courage, activity, and force were wanted—they had no equals." He also added that "they had never known discipline, and they were beyond measure jealous of restraint." Adams's patrician views of the Scotch-Irish were no doubt influenced by his famous forebears' tribulations with some of the more resonant examples.

The Scotch-Irish embodied all those traits that have since been identified as American. They were God-fearing—a Protestant God, of course—hard-working, puritanical, quick-tempered, somewhat insular, and, although devoted to education, often anti-intellectual.

John Houston was typical of the breed. His plantation prospered, and he became one of the most honored men in the new settlement. He was a model of civic duty and Presbyterian rectitude. The Houstons attended the Old Providence Church, about five miles from their plantation, but true to the prickly nature of the Nonconformists, friction arose in the Old Providence congregation. Houston and his faction separated from Old Providence and founded the New Providence Church nearer his home. Old Providence Church and New Providence Church are still active congregations.

Presbyterianism as practiced in the eighteenth century was arduous if not downright onerous. Sunday services lasted from ten in the morning until sunset with only a one-hour break for dinner. During communion, meetings could last for days with several ministers participating.

Beyond this rigorous form of worship, other aspects of the religion made it difficult. There was little social life outside the church and the family. The men did get together for hunting parties or to fight the Indians, and they congregated on court days or at the store or the mill. Some of them even patronized the ordinary—the tavern—but whiskey was problematical. It was all right to distill it and sell it for cash, but home consumption was frowned on. Dancing, of course, was forbidden; and even serving hot coffee on Sunday was considered a desecration.

The founding father of the American Houstons thrived on the asceticism of his religion. Perhaps it made him strong not only spiritually but also physically. He died in 1754, at age sixty-four, while clearing land on his plantation. He was killed by a falling tree limb that pierced his skull. John Houston was buried in New Providence Church cemetery, alongside other staunch Presbyterians.

Houston had ensured that his wife, Margaret, would be taken care of for the rest of her life and even designated what part of the house she was to have for her own use. His principal beneficiary, however, was his youngest son, Matthew, who was to take possession of the estate when he came of age.

James Houston, who had stayed behind in Ireland, was dead, but the oldest surviving son, thirty-four-year-old Robert, did not benefit from primogeniture, the custom of the day. In fact, he is not even mentioned in John Houston's will. Robert already owned considerable property on nearby Timber Ridge, no doubt financed by his father, and perhaps the old patriarch thought that was enough. Or Nonconformism might have played a role.

Robert was instrumental in founding yet another Presbyterian congregation at Timber Ridge. The original meeting house was a rough log building that served the congregation as church and fort against Indian attacks until 1756. In that year the congregation moved two miles south to land acquired from Robert Houston.

Although Robert, like his father, was a stalwart of the community, he was clearly not much of a philanthropist, even for his church. He did not donate the acre of land for a church and burial ground. He sold it to the congregation for five pounds. There they built a more substantial stone building, about a hundred yards from Houston's house.

Robert set about adding to his Timber Ridge plantation and consolidating the family position in Virginia. His wife, Mary Davidson, was the daughter of Samuel Davidson, another well-to-do Scotch-Irish planter and, of course, a Presbyterian. Robert's two-story house with white columns and a gallery sat on a hill overlooking his large holdings at Timber Ridge and the Presbyterian church. An impressive house still sits on the foundations of the old house, and the stone Presbyterian church survives, with its cemetery filled with early Scotch-Irish settlers and their descendants.

Robert put together impressive holdings, but he was not as robust as his father. In September 1760, "being sick and weak of body," he made out his will. He died the following spring, leaving a widow and eight children. He was forty-one years old.

Robert Houston's estate included just twelve pounds in cash. His real worth was in his property, and that went to the sons. He left plantations to the two eldest, James and John, but Timber Ridge itself went to his youngest son, Samuel, who was still a boy.

Samuel could have been the favorite or perhaps, equally likely, this was the best guarantee that Robert's wife, Mary, would be looked after. Decrypting a last will and testament is a risky business at best. Whatever Robert Houston's reasoning, and it certainly was not in line with custom, it echoed that of his father.

Court records reveal that a James Houston was something of a delinquent. He was fined for killing a deer, public swearing, and setting the woods on fire. Very probably this was Robert's son James, to whom he left two hundred acres adjoining the Timber Ridge property. (Maybe this was Robert Houston's method of making sure that the family would keep an eye on James.) His brother John was given a mere ninety acres on Colliers Creek, about fifteen miles west.

In line with eighteenth-century tradition Robert's daughters fared less well in the division of the estate. The eldest had already received her share, probably a dowry, so she was left only five shillings. The other four daughters, Anne, Esther, Margaret, and Mary, divided equally two-thirds of Robert's household goods and cash. The other third went to their mother.

Each daughter wound up with goods worth less than ten pounds, the value of their father's best horse. Marriage was therefore their only recourse, but in frontier Virginia marriage was possible even with a small dowry.

While the Houstons were improving their position in Virginia, the long-simmering hostilities between France and England boiled over into the so-called French and Indian War, the American arm of that larger conflict, the Seven Years' War (1756–63).

The war might be said to have begun as early as June 21, 1752, when the French attacked the trading post at Pickawillany in Ohio, but a more commonly accepted beginning is the victory over the French on May 28, 1753, at Great Meadows, in Pennsylvania. Great Britain and France had, of course, been struggling for control of North America since King William's War in 1689.

On July 8, 1755, at Draper's Meadows, now Blacksburg, Virginia, the Shawnees murdered the inhabitants and burned the settlement. The very next day, a British-American force was routed by the French and Indians at Fort Duquesne, in Pennsylvania. After this debacle at the Forks of the Ohio, the British regular army abdicated its responsibility to defend the frontier, and Virginia had to raise a militia to defend itself. Twenty-three-year-old George Washington was appointed commander.

The hit-and-run attacks of the Indians up and down the Shenandoah Valley were impossible to anticipate or defend against. In one famous raid in 1757, only a few miles from Timber Ridge, the Indians carried off women and children. A Mrs. Renick managed to escape, but her small son grew up with the Indians and became a chief of the Miamis. Another woman, a Mrs. Dennis, was a prisoner until she managed to escape in 1763. She slipped away from her captors and floated across the Ohio River on a log. She then struggled over the mountains on foot to her home in Virginia.

Young Washington was a hero even then to his fellow Virginians. Aided immeasurably by his Scotch-Irish militiamen, he vigorously waged war against the Indians. Perhaps the young commander was further inspired to secure the frontier because of his ownership of almost fifteen hundred acres in the Shenandoah Valley.

The French and Indian War ended with the defeat and expulsion of the French, but the Indians, exhorted and aroused by the charismatic Ottawa chief Pontiac, continued their depredations. There were terrible and bloody raids at Kerr's Creek and Big Springs in 1763.

It was largely through their own efforts that the colonists pacified the frontier, which gave them a new sense of power over their own affairs. Had they not, they reasoned, been pretty much the authors of the victory, with almost no help from the British? The inhabitants of the valley had always suspected that they were considered little more than a buffer against the Indians. Now an ungrateful British government began to implement political and mercantile policies that could only exacerbate problems that had been brewing for a century.

In Virginia the old animosities between the Presbyterians and the Anglicans had never disappeared. The Anglicans of the Tidewater and Piedmont appeared hardly different from their despised counterparts in England. Conversely, the worldly, cosmopolitan, sophisticated Easterners were contemptuous of the straitlaced puritanical Westerners, with their austere ways and their heavy Scottish speech. As the luxury-loving Anglicans of the Tidewater took their pleasure so did the Presbyterians of the valley find satisfaction in their austerity.

This was especially evident in the architecture. John Sergeant Wise, an early traveler to Lexington, complained of the hard-looking blue limestone streets and the stiff and formal red brick houses with their severe stone trimmings and plain white pillars and finishings. "The grim portals of the Presbyterian church looked cold as a dog's nose," he said.

The previous century had been one long religious confrontation, and the English thought they had rid themselves of these troublemakers once and for all. But the Puritans were stirring things up again in the colonies. George III called the American Revolution "a Presbyterian war," and Horace Walpole wryly observed, "There is no use crying about it. Cousin America has run off with a Presbyterian parson, and that is the end of it."

When war came, Robert Houston's principal heir, Samuel Houston, became an officer and paymaster in Daniel Morgan's famous Virginia Rifle Brigade in the Continental Army. Morgan's Brigade was present at Burgoyne's surrender at Saratoga and was in action at the battles of Cowpens and Guilford Courthouse.

Samuel Houston was a dashing, romantic figure, and he seemed particularly so to Elizabeth Paxton, the beautiful daughter of another Scotch-Irish family. The Paxtons had also immigrated from Northern Ireland to Pennsylvania and then on to Virginia to settle among their coreligionists in the Shenandoah Valley. Elizabeth's father, John Paxton, was said to be the richest man in Rockbridge County. Most of his income came from farming, but in 1761 he was granted a license to operate a tavern. Presumably he had no difficulty in keeping separate his Puritan conscience and his Scottish entrepreneurial spirit.

The area west of the mountains was not quite the raw frontier it appeared to the more effete Virginians of the Tidewater. The residents were not as backward as pictured by the more advanced Easterners. The Paxtons and the Houstons were not aristocrats by the standards of the Tidewater, but they were of that class of country squires that constitute a local gentry—admired, respected, and treated with deference by their neighbors.

Major Samuel Houston and Elizabeth Paxton were married. John Paxton, like all fathers, may have hoped for a better match for his beautiful daughter, but the Houston estate at Timber Ridge was a considerable property, and in the euphoria of the victory over the detested British a handsome Continental soldier no doubt was seen by most of the Scotch-Irish in the valley as a good match.

After the Revolution, the regular army was reduced to only eighty men. Experience with British troops had taught Americans that a large standing army was a potential threat to liberty. Major Samuel Houston, however, had found military life congenial. His primary interest was soldiering, not farming. With the regular army closed to him, he had to settle for a career as an officer with the Virginia Militia.

———

Elizabeth Paxton and Samuel Houston had a happy marriage, in spite of the frequent absences of the major. Elizabeth was by all accounts a remarkable woman. She was intelligent and sensible, and she was strong-willed. Roman matron is a description often encountered. She instilled in her children a love of learning and a respect for what the Tidewater called the finer things.

After ten years of marriage and four sons—Paxton, Robert, James, and John—she gave birth to her fifth child, another son, on March 2, 1793. Sam Houston was born in the columned plantation house built by his grandfather, Robert Houston, not in the modest log cabin of the Houston legends.

Major Samuel Houston, a hero of the American Revolution, was at home for the birth of this new son and namesake, who would, in a far-off place called Texas, be a hero in another revolution and bring lasting glory to the Houston name.

Young Sam Houston had a typical boyhood on the edge of the frontier. He helped out on the plantation, but like his father he had little interest in farming except as a romantic ideal or, later in life, as an investment. He preferred roaming the woods and fields, fishing and swimming in nearby Mill Creek, and hunting in the forests of the Blue Ridge.

During his father's absences, his older brothers acted as surrogates, but as his mother's favorite he knew very little discipline. Besides, until he was about ten, Elizabeth Houston was always caring for a new baby or else was pregnant with another or both. After Sam was born, Elizabeth Houston had one more son, William, and then, at last, daughters—Isabella, Mary, and Eliza.

Down the hill from the Houston house at Timber Ridge was a small country school, a so-called field school. It occupied the building once used by Liberty Hall Academy, the school that evolved into Washington and Lee University. At the late age of eight, Sam began his sporadic education at this little school. He learned to read and write and do some arithmetic, but, as was typical of the eighteenth century, he received the better part of his education at home.

His father had a small library, and Elizabeth Houston encouraged Sam in his studies. History and geography were special favorites, and the boy spent hours with Brown's *Gazetteer,* Morse's *Geography,* and Rollins's *Ancient History.* Perhaps it was Morse and the map of the Spanish empire that made young Sam aware that there was a place called Tejas.

Even closer than the school to the Houston house was the Timber Ridge Presbyterian Church. It had been fifty years since great-grandfather John Houston had founded New Providence and his grandfather Robert Houston had founded Timber Ridge, but the Presbyterian churches in the valley had not relaxed any of the rigid Old World rules governing public worship and private behavior.

Every Sunday Elizabeth Houston and the major, when he was home, gathered their family together and the eleven Houstons walked the few feet from their house to the stone Timber Ridge Church for services. It was an agony for Sam to spend almost the entire day every Sunday being threatened with the fires of hell and eternal damnation.

Major Houston, in spite of his eminence in the community and the Houston religious legacy, once ran head-on into the more conservative elements in the church—not that anyone in the congregation could be accused of being particularly liberal. He was charged with disturbing public worship at Timber Ridge.

During the Sunday service, August 4, 1805, Ann Henderson was suddenly seized by a religious fervor and began to dance. The shocked major rose from his seat and took the woman outside to try and calm her down. These public displays, called "the jerks," were not unlike speaking in tongues.

The practice had become something of a fad among the religious ecstatics at Timber Ridge, and they were much offended by Major Houston's interference. They felt that Ann Henderson should have been left alone to dance out her religious rapture, and they brought charges against Houston. After an airing, the charges were quietly forgotten.

The road that passed within a few yards of the Houston plantation was the old Indian Warrior and Trading Path, which ran from northern Virginia to the Cherokee Nation in the Southeast. Each day young Sam heard the clatter and racket of the great migration of settlers as they passed Timber Ridge, heading south and west.

The path had once been part of the centuries-old network of Indian trails, or warpaths, which connected much of North America. It was a natural route down the valleys and river bottoms west of the highest peaks of the Appalachians, and the white settlers and traders expropriated it for their own purposes, building roads over the path and forts and settlements on the sites of the old Indian encampments.

Seven miles past Timber Ridge the road went through the market town of Lexington, the center of social and economic life for the county. In 1778, Rockbridge County was carved out of Augusta and Botetourt counties and Lexington laid out as the county seat. It was there that farm products and implements were sold or swapped, horses traded, gossip exchanged, and court was convened.

The little town was destroyed by a fire in 1796, but rebuilding began immediately. Oddly enough, the first church was not constructed until 1802. The congregation worshipped at the courthouse. There was such a thin line between offending God and offending the state that perhaps this practice may have been a great convenience for the magistrates and the church elders, who were often one and the same.

Although it was twenty-four years before Lexington had a proper Presbyterian church, the town was quick to erect the other public symbols of moral order and righteousness. A pillory and stocks were set up in the middle of the town at a very early date.

In spite of fires, rebuilding, and the Civil War, the small valley town has kept its late-eighteenth-, early-nineteenth-century aspect. John Sergeant Wise's austerity and coldness now appear, with the patina of age, as simple dignity, restrained beauty, and warmth.

Young Sam was especially fond of visiting his cousin Matthew Houston at his plantation at High Bridge, fifteen miles south of Timber Ridge. Matthew's grand house sat by the main road to the south, which was handy in that he used the lower floor as a general store. He was also a successful planter and he operated a mill on nearby Cedar Creek.

Matthew's Red Mill was just upstream from the great geological wonder owned by Thomas Jefferson, the Natural Bridge. Jefferson had bought the bridge and the surrounding 150 acres for 20 shillings in 1775, and in his *Notes on the State of Virginia,* he called it "the most sublime of Nature's works. . . . You involuntarily fall on your hands and feet, creep to the parapet and peep over it." He also found that looking down into the abyss gave him violent headaches.

One is awed by the thought of the author of the Declaration of Independence falling on his knees before anything, but the limestone arch does afford a dizzying prospect of Cedar Creek flowing 215 feet below. Young Sam and his friends also crept on their hands and knees to the edge and were scared witless just like the great statesman and scientist.

Houston's knowledge of the French and Indian War, the American Revolution, the Federalist period, and the new United States was gained directly from people, beginning with his own father and Cousin Matthew, who actually knew firsthand of the battles, the Indian raids, the congresses, and the conventions. The stories and exploits of the great Virginia heroes were still fresh.

The Treaty of Paris, which ended the War of Independence, was signed less than ten years before Sam's birth, the Constitution ratified only five years before, and George Washington was just about to begin his second term. Many of the patriots in the valley knew Washington, Jefferson, and Madison personally. Jefferson's Monticello and James Monroe's Highlands were only sixty miles from Timber Ridge and Madison's Montpellier less than twenty miles farther on.

Those great Virginians whose names are synonymous with the term Founding Fathers occupied the presidency for twenty-eight out of the first thirty-two years of Houston's life, and their legacy was never forgotten by him.

On a cold December day in 1799, Major Houston came home to Timber Ridge wearing a black band around the left sleeve of his uniform. George Washington had died at Mount Vernon. The symbol of mourning for the father of his country made an indelible impression on the six-year-old boy. "The first manifestation of grief and sorrow ever made upon my mind or that impressed my heart with sensibility was the crepe I saw worn upon my father's arm, doing honor to the memory of Washington, after his decease," Houston emotionally recalled sixty years later.

Major Houston was away a great deal during Sam Houston's boyhood, but his absences were always brief. He was in charge of inspections of fortifications along the frontier, but the only real threat was from the Indians whose raids were generally confined to areas farther south.

Elizabeth Houston ran the plantation, aided by her children, relatives, servants, and slaves. A typical plantation was self-sufficient. All food, whether vegetables, grain, meat, milk, or eggs, was grown or produced on the place. Cattle and horses were bred and traded. Cloth was woven and clothes were made. Even shoes were made at home. Surplus products were sold or bartered, but little cash money changed hands. The major cash crop was, of course, tobacco, but corn and wheat were increasingly important. There was also money generated by distilling whiskey.

Financially precarious during the best of times, plantation life was doubtless made more so by a part-time patron who had abdicated domestic responsibilities to his wife. Major Houston also had pressing financial needs of his own. Because officers paid their own expenses in the Virginia Militia, his military career was a financial drain on the plantation.

One tradition holds that Samuel and Elizabeth Houston were faced with financial ruin in 1806, and the major had to resign his commission and sell the Timber Ridge property. They then bought new land, in the eastern part of the new state of Tennessee. Allegedly they were forced in their early middle age to make a new start in life. The proverbial journey "from shirt sleeves to shirt sleeves in three generations" had taken place.

There is no hard evidence that they were in such dire financial straits, but a chilling inference can be drawn from the inventory of Major Houston's estate. He owned slaves, and five of them are listed in the inventory, two women and three children. No men's names appear. Did he sell the father or fathers of the three children to pay off his debts?

Land in Tennessee cost a fraction of the price of land in Virginia, and millions of acres had been opened up for settlement, sometimes by not so legal means. If the Houstons were in financial trouble, the sale of Timber Ridge and a move to Tennessee could indeed have assured that their family would have a more prosperous future.

Samuel Houston's will, dated September 22, 1806, does refer to his heirs moving "to some new country" and buying land there "on the best terms," but the wording is speculative, conditional. What is not speculative or conditional is that he still owned Timber Ridge when he made out his will.

Major Samuel Houston died suddenly, while on an inspection tour. He was about forty miles west of Timber Ridge, at an inn near present-day Callaghan, Virginia, in Alleghany County. The date is generally given as 1806, but it is more than likely that he died sometime in 1807, for late that year, on November 6, Elizabeth Paxton Houston and her sons James and John appeared at the courthouse in Lexington as executors of the estate.

Samuel Houston left the bulk of his property to Elizabeth, but it is clear that his son John was the favorite of his many children. He left him his sword and two of his "horse creatures," one of them the major's own mount, a sorrel. And in the event of Elizabeth's death, John Houston was to receive two shares while the other children, including the daughters, were to have one share each.

Elizabeth Houston, who had held family and property together for her soldier husband, was now faced with a new challenge, but she was more than equal to the task. She sold the plantation for a thousand pounds to John Kinnear, a Timber Ridge neighbor, and decided to reinvest in property in east Tennessee, near the little town of Maryville. She had many relatives and friends already there, so she would not be alone.

The Houstons had traveled from Scotland to Northern Ireland to Pennsylvania to Virginia and now they were again on the move. Religion had played a part. And economic necessity had certainly had a hand in the family's wanderings. But there was also a restlessness in the Houstons, which was manifest in its most famous member. For young Sam, the removal to Tennessee presaged his own future. There would be many such moves in a lifetime of dislocations.

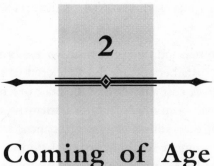

2

Coming of Age
in Tennessee

THE HOUSTONS, with their little two-wagon caravan, had themselves become part of that exodus that Sam had seen go by Timber Ridge on the old Indian warpath. Steeped in tales of war, adventure, and exploration, he was now embarked on his own great expedition into a new world.

Elizabeth and her children and servants traveled in company with others. The trip was arduous and potentially dangerous, but the road was busy from sunup to sundown. There were always other groups in sight. Immigrants by the thousands, traveling by wagon, horse, or on foot, flooded the trail to Tennessee, Kentucky, and the Carolinas—all drawn by one thing, cheap land.

The road in some places was wide and hard packed, in others it was not much better than the original Indian path. There were ferries at the major river crossings, but small streams had to be forded. Even the slightest rain turned the road into a muddy track, and in dry weather the air was filled with a fine choking dust. Horses, cattle, sheep, goats, pigs, even flocks of turkeys were driven over the trail to market.

Inns and taverns were scattered along the route, but they were primitive affairs designed to serve mule skinners, drovers, peddlers, and other itinerants. The Houston boys were therefore on constant guard over their mother and their sisters, the youngest of whom, Eliza, was only seven years old.

At a famous landmark, the Block House, a few miles north of the Long Island of the Holston River, in northeast Tennessee, the road diverged to the west to join up with Daniel Boone's famous Wilderness Road. For thirty years Boone's road, which also followed another Indian trail across the Cumberland Gap to Kentucky, had been the principal overland route to the west.

Twenty miles to the east of the Houston's route was Fort Watauga, founded in 1771 by James Robertson, the North Carolina Regulator leader. When that early rebellion against the British was crushed, Robertson moved a group of settlers west over the high mountains into the fertile valley of east Tennessee.

The settlement of east Tennessee was much slower than what was occurring farther up in the Shenandoah Valley in Virginia. The first permanent white settler, a Virginian named William Bean, arrived only in 1768. His homestead on the Watauga was just south of the Virginia border. The North Carolina mountains presented a much more formidable barrier than that between the valley of Virginia and the Tidewater. An even greater obstacle, however, was the Cherokee Nation, which claimed all of east Tennessee, western North Carolina, north Georgia, northern Alabama, and parts of South Carolina. Fur traders visited the area regularly, but the British attempts to get along with the Indians ended in disaster at Fort Loudoun.

Robertson and the Wataugans leased their lands from the Cherokees, but the white settlers could not be content with remaining on the lands covered in the agreement. They gradually began moving onto other Indian lands. The sporadic violence between Indians and whites became open warfare when the Cherokees aligned themselves with the British during the revolution.

Robertson was fearless, and he and his great friend and colleague, John Sevier, waged all-out war against the Indians. Robertson was fond of calling himself the advance guard of civilization and he soon pushed on from Watauga and founded Nashville. His and Sevier's efforts led to statehood for Tennessee in 1796 and Sevier became the first governor.

Robertson's son, Felix, and his nephew, Sterling, observed the family tradition of carrying civilization to the West. They helped to settle Texas.

Houstons were also important in the founding of Tennessee. The

Reverend Samuel Houston, the famous pastor of the High Bridge, Virginia, Presbyterian Church, preached in Maryville, Tennessee, as early as 1772. Indeed, Maryville's first church, built in 1786, was named New Providence Church and its first minister came from Rockbridge County.

Robert Houston was sheriff of Knox County in 1793 and James Houston, one of the most distinguished of the early settlers, was in Blount County by 1783. His Houston Station, a log fort, was six miles from Maryville, and in 1785 he and a handful of neighbors defended it against a war party of over a hundred Cherokees.

James Houston was a delegate from Blount County to the 1796 constitutional convention at Knoxville, which led to statehood. It was this convention, allegedly at the instigation of Andrew Jackson, that adopted the name Tennessee for the new state. The name comes from the Cherokee name, Tanasi, for the great river that flows through most of the state. Houston was also a member of the first Tennessee state legislature.

———

After crossing the Holston River, the Houstons continued their way south, down the broad valley of east Tennessee. They must have felt right at home in that landscape that so much resembles the Virginia valley they had left behind.

Spring was upon them, and this season in the southern Appalachians, particularly along the foothills and the slopes of the Great Smokies, is one of the supreme glories of nature. Dogwoods first whiten the slopes and then flame azaleas turn them to fire. Lady's slipper, trillium, dogtooth violet, bloodroot, and dwarf iris carpet the ground.

In a few more days, they crossed the French Broad River, which cuts through the gorges from North Carolina and joins the Holston at Knoxville to form the Tennessee. The highest peaks of the Great Smokies now began to appear on their left. They had never seen mountains so high.

In another day or two they were home, after three weeks on the road and over three hundred miles. They had averaged a more than respectable fifteen miles a day.

The new Tennessee property was situated on Baker's Creek, about ten miles south of the little settlement of Maryville, in Blount County.

Just five miles further south of the Houston homestead was the Little Tennessee River, the border of the vast lands of the Cherokee Nation.

James Houston's property was nearby, and Margaret Houston and her nine children were at first dependent on him and other relatives and friends for food and shelter. While they easily but of necessity accepted the traditional aid accorded to newcomers on the frontier, they also began immediately to make themselves self-sufficient, an even stronger frontier tradition.

———

The very word *frontier* conjures up images of privation, loneliness, danger, and isolation. History, however, tends to be written by those who are unfamiliar with, and thus tend to overemphasize, physical hardship. The primary danger to men and women on this frontier came from the hostile Indians. Otherwise, in many basic ways, life differed little from that in the eastern settlements.

A dependable and safe water supply, sewage disposal, and adequate medical care were almost unknown in the early nineteenth century no matter where one lived. The great eastern cities of Boston, Philadelphia, and New York had none of these amenities until the fifth decade of the century or even later. Water was drawn from wells, lakes, or streams. Diseases such as typhoid, hepatitis, and dysentery were common in both cities and isolated settlements.

The universal fuel was wood, and vast amounts were needed year round for cooking. In the winter the demand increased manyfold. A plume of woodsmoke was a permanent fixture above every house no matter what the season. As settlements grew, so did the cleared land around them. The deforestation of America was halted only by the discovery and exploitation of the great coal reserves.

———

The growing season is a long one in east Tennessee, but autumn can come early and there was great urgency to build a house and plant crops. There were over a dozen people to feed and shelter, so it was essential that they be settled before the following winter.

The Houston house was initially a simple, one-story log structure built on a slight rise overlooking the meadows and fields along Baker's Creek. Over the years it would grow into a substantial, well-furnished two-story home. Two pieces of Elizabeth Houston's furniture survive, a poplar lift-top, stand-up writing desk and a small cherry corner cupboard. Both are spartan in their simplicity but they also show the quality of Tennessee frontier craftsmanship.

Sam was obliged to help out more on the farm than he had in Virginia. There were slaves, it is true, but they were too expensive to buy and maintain for subsistence farming. A sale registered at the Blount County Courthouse in 1805 shows that a twenty-six-year-old black man was sold to James Houston for $500, a tremendous sum for that time. Slavery as an institution therefore never caught on in such areas of the South as east Tennessee, which did not have thousands of acres of tobacco and cotton to harvest.

As in Virginia, Sam was more interested in his books, and he enrolled at the Porter Academy, which had been opened in Maryville in 1806. Like all schools of its type, the academy was founded to teach the basics of education. Its curriculum was not an ambitious one. But Sam "devoted all the time he could spare to the studies of a rude frontier school."

One book can change a life, provide inspiration, give purpose and direction. At the "rude frontier school" Sam Houston fell under the spell of such a book—Alexander Pope's translation of *The Iliad*. The young dreamer was transported. Here was everything—myth, history, poetry, heroism, valor, and, perhaps most important of all, soaring rhetoric. It would be hard to overestimate the effect of the great work on the young Houston.

Pope's rendering has been superseded by more faithful and correct translations, but it still holds its own after almost three centuries. Houston returned to it again and again throughout his life, and he maintained that he committed over a thousand lines of the epic to memory.

Fired up by the stories of Achilles, Hector, Ajax, and Odysseus, he developed an intense interest in the Classical world. He determined to commence the study of Greek and Latin, but the schoolmaster refused, thinking his precocious pupil not equal to the task. This lack of foresight, a common failing of pedagogues and pedants, cost the teacher his best pupil. Sam walked out of the school, and there ended his formal education. He was sixteen years old.

Houston later said his education could not have amounted to more than six months total. He was, of course, exaggerating. However, in the eight years he attended school, sessions never lasted more than three or four months so he probably had about a third- or fourth-grade education.

His brothers, in despair over his renunciation of formal education and his disdain for the agricultural life, put him to work in a dry goods store. Some sources say that the store was in Kingston, on the Tennessee River, about fifty miles from Maryville, and was run by a member of the Rogers family. Houston, however, did not meet any of the Rogers clan until later. Others say a Mr. Sheffy owned the store, which was in Maryville, and Houston was apprenticed to him in 1811. This too is impossible in the light of subsequent events.

In any case, it makes little difference where the store was and who the owner was. The brothers Houston had misjudged their rebellious sibling. This time he did not just walk out. He ran away, a flight that would forever change Sam Houston and, in due course, much of history.

His brothers began immediately to search for him, but it was several weeks before Sam was found. The Baker's Creek community, indeed the whole county, was dumbfounded. He was living with a band of the Cherokee Indians on Hiwassee Island, ninety miles away at the juncture of the Hiwassee and Tennessee rivers, not far from present-day Dayton, Tennessee.

On the western shore of the Tennessee, opposite the island, was a United States Army post established to prevent whites from encroaching on the Cherokee lands and also to encourage trade between the Indians and the settlers.

The leader of the Hiwassee Cherokee, which numbered about three hundred men, women, and children, was Chief Ooleteka—called John Jolly by the whites. Hiwassee Island, or Jolly's Island, had been home to various Indian groups for hundreds of years. Ooleteka's band had been settled on Hiwassee Island for about twenty or thirty years when Houston joined them.

These Indians were part of the Overhill Cherokee, who years before had crossed over the mountains into Tennessee. The majority of the tribe still lived to the east of the high mountains.

The Cherokees, one of the Five Civilized Tribes, were the most assimilated and progressive of the native American groups. They viewed themselves as a chosen people, and they had developed a mythology and rich oral tradition which seemed to bear this out.

In the Cherokee cosmogony, the world is an island in the middle of a great sea. The island is suspended at the cardinal points—north, east, south, and west—by cords attached to a solid rock sky vault. At the exact center of this world-island reside the Yunwiya, the "real people" or the "principal people." The white man gave the popular name *Cherokee* to the Yunwiya. It is probably derived from the Creek word *tciloki,* meaning "people of a different speech."

According to the Cherokee mythology, at the end of time the cords holding up the world will break and it will sink into the water. This association of water with the end of the world was a source of great fear. Creeks and rivers became the abodes of evil spirits.

The great naturalist and traveler William Bartram visited the Cherokee country in the spring of 1775, venturing as far as the town of Cowee, or Kawiyi, in western North Carolina, just a few miles over the mountains from Tennessee. Bartram traveled on horseback, and, except for occasional brief periods, was alone. He extolled the region and its inhabitants in his classic *Travels.* Generations of scientists and writers have since been indebted to him—not only for observations but for his lyrical descriptions of the countryside, its flora and fauna, and the Indian tribes. The *Travels* was greatly admired abroad. Chateaubriand had a copy and it influenced the work of both Coleridge and Wordsworth.

Few people have succeeded so well as William Bartram in evoking the great beauty of the region. Strawberries did not just grow wild in the fields. They grew "in painted beds of many acres . . . their rich juice dying my horses feet and ancles."

On his journey to the Indian towns he passed through "one of the most charming natural mountainous landscapes perhaps any where to be seen." The ridges and hills rose "grand and sublimely one above and beyond another, some boldly and majestically advancing into the verdant plain, their feet bathed with the silver flood of the Tanase."

Meanwhile, "others far distant, veiled in blue mists, sublimely mount aloft, with yet greater majesty lift up their pompous crests and overlook vast regions." It is one of the earliest descriptions we have of the Great Smokies.

Bartram's Cherokees were filled with "divine simplicity and truth, friendship without fallacy or guile, hospitality disinterested, native, undefiled, unmodified by artificial refinements."

Crossing the mountains, he met on the trail the great Cherokee chief Attakullakulla and his splendid train of retainers. Attakullakulla had been taken to England forty-five years before with a group of Cherokee chiefs and created a sensation in London society. He had even been painted by Hogarth. The experience had not corrupted him, however. He retained his noble native ways, which impressed Bartram profoundly.

Bartram's account of his stay with a local chief is particularly good.

> Tobacco and pipes were brought, and the chief filling one of them, whose stem, about four feet long, was sheathed in a beautiful speckled snake skin, and adorned with fathers and strings of wampum, lights it and smokes a few whiffs, puffing the smoak first towards the sun, then to the four cardinal points and lastly over my breast, hands it towards me, which I cheerfully receive from him and smoaked. . . .
>
> This prince is the chief of Whatoga, a man universally beloved, and particularly esteemed by the whites for his pacific and equitable disposition, and revered by all for his exemplary virtues, just, moderate, magnanimous and intrepid.

Bartram's encomiums notwithstanding, the Cherokee had lost none of their ability to wage war, even though it had been many years since they had given up a nomadic existence for a settled agricultural life. It is remarkable that he got out of the Cherokee country with his skin or his scalp. But there was nothing to fear from this slight, peaceful man the Seminoles called Pukpugee, "flower hunter," who cared little for anything outside nature. In all his journals, there is no mention of the ongoing Revolutionary War.

The Cherokees had resisted white encroachments on their territory for two centuries, allying themselves with anyone who could help guarantee the integrity of their widespread domain. The dozens of Cherokee towns with their farms and orchards were scattered over an area of hundreds of square miles.

The Cherokees went to war against the Americans alongside the British. They suffered greatly for this inevitable but disastrous alliance.

When the Revolutionary War ended, their towns and villages had been destroyed, their crops burned, their orchards cut down, hundreds of their bravest men were dead, and their domain was much reduced.

The destruction of the Cherokees as an eastern nation now was only a matter of time, but they continued to resist, chiefly by raiding outlying settlements and isolated farmsteads. These attacks were, for the most part, the work of the Chickamauga branch of the Cherokee, but the white settlers made no effort to differentiate between the various bands.

One particularly grisly incident occurred on August 30, 1793, in Washington County, Tennessee. Two Indians murdered farmer Philip Hutter, scalped his wife and left her for dead, and then cut off the head of his daughter and carried it away. But the whites were no less barbarous, and their acts of reprisal could be equally monstrous.

In 1799 two Moravian missionaries, Abraham Steiner and Frederick C. De Schweinitz, journeyed to Tennessee to save the souls of the Cherokees. They stopped over at the Tellico Blockhouse on the Little Tennessee River, inside the Indian lands. The commandant and his wife entertained them in their comfortable two-story house. "Here we had a delightful view. One can see several miles up the [Little] Tennessee, with its charming islands covered with countless peach-trees."

Across the river from the spot where these gentle travelers admired the view stood the ruins of Fort Loudoun, where the Cherokees had besieged the British outpost for five months in 1760. After the British regulars and American militia surrendered, the fort was burned.

The next day the Indians had a change of heart, prompted no doubt by the fact that the British had executed twenty-three of their tribe. They fell upon the withdrawing soldiers and killed about thirty of them. As always on the frontier it was often hard to tell who was avenging whom and for what.

The circle of violence had seemed impossible to break, but the unremitting war threatened to kill off the tribe entirely. There were just not enough Indians to fight the increasing number of whites. Peace came to the frontier. The peach orchards on the islands in the Little Tennessee were both a monument to the success of pacification and the destruction of a way of life.

———

Peace also brought assimilation of the Cherokees and intermarriage with the whites. The Cherokee leaders Sam Houston first encountered were almost all of mixed white and Indian ancestry and contrary to the popular modern image they, like their white neighbors, were shopkeepers, planters, and slaveholders.

The idea of the Noble Savage, at one with nature and uncorrupted by civilization, has engaged man's imagination since antiquity. In the late eighteenth and early nineteenth centuries, the beginning of widespread industrialization, the idea gained new power and attracted new adherents. Sam Houston wholeheartedly embraced this romantic image. For him Ooleteka was the embodiment of the Noble Savage and was the physical and spiritual descendant of Attakullakulla and the Chief of Whatoga. Another noted botanist and traveler, Thomas Nuttall, said Ooleteka was "a Franklin amongst his countrymen."

Ooleteka's Hiwassee Island village, probably the Coyacua referred to by early travelers, was a pale reflection of the great town of Cowee. That Cherokee capital, which was burned by the Americans a year after Bartram's visit, had comprised over a hundred dwellings and a council house that held hundreds of people. Still, Hiwassee had a sizable council house, which served as the center of government and festivities, and numerous log dwellings. Many of the young people of the settlement had been taught to read and write by the missionaries.

The Cherokee had a passion for dancing, with both the men and the women taking part. The dances were celebratory and religious, but they were often lascivious as well. Houston, throughout his life, liked to dance, and his enthusiasm for it was probably born on this island in the Hiwassee River. There is no way that he could have acquired the taste among the puritanical Presbyterians.

Ball games were another great Cherokee diversion. The Indian ball game, which is still played by the Cherokee, has since evolved into the modern lacrosse, but the collegiate version is a great deal tamer than the often violent Indian sport.

When his brothers finally found him, Sam told them that he preferred "measuring deer tracks, to tape—that he liked the wild liberty of the Red men, better than the tyranny of his own brothers, and if he could not study Latin in the Academy, he could, at least, read a translation from the Greek in the woods, and read it in peace. So they could go home as soon as they liked."

Houston remained with the Cherokees for the better part of three years. He did return home from time to time but only to get new clothes. On one of these trips, he was fined five dollars for "annoying the court with the noise of a Drum and with force preventing the Sheriff and Officer of the Court in the discharge of his duty."

Sam and Captain John B. Cusack, who was fined ten dollars, had gotten carried away during a muster of the militia in front of the Blount County Courthouse. No doubt fueled by whiskey, they had decided to serenade the court.

Ooleteka became more than a surrogate father to young Sam. In fact, he adopted him, giving him the name Kalanu ("The Raven"). The Cherokee leader was the first of many older men who would be both friend and mentor to Sam Houston. And young Houston, in turn, recognized Ooleteka to be what he truly was, a prince, not unlike those of the history, legends, and myths that filled Sam's head. Like those princes, Ooleteka did succeed to a kingdom. In 1820, he became the principal chief of the Cherokee Nation.

The raven, *kalanu,* was not often seen in the mountain home of the Cherokee. It does not figure much in the Cherokee folk tales except for the grisly legend of the Raven Mocker, a witch who appears to a dying person to take his life and eat his heart. *Kalanu* was most generally taken as a war title and perhaps that is why Ooleteka conferred it on Houston, or Houston chose it, as his Cherokee name.

At Hiwassee, Sam also made friends with the Rogers family, who lived a few miles away on Rogers Creek. The patriarch, John Rogers, was one of those Scottish traders who had lived so long among the Cherokees that they had become quasi-officials. They were particularly influential in dealings with the British governors during the colonial era. The Indian trade was important to the economies of the colonies, and there are accounts of great pack trains of over a hundred horses traveling between Virginia and the Cherokee Nation.

Most of the traders were married to Indian women and their descendants became powerful tribal leaders. Rogers's wife was the sister of Ooleteka. His children were tutored by a white man, George Barbee Davis, and they may also have attended the nearby school founded by missionaries in 1804.

John, William, and Charles Rogers became close companions of Sam Houston. The tall, auburn-haired teenager with the piercing blue-gray eyes was a striking contrast to his darker Cherokee brothers. Together they hunted, trapped, and fished, and they taught Sam many of the Cherokee customs and practices. The boys often journeyed the few miles up the Hiwassee and the Little Tennessee to hunt and fish in the vastness of the Great Smokies.

In addition to Indian lore, Sam became adept in the art of woodcarving. All his life he carried small pieces of wood and a pocket knife. He whiled away the time, whether on riverboats or the floor of the United States Senate, carving small and intricate pieces. For female admirers he often carved little baskets out of peach pits.

John Rogers had another child, a daughter named Diana. Cherokee tradition maintains that she and young Sam became lovers this early on, but Diana Rogers was only a child at this time. Even if she were older it is doubtful that the Cherokees would have countenanced such a relationship, although the Indians were more open-minded than the Presbyterians whom Houston had fled.

Our old friend Bartram gives us some indication of how closely watched were the young Cherokee girls. One day on his journey, he and a companion ascended a ridge from where they "enjoyed a most enchanting view." Below them were "companies of young, innocent Cherokee virgins," picking strawberries or reclining "under the shade of floriferous and fragrant native bowers . . . disclosing their beauties to the fluttering breeze, and bathing their limbs in the cool fleeting streams."

When Bartram and his companion, a trader, having become "warmed and excited" tried to take "a more active part in their delicious sports" some "envious" Cherokee matrons "who lay in ambush" sounded the alarm.

This account reveals much of how far this Philadelphia Quaker had strayed from the paths of righteousness, but more importantly it shows that young Cherokee women were not fair game for white men. Even though the Cherokees were watchful of their young women, they cannot have compared to the straitlaced Presbyterian community that Houston had fled.

Whatever their relationship at this time, Diana Rogers, or Tiana as she is popularly known, and Sam Houston would not see each other again for almost twenty years, when he again fled to the Cherokees.

Houston's forest idyll now had to end. He could not live with his adoptive father forever, and, in fact, he was needed at home. His sister

Isabella, who had never been strong, died soon after they arrived in Tennessee, and his brother Paxton had died of the tuberculosis that had afflicted him since childhood. Elizabeth Houston had now lost her husband and two of her children.

Young Sam was going to have to learn to make a life for himself with his own people and, in particular, with his own family. He was nineteen years old and he had matured in many ways. He had learned the ways of the Indians, their language, and most important of all their psychology. Houston also adopted a useful Cherokee custom. He began to refer to himself in the third person, a device that would later drive political adversaries to distraction.

The fierce attachments and loyalties formed on Hiwassee Island lasted a lifetime and had a most profound influence on Houston the public and private man. Years later, as Houston was reminiscing about this formative time he remarked that "there's much that was sweet to remember in this sojourn among the untutored children of the forest."

When Sam rejoined the white community, he had to make a living of some sort. He had lived on credit for almost three years and owed money to his family and to the merchants of Maryville. He not only had to pay off his debts but be self-supporting—a dual task that plagued him his entire life.

An improbable opportunity presented itself, no doubt through the offices of his mother who was still determined to make something of her wayward son. Two prominent early settlers of Maryville, Andrew Kennedy and Henry McCulloch, had established a school about five miles northeast of the town in 1796. Kennedy attended church with Elizabeth Houston at the Baker's Creek Presbyterian Church.

Kennedy and McCulloch built their little school building in the middle of rolling farmland with a spectacular view of the nearby mountains to the east. It was a one-room, dressed-log building, chinked with clay. On two sides of the building some logs were left out and inside shutters installed. These gaps in the walls served as windows. A stone fireplace provided any necessary heat. It was a delightful site, and even today the spring used by the students still bubbles up on one side of the property and flows into the nearby creek.

As in all such backwoods communities, it was hard to attract teachers and once they were there to keep them for more than a single term. When Sam returned home, the school had no master. Kennedy needed a teacher. Elizabeth's son Sam needed a job. The two needs were joined.

Much has been made of Houston's becoming, with his seemingly meager education, a schoolmaster. But it must be remembered that teaching was not then the arcane and cabalistic profession it has become. Sam knew the basics of reading, writing, and arithmetic. He knew history and geography. He was a persuasive and convincing speaker all of his life. If these qualities are combined with the requisite enthusiasm, then teaching becomes possible for anyone.

It was a great distance from the Houston homestead on Baker's Creek to the school, about fifteen miles. This necessitated Sam's boarding with various pupils' families, but this was soon arranged. He became a teacher.

Houston charged his pupils a tuition of eight dollars—considered extremely high for the time. It was payable one-third in cash, one-third in corn, one-third in cotton cloth of various colors. This last was for his shirts, and it is the first evidence of that life-long fascination with colorful attire that not only bordered on the eccentric but often crossed over the line. He wore his hair Indian fashion, with a long queue down his back.

The school was a success and in spite of the high fee attracted a large number of students. As many as eighteen people—boys, girls, and even middle-aged men—crowded into the little building at one time. Nine of Kennedy's children attended. On warm days sessions were held outdoors under the trees, and the students and teacher shared the meals brought from home.

Houston later said that his tenure as a schoolteacher was the most satisfying time of his life. If so, it was a brief satisfaction. He abandoned the school after teaching about six months in 1812.

Just as *The Iliad* opened his mind to poetry and the classics, so did teaching make Houston aware of his gifts as a public speaker and his ability to hold an audience. It also made him aware of his deficiencies. He therefore attempted to pick up with his own delayed education at the Porter Academy, but he was defeated by mathematics. As he recalled years later, he "undertook to dive into the secrets of geometry, but Euclid had little charms for a mind like his, and he threw it by to seek some more congenial pursuit."

So at the age of twenty, Sam Houston was faced with the question that he had been avoiding for years. What "congenial pursuit" was available? The answer came from beyond the mountains.

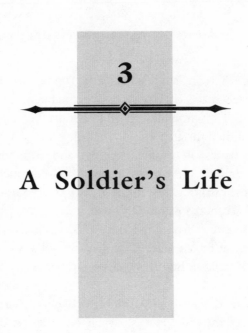

3

A Soldier's Life

F OR OVER TWENTY YEARS the new United States had been caught
between the quarrelsome British and the fractious French in their
ceaseless squabbles. America was a major trading partner of each nation
and both John Adams and Thomas Jefferson had tried to maintain a
fragile neutrality. They generally succeeded only in provoking one or the
other of the great powers or both at the same time.

Jefferson's chief contribution was an embargo forbidding trade with
either of the belligerents. The policy effectively destroyed the commerce
of much of the United States. Everyone, from manufacturers to small
farmers, suffered from what turned out to be one of the most ill-advised
policies of any president in American history. The Jeffersonian pox on
both your houses hurt only his own house.

The British impressment of American sailors, confiscation of vessels
by both nations, and British intrigues among the frontier Indians further
increased tensions. In addition the British delayed removing themselves
behind the lines set forth in the 1783 treaty ending the Revolution.
Americans were justifiably suspicious that the British felt the boundaries
were renegotiable or, worse, were awaiting a suitable opportunity to
reestablish themselves in their former colonies.

Another important element was the considerable sentiment among

American expansionists to expel the British from Canada and the Spanish from Florida. The United States could thereby expand both to the south and the north.

And there was a factor often overlooked by historians as too emotional, or not quantifiable, or not subject to easy analysis. Call it spite or simple malevolence, it played an important role in the relations between England and the United States. There was the simple desire for many in the British government to see the young republic fail.

On June 18, 1812, President James Madison, urged on by the bellicose group called the War Hawks, signed a declaration of war against Great Britain. The United States thus entered in the War of 1812, the American arm of yet another European war. In fact, in that same month, Napoleon's Grand Army marched into Russia.

The war was far from popular either in Great Britain or the United States, which was reflected in the way Congress voted on the declaration. In the House of Representatives the vote was 79 to 24 and in the Senate it was 19 to 13. These are thin majorities to wage all-out war against any powerful nation.

In Great Britain economic distress caused by years of warfare was widespread and had forced His Majesty's government to reexamine the hateful policies toward the former colonies. The declaration of war was therefore met with great surprise and dismay in many quarters. It was generally viewed as unnecessary, unwise, and even foolish. However, with the French emperor and his troops otherwise engaged, the British could turn their full attention to their former colonies.

Recruiters were active in Tennessee, and in March 1813 they appeared in Maryville. They paraded up and down with a fife and drum and finally set up shop in front of the courthouse. The recruiting officer placed some silver dollars on the drum. A dollar was the bounty for new recruits, and anyone interested in enlisting stepped up, picked up a silver dollar, and was in the army.

Houston, who happened to be walking by with a friend, on the spot "quit the peaceful walks of scholastic life at the age of twenty years & enlisted in the 7th Regt of Infy."

His family and friends were outraged that the son and namesake of a military officer had signed on as a common soldier. They might be frontiersman and farmers, but they were well aware of their place in the world.

"And what have your craven souls to say about *the ranks?*" Houston righteously responded to their jibes. "Go to, with your stuff; I would much sooner honor the ranks, than disgrace an appointment. You don't know me now, but you shall hear of me."

As for his mother, the widow of the major, her reaction, again according to Sam, was more sympathetic. "There, my son," said Elizabeth Houston, "take this musket and never disgrace it: for remember, I had rather all my sons should fill one honorable grave, than that one of them should turn his back to save his life. Go, and remember, too, that while the door of my cottage is open to brave men, it is eternally shut against cowards."

Although one must allow for Houston's famous gift for embellishment, it is not difficult to imagine Elizabeth Houston saying something close to this. This was, after all, the woman who ran a plantation by herself, moved her large family over three hundred miles through wild country, and then made a new home for them on the frontier. She gave her favorite son a gold ring, which he wore until his death. There was but a single word inscribed inside the band—*Honor*.

Houston's brother Robert enlisted in the army as well, and presumably Elizabeth Houston's homilies extended to him. Sam, although devoted to his family throughout his life, made no mention in the memoir compiled so many years later of his brother's army career or his exploits, if there were any.

Robert Houston's life, however, came to a melancholy end. Years later he alighted from a stagecoach on the Brownsburg Road near New Providence Church, back in Virginia, and blew his brains out with a pistol. The church refused to let him be buried in consecrated ground and he was interred in the roadway outside the cemetery.

Sam Houston was not an enlisted man for long. From Fort Hampton, Alabama, on September 15, he wrote to Secretary of War John Armstrong, "Your notification of my appointment of Ensign in the Service of the United States I received by last Express, and is accepted. I shall report myself to Col. Williams accordingly." He signed the letter "Samuel Houston Ensign 39th U.S. Regt. Inf."

Houston's appointment to ensign was officially dated July 29, 1813. In less than six months he was promoted a second time, to third lieutenant. This appointment was officially dated December 31.

Thirty-one-year-old Thomas Hart Benton was a colonel in the 39th

Regiment. He immediately recognized, as he recalled many years later, the special qualities of the handsome twenty-year-old soldier, and, in Benton, Houston collected one more mentor and lifelong friend and ally. Another Tennessean who signed on at the same time and served with Houston was a tall, lanky twenty-seven-year-old frontiersman named David Crockett.

The war in the Southeast was primarily a war between the whites and the Creek Indian allies of the British. The Creek leader, Red Eagle, was a half-Scot known to the whites as William Weatherford. Inspired by the great Shawnee leader Tecumseh and his brother, the Shawnee Prophet, Red Eagle and the Creeks believed that they had been chosen to drive the white man from their lands.

Tecumseh and the Shawnee Prophet traveled from the Northwest Territory to Florida seeking to forge a confederation of all the eastern tribes. They saw the British as the means to that end. Tecumseh inveighed against tribes who had sold out to the white man. All the land was the common property of the red man and no one had the right to part with it. "Why not sell the air, the clouds, and the great sea," he said. "Did not the Great Spirit make them all for the use of his children?"

Tecumseh's words incited the Indians, but the Creeks split over whether to fight the whites. The Red Sticks, so-called because they painted their war clubs a brilliant red, chose the warpath. Another faction sided with the Americans. The Creek Nation thus engaged in a civil war as well as a fight with the Americans. The British, who were certainly no tools of the Indians, quickly took advantage of the situation on the frontier and determined to arm the Red Sticks.

On August 30, 1813, over a thousand Creek warriors under Red Eagle easily overwhelmed a poorly prepared and almost defenseless Fort Mims, forty-five miles northeast of Mobile, Alabama. Mims was little more than a flimsily fortified house and stockade, but the military troop and civilians from outlying districts who had sought refuge there took so few precautions that they invited disaster. They even left the gates open.

The Red Sticks massacred nearly five hundred whites and burned the fort. Their action was typical of the vicious warfare carried out by Indians against whites and whites against Indians—the one determined to protect and hold on to ancestral lands, the other just as determined to take over the land and settle it.

Governor Willie Blount of Tennessee had railed loudly and often for the Creeks, indeed all Indians, to be annihilated. The Fort Mims massacre lent new urgency to his shrill diatribes, and he called on Andrew Jackson, Major General of the Tennessee Militia, to prosecute the war.

Jackson was at his plantation, The Hermitage, recuperating from gunshot wounds inflicted in a brawl with Thomas Hart Benton and his brother. Jesse Benton had come off second best in a duel with one of Jackson's protégés, William Carroll. He had been wounded in the buttocks, and Jackson's ridicule of the embarrassing wound had made him even angrier. The Bentons encountered Jackson at the City Hotel in Nashville, and in a terrible shoot-out Jesse Benton shot Jackson in the left arm and shoulder.

After several months, Jackson was able to sit a horse, although his arm was still in a sling. On October 7 he joined his troops in Fayetteville, and they headed south into the Creek Nation. From his headquarters at Fort Strother, on the Coosa River in northeastern Alabama, Jackson began a campaign that was singular in its ferocity and viciousness. In less than a month, his troops had killed more than five hundred Indians, most of the engagements little more than massacres.

The battle at Tallushatchee, on November 13, was typical of the cruelty. Even Jackson's own men were sickened by the killing and mutilation of the Indians. The inhabitants of the Indian town were slaughtered in their houses where they had taken refuge. "We found as many as eight or ten bodies in a single cabin," reported a lieutenant. "Some of the cabins had taken fire, and half-consumed human bodies were seen amidst the smoking ruins."

Even in such brutal wars exceptional acts of humanity can occur. After the battle, the Tennesseans rescued an infant, who was less than a year old, from the arms of its dead mother. Jackson fed the tiny baby boy sugar water to keep him alive and then sent him to his wife at The Hermitage. He and Rachel Jackson raised the boy as their own son.

Third Lieutenant Houston and the 39th Regiment arrived at Fort Strother on February 13, 1814. Jackson welcomed this unit of the United States regular army to his command. Professional soldiers could help him whip his ragtag and still raw Tennessee State Militia into shape. Houston took an active part in helping the general train his troops to be real soldiers. The Indians had begun to fight back with some success and Jackson's army had been forced to retreat north and reorganize.

Sam Houston's public career began here in the backwoods of Alabama, with his first meeting with Andrew Jackson, who became his mentor, example, and guide in politics, war, and life. Jackson was already forty-six-years-old and had served terms in both the House of Representatives and the U.S. Senate. He had also been a successful lawyer, judge, land speculator, and planter.

Jackson was equally well-known for his temper, his drinking, and, of course, his dueling. Anger, inebriation, and pointing a pistol at someone with the express purpose of killing him are hardly to be applauded, but Jackson also was a man of great courage.

Judge Jackson once left the bench and personally arrested a murderous backwoodsman who had stormed out of his court and terrorized the sheriff and a posse. When the criminal asked why he had surrendered to Judge Jackson when he had held off the sheriff and his men, he replied that it was because he had looked the judge in the eye and "I saw shoot." Jackson meant it.

Sam Houston had "shoot in his eye" also. He and Jackson had a natural affinity. Their lives and careers were strikingly parallel as they unfolded. Some of these events are attributable to coincidence, but what is more likely is that the younger man began immediately to emulate his idol.

Fort Strother, a wooden stockade in the Alabama wilderness, was now home to a group of men who did much to shape and change the course of American politics, history, and folklore. Andrew Jackson, Sam Houston, Thomas Hart Benton, John Eaton, James Gadsden, William Carroll, William Lewis, and Davy Crockett were all there.

Chief Red Eagle's principal captain was Menewa, the commander of the Red Sticks. For months the Creek refugees from the war had been gathering at Tohopeka, at a bend in the Tallapoosa River—Horseshoe Bend—near present-day Alexander City, Alabama.

By the middle of March, the Creek town on the riverbank had over three hundred log houses and more than thirteen hundred inhabitants. About a mile back from the river, at the top of a long slope, the Creeks erected a double-walled log and earthen breastworks. It extended across the entire neck of the peninsula formed by the sharp bend in the river. The fortification faced a wide field and behind it the land fell away sharply to the river and the village. The rear of the Indian force and the village were thus protected by the river. Any invading force had to come at them directly overland and fight them at the breastworks.

On March 14, Sam Houston and the 39th left Fort Strother and headed south for Horseshoe Bend. The troops boarded flatboats and descended the Coosa River to a point about forty-five miles west of the Red Stick fortress. Here they established an advance base, which they named Fort Williams.

Jackson and his main body of troops—a force of about 2,000, including 500 Cherokees and 100 friendly Creeks—rendezvoused with the 39th at Fort Williams. The entire force then set out overland to attack the Red Sticks at Horseshoe Bend. The troops were ready and the excitement of finishing off Red Eagle and the Red Sticks once and for all, in a great battle, enabled them to endure, even perhaps enjoy, the hardship of the march.

The Cherokees numbered among their contingent the leading men of the tribe. Present at the Horseshoe were Junaluska, Sequoyah, Major Ridge, John Ross, and the grandson of Attakullakulla. Houston's knowledge of Cherokee and the fact that he was the adopted son of one of the chiefs was of great aid to Jackson and the American cause.

Jackson's forces arrived at Tohopeka on March 26. Awaiting them behind the double-walled breastworks were a thousand hardened and determined Creek warriors. In the village on the river several hundred women and children huddled in the log houses. Jackson placed his two cannons on a low rise overlooking the breastworks and deployed troops on the opposite shore of the river around the entire bend.

The next day, at half past ten, a two-hour artillery barrage began from a distance of only eighty yards. Many of the Creeks were killed, but the stockade was not breached. The defenders also fought off the direct attacks by the Indian allies of the whites.

Meanwhile, on the shore opposite the Creek village, a group of Cherokees decided on a bold maneuver. They swam the river and returned with enough of the Creek canoes to ferry a fighting force across. They were thus able to mount an attack on the village and the main Creek force from the rear.

When he saw the smoke from the burning houses, Jackson realized, to his great surprise, that he had a force to the rear of the barricaded Creeks. He immediately ordered a full-scale, direct assault on the breastworks, which pinned the Creeks between two armies.

The 39th Regiment led the charge. Its commander, Major Lemuel P. Montgomery, was instantly killed on top of the wall. Houston was just behind Montgomery and, shouting to the men to follow, scaled the wall. He too was felled, by an arrow embedded in his thigh, but he was inside the Indian fort and his men were streaming in behind him.

Houston summoned a subaltern to pull the barbed arrow out, but he failed twice to do so. Threatening the hapless subordinate with his sword, Houston ordered him, "Try again and, if you fail this time, I will smite you to the earth."

On the third try, the arrow came out, but the torn flesh and loss of blood obliged Houston to cross back over the wall to have his wound dressed. Although he begged to rejoin his men, Jackson, who had witnessed his heroism, ordered him to withdraw entirely from the battle.

The Creeks were equally heroic, but their defense also had a religious fervor, a mystical element. Had not the Shawnee Prophet promised that the Great Spirit would intervene and give them victory over the whites? They waited for the promised miracle. The shamans and holy men called on the Great Spirit for help and exhorted the warriors to fight on. The sky suddenly clouded over. Could this be the sign? It was only a spring rain. The darkened sky was a portent of destruction, not victory.

The Creeks began to retreat to the river, where they were slaughtered by the sharpshooters lined up on the opposite shore. A small force took advantage of a natural redoubt formed by fallen logs and brush on the steep slope between the breastwork and the river. Jackson called for volunteers to dislodge them.

Houston, who had rejoined his unit, grabbed a musket and led the charge. Five yards from the redoubt, he received two rifle balls in his right shoulder. He called to his men to follow him, but they did not and he sank alone to the earth, unconscious and near death. The remaining Creeks were dislodged only when the logs and brush were set afire.

The severely wounded, unconscious third lieutenant was carried back to the surgeon. With a probe and forceps, the doctor was able to remove one of the rifle balls from Houston's shoulder. He left the other ball. It made little difference. The young soldier was finished and would probably die before daybreak. The wounded with a better chance to live must be looked to first.

Houston's comrades left him where he lay. He spent the night on the damp ground, suffering the agonies of three serious wounds. Excruciating pains swept through the shoulder ravaged by the rifle balls and the upper leg torn by the barbarous Creek arrow. When the sun rose he was still alive and had rallied slightly.

A litter was prepared, and the desperately injured man was loaded onto it. The journey home began. It took more than two months for Sam to reach his mother's house on Baker's Creek. When he was brought to her door, Elizabeth Houston had no idea who he was. It was only by his eyes, she said, that she realized that the pale, skeletal apparition was her son Sam.

———

The bloody battle of Horseshoe Bend ended the Creek War and the Creek Nation. The bodies of almost a thousand warriors lay in the smoking ruins of the barricade, among the charred logs of the redoubt, on the open slopes leading down to the razed village, or floating in the Tallapoosa. In a letter to Rachel, Jackson said, "The carnage was dreadfull." He did not add that he had added to the butchery by ordering his men to cut off the noses of the dead Indians as a way of accurately counting the number killed.

The 39th Regiment, as the leaders of the assault, suffered most of the casualties: twenty dead and fifty-two wounded. The Tennessee Militia, which comprised two thirds of the entire force, lost only eight men. Twenty-three of the friendly Indians died.

The Battle of Horseshoe Bend was one of the most important battles of the War of 1812. It ended the threat of an alliance of the Indians and the British, who were prepared to arm the Creeks heavily. Such a coalition would have been a disaster to the entire southern half of the United States.

Red Eagle realized his cause was lost, and he surrendered to Jackson two weeks later. He walked unarmed, unannounced, and unafraid into Jackson's camp, Fort Jackson, just north of present-day Montgomery. The Hickory Ground, the most sacred site in the Creek Nation, was nearby.

Red Eagle's bravery in coming to the fort—every white man in a thousand miles wanted to kill him—impressed Jackson mightily and he released him, after Red Eagle had promised to intercede with the other Creeks to stop the war and lay down their arms. He kept his word, but most of the other leaders had already fled to Florida, where they joined up with the Seminoles in their war against the whites.

The friendly Creeks, who had fought beside the whites and the Cherokees, fared no better than their unassimilated and warlike brothers once the fighting ended. On August 9, 1814, in return for their services, they were forced to sign the Treaty of Fort Jackson, in which they ceded twenty million acres of their ancestral lands to the United States.

And what of Red Eagle, who had led his people to disaster? True to his word, he forsook the Indian cause, not that there was much of one left. He again took up the ways of his white forebears. Once again William Weatherford, he lived on and died a successful and well-to-do planter in Monroe County, Alabama. He even visited Jackson at The Hermitage. Jackson, whose hospitality was boundless, understood the lessons of history and how easily their situations could have been reversed.

Would Red Eagle have spared Old Hickory? The Red Sticks were not noted for honoring their enemies' bravery. On the contrary, a brave warrior could expect a particularly grisly death if captured.

But history is rich in ironies. Weatherford, whose braves murdered almost five hundred people at Fort Mims, is commemorated by a monument about ten miles from the site of the massacre.

———

The doctors in Tennessee were certain that Houston could not live and certainly could not survive an operation. The second rifle ball was left in the shoulder. Sam's convalescence was long and difficult, but by late summer he was able to ride, and he set out for Washington, D.C., to seek better medical aid. He was also on a perhaps more important mission—to secure his future in the army.

The British plans in the Southeast had gone awry, but they were pursuing the war more aggressively in the North. They had no European distractions. The war on the Continent was over. Napoleon had been defeated and exiled to Elba.

A British army of four thousand landed on the shores of Chesapeake Bay, at Benedict, Maryland, on August 19, 1814, and marched on Washington. In one of those acts of warfare that is guaranteed to rouse the populace and certify the barbarism of the aggressor, the British vengefully burned both the White House and the Capitol on the night of August 24–25. Jefferson wrote to Lafayette that the act "has merely served to immortalize their infamy."

Jefferson's condemnation was justified, but American troops had done much the same thing a year earlier in Canada. An invasion force attacked York and burned the Parliament building and the home of the lieutenant governor.

Houston arrived in Washington soon after the British had done their spiteful best to raze it. He saw firsthand the blackened ruins of the seat of Congress and the president's home. The sight was indelible and Houston could describe it in detail to his last days.

From Washington, Sam went on to his birthplace in Virginia. He spent the winter with loving and solicitous relatives who nursed him back to health. In February 1815 he headed back down the Shenandoah Valley to Tennessee—over the same route that he had traveled as a fifteen-year-old in 1808.

Peace negotiations had been taking place between the Americans and the British since the beginning of the war, when the Russian tsar, Alexander I, had offered to mediate and had so instructed the American minister to Russia, John Quincy Adams.

A peace conference was finally convened in Ghent, Belgium, in August 1814. The American delegation included Adams, Henry Clay, and Albert Gallatin. The British delegation was less exalted. After all the Congress of Vienna was taking place at the very same time. The rearrangement of Europe was more important than the sideshow in America.

Demands and concessions were radically influenced by dispatches from America, which took at least a month. The British were after territorial gains and the news of the burning of Washington gave them hope that the Americans would be more malleable.

The rights of the Indians and their lands were a major sticking point at Ghent. The British, to their credit, did try to protect their allies, but their main aim was to use the Indians as a buffer between the United States and Canada. This goal proved futile. The United States would never agree to set aside land for a group that most Americans viewed as savages, especially those tribes that had sided with England in the war.

The British did not pursue the Indian issue nor any other that might lead to a continuation of the war, and the Americans reciprocated by not pressing for the resolution of the very issues that had caused the United States to go to war in the first place—in particular, the impressment of American seamen and the boundary disputes.

The British had another compelling reason to cease hostilities. The Duke of Wellington himself, when offered the American command, had expressed doubt about any successful military conclusion.

The peace treaty was signed on Christmas Eve. It was little more than a paper documenting the end of a war that no sensible person had wanted and restoring the *status quo ante bellum*. The report of the signing of the treaty reached Washington on February 11, 1815. Houston probably heard of the end of the war while he was still in Virginia.

The greatest battle of the war was fought two weeks after the signing of the Treaty of Ghent. Houston's old commander, Andrew Jackson, defeated the British at New Orleans on January 8. Wellington's brother-in-law, Lord Pakenham, did not share the Iron Duke's view of the American war and accepted the command of the British forces in the southeast. He was killed before the American fortifications at New Orleans.

With this resounding victory, Old Hickory stepped onto a greater stage than anyone but Jackson himself, and probably Sam Houston, could have imagined. The country was delirious with joy over Jackson's triumph. It would not know for another month that the war was over and a peace treaty had been signed, but it didn't really matter. The British had been defeated again.

The disaster at New Orleans did no real damage to the morale of the British. Within months Wellington defeated the temporarily revivified Napoleon at Waterloo and the second American war soon became a footnote in British history. But both England and the United States were relieved that the war was over. It had been a failure of arms for both sides. It did, however, have a major political and psychological effect in the United States. American expansion to the west could now proceed, unimpeded by the British and the Indians, who were finished as a major threat.

On the political side, the sectionalism that had threatened the republic from its birth had been invoked by the New Englanders who opposed the war. Their arguments were later used to good effect by Southerners to defend slavery and oppose the tariff.

And, of course, the war eventually raised Andrew Jackson to the

presidency and inaugurated a completely new idea of the role of the
people, particularly people from the West—the frontier—in participa-
tory democracy. Although they managed to hang on for a few more
years the war finished the Federalists, who had opposed it, as a major
party.

Houston and his neighbors in Tennessee, who were "all Republicans," were gratified by the peace with England, but Sam worried that
he would be dismissed from the army with most of the other officers.
His worries were understandable. His heroism at the Battle of
Horseshoe Bend had earned him a promotion to second lieutenant on
May 20, but what chance did a seriously wounded man have of being
retained in an army that was being completely reorganized and much
reduced in size?

His ambition and his much improved health encouraged him to press
his case to powerful politicians and cabinet members. From Maryville,
on March 1, 1815, he wrote to Congressman John Rhea of Tennessee
that "it is my wish to be continued in the army I have fought & bled
for my country in consequence of which I am in measure rendered unfit
for other business. . . . I entered the army at a time I had not friends
to patronize me & by my own merits or good fortune have been
promoted & I think it consistent with a virtuous Government to reward
bravery & merit both of which I claim."

A second letter, written the same day was addressed to Secretary of
War James Monroe. "I have given proofs of my Valour & fidelity in the
cause of Liberty and in return I carry honorable scars," said Houston,
"for no less than two wounds did I receive at the Battle of Tohopeka
one by an arrow, & another by two rifle balls which lodged in my
shoulder & have since been extracted & I am now so recovered as to
do active service.

"You no doubt will think proper to make yourself acquainted with my
private character," he continued. "I refer you to the delegation from
East Tennessee, I have the pleasure of an acquaintance with some of the
members. I have not influential relatives to support me with their influence & if merit does not support me, I must sink."

A third letter went to Senator Joseph Anderson of Tennessee. "I have
evinced to the world that whenever it is necessary to risk my life for the
safety of my country that I will do it," said Sam, "& Sir if you feel

yourself justified in using your influence to have me continued in the army you may rest assured that I will be ever grateful for the same."

He dispatched all three letters the next day, his twenty-second birthday. They demonstrate that Houston had developed considerable political wiles. It is certainly questionable that he was as alone in the world as he maintained. He knew very well, even at this young age, which strings to pull and who could be helpful.

He nevertheless spent an anxious two months waiting for a reply. He had not heard anything by the end of April when he wrote an old Virginia friend, Captain Alexander Campbell, about his plans. He knew he had to make a living but supposed it "impracticable for a disbanded officer to marry, for the[y] will be regarded as cloathes, out of fashion, not worn or much altered before the[y] are worn but I will not despond before I am disappointed, and I suppose that will be some time for I will not court any of the Dear Girles before I make a fortune and if I come to no better speed than I have done heretofore, it will be some time."

Houston's lobbying efforts were successful. He was accepted for regular duty in the 1st Infantry on May 17, 1815, and he reported for duty in Nashville on July 4.

He was posted to New Orleans, and in September he and a companion, Edward White, set out in a small skiff from Nashville. They traveled northwest on the Cumberland, through western Kentucky to where the river joins the Ohio, and then down the Ohio to the juncture with the Mississippi.

Houston, as was his custom throughout life, chose his traveling companion carefully. The twenty-year-old White had just graduated from the University of Nashville and was on his way back to his home in New Orleans to study law. His subsequent career in some ways resembled Houston's. He served in Congress and was governor of Louisiana. His son became chief justice of the United States.

River journeys, whether Huck Finn's on the Mississippi or Siegfried's on the Rhine, always engage a romantic imagination. Houston no doubt conceived and planned this particular trip, seeing himself and his companion as nineteenth-century argonauts. Even allowing for his decoration of the tale years later it is still an appealing nineteenth-century interlude.

Sam took along "in his frail bark, with which he threaded the vast solitude of the father of waters, a choice but small library." His mother had given him a Bible, and he had his old copy of Pope's translation of *The Iliad*. In addition he carried an edition of Shakespeare, some works of the English poet Mark Akenside, and copies of *Robinson Crusoe, The Vicar of Wakefield,* and *The Pilgrim's Progress*.

The works were, and are, standard items, with the exception of Akenside, a now forgotten eighteenth-century poet who was also physician to Queen Charlotte. Akenside's most famous work, *The Pleasures of Imagination,* no doubt appealed to Houston who always took pleasure in the imagination. And Houston almost certainly saw parallels between Friday, Crusoe, the Cherokees, and himself. Had he not been marooned, although voluntarily, in the Cherokee Nation with his own noble children of nature?

Near Natchez, the voyagers came across an astounding sight, a vessel belching fire and smoke. If this was, as Houston later reported, the first steamboat to traverse the Mississippi, it was the *Enterprise,* which was headed downstream to New Orleans. The young officers immediately decided to sell the skiff in Natchez and book passage. Eight days later they arrived in New Orleans.

New Orleans had been ruled by both France and Spain, and it retained much of both these cultures. Most of the population was still Spanish or French, and it was arguably the most cosmopolitan city in America. The War of 1812 had made the city stable and its growth was explosive. Within a few years it became the greatest port in the country, serving the entire western region.

Houston, in his recollections, passed briefly over this period. He called it "a winter of great suffering" caused by the removal of shattered bone from his shoulder. He was confined to the barracks most of the time and spent his evenings reading.

Many years later, when Houston was telling the story of his time in New Orleans, it was important that he be seen as abstemious. The issue of intemperance followed him throughout his political career. The more likely story is that in spite of pain from his war wounds, which did plague him, Houston readily plunged into the social life of New Orleans.

Young officers have ever been in demand, and in postwar New Orleans they must have been the very center of attention. Given his personality, Sam would have seen this as not only the duty but the right of a young war hero.

In politics and war, Sam Houston preferred the company of older men. Otherwise he would rather be with beautiful young women. It would have been difficult for him not to put on his dress uniform and go out on the town. He was charming, handsome, and a good talker. The parties, balls, and dinners, the restaurants, coffeehouses, and brothels of New Orleans were a great temptation to a twenty-two-year-old from the mountains of east Tennessee.

He also spent some time writing letters. Houston felt that his promotion to second lieutenant should have been dated March 28, 1814, instead of May 20. Two officers who outranked him were killed at Horseshoe Bend on March 27. If his appointment had been made immediately, he would have advanced two places and thus now be the ranking second lieutenant in the United States Army.

Houston pursued this point doggedly, but unsuccessfully, throughout his time in the army. It was a matter of principle, but he was also probably right. As it stood, he was next to last on the list of the 1st Regiment of Infantry. He, of course, wanted to be first. Neither the secretary of war nor Andrew Jackson, who at Houston's request intervened in January 1817, was able to change the order of rank.

However Houston spent the New Orleans winter—out and about, or in monastic retreat with the classics, or having his wounds treated—he remained there only until the following spring. In April 1816, he sailed for New York City.

———

Houston may have traveled to New York for further medical treatment, but there is no documentation for this. There was no army hospital in the city, and any treatment that his wounds required was available in any number of other places in the United States of 1816. Therefore this visit remains something of a mystery. Perhaps he was simply on leave from the army. In any event, Houston "sojourned some weeks and improved in his general health" in New York.

New York, in 1816, was not yet the cultural and commercial capital of the United States, but it had already taken on those cosmopolitan and brash airs that remain its defining characteristics. Houston developed a taste for the city and made many friends there. He visited New York often throughout his life.

Houston returned to active duty sometime in the fall of 1816. As was his habit, he traveled south by way of Lexington to see his Virginia relatives, in particular Cousin Matthew at High Bridge. He then went on to Maryville, where he had a long rest at his mother's house on Baker's Creek.

After the War of 1812, the United States Army was reorganized into two sections, the Northern Division and the Southern Division. The command in the South automatically went to Andrew Jackson. Old Hickory was even allowed to set up his headquarters at The Hermitage. He thus enjoyed the life of a military commander and a Tennessee planter at the same time. He could indulge his twin passions—raising horses and running an army—without leaving home. His staff was quartered on the estate.

Houston reported for duty in Nashville and was warmly welcomed by his old chief. The Hermitage had become the center of political as well as military life and Jackson was surrounded by representatives from both worlds. And, as was his custom, he put them up at his home.

The Hermitage in 1817 was a collection of log cabins used for family quarters, staff and guest quarters, kitchens, and storage. It was not until 1819 that the Jacksons began the brick federal style house that eventually evolved into the beautiful Greek revival mansion that is so familiar through photographs and prints. The earthy and colorful Old Hickory would never recognize his home today. It has been sanitized, made respectable, the rooms embalmed and entombed behind sheets of glass.

The adoration by the public for Jackson had, if anything, only increased since the war, and there was already talk of his running for the presidency. A small, tightly knit group of Tennessee advisers—John Eaton, John Overton, and William B. Lewis—was already in place. James Gadsden, Jackson's aide de camp, was also in residence. A patrician South Carolinian who had graduated from Yale, Gadsden nevertheless fit right into the circle. Houston happily became an acolyte in the budding movement that became Jacksonianism.

Thirty-three-year-old William Berkeley Lewis was another transplanted Virginian. He had served as quartermaster in the War of 1812 and fought at both the Horseshoe and New Orleans with Jackson. He was further tied to Jackson through his marriage to Jackson's ward, one of the Lewis sisters, daughters of a wealthy Tennessee planter. The two girls were just two of the many young people taken in by the childless

Andrew and Rachel Jackson. William and Margaret Lewis lived at their plantation, Fairfield, just down the road from The Hermitage.

John Eaton was born in North Carolina in 1796, but he had grown up on a 4,800-acre property in Tennessee. He also served under Jackson in the War of 1812, and when Jackson's aide and biographer, John Reid, died, Eaton stepped in and finished the biography. He produced a work that is historically valuable, sycophantic, full of flattery, and dull. It was also hugely successful. Eaton married the other Lewis sister, Myra, and they lived at The Hermitage.

The third member of the Tennessee triumvirate was John Overton. He had immigrated from Virginia to Kentucky where he studied law. The young attorney boarded with a Mrs. Robards, whose son, Lewis, was married to a Rachel Donelson, whom he had met in Nashville, Tennessee.

Rachel Robards was vivacious, flirtatious, outgoing, and pretty. She loved parties, dancing, singing, and telling stories. She could also ride and shoot as well as most men and better than many. All of these attributes were not a cause for celebration by her pathologically jealous husband, however. They only agitated him. Lewis Robards's jealousy finally got the better of him, and he sent Rachel home to her mother in Nashville.

About 1788, Overton left Kentucky and moved on to the raw frontier town of Nashville, which was little more than a collection of log houses and forts on the Cumberland River. He boarded with Mrs. John Donelson, Rachel Robards's widowed mother. Rachel's father, John Donelson, had been killed and scalped by Indians while out surveying land near Nashville.

Soon after Overton's arrival, Andrew Jackson came to town. Tennessee was still part of North Carolina, and the twenty-one-year-old Jackson had been appointed prosecuting attorney for the western district. Mrs. Donelson's boardinghouse was recommended to him, and there he met the woman who made him supremely happy and the man who made him president of the United States.

Rachel Robards and Andrew Jackson began a flirtation that quickly got out of control. When Rachel's husband left her for good and moved to Virginia, she and Jackson were completely free to continue their affair.

In the summer of 1791, Jackson received word that Lewis Robards had divorced Rachel in Virginia. He hurried to Natchez, where Rachel was visiting, and they were married. They returned to Tennessee and settled down in Nashville.

In 1793 they were astounded to learn that Robards had not been granted a divorce in 1791. He had only instituted proceedings. The final divorce had just been granted—on grounds of adultery and desertion. In his suit, Robards alleged that Rachel had left him and had been living with another man for two years.

Had they been victimized by the jealous Robards and married in good faith in Natchez? Or did Rachel knowingly commit bigamy? Whatever the answer, the scandal had to be contained.

John Overton had become Jackson's closest friend, confidant, and business associate. He immediately proposed a solution. In January 1794, Andrew Jackson and Rachel Robards went through another marriage ceremony. They were now legally man and wife, and the scandal was buried. It was by no means dead, however. Thirty-five years later, it was dug up by Jackson's enemies and dragged about in the midst of a presidential campaign.

Andrew Jackson's friends knew that Tennessee could not hold him. Lewis had said as much soon after the Battle of New Orleans back in 1815. Jackson clearly had a higher destiny, the fulfillment of which seemed only a matter of time. However, this was the Era of Good Feeling. The new president, James Monroe, had united the country and was wildly popular. His election to a second term was inevitable. The earliest that Jackson could run for president would be 1824, which gave Lewis, Overton, and Eaton plenty of time to organize their coup.

Overton's adroit handling of the marriage scandal had demonstrated his loyalty and political acumen. Now he had joined forces with Eaton and Lewis to form the most politically astute trio in the United States. They set about to do nothing less than change the way presidents were made or elected. At first they underestimated the old guard and suffered a stunning setback. But the next time out, they left nothing to chance.

At The Hermitage, the discussions of the great issues of the time— the future of the Bank of the United States, slavery, the tariff, Jeffersonian democracy and the role of the people, westward expansion, and Indian removal—must have been intoxicating for an ambitious twenty-four-year-old. This was especially so when the unstated, perhaps, but underlying purpose was preparation for Jackson's assumption of the presidency of the United States.

The goal may have been more subliminal than conscious to the future candidate, as he later maintained, but it certainly shimmered like the Holy Grail to the others. Houston called his three early years with the Cherokees his "university of the woods." The Hermitage became Sam Houston's political university.

There was also a softer side to life at The Hermitage, isolated from the rough and tumble of politics and war. She still smoked a little pipe and could not write a proper sentence, but Rachel Jackson was far removed from her hell-raising youth on the frontier. She was now mistress of a great estate and the wife of America's hero.

Rachel Jackson welcomed Sam Houston to her home and became a second mother to him. She doubtless recognized in this young officer many of the qualities—some of them not necessarily admirable—that had drawn her to another young man thirty years before. She was forever after Houston's beloved "Aunt Rachel."

On May 1, 1817, Houston was promoted to first lieutenant. Not only was he now among the inner circle at the commander's headquarters—a great personal favorite of Old Hickory and clearly enjoying the esteem of his colleagues—but his military career was firmly back on track.

That summer in Tennessee he enjoyed a wonderful idyll. His health was good and there was much to do in Nashville and the surrounding countryside. Jackson's stable was just one of many and races were held regularly. Everyone attended and wagered. There were also fox hunts and bloody cockfights. General Jackson heartily took part in all of them.

During this time Houston was initiated into the Masonic Order. Almost all of the eminent men of the time were Masons, and the order was especially powerful in the South. Washington, Jefferson, Madison, Monroe, and, of course, Jackson were all members. Houston joined the Masons in Nashville, at Cumberland Lodge No. 8, on April 19, 1817. He took his first degrees on June 25 and became a Master Mason on July 22. Masonic connections proved to be extremely valuable to Houston throughout his life.

Andrew Jackson in the War of 1812 had eliminated the Indians as any real threat to the whites in Tennessee. The Indians in Florida were another matter. They were still hostile and if stirred up and armed by the Spanish could be a threat to the Southeast. At The Hermitage, Jackson laid plans to march south and eliminate the Indian problem once and for all.

The peaceful tribes closer to home posed a much different problem for the whites. The Indians still occupied millions of acres of territory that extended over large parts of five states. War could make the problem easier and eliminate the moral issue. Whites could defeat the Indians and then take their land as spoils of war, as they had done after the Revolution and the War of 1812. The Indians had powerful friends, however, so an offensive war against them was out of the question. More devious measures were called for—measures that would strain both credulity and morality.

There were between six thousand and seven thousand surviving Creeks. In spite of the cession of twenty million acres of their land in 1814, they retained a like amount of territory to roam in. The Cherokee Nation, which was spread out over North Carolina, Tennessee, Georgia, and Alabama comprised a similar amount of territory with perhaps twelve thousand inhabitants. Then there were the Choctaws and the Chickasaws with their immense holdings.

In the American Southeast in 1817 there were some twenty-five thousand Indians living on thousands and thousands of square miles of land, all of it coveted by the whites. Why should so few people, it was argued, be entitled to so much land? Removal was seen as the only solution.

The Cherokees had signed the first treaty with the new United States in 1785, which was both a treaty of peace and a boundary settlement. The whites immediately ignored the treaty and began settling on Indian land. As pressure for Indian land steadily increased, white squatters were supported in their illegal acts by the state governments.

The Indians, of course, defended their lands, which led to intermittent and always bloody warfare. The federal government attempted to protect the Indians and honor the treaties. By and large the efforts were futile, and a new round of treaties would be negotiated. The Indians would be temporarily secure until a new wave of white settlers began to press in on them.

Removal of all the Indians beyond the Mississippi had been advocated for years. Thomas Jefferson, a strong proponent of the policy, sent a delegation to inspect land in the Arkansas Territory as a possible site for settlement of the eastern tribes. The commissioners reported favorably on the area, and in 1809 the first band of eastern Indians left for the west.

The time for the idea that all the Cherokees should move west had now come. On July 8, 1817, General Andrew Jackson, General David Meriweather, and Governor Joseph McMinn of Tennessee negotiated a treaty with the Cherokees for cession of their lands and the beginning of the removal of the tribe. There was only one problem. The majority of the Indians were dead set against giving up any more land and, in particular, against leaving their ancestral lands and heading west.

In the Cherokee mythology the spirits of the dead traveled to the west, and rivers and creeks were paths to the underworld. Therefore any travel to the west, and especially by water, was dangerous.

In the autumn of 1817, Andrew Jackson charged Sam Houston with a most important mission to his old friends the Cherokees, in particular to his adoptive father, Ooleteka. Houston was to persuade the Indians to relinquish their lands and move to the Arkansas Territory.

On October 9, Colonel Return J. Meigs, the federal agent, wrote to Houston, at Jackson's behest, appointing him subagent to the Cherokees. Meigs was a Revolutionary War hero who had been with the Cherokees since 1801. He was well respected by the tribe and always had a serious interest in their welfare. He lived among them until his death at the age of eighty-two. He died of pneumonia contracted by sleeping outdoors in a tent after giving up his warm indoor quarters to an old Cherokee chief.

Houston was ordered to proceed to Hiwassee and carry out Meigs's dictum that "the emigrants are not going from home; on the contrary they are going home in the best sense of the word." Sam enjoyed the complete confidence of Andrew Jackson, and he knew firsthand what the United States military was capable of and what the feelings of his fellow whites were toward their Indian neighbors.

The powerful forces of racial animosity and greed for Indian lands had been loosed, and the Indians would be driven off their lands by the whites sooner or later. Houston had to convince the Cherokees to follow the example of John Rogers, who had already left for the west with a large contingent of the Overhill Cherokee.

By December 18, Sam was back on the Hiwassee at the Cherokee Agency, near present-day Calhoun, Tennessee. The agency was only a few miles upriver from Hiwassee Island. The reunion with his Indian father was joyful but bittersweet. Had the Raven returned as a friend or a traitor?

If a fair settlement could be reached and a fair exchange of land negotiated, Houston argued, then it was in the best interests of the Cherokees to move to the west, where they were guaranteed they could live in peace. The guarantee was backed up by the might of the United States Army, of which Houston was the representative.

As soon as Houston reported in, he wrote to Jackson. In a touching and idealistic letter he confided to the white chief that although he was ill he had tried to do his duty. It is clear that his first concern was the welfare of his old friends. How could the Indians leave in the winter if there were not enough blankets for them? he asked. Besides only heads of households were entitled to blankets, which meant that many of the Indians would not receive them.

Even worse than the meager supplies set aside for the trek to the west was the selling of whiskey to the Indians. However, Houston was most upset by the profiteering of the agents and traders. "Is it compatible with the duties of an Agent of the Government to be engaged in Mercantile speculation?" he asked Jackson.

On December 28, Houston was a bit more optimistic about his mission in a letter to Secretary of War John C. Calhoun, whose department administered Indian affairs. He appealed for more blankets for the Indians because there are "no more than will enable them to move in circumstances barely tolerable."

He also revealed a characteristic high-handedness and self-confidence that are all the more remarkable when one remembers that he was not yet twenty-five years old.

He reported to Calhoun that he had moved the depot from the garrison to the agency. He could thus prohibit the sale of alcohol, which was forbidden on agency land. The Cherokee, according to Houston, could not drink the white man's liquor without getting hopelessly drunk for a good reason. The Indians had little tolerance for liquor because they seldom had access to it. And when they did they tended to drink up every drop. No matter what anyone's race the results are fairly predictable and disastrous.

Houston was disarmingly frank about the outright bribery involved— the blankets, tools, and other goods that the Indians were to be given if they would emigrate. Many Indians "had no intention of emigrating to Arkansas, until they came here and caught the contagion, which, in a short time will be epidemic." He reported that he had five hundred ready to go, including Ooleteka and his band of a hundred Hiwassee Cherokee.

The Cherokees who had already settled in the Arkansas Territory were worried, and rightly so given the white man's history. The boundaries of their new lands in the West often overlapped those held by the native western tribes. A delegation of chiefs was dispatched to Washington to press for the federal government's guarantee of their boundary rights and also to press for their recognition as an independent tribe.

The delegation, led by the venerable Chief Tahlohntusky, Ooleteka's brother, passed through Tennessee on its way east to the capital. Governor McMinn ordered Houston to accompany them, and he sent along detailed instructions for the journey—where to stay, how much to spend, how to behave.

Most important of all, the governor wanted no reports of drunkenness. This last may have been a prime example of gubernatorial hypocrisy, since McMinn reportedly had his own problems with liquor. Or perhaps it was because he knew firsthand what he was talking about that McMinn was so explicit. In any event, McMinn, unlike Jackson, obviously had some doubts about a twenty-four-year-old carrying off the mission.

The delegation arrived in Washington in February and was lodged at Brown's Indian Queen Hotel. The delegations from the dozens of Indian tribes were an everyday sight in the capital. The Indians enjoyed the festivities arranged for them and, of course, the presents they were given by the government officials.

In return the Indians gave their white hosts their money's worth. The tribal leaders appeared at receptions in full regalia and paint. Buffalo robes, feathers, and horns were not uncommon sights. One chief showed up at a party with his entire face painted a brilliant yellow.

On this trip to Washington, Houston had his first personal encounter with that commonplace of American political life—ambitious men trying to destroy the careers of other ambitious men. There were no formal charges, but Houston was accused of two things.

At Hiwassee, he was supposed to have prevented a force of Cherokees from marching to join up with General Edmund P. Gaines, who was fighting the Seminoles in Florida. Further, he had not intervened to stop the smuggling of black slaves from Florida into the Creek Nation but in fact had engaged in the illegal slave trade himself.

No one ever really got to the bottom of this, but since the smuggled slaves were found near the Creek Agency, that agent may have played a role. As for who started the rumors, there is little doubt—Houston's old commander, General John Williams. He was now a United States senator from Tennessee and an enemy of Andrew Jackson. Jackson was the real target. Houston was a target of opportunity.

Houston easily cleared himself of the false charges, but they were bitter reproofs for a man who felt that he had been slighted by an ungrateful government. He had after all spent an arduous winter, in ill health, effectively carrying out government policies that he had only half believed in. He wanted no more of it.

In a characteristically impulsive action, he resigned from the army while he was still in Washington. He sent a one-sentence letter to General Daniel Parker on March 1, 1818, submitting his resignation, effective immediately. The next day was his twenty-fifth birthday.

Although he had submitted his resignation, Sam appeared with the Indian delegation for their appointment with Secretary of War Calhoun and a reception with President Monroe on March 7. But he did not appear as a subordinate military officer for the meeting with the starchy Calhoun. Sam was in full Indian dress. Calhoun was outraged. The Era of Good Feeling did not extend to outré costumes.

Calhoun welcomed the Indian chiefs and promised them that the Arkansas lands would be theirs in perpetuity. He assured them that the overriding concern of the federal government was to protect the Indians from unscrupulous people.

The chiefs then adjourned to the next room to be received by the president. Calhoun asked Houston to stay behind and then proceeded to give him a thorough dressing down. No one had a finer sense of noblesse oblige and the white man's burden than Calhoun.

Houston kept his temper, although he was seething with rage when he joined the reception. His buckskin leggings and colorful hunting shirt were a startling contrast to the president's attire. Monroe, that son of the eighteenth century, customarily wore black knee breeches, black silk stockings, and his hair long, tied with a black ribbon. For ceremonial occasions, and these Indian receptions were designed to impress, he often switched to buff knee breeches and a blue coat, the uniform of the Revolution.

Monroe's role with the Indians was largely ceremonial—the Great

White Father. He had long since had his fill of this endless parade of Indians through Washington, but he dutifully received them. He left the details to Calhoun, who was certainly no friend of the red man.

The western Cherokee mission was only partially successful. The delegation was guaranteed their lands, but they were not accorded recognition as a separate tribe. The federal government had no intention of creating more Indian tribes. The long-range plan was for the eastern Cherokee to join their western brothers as soon as possible.

Sam Houston's military career ended in Washington. He left the capital as a civilian. He nevertheless fulfilled his obligation to his Indian friends and accompanied them south as far as his home in Tennessee. His bitterness, even hatred, toward John Calhoun would never abate.

Civilian Sam Houston faced an uncertain future. After five years in the army, he had very little to show for his efforts other than his wounds. He was unemployed, uneducated, and in debt to friends and family. His only training and experience had been in the military. He did have resources, however, and they were those that often count the most. Sam Houston had influential and supportive friends.

4

Congressman Houston

B Y THE END OF MARCH 1818, the young veteran was back on Baker's Creek. It was to be a brief visit, however, for Sam had decided on a new career. He would study law, that traditional occupation of the would-be politician.

Law schools were still a rarity in America. Harvard Law School, for example, was only a year old. The custom of the time was to read, or study, law in the office of a practicing attorney to prepare for the bar.

Houston's family and his old friends in Nashville found him a suitable mentor. In fact it is unlikely that anyone else was even considered. Judge James Trimble, the distinguished Nashville barrister, agreed to take Sam Houston as a legal apprentice.

The Trimbles had known the Houstons for decades. Judge Trimble's grandfather, Moses Trimble, witnessed the will of Sam's grandfather, Robert Houston, in 1761, and another Trimble was pastor of the Timber Ridge Presbyterian Church.

James Trimble was himself born in Rockbridge County in 1781, but as a young man had moved on to Tennessee. He was practicing law in Knox County when the Houstons arrived in neighboring Blount County in 1808. He organized the circuit court in Blount County in 1810, and a Robert Houston and a James Houston, probably Sam's brothers, both served as clerk of the court.

Another older and influential man had now entered Houston's life at a particularly critical juncture. In June 1818, Sam began his studies with Judge Trimble at his Nashville office. Sam, who six years before had been defeated by Euclidean geometry, now readily took to a demanding course of legal studies. The judge's course was designed to take at least a year to complete, but Houston, "after a few months' severe study, was admitted to the bar."

———

Houston's intensive study of the law did not preclude the pursuit of pleasure. He took an active part in the social life of Nashville, and in particular in a short-lived theatrical company founded by a twenty-three-year-old actor and budding impresario named Noah M. Ludlow. This colorful character had arrived in Nashville the year before after a tour of western America with Samuel Drake's company.

The Dramatic Club of Nashville attracted many prominent men of the town. John Eaton was a member and Andrew Jackson was an honorary member. However, Houston was the only one who actually appeared on stage. He took the part of the villanous, Iago-like Glenalvon in John Home's *Douglas*. "Never were vice and virtue poised so ill/As in Glenalvon's unrelenting mind." In Louis-Sébastien Mercier's *Point of Honor* (*Le Deserteur*), Sam was the noble Chevalier St. Franc, faced with the terrible dilemma of executing his own son, the deserter of the title, or allowing him to escape.

Ludlow said that Sam was "the *largest*, if not the most gifted with dramatic ability," of anyone in the company. He added that he had "never met a man who had a keener sense of the ridiculous"—no doubt referring to Houston's role as a drunken porter in *We Fly by Night*.

Ludlow moved on to New Orleans at the end of 1818, and the Dramatic Club folded. Houston thus had to give up acting, but the theatrical flair would stay with him all his life.

Houston's theatrical career ended just about the same time that his legal career began. Early in 1819, Sam wound up his studies with Judge Trimble and was admitted to the Tennessee bar. He was looking around for a place to settle when Isaac Galladay, the postmaster in Lebanon, Tennessee, offered him an office for a very low rent.

Sam thus opened his first law practice in a small log building just off the main square in a little town about thirty miles from Nashville and an equal distance from Murfreesboro, which was the capital at the time. Tennessee, like most of the states and indeed the United States itself, had the usual problems with deciding where its capital should be. Knoxville had already served twice and Nashville once. The issue was not settled until 1834.

Houston was perfectly suited for his profession. He was tall, good-looking, clever, affable, and had a brilliant oratorical style. He was thus settled in and thriving when a major political and historical event occurred in Tennessee.

President James Monroe had decided to visit the southern and western states—a royal progress through his domain. Two years before he had toured the North to great acclaim from the huge crowds. This trip was part fence-mending and part further consolidation of the hold the Jeffersonian Republicans had on the country. He would, of course, come to Tennessee and visit the most popular man in the United States at The Hermitage.

Houston had last seen the president when he had appeared in Indian dress at the Washington reception for the Cherokees in March 1818. Sam now presented another image to the patrician Monroe—that of a respectable Tennessee attorney.

Houston's private practice led to public service almost immediately. Within just a few months, although he no doubt felt it should have been sooner, Sam was elected district attorney of Davidson County. In October 1819, he left Lebanon to return to the brighter, but by no means bright lights of Nashville, the county seat.

His tenure as district attorney, by his own admission in his 1855 *Short Autobiography,* was effective because "his powers of generalization and his sound judgment . . . gave him an advantage over his seniors." But success was apparently his only reward. Weary of the "profitless discharge of the unceasing duties," he returned to private law practice. On December 26, 1821, he placed an advertisement in the *Nashville Whig:*

> Sam Houston attorney at Law. Having removed to an office second below A. Kingsley's Esq. on Market Street, can be found at all times where he ought to be.

Houston, meanwhile, was advancing himself in two seemingly disparate organizations. He regularly attended meetings of the Tennessee Antiquarian Society and he rose in the Tennessee State Militia. Soon after his arrival in Davidson County, he was made a colonel in the militia. Promotion to adjutant general followed quickly. In October 1821, he was elected major general by his fellow soldiers. He was both honored and gratified, but then how could he not be? His father, even after a lifetime of service, had never gone beyond the rank of major.

Popular election of officials was in the American tradition, but Houston, in spite of his own elevation by the militia, disapproved of the election of military officers and always spoke against it. It was damaging to morale and discipline in a properly run military organization. Houston, of course, believed in democracy—for civilians. It was detrimental to an army.

As major general, he had Andrew Jackson's old job as head of the militia, a position that had propelled Jackson to national prominence. The ambitious Houston was well aware of the importance of the job and the parallel with his hero Jackson.

Houston now divided his time between Murfreesboro, the headquarters of the militia, and Nashville, where he had his law practice. He was still a bachelor and the Nashville Inn was his chief residence. The inn was the center of public life in the Tennessee capital. It was popular with state legislators, and visiting dignitaries were put up there. It was also a place where plots were hatched and feuds and quarrels were born—fueled by gallons of good Tennessee sour mash whiskey.

The inn became not only Houston's home but his club and favorite place of entertainment. Just after Christmas in 1822, he was host of a holiday Masonic ball at the inn. Houston was the most eligible man in town. Major general of the militia, successful lawyer, and rising political figure, he was clearly a man on his way up. He was twenty-nine years old.

Nashville had been founded on speculation by James Robertson. His son, Felix, the mayor of Nashville, carried on the tradition. With a group of prominent Tennesseans, who were interested in Texas land speculation, Felix Robertson had formed the Texas, or Nashville, Association. Sam Houston was an active member. In April 1822, the association's representative, Robert Leftwich, arrived in Mexico City to petition the federal government for a land grant.

At about this same time, a German Jewish traveler named Adolphus Stern arrived at the Nashville Inn. He and Houston took an instant liking to each other. Their friendship endured until Stern's death thirty years later.

Whether Stern was then on his way to Texas, where he would become a central figure in the revolution and the republic, is not clear. But he was definitely settled at Nacogdoches by 1824.

Texas had also caught the eye of other entrepreneurs by this time, most notably Moses Austin. On January 17, 1821, Moses Austin's petition to settle three hundred families in Texas was approved by the Spanish authorities. Moses Austin, unlike his biblical namesake, did at least visit the Promised Land. But he died in June 1821, three months after receiving the good news from Monterey.

Austin's son, Stephen F. Austin, took up his father's work and in December 1821 the first sixty families arrived at his new colony on the Brazos River, about sixty miles northwest of present-day Houston. The settlement of Texas by Americans had seriously begun when Houston resumed law practice in Nashville.

————

Meanwhile Andrew Jackson and his little band of advisers continued their plans to win Old Hickory the presidency. Jackson had added to his military reputation with his victories in the Seminole War in Florida, and his standing with the American public was highter than ever. He would have to wait until 1824, however, to seek election.

Monroe had, of course, been reelected in 1820. Perhaps reannointed might be a better description of the election. He received all the electoral votes but one, cast for John Quincy Adams by a spoilsport from New Hampshire.

The Hermitage was no longer a collection of log cabins. It was now a two-story, Federal-style brick house with four large upstairs bedrooms for guests. Houston was now part of Jackson's inner circle, along with a newcomer to Tennessee, James K. Polk. A North Carolinian by birth, Polk had just set up his own law practice in Columbia, about thirty miles from The Hermitage. He soon became an ardent Jacksonian.

Jackson was building a powerful machine, and he needed a slate of attractive political candidates who would help him take over the newly evolved Democratic party. The election of 1824 was to be the beginning of a new era in American political life. Both Houston and Polk were obvious choices to run for office.

Andrew Jackson faced more formidable obstacles to election than any candidate in American history. Every president had been an aristocrat— four from Virginia and two from Massachusetts.

Tennessee, that outpost of the West, promised reform of the system. The Tennessee constitutional convention of 1796, in which Jackson had a leading role, drafted a constitution that was more democratic than that of the United States. It guaranteed universal manhood suffrage, even for free blacks. Jefferson had called it the "least imperfect and most republican" of any constitution.

A new political constituency was being forged and Jackson and his circle would command its loyalty. Though all of them had been born in the old colonies or original states, they had little in common with the eastern seaboard establishment. They were of the frontier. Their lives had been shaped by what they viewed as the real America, which must be restored to the people.

Houston, the natural lawyer, the instinctive stump speaker, was chosen to run for the U.S. Congress from Tennessee's Ninth Congressional District in the 1823 election. He ran with no opposition, which is hardly surprising. Who would have the temerity to run against the hand-picked candidate of General Jackson and the governor? Houston received 100 percent of the votes cast. But it was a vote in the state legislature that, for the time being, was much more important than Houston's own lopsided race for a House seat.

William Lewis was hard at work to secure the Democratic nomination for Jackson in 1824. After his first wife died Lewis had remarried, and he now traveled to North Carolina to persuade his father-in-law, Senator Montfort Stokes, to endorse Jackson and to convince the North Carolina legislature to do the same.

Stokes was pledged to support Calhoun, but he did agree that if the South Carolinian dropped out he and the North Carolina legislature would support Jackson for the nomination.

Back in Tennessee, Lewis had a more difficult problem. Jackson ally John Eaton held one Senate seat, but the other was held by Jackson's bitter enemy, John Williams, who was up for reelection. Since there was no strong opponent the legislature, which then elected United States senators, would almost certainly return Williams to Washington, which would be a fatal blow to Jackson's presidential plans. How could Lewis convince other state legislatures to endorse Jackson if his home state was sending a virulently anti-Jackson man back to the Senate?

Lewis and Overton devised a brilliant scheme. Andrew Jackson himself would run against Williams for the United States Senate. It was foolproof, and Jackson got all but twenty-five votes. Jackson's power was such that of the twenty-five legislators who voted against him twenty-two lost their seats in the next election.

Houston left for Washington in October 1823 to serve in the Eighteenth Congress, which convened on December 1. He took with him a letter of introduction from Jackson to Thomas Jefferson. The Sage of Monticello was eighty years old, but his health was good and he rode his horse almost every day. Jefferson was always eager for news from the West and in particular the Jackson camp.

The canny old philosopher politician had followed Jackson's career and grasped intuitively that here, perhaps, was a future president. It was Jefferson's advocacy of investing the power in the common man that had made Jackson possible, after all. But Jefferson, given any choice in the matter, would have chosen a much different sort for his experiment.

As vice-president, he had presided over the Senate when Jackson had first appeared there in 1797. His chief memory of Jackson then was his anger, which was so great that it often rendered him unable to speak on the Senate floor. Jefferson felt that Jackson had no doubt mellowed but he never liked him much. "His passions are, no doubt, cooler now," said Jefferson; "he has been much tried since I knew him, but he is a dangerous man."

While in Virginia, Houston also called on Miss Sophia Reid, the granddaughter of a Tennessee friend, Abram Maury, but "I had not time to make a long stay there, as I wished to have done," he said. If a romance with Miss Reid was in the air, it soon dissipated. No more is heard of her.

Congressman Houston rented rooms at the boardinghouse of a Mrs. Wilson, while senators Eaton and Jackson were lodged at O'Neill's Tavern. The proprietor's pretty daughter, Margaret O'Neill Timberlake, was also living at O'Neill's. She was married to a naval officer and while her husband was at sea she helped her father with the hotel, often playing the piano for the guests.

In many ways the situation was reminiscent of that at Mrs. Donelson's boardinghouse in Nashville back in 1788. Jackson's protégé, John Eaton, now began his own affair with a married woman at her family's boardinghouse.

The one thing in Washington that Houston disliked from the beginning was the press, an antipathy he shared with most public figures. He soon wrote to a friend in Tennessee, "I will not pretend to give you news at this distance when we have so many smart Editors in this part of the country—I say smart because many of them are so sagacious that they will not state facts, but make them to suit their own wishes."

Jackson's appearance in Washington was more like that of a head of state than a senator. He was "much courted, by the Great as well, as the Sovereign folks," noted Houston approvingly. Old Hickory also had not yet set foot in the Capitol, which was not surprising. The Senate was not on his mind. He was there to pursue the presidential nomination, and as Houston observed, "He will not do anything out of his fixed course."

When Jackson did decide to enter the Senate chamber he ran into Thomas Hart Benton, one of the two senators from the new state of Missouri. The two former friends had not seen each other in ten years. The two men put aside their old animosity in the interest of the party and Jackson's presidential aspirations. Benton once again was a staunch Jacksonian.

There seemed to be a disproportionate share of political giants abroad in the land in 1823. They roamed the halls of the Eighteenth Congress, they inhabited the White House, and they were even in the cabinet. Perhaps the issues of the day were such that they produced men of stature to deal with them, or at least to define and debate them.

Clay, Webster, Van Buren, Benton, and Jackson were in the Congress. Monroe was in the White House and both Calhoun and John Quincy Adams were in his cabinet. John Marshall still headed the Supreme Court. Jefferson, Madison, and John Adams from their retirement commented regularly on public affairs.

The extension of slavery or its abolition, Indian removal or assimilation, states' rights or a stronger federal government, free trade or a more restrictive tariff were unresolved issues that threatened the viability of the nation. There was also the continuing debate over the proper role, if any, for a government-sanctioned Bank of the United States. And what was the proper role of the United States abroad, particularly in Central and South America?

No domestic issue was as inflammatory as the extension of slavery into the new states. All of the states north of Maryland and Delaware had abolished slavery, which had been relatively simple since there was no economic imperative involved. The agricultural South was a very different matter. Slavery had been institutionalized and much of the agrarian economy depended on it.

Southerners, therefore, had a vested interest in not only preserving the "peculiar institution" but in expanding it. Otherwise it was only a matter of time, as new states were admitted to the Union, until the slave states would be hopelessly outvoted in the Congress. The slavery faction felt that it was fighting for its very life. In 1819, the slave and free states were balanced in the Senate, but the equilibrium was threatened by the proposed admission of Missouri.

The so-called Missouri Compromise of 1820, masterminded by Henry Clay of Kentucky, while it did not resolve the issue, at least deferred it for years. Missouri was to be admitted as a slave state, Maine as a free state, and in the remainder of the Louisiana Purchase slavery was prohibited north of 36° 30'.

The crisis was averted, but everyone had been finally forced to recognize the depth of feeling on both sides. They had looked into the abyss. Southerners had served notice that secession from the Union was a very real possibility. The antislavery forces had countered with the threat that they were as equally determined not only to prevent the spread of slavery but to abolish it entirely in the United States.

When Thomas Jefferson received news of the compromise, he said that "this momentous question, like a firebell in the night awakened and filled me with terror. I considered it the knell of the Union." Here began in earnest the struggle that would end, perhaps could only end, in civil war.

President Monroe felt that the best solution to both the slavery question and the Indian question was resettlement. Geography could thus solve two of the greatest problems confronting the United States. The blacks would be sent back to Africa and the Indians would be moved to the West. Many other eminent men, who should have known better, agreed with Monroe, most notably James Madison and Thomas Jefferson.

Both Monroe and Madison endorsed the work of the American Colonization Society, which was instrumental in the founding of Liberia. The colony on the west coast of Africa was to be the immediate home for newly freed blacks. When slavery was eventually abolished millions more would join them there. The capital, Monrovia, was named for the president.

The resettlement of American blacks in Africa was doomed from the beginning because of the vast numbers of people involved, the great expense, and the uncongenial location of the African colony. The plan was never completely abandoned, however, and continued to engage even thoughtful and well-meaning people of both races for decades.

The slavery issue defeated men of the most humanitarian impulses, who otherwise always acted in the best interests of others. The most resonant example of those who said one thing and did another was Thomas Jefferson. He was the exemplar of the old "do as I say, but not as I do" school of political philosophy.

He had helped rewrite the Virginia statute that in 1778 abolished the slave trade. Unfortunately the statute also prohibited free Negroes from entering Virginia and forbade emancipated slaves from remaining in the state for more than a year after receiving their freedom. If free Negroes entered Virginia or remained there illegally, they were to be considered "out of the protection of the laws"—a nice turn of phrase that translated into their being arrested and auctioned to the highest bidder.

Jefferson also tried to save himself from financial ruin by breeding slaves. As in all his endeavors he went about it with as much scientific rigor as was possible. He was very explicit in his orders to his overseer about caring for women of childbearing age and reducing infant mortality. A child "every 2. years is of more profit than the crop of the best laboring man." In 1822 there were 267 slaves at Monticello.

Jefferson, like many men of the time, felt that the Negro race was inherently inferior. He also felt that no race should be enslaved. Thus he advanced another scheme to eliminate slavery. The federal government would buy all slave children and bring them up and educate and train them. They would then be shipped to Haiti. He lamented the cruelty of separating these children from their parents, but as he put it, "The separation of infants from their mothers, too, would produce some scruples of humanity. But this would be straining at a gnat and swallowing a camel."

When Jefferson died he freed only five of his many slaves. All the others were left to his heirs. His action did not go unnoticed by the defenders of slavery. Philosophically, and no doubt morally, Thomas Jefferson was opposed to slavery, but like so many men of his class he too much enjoyed the advantages derived from it to advocate sudden and total abolition. Of all the founding fathers, only George Washington actually took steps to free his slaves.

Fortunately neither Jefferson's, Madison's, nor Monroe's place in history is based on their suggested solutions for the slavery question. Monroe is more deservedly remembered for a policy expounded in his annual message to Congress, delivered the day after Congress convened, December 2, 1823.

Houston was present to hear what became a basic principle of American foreign policy spelled out to the Congress and the world for the first time. The United States would not interfere in the affairs of Europe, but at the same time America would not countenance European intervention in the Western hemisphere.

The other major foreign policy initiative of the Monroe administration, the Adams-Onís Treaty, had been negotiated earlier. Secretary of State John Quincy Adams had skillfully used the threat of American arms, in particular the threat of General Andrew Jackson, to exact tremendous territorial concessions from the Spanish minister, Luís de Onís. The United States acquired all of Florida, and Spain and the United States agreed on the northern boundary of the remaining Spanish possessions in North America.

Treaties, when ratified, theoretically at least lay issues to rest and become the law of the land. Adams-Onís, like so many of its predecessors and successors, did no such thing, except for the status of Florida. A great many Americans had always believed that the northeastern province of the Spanish colony of Mexico—Tejas—had been part of the original Louisiana Purchase and had been United States territory since 1803. The treaty did not change their minds.

Andrew Jackson was certainly one of those who thought Texas was American and so was Sam Houston. Jackson, whom the Spanish called the "Napoleon of the Woods," was aching to throw the Spanish out of North America entirely, even to invade Mexico if necessary. However, as governor of Florida, Jackson was consulted by Adams and he had agreed to the boundaries set forth in the treaty. He later denied that he had done so. The Adams-Onís Treaty and Jackson's later recantation would have profound effects on Sam Houston's future.

————

The thirty-one-year-old freshman congressman from Tennessee wasted no time in calling attention to himself in the House of Representatives. The Greeks had risen up against their Turkish masters and their cause had captured the attention of the world. The people of *The Iliad* were suffering and Houston answered their call. He rose before his colleagues on January 22, 1824, to deliver a ringing and elegant speech on behalf of Greek independence.

He realized that the United States could not give direct aid to the Greeks, but recognition by the United States would give them courage in their struggle with the Ottoman Empire. We had done so when the colonies in South America had revolted against Spain, and we should do no less even though Greece was half a world away. "The principle is the same. Principles remain unchanged and eternal. The distance of the people from us does not alter the principle," said Houston.

With the exception of this speech. Houston's first congressional session was uneventful and when it ended he returned to Tennessee and the first order of business, the presidential campaign of Andrew Jackson. Campaigns were still fairly simple affairs. Very few people were involved, and the candidates themselves did no campaigning at all. Jackson's lieutenants had lobbied heavily while Congress was in session and they now went to work in the various state legislatures where so much of the power lay.

There were five candidates: Secretary of State John Quincy Adams, Secretary of the Treasury William H. Crawford, Secretary of War John C. Calhoun, Speaker of the House Henry Clay, and Andrew Jackson. Calhoun withdrew early from the race for the presidency, but his name was on the ballot as the vice-presidential candidate for both Adams and Jackson. Whichever of the two favorites won would have this Southern Trojan horse in his administration.

Houston had, of course, to make a living and for much of the early part of the summer was involved with his law practice. He was "at court continuously," he said. Then in August he became seriously ill.

"I am just out of sick bed," he wrote to his cousin John H. Houston in Washington. "This season is without any parallel here, for disease of the most fatal character. We have lost some of our best citizens, and some distinguished for talents. I will not describe the disease particularly, but only state that most persons become yellow when attacked—yet it is not termed 'Yellow fever.' "

Judging from his description of the disease and the fact that the following January in Washington it flared up again and he complained of a "torpid liver," Houston was probably suffering from hepatitis.

Politics, even the election of his friend Jackson to the presidency, if one judges from the available correspondence, was second to romance between sessions of Congress. Sam had met a young woman from Cheraw, South Carolina, but he was extremely discreet about it. He referred to her only as "Miss M," and he cautioned his Washington cousin, "Say nothing of this thing to our friends in the City."

Miss M was Mariah Campbell, the sister of a young South Carolina congressman, Robert Campbell. Their father, Captain Robert Campbell, was a British officer who had fought against the Americans in South Carolina during the Revolution. Ironically, he had been in charge of a contingent of American prisoners that had included Andrew Jackson. Captain Campbell was so taken with South Carolina that after the Revolution he returned and settled in Marlboro County.

Houston met Mariah in Washington, where she acted as hostess for her bachelor brother, and immediately fell in love. He asked her to marry him but she refused and when she returned home he followed her. In early November 1824, he wrote to his cousin from Morganton, North Carolina, where he had stopped over on his way to South Carolina. Mariah Campbell received him but still nothing was resolved and he went on to Washington for the next session of Congress.

———

The second session of the eighteenth Congress, which convened in December 1824, began auspiciously enough. Lafayette was on his grand tour of the United States, and almost the first order of business was the emotional welcome given to him by the House and Senate. Houston was a member of the group that escorted Lafayette into the House chamber and later joined with other representatives and senators in voting Lafayette $200,000 in recognition of his services to the revolution.

Since Lafayette was staying at the same house as Andrew and Rachel Jackson, Houston also had ample opportunity to socialize with him while he was in Washington. He would see him again the following spring when Lafayette came to Tennessee to stay with Jackson at The Hermitage.

The great French friend of democracy was also able to witness an event that must have troubled him greatly.

The 1824 presidential election resulted in no electoral college majority for either of the candidates. Jackson received the most votes, 99. Adams was second with 84. Crawford had 41 and Clay 37. The election therefore had to be decided by the House of Representatives. Clay threw his support to Adams, who became the sixth president of the United States.

Adams moved immediately to appoint Clay secretary of state. He thus paralyzed his presidency and poisoned the political well. Jacksonians, and most of America for that matter, were convinced that Adams and Clay had struck a "corrupt bargain." Clay had delivered the votes in the House in return for the office of secretary of state—an office that had already served four of the first six presidents as a springboard to the presidency. Jackson raged that "the *Judas* of the West has closed the contract and will receive the thirty pieces of silver."

Would men of the stature of Clay and Adams have struck such a bargain? Was their lust for power so great and their conviction that only they knew what was best for the people so firm that they were willing to thwart the will of the very people they were sworn to serve? These questions have been debated since 1825.

The truth most certainly is that Clay so disliked and distrusted Jackson that he would have given his votes to anyone, and for nothing. But his desire for the presidency was great enough that he was willing to run the risk of destroying his reputation. So he delivered Kentucky, in which Adams had not received a single electoral vote.

Adams knew his man, and Clay bore out Adams's assessment of him three years before. "Clay is an eloquent man, with very popular manners and great political management," said Adams. "He is, like all the eminent men of this country, only half educated. His school has been the world and in that he is proficient. His morals, public and private, are loose, but he has all the virtues indispensable to a popular man."

John Quincy Adams knew instinctively that not even the presidency was worth compromising his integrity. But he did not follow his instincts. His Brahminism prevailed. He was convinced that his learning, wide-ranging government experience, and social background made him a far better choice to lead the country than a barely literate "military chieftain" from the backwoods.

He no doubt believed that the charge that he had bargained with Clay for the presidency—which historian Robert Remeni has called "the theft of the government"—would soon be forgotten and the people would go about their business. It was a disastrous miscalculation and wrecked Adams's administration.

In the House of Representatives, Houston reviled the new president and his secretary of state. Jackson had lost for now, he reported to his constituents in Tennessee, but eventually the people would decide "whether their voices shall be heard and their rights respected, or whether they will tamely yield those inestimable rights to the unhallowed dictation of politicians, who may choose to barter them for their own individual aggrandizement, or otherwise dispose of them contrary to the known will of their constituents."

Henry Clay asked for a House investigation into the charges that he had conspired with Adams, but Houston felt that the courts were the proper venue. The Congress should not "become a court for the trial of personal altercation and disputes."

In the same circular sent to his congressional district in which he condemned the election of 1824, Houston also explained his vote for the tariff bill of that year. He was also up for reelection so the report was a mixture of campaign rhetoric, statesmanship, and civics lesson.

Houston was joined by only one other of the seven Tennessee representatives in voting for the tariff bill, but both Jackson and Eaton supported it in the Senate. These four were clearly not representative of that narrow sectionalism that affected so many of their colleagues.

Customs duties and land sales were the only sources of revenue for the federal government. Land sales had been depressed since the Panic of 1819 so there was great pressure to increase the tariff.

Southerners and Westerners generally felt that an increase in the tariff on manufactured goods was at their expense. Neither the West nor the

South had factories and a great percentage of their manufactured goods came from abroad. Prices could therefore only go up.

However, an increased tariff could help to raise the badly needed funds for the internal improvements propounded by Henry Clay in his visionary "American System." If Clay proved to be right, then everyone would benefit. Manufacturing would grow. New markets would be created and access improved. Surplus agricultural products would find buyers.

"I gave to this measure my cheerful support, and am confirmed in the opinion which I then entertained of its policy, from its salutary effects upon the country," Houston wrote. "I am aware that in Tennessee as well as every other State, there is diversity of opinions on this subject. This is not to be wondered at, when we reflect with what reluctance men generally yield their accustomed theories and practices for new ones, however improved.

"It would be a source of much satisfaction to me, could I believe that this subject is fully comprehended, by all who condemn its policy," he lectured his constituents, "but when I see many of the ablest statesmen here, who array their sectional interests against the general good, I fear that their seducing arguments may have improperly influenced some, who would disdain to persevere in error, when that error became apparent."

Here at the age of thirty-two, Sam Houston set forth a philosophy of government that sustained him and that he consistently followed throughout his political career. It also brought him down in the end.

———

In February 1825 Sam wrote a friend in Tennessee, "For my single self I do not know yet the sweets of matrimony, but in March or April, next I will." Although Sam wanted very much to marry, clearly his political career was more important. "To have been married on my way here would not have answered a good purpose," he said. "My errand here is to attend to the business of my constituents, and not to spend 'honey moons.' " He ended with a typical Houston flourish. *"Every thing in good season!"*

On March 12, Houston was again on his way south for another reunion with Miss M. He was in Cheraw for over a month, but there were still no marriage plans. On the contrary. On April 20, he wrote to Cousin John from Lancaster, South Carolina, "I am this far on my way west, in the full enjoyment of the sweets of single blessedness."

Politics had intervened again. Sam was being pressed to run for governor of Tennessee, and even if he did not he would have to campaign for reelection to the House. He also had made no arrangements for a house or quarters for himself and Madam, as he had begun referring to Mariah Campbell. She would be in Nashville, alone among strangers, while her husband was away campaigning. They had therefore decided to put everything off.

"I left there with a promise to return next fall, by the first of November. I intend to do so, let what may take place," he wrote to John Houston. Not so incidentally, perhaps, Houston was also involved in a legal case in Marlboro County, for a fee of one thousand dollars. The court date was November 1, 1825.

Houston decided against running for the governorship and instead decided to seek reelection to Congress. He did go back to South Carolina to try the court case and collect his fee, but there was no more talk of his marrying Miss M, or Madam. Mariah Campbell eventually married David G. Coit, a Connecticut lawyer who had settled in Cheraw.

Houston did not face serious opposition to his bid for reelection to the House in 1825. Either the tariff issue did not matter to enough of the voters in his district to make a great difference or else he and Jackson and Eaton had convinced them that it was a good idea. Then again perhaps Jefferson was right. An educated and informed electorate will follow the right course.

When Congress reconvened in December 1825, the political atmosphere was poisonous. The war between the supporters of Andrew Jackson and the Adams–Clay faction began immediately.

Adams's first annual message, delivered December 6, was replete with first-rate ideas and has been called one of the great presidential messages to the Congress. He called for an activist government that would build roads and canals, promote public institutions of learning, and nurture scientific investigation.

His opponents, even though they advocated many of the very same things, derided Adams as a visionary fool. They charged that the president's proposals were not only unnecessary and wasteful, they were also unconstitutional.

Three weeks after his annual message, Adams notified the Senate and the House that he was sending a delegation to the Panama Congress called by Simón Bolívar. The president did not have to seek congressional approval, but he also did not want the hostility of the Congress. On February 2, 1826, Houston, who was Jackson's point man in the House, delivered the Jacksonians' reaction.

His lengthy attack, dripping with sarcasm, is a fair example of the isolationism and anti-intellectualism of which the Jacksonians have sometimes been accused. It was a frankly political assignment, which Houston carried out brilliantly, but it did not do him much credit.

In a letter to a friend, from whom he was afraid he had become estranged, Houston once remarked, "I was truly alarmed least some 'snake had come across de Road for to make distarbance.'"

President Adams would certainly have understood that little joke and could have applied it to the Jacksonian "snake" that was making a great "distarbance" on Capitol Hill. An American delegation was sent to Panama, but it arrived too late to take part, so the first great opportunity for inter-American cooperation was lost.

Houston's speech against participation in the Congress of Panama is filled with the sort of propaganda that was used with such effect ten years later to drum up support for a revolution against Mexico. His Presbyterian background, his Masonic training, and his devotion to the Declaration of Independence and the Constitution all contributed to his fear of a state religion. Houston was unforgiving about what he saw as the stifling, anti-libertarian influence of the Catholic church in South America. There could be no freedom as long as the church had any control over the people and the government.

Houston also rose in the House that session to speak against paying Massachusetts for the services of the state militia in the War of 1812. He argued with great passion and stirring nineteenth-century rhetoric. Politics and strongly held beliefs were one. He reminded the House, in case anyone had forgotten, that the country was legally at war, had been invaded by a foreign power, and that Massachusetts had not come to the aid of the country except to defend its own borders. Further the governor and legislature had been the leaders in consorting with the enemy, defying the authority of the president, and calling the infamous Hartford Convention.

No doubt many of those who during the war were "more politic than valiant" were in the House chamber as Houston, appalled that any federal money should be paid to Massachusetts, thundered like an Old Testament prophet. He heaped fire and brimstone on the "pious Governor and his patriotic Legislature" who did not send aid "when our towns and villages were burning—when our matrons and virgins were violated—when even little babes were butchered, our altars abused, the symbols of our worship broken, our sanctuaries profaned, our soil prostituted by the footstep of a mercenary foe, and our Hall of Legislation a heap of smoking ruins."

The speech demonstrated that Houston's oratorical style was perfected. He was, of course, a born orator who could speak extemporaneously for any length of time on almost any subject. This was an art required of political figures, and the better ones were those who had grown up in a rigid religious atmosphere where the preacher or minister, without a text or notes, was expected to speak for hours to his congregation.

Houston's jeremiad against relief for Massachusetts could very well have been his last speech to the House of Representatives if it had not been for good marksmanship, Andrew Jackson's tutoring, and Houston's usual good fortune.

Dueling, although condemned by most civilized men in America, had been a familiar method for settling personal disputes since at least 1621, when there was a duel in the Plymouth Colony of all places. In the nineteenth century these affairs of honor seemed to take on more respectability or at least involve more well-known figures. The most famous encounters were the killing of Alexander Hamilton by Aaron Burr in 1804 and the death of Stephen Decatur at the hands of James Barron in 1820.

Andrew Jackson himself was involved in at least three duels, counting the street brawl with the Bentons. The most notorious was the duel with Charles Dickinson in 1806. Jackson's studied, some said cold-blooded, killing of Dickinson almost ruined his public career, but he was unrepentant. Now, almost unbelievably, the most famous and revered man in America, a man who was just waiting out Adams's tenure to assume the presidency of the United States, agreed to involve himself in an act that was not only illegal but could lead to a charge of murder.

In early 1826, the postmastership in Nashville became vacant and the brother of Henry Clay's son-in-law, John P. Erwin, was nominated by President Adams to fill the vacancy. In March Houston wrote the president decrying Erwin's nomination and putting forth another candidate who had the endorsement of six hundred citizens of Nashville and the representatives to Congress.

During this time Houston suffered another recurrence of the "torpid" liver, which periodically flared up. He was so ill in April 1826 that he was "too much indisposed to write." His letters had to be taken down by a friend. His illness did not distract him from his campaign against Erwin's appointment, however.

Typically, he did not stop with nominating his own candidate for postmaster in Nashville. The opposition candidate had to be destroyed—especially since he was tied by family to the despised Clay. "Mr. Erwin is not a man of fair and upright character," Houston informed Adams. Further, the nominee did not pay his debts, had defrauded his creditors, and was even seen spying through the window of a political opponent late at night.

Erwin, of course, got the job. How could he not? His brother's father-in-law, after all, was the secretary of state. Houston's remarks were passed on to him, and he wrote accusingly to Sam on August 17. Houston was back in Nashville, and he replied immediately. There was no denial. He readily admitted that he had, indeed, made statements impeaching Erwin's integrity. "I then believed them true," said Sam, "and nothing has since transpired to induce an alteration of the opinion then entertained."

Nashville, in spite of its overlay of civilization, still loved a good fight and for weeks was in an excited state over the Houston-Erwin affair. Erwin published his version of the dispute in the local newspaper, and he was not without his partisans. A Missourian named John Smith took up Erwin's cause and on September 8 attempted to present a written challenge to Houston at his room at the Nashville Inn.

Sam wanted no part in a duel. There was nothing to be gained. His reputation could only suffer or worse he could be maimed or killed. He did not even know this John Smith. With his friend Colonel McGregor, Houston worked out a flimsy solution that he hoped would head off a confrontation.

When Smith showed up at the inn, Houston quickly turned him over to Colonel McGregor and withdrew. The colonel told Smith that this was an internal affair and since he was a resident of another state he could not accept his challenge on behalf of Houston. Smith was taken aback by this specious legalism—dueling was against the law in Tennessee no matter where you came from—but he asked for time to think it over.

Within the hour, Smith returned armed and he confronted Houston in front of the Nashville Inn. Sam assured Smith that McGregor was acting on his instructions, but agreed to accept the note through McGregor.

A crowd of bystanders, which no doubt was eager for a repeat of the Benton-Jackson affray of 1813, hovered expectantly on the sidewalk nearby. With them was another friend of Erwin's, General William A. White. The general interposed himself in the quarrel, "which led," as Houston said, "to some altercation between him and myself."

A quarrel with Smith, a perfect stranger, was very different from a quarrel with someone whom Houston knew well and detested. There had been bad blood between Houston and White for years. White was anti-Jackson and had not supported Houston's hero in the 1824 election. All the same, Houston certainly did not want to kill him.

The situation had now deteriorated into a quarrel between White and Houston. The original reason for the duel, the argument with Postmaster Erwin, was forgotten. Smith decamped for his home in Missouri. A challenge was issued and accepted, and a date was agreed on.

The old duelist Jackson offered Sam his expertise, and Houston rode out to The Hermitage where he practiced in a field near the house with Jackson looking on and advising him.

Even issuing a challenge was a breach of the peace in Tennessee and culpability increased from there. The final outcome could be a charge of murder. Kentucky was less punctilious. Or at least if the duel were held across the border the Tennessee authorities could not arrest the congressman or the general.

At dawn on Thursday, September 21, the adversaries faced each other on the dueling ground about six miles south of Franklin, Kentucky.

White had stayed a few miles away in Sumner County, Tennessee. Houston spent the night in Simpson County, Kentucky.

After a sleepless night, he rose in the dark and dressed by candlelight. He was resplendent in a ruffled shirt, satin vest, and a hunting jacket. Around his waist he wore a brilliant red sash with elaborate beadwork and a huge silver buckle. His hat was a broad-brimmed black beaver. When all was in order, he and McGregor had a shot of Tennessee whiskey and mounted their horses. Houston rode a majestic dapple gray.

The resolution of the affair was swift and violent. White fired and missed. Houston, following Jackson's advice, bit down on the lead bullet he held between his teeth to steady his aim. His shot found its mark. White fell to the ground, wounded in the groin. "Thank God my adversary was injured no worse," Houston remarked later.

General White lived, but the duel was used by Houston's enemies for years in their attempts to discredit him. Kentucky turned out not to be so cavalier about people shooting each other. There was a grand jury indictment, and Governor Joseph Desha requested that Houston be extradited from Tennessee "for having feloniously shot and wounded" General White.

Since Governor Desha was firmly in the Jackson camp by this time, his request was not taken seriously by the Tennessee authorities. There was no attempt to arrest Houston and bring him to trial. However, the issue was raised during his campaign for governor, but with his usual skill he turned the defense of his honor to his advantage.

Ironically, he could have been arrested and tried by Tennessee authorities. There is strong evidence that the dueling ground was not in Kentucky at all, but lay just inside Tennessee.

Houston did suffer one setback from the wounding of White. The Cumberland Lodge suspended him for a year for fighting a duel with a fellow Mason. Eventually this was reversed and Houston was welcomed back as a loyal and devoted member of the Masonic Order.

———

The Houston–White affair was the important news in Tennessee, but there was another duel in 1826 that involved much higher placed government figures. However, it too sprang from the same source and further underscored the underlying distrust and even hatred in Washington and the country.

Henry Clay had finally reached the breaking point over the slanderous and libelous remarks about his part in the election of 1824. Particularly irksome to the secretary of state was John Randolph of Roanoke, a master of the scathing and witty remark. The brilliant but unpredictable Randolph amused his colleagues, but one never knew which way he would strike. He had once called Jefferson "St. Thomas of Cantingbury."

Randolph had moved from the House to the Senate in 1825, where he continued his guerrilla war against Adams and Clay. He called them "the coalition of Blifil and Black George, of the puritan with the blackleg." Clay challenged him and they met on the banks of the Potomac River opposite Georgetown on April 8.

On the first firing, each man missed, but on the second round Clay shot a hole in Randolph's coat. According to the rules, Clay had received his satisfaction, but the duel did not end their enmity. Nor was it a comic operetta affair. It was a deadly serious exchange of gunfire and a true reflection of the high political passions of the time.

Dueling was so common that it was clear that a simple law was not enough to put a stop to it. Public revulsion finally was so great that a ban against dueling was written into the revised Tennessee Constitution of 1834. Anyone who fought a duel, or who aided or abetted dueling, or who sent or accepted a challenge was barred from holding public office.

————

Houston was back in Washington for the opening of Congress in December 1826. He probably saw the end of the year with a great sense of relief. A serious illness, petty but demeaning quarrels with other members of the Jackson circle, and the duel with White had ruined the stay in Nashville.

He still clung to his Jacksonian rock, however. "My firm and undeviating attachment to Genl Jackson has caused me all the enemies that I have," he said, "and I glory in the firmness of my attachment to Jackson and to principle. I will die proud in the assurance, that I deserve, and possess his perfect confidence."

He had made good on his announcement to a friend back in January that he must be seen "less frequent in the Lady World than I have been. I must keep up my Dignity, or rather I must attend more to politics and less to love." Indeed, there seem to have been no distractions from the "Lady World," but his close attention to politics had almost got him killed.

This was Houston's final session in the House. He again was being urged to run for governor of Tennessee. There were more battles to fight on behalf of Andrew Jackson, but there was no shortage of partisans. Fellow Tennesseans James K. Polk and John Bell would be in the House to carry on the war against the Adams administration.

Many Americans truly believed that the presidency of John Quincy Adams was illegal. He had after all received only 30 percent of the popular vote in 1824. Adams therefore could only be reelected in 1828 if through some miscalculation Jackson destroyed himself as a viable candidate.

Houston, probably owing to his own volatile nature, was worried that Jackson might make some slip that would be his undoing. His fears were soon realized. Secretary of the Navy William Southard's intemperate remarks about Jackson's handling of the defenses of New Orleans had been reported back to The Hermitage. Predictably, Jackson exploded and wrote an abusive letter to the secretary. He wisely sent the letter, unsealed, to Houston for his opinion.

Houston returned the letter to the Old Chief on December 13, 1826, with a gentle admonition. "It is now a desirable matter with all your friends, to keep you out of collision, as to things said and done," he said. "If you shou'd write directly thro me to Mr. Southard, I pray you, to let it be in the mildest, calmest tone of expression."

Jackson took Sam's good advice and wrote a calmer letter. Houston passed the letter on to Southard, with the clear instructions that all future correspondence between Southard and Jackson must be sent through him. Southard sent his reply to Jackson through Houston, but it was sealed.

Houston returned it, again reminding the secretary that he could not forward letters to Jackson that he had not read. Southard insultingly replied that he would make other arrangements to get letters to Jackson.

Southard's rebuff struck Houston as an attempt to lure him into a quarrel with the cabinet. Their aim "is to get me to *cut* some *capers*," he wrote to Old Hickory. He did not rise to the bait, but he delighted Jackson by saying that Southard's behavior could "justify me under almost any other set of facts asking him *personally,* if he intended disrespect to me, and if he was not prompt in denying, *slap his jaws!*"

Sam never missed an opportunity to buttress the general, though the supremely confident Jackson rarely needed any moral support. Jackson's quest for the presidency must remain uppermost, and the Adams administration left to destroy itself.

"Like the wounded serpent, when they find that, their adversary, is beyond the reach of their fangs, they will be compelld, in the anguish of disappointment to strike themselves; and of *their own* poison— perish!" Houston wrote Jackson. "You loose no friends, but gain daily! It will be so until the great day of deliverance to our country arrives."

Three days later Houston attended the gala dinner in Washington celebrating the anniversary of the Battle of New Orleans. Jackson's fame and reputation flowered anew each January 8. These annual nationwide celebrations were an important and emotional way for Jackson's friends and admirers to keep his name before the public in preparation for the epiphany planned for March 4, 1829.

In the House, Houston continued the Jacksonian war on the Adams administration. When the secretary of state awarded new contracts for printing of the government laws to newspapers friendly to the administration, it was not flagrant political patronage, but it nevertheless gave the Jackson camp more ammunition to use against Adams.

Again Houston was chosen to be the sword carrier in the House. The people, he thundered on February 2, 1827, "are not situated like the Secretary of State, who stands aloof, and uses his power for his personal purposes, regardless of any expression of the People's will. . . . Mr. Speaker, I have no objection to the principle which urges me to promote my friends. . . . But, then, Sir, I would be very careful who my friends were."

Adams and Clay could not make the patronage issue go away and on February 16, Houston again took the floor. His extended speech ran over into the next session and was a masterpiece of political invective and campaign oratory. The strategy, of course, was not only to wreck Adams but to build up Jackson. Of Jackson, Houston said, "Cincinnatus like, he has gone back to the plough, and devotes his hours to those rural occupations which are ever most congenial with the Republic, and most truly beneficial to the great body of the People."

Houston's fellow legislators by now had begun to expect great blasts of oratory from their young colleague from Tennessee. He was allowed to go on, after one recess, until the end of the day's session. The next day, refreshed, he began again. It was great theater. Houston invoked Jefferson, Madison, and Monroe. He belittled the president as not being the equal of his famous ancestors. He called down God's wrath on Federalists, Whigs, and other "Tories." He managed to mention Greece, Rome, Troy, even Nazareth. Catiline, Sinon, Cato, and Cicero, Scott, Perry, Jackson, and Lafayette were summoned. And he quoted not only doggerel supposedly written by the president but lines from *The Iliad*.

The printing contracts stood, of course, but the administration was further damaged. The Jacksonians in the House and Senate, in the statehouses and legislatures had a more than ample supply of crosses and nails for the ongoing crucifixion of Adams and Clay. And they never let up for the entire four years.

On March 14, Houston was still in Washington and gave the impression by ordering a newspaper subscription to be mailed home that he was planning to run for reelection to the House. He asked that a triweekly Washington paper be sent to Nashville during the recess and "at the commencement of the next session of Congress" he would make arrangements for a daily paper to be delivered.

Houston then added, somewhat disingenuously, "If any thing occurs of importance in the course of the summer I will let you know."

5

Governor Houston

A**S SOON AS** the Congress adjourned, Sam Houston headed south for
Tennessee. At Andrew Jackson's insistence he had agreed to run
for governor. The incumbent, William Carroll, was ending his third
consecutive term in office, the maximum allowed under the Tennessee
Constitution. Houston was the obvious choice to ensure that the governor's chair would remain a Jacksonian preserve.

Tennessee had the usual qualifications for running for governor—
citizenship, age, sex, and race—but also required that a governor had to
own at least five hundred acres of land. So Houston must have had
considerable property in East Tennessee or someone—Overton, Jackson, or Lewis perhaps—arranged for him to buy or have enough transferred to him to qualify.

Billy Carroll had met Andrew Jackson soon after he arrived in Nashville from his native Pennsylvania, sometime around 1810. They had
been friends since. And like many of the inner circle, he had served under
Jackson in the War of 1812. He was at both Horseshoe Bend and New
Orleans, where he had distinguished himself. And it was he who had
drawn Jackson into the brawl with the Bentons.

Billy Carroll had also been careful to acquire that other honor that
guaranteed political advancement in Tennessee—major general of the
Tennessee Militia.

By any measure, Carroll was an able and respected governor, and if it were not for the term limit clause in the constitution he would have stayed in the job. The only other wish he had—and it was a strong one—was to become a United States senator. Alas, that avenue too was closed. John Eaton was reelected to the Senate by the Jackson-controlled legislature in 1826 and Hugh Lawson White, Tennessee's other senator, was not about to make way for anyone.

Carroll enthusiastically supported Houston in the governor's race, which he handily won, but he viewed Houston as simply a caretaker. Sam was to keep the governor's chair warm for Billy for two years and then return it. Billy Carroll could then resume running Tennessee as he had in the past. Cracks began to appear in Jackson's grand edifice.

Andrew Jackson had absolute control of Tennessee politics, but personal ambitions were beginning to undermine Old Hickory's "Tennessee Dynasty." Carroll was 39 years old, Houston was 34, Polk was 32, and Bell was 30. How could the political offices be so arranged and a timetable worked out so that all could climb the ladder with a minimum of discord. Perhaps, in time, one or more or all might become president of the United States.

Granted that Jackson himself was not yet president, but there was little doubt in anyone's mind that the election of 1828 had been settled by the infamous vote in the House of Representatives in 1825. The cunning Old Hickory was already thinking far ahead, even perhaps generations ahead. He had always surrounded himself with intelligent and ambitious acolytes, protégés, and disciples. Jacksonianism was for the ages not just two terms. Those who succeeded him were to carry on his political and social program. Jefferson had done that very thing in Virginia. Why might it not be possible in Tennessee?

Jackson's grand plan was based on the fact that the people and the power structure were shifting to the southwest and west, and what would become known as Jacksonian democracy was their movement. Jackson was out to ensure that it would be a long-lived one. In 1827, thanks to William Carroll, John Bell, James K. Polk, and Sam Houston, among others, this seemed an intoxicating possibility.

Some of Jackson's dream was realized. Both Polk and Bell served as Speaker of the House, and Polk did become president of the United States. Carroll served three more terms as governor. Bell, however, was less committed to the Old Chief than the others and began to flirt with the Whigs.

His final break with Jackson came when Jackson chose New Yorker Martin Van Buren over Hugh Lawson White for the presidency in 1836. Bell bolted to the Whigs who took control of Tennessee and controlled politics in the state for years.

Later, in the U.S. Senate, Bell reconciled with Houston, but slavery, sectionalism, and outright class warfare had done their damage by then. In 1856, Houston said that "the parties themselves have no distinctive character. They have faded, become extinct, and expired." He and Bell, the remaining early bulwarks of Jacksonianism found themselves competing against each other for the nomination of a fringe party.

Bell defeated Houston for the Constitutional Union party presidential nomination in 1860. He carried just three states and received only thirty-nine electoral votes. But the Civil War effectively derailed Jacksonianism until the end of the century.

In 1827, however, the future looked bright and the possibilities limitless. Houston had just finished two successful terms in the House, and now his election as governor proved he had a broader, statewide appeal. Granted he had run with the support of both Jackson and Carroll, but he had waged a campaign marked by an indelible personal style.

He stumped the state in an apparently endless change of costume—shiny black trousers, red sashes, wide brimmed beaver hats, multicolored Indian hunting shirts—always riding a magnificent horse. His populist, Jacksonian message was equally appealing. In the August election he was an easy winner.

Houston was inaugurated as the sixth governor of the state of Tennessee on October 1, 1827. In his address he offered an olive branch to states' righters. While he was bound under law to support the U.S. Constitution and the preservation of the Union, he was also obliged to preserve the rights of the state. Surprisingly, the whole speech was only about six hundred words long. Given his reputation for public speaking, the crowd must have been perplexed indeed.

Two weeks later, in his message to the legislature, he was back in form. He called for state support of internal improvements such as roads, bridges, canals, and waterways; government promotion of commerce and trade; relief for poor homesteaders or squatters in east Tennessee who could not pay for their land; and a fund to set up a public school system.

His emphasis on support for broad public education was undoubtedly motivated by his own feelings about glaring deficiencies in his own education. He wanted to ensure that "the road to distinction in every department of science and moral excellency [would] be equally open to all the youth of our country."

The speech was a practical blueprint for growth and an eloquent call for government intervention, albeit on the state level. Ironically, many of the ideas seem to have been lifted from John Quincy Adams's first message to Congress. But unlike Adams and like Jefferson, Houston still felt that all of these things should be done on a state level and not by the national government.

Houston's administration was mainly a continuation of the policies of his predecessor. There were no sharp turns in policy and nothing even resembling a departure or break. Any strains that occurred were minor and caused by the clashes of ambitious personalities and not by policies. There were no major clashes, however. Everyone was subordinate to the greater good of ensuring the election of Andrew Jackson as president in 1828.

The hero of the War of 1812, the Seminole Wars, and the 1824 Election War with Adams and Clay was still the most popular man in the country. The defeat of the British at New Orleans was a defining moment for great numbers of Americans, and annually it was kept fresh in their minds.

The celebration planned for New Orleans in 1828 was noticeably different from the others. It was after all an election year and the guest of honor was not only the conqueror of the British but the favored candidate. For the men who were running Jackson's campaign the trip was a heaven-sent opportunity.

However, Jackson's natural dignity and his sense of honor ruled out using the celebration to advance his candidacy. His advisers had to go along with his wishes, but they did not have to worry. The journey to New Orleans aboard the *Pocahontas* was a long celebratory campaign parade down the Mississippi River. Groups seemed to appear from nowhere to line the river bank for a glimpse of their idol. Rivermen fired their rifles in salute. At each fueling stop, great crowds gathered to cheer Old Hickory. Little children who were held up to see the great man talked of it when they were old.

The Jackson entourage was made up of old friends and political colleagues except for one newcomer. They were joined in Nashville by James A. Hamilton, who had been sent from New York by Martin Van Buren and the Tammany Society to confer with Jackson. The Tammany ambassador was proof that the Jackson candidacy had more than regional appeal.

Hamilton had a considerable political legacy of his own. He was the third son of Alexander Hamilton. Jackson and the rest of the party took to the urbane and witty New Yorker immediately, and while Jackson was sincere about no public displays, in the privacy of the boat there was no harm in doing a little politicking.

When the *Pocahontas* reached New Orleans, it seemed as if the entire city, thousands upon thousands of people, had turned out to greet Old Hickory. Jackson had to respond to this great outpouring of affection. Standing bareheaded and alone at the stern rail, he received the tributes of the crowd.

Houston's return to New Orleans was itself a personal triumph. He had left the city in 1816, a still-ailing young soldier with an uncertain future and few prospects. In the intervening twelve years he had risen to major general in the militia and served two terms in the Congress. He now stepped ashore as the governor of Tennessee.

New Orleans was more hedonistic than ever, and the anniversary gave the fun-loving populace yet another reason to rejoice. The bachelor governor revisited his old haunts and showed his more adventurous companions around the city. While the speeches droned on during the public dinner, he and Hamilton sneaked out to a quadroon ball being held in the hotel. The balls were lavish entertainments sponsored by rich Creole planters for their beautiful quarter-black mistresses.

At one of the more conventional festivities, Houston met a Mrs. Nathan Morse, who lived on Rampart Street. At her request, he sent her a lock of General Jackson's hair when they returned to Nashville. Addressing her as "Mrs. Colonel Morse," he said, "From the veteran Warrior's brow the enclosed lock was taken, and regarded by him as a high compliment, from a lady, possessing so many charms and so much excellence as Mrs. Morse! Genl Houston begs leave to assure Mrs Morse of his most affectionate recollection."

A lock of hair was a favored memento of the times, and not so unusual, but Sam Houston's clipping a bit of Andrew Jackson's hair cannot have been a common occurrence. However, the "veteran Warrior" happily obliged his young friend the governor and his Creole lady of "charms" and "excellence."

Sam Houston was, of course, in New Orleans primarily as a friend of the Jackson family, which needed the support of good friends more than ever. The election campaign had taken a particularly vicious turn early on. The Adams-Clay camp embarked on a scurrilous course to destroy Jackson and nothing was considered off-limits. Everything was dredged up, but nothing was as damaging as his disputed marriage back in the 1790s.

The country was thunderstruck. The man of the people was accused of adultery and licentiousness and his wife of bigamy. The slanders had begun as early as 1826 and reached a crescendo in the spring of 1827. Jackson wrote Houston a fiery but sad letter defending Rachel, "the aged and virtuous female," but swearing vengeance against Clay and his *"pander heads."*

Rachel Jackson accompanied her husband on this triumphal return to the scene of his greatest victory, but she cannot have gotten much joy out of it. Her health was poor, and she stayed in her cabin most of the journey. The adulation, the invasions of privacy, the screaming crowds frightened her. She turned away from this horrifying glimpse of what her life was to be like as the president's wife.

And now in New Orleans she found herself the object of acute interest. The sophisticated women of the city were gracious and accommodating and she managed to hold her own with them. Rachel Jackson was not a worldly sophisticate, however, and her beauty had long since been sacrificed to illness and hard work. She was now a plain, matronly, sixty-year-old—a religious, even pious woman whose only real interests were her husband, her home, and her extended family.

The return journey up the Mississippi was as tumultuous as the trip down, perhaps more so. Lookouts were posted downriver and they sped to the river towns and landings to herald the coming of the *Pocahontas,* with Old Hickory aboard. A friend witnessed Jackson's passage up the river and wrote to James K. Polk in Washington. "Genl Jackson passed up by Vicksburg a few days since accompanied by Gov. Houston, Judge Overton, and a few others. . . . The people in this state and Louisiana worships the Hero as a god on earth."

The next nine months of 1828 were taken up with the presidential campaign. Houston with his flair for language and writing turned out speeches and broadsides and helped in answering each new charge and libel as it was hurled by the supporters of Adams. He also stumped the state for Jackson. On July the Fourth he attended a large celebration at Carthage and the next day he was present at a "dinner supper and ball" in Hartsville.

The most scurrilous campaign in American history seemed as if it might never end. But end it did—in vindication and triumph for Andrew Jackson. His enemies had been brought low and his friends would be rewarded.

Jackson's joy was short-lived, however. On December 22, the day before a great victory celebration planned in Nashville, Rachel Jackson died suddenly at The Hermitage.

Her funeral on Christmas Eve was attended by ten thousand people of every class and description. A hush fell over the vast throng as the cortege, led by Sam Houston, left the mansion and came down the walk to the burial place in Rachel's garden. The servants filled the Tennessee air with their wails and keening, and the old warrior himself broke down and cried at the graveside.

Houston was nearly as devastated by the death of Rachel Jackson as the president-elect, and he was just as certain as he that her death had been brought on by the viciousness and calumny of their enemies. During the next month he helped sustain Jackson, whose grief was such that it became a great worry to his friends.

The stricken president-elect spent day after day working on the design of the memorial for his dead wife and composing an epitaph. One line of the long inscription on the small marble temple he erected over her grave stands out above the others. "A being so virtuous, slander might wound but could not dishonor." Jackson swore to make his enemies pay for what they had done to his wife. Sam Houston would help him.

Meanwhile, Governor Houston's personal life had taken a happy turn, which he had earnestly sought for years. He was going to be married. Andrew Jackson was a great soldier, a great politician, and a great leader. But he did not bring to affairs of the heart that great good sense that he exhibited in war and government. He was something of a meddler and a matchmaker in the lives of his friends.

Jackson's happy marriage led him into the trap of believing that everyone could enjoy the same bliss and that marriage was a private affair between two individuals, even if one of them was a public figure. Experience had certainly taught him a different lesson, which he ignored.

In the autumn of 1828, his advice to John Eaton and Sam Houston, two of his most trusted subordinates, led directly to two of the most celebrated scandals of the century. Jackson's marriage to Rachel Donelson was a third. All three affairs have been debated and discussed for a century and a half.

While Senator John Eaton was visiting his home in Tennessee, he sought Old Hickory's advice about whether to marry Margaret O'Neale Timberlake. Jackson knew Peggy very well, and he also knew of the rumors that she had been Eaton's mistress for years. Indeed, he might have known that they were more than rumors. Nevertheless, he told the senator by all means to marry her and the sooner the better. John Eaton returned to Washington and married the widow Timberlake on January 1, 1829.

When Eaton joined Jackson's cabinet as secretary of war, many government wives, led predictably by Mrs. Calhoun, refused to receive Peggy Eaton, the adulterous daughter of a tavern keeper. The uproar divided the government and hamstrung the Jackson administration. The brouhaha ended only with Eaton's resignation in 1831.

Jackson's other foray into matchmaking in 1828 had an equally disastrous outcome. Sam Houston's career, he felt, would be blocked unless he had a wife. Sam had gone far in his thirty-six years, but he would not go much further without the steadying influence of a wife and family.

Houston was vulnerable to any number of charges from political opponents, and they never hesitated to invent what they could not stir up. He had just seen what dedicated political enemies could do. He served in the trenches in the ongoing war with Adams and Clay. He sat in on campaign strategy meetings in Washington and Tennessee, and he knew firsthand the underside of politics and what men would do to get elected and to destroy their opposition.

Houston had only to reflect on what damage had been done to

Jackson, and he had been happily married to the same woman for thirty-eight years. God knows what charges could be leveled at a thirty-six-year-old bachelor with a reputation for drinking, carousing, and promiscuity.

Eliza Allen was a very pretty twenty-year-old woman from nearby Gallatin. Her family were Tennessee aristocracy. John Allen was a well-to-do planter and a close friend of Andrew Jackson, who was often a guest at his plantation, Allenwood, on the Cumberland River.

Robert Allen, John's brother, served in Congress with Houston, and he introduced Sam to the family. His niece Eliza was then a schoolgirl. Sam became a frequent visitor to the Allen plantation, and he had watched the little girl grow up into a confident and poised young woman. She had a good education, much better than Houston's, and she was both intelligent and strong-willed.

John Allen had ambitions for his blond, blue-eyed daughter, and he concurred with everyone else that a marriage to the governor would be a perfect match. There may have been concern about the great difference in their ages, but no one spoke of it and Allen did not let it affect his enthusiasm. The Allens were happy for their daughter and, no doubt, especially for themselves. Governor Houston was clearly a man on his way to great things, maybe even the presidency.

Eliza Allen was not completely free, however. She had another suitor, and she very likely had secretly promised to marry him. His name is not known for certain, but it is more than probable that he was a young attorney named William Tyree. Their courtship was hopeless and marriage was out of the question. Will Tyree was dying of tuberculosis.

Like most parents whose child is presented with what they consider a great opportunity, the Allens pressed Eliza to accept Houston's proposal. Eliza Allen relented and in the autumn of 1828 she agreed to marry Governor Sam Houston. If ever there was an arranged marriage it was this one.

Andrew Jackson was delighted with the upcoming marriage, but he could not be present. He had delayed his journey to the capital much too long, and a winter drought had already made the Cumberland River barely navigable. Farther north, on the Ohio River, a sudden freeze could halt all traffic.

Jackson left for Washington on Monday, January 19, 1829, on the steamboat *Pennsylvania*. The boat had arrived on the Cumberland the day before to board the president-elect and his party, but Jackson intuitively knew that if he departed on Sunday the faithful would raise a ruckus.

Houston said good-bye to the Old Chief at The Hermitage landing. Billy Carroll was also there to see him off. Houston and Jackson doubtless discussed the upcoming elections, and Houston left the *Pennsylvania* encouraged to seek reelection as governor. But politics had to be put aside, at least temporarily, for the wedding was only three days off.

On Thursday evening, January 22, in the drawing room at Allenwood, Sam Houston married Eliza Allen. The weather had turned colder and snow threatened. Most of the local gentry had turned out, at least those who were not either in Washington or on their way there to prepare to run the country.

The guests stood before the blazing fireplaces and sipped refreshments passed round by the Allen house slaves. They quietly discussed the tragedy at The Hermitage and the departure of the president-elect for Washington.

They also spoke of Billy Carroll's wedding gift. The day before, in the *Nashville Banner and Whig,* he had announced that he would seek a fourth term as governor. Also it cannot have gone unremarked that the same Presbyterian minister, the Reverend William Hume, who had just buried Rachel Jackson, was now preparing to marry Eliza Allen and Sam Houston.

The guests marveled at the beauty of the young bride in her long white dress. She smiled up at the tall handsome groom. Her beautiful face was aglow from the soft light of the candles. John Allen was understandably proud as he gave his twenty-year-old daughter to the thirty-six-year-old governor. Everyone agreed that it was the best possible of matches.

After a long and elaborate dinner and many tributes to the bride and groom, the guests went out into the cold night. Sam and Eliza retired to the room prepared for them at the Allens'. Although this was no doubt the custom, given the difficulty of travel, it would be hard to imagine a more awkward beginning for a marriage.

Eliza Allen was very much a young woman of her time. Sheltered and protected by her doting brothers and her father, she had little or no experience of the world. Sam Houston was sixteen years older, and he had known every kind of experience. He had lived in Indian villages, on army posts, and in large cities. He had slept in tents, mansions, boardinghouses, and taverns. He had fought battles and duels. And the women he had known were just as varied—patricians and white trash, whores and unfaithful wives, Creoles, Indians, mulattoes, and black slaves.

It has been rumored over the years that Houston attempted to introduce his bride to the sexual practices of the Indian nation or the New Orleans bordello in their marriage bed. This is unlikely, given his legendary deference to women. What is not unlikely is that Eliza was filled with revulsion at what terrible damage had been done to Houston's body by the arrows and rifle balls of the Creek Indians.

Houston's wounds never healed properly and he suffered from them throughout his life. The Creek arrow had caused great damage to his thigh, and his right shoulder was covered with the great purple and red scars from the lead shot and the crude probing of the army surgeons. In his *Life of Sam Houston,* C. Edwards Lester said, "Sometimes these sufferings are intense, and he will never be free from them while he lives, for no surgical skill has ever been able to close up that wound. It has discharged every day for more than thirty years." Accepting this required an understanding and tolerance that the young bride did not possess.

In any event Eliza Allen, on this night of January 22, no doubt realized the enormity of her mistake. Nevertheless, she rose the next morning and set out for Nashville with her husband. They traveled on horseback, accompanied by the two daughters of Martha Martin, who lived at nearby Locust Grove. A light snow was falling.

They rode through the still, whitening landscape for a few miles, but the snowfall soon became heavier. When they reached the Martin place, it was obvious that it was not possible to proceed on to Nashville. They had to stop off for the night.

The next morning dawned clear and cold, and Houston rose early and went downstairs. When Eliza came down later she stood in a window watching the governor and the Martin daughters in a snowball fight. Martha Martin remarked that Eliza should go out and help the governor as her daughters seemed to be getting the best of him.

"Looking seriously at me, Mrs. Houston said: 'I wish they would kill him.' I looked up astonished to hear such a remark from a bride of not yet forty-eight hours, when she repeated in the same voice, 'Yes, I wish from the bottom of my heart that they would kill him.' "

Later at breakfast, "Mrs. Houston joined but little in the conversation," said Mrs. Martin. The couple then continued on their leisurely but troubled way. They spent two days with a cousin of Sam's near Nashville and then settled in on the second floor of the Nashville Inn.

Houston responded to the challenge from Billy Carroll on January 28. He would seek reelection. Even then, officeholders spent an inordinate amount of time looking to the next election. Houston had been in office only sixteen months and he had eight months to go in his term. He had been successful, but there was much more to be done and his recent marriage would be a great help.

The women of Tennessee, at least the married ones, were happy that Sam Houston had finally settled down. The men were too, and not a few of them envied the governor his beautiful young wife. A Nashville woman, employing one of those epigrams that often serves to fix a person permanently in the public's mind said, "Two classes of people pursued Sam Houston all his life—artists and women." For better or worse, this romantic image has been his ever since.

Sam had written to his cousin John in Washington that he planned to be in the capital on March 4, the day Jackson was to be sworn in. Now, in late January, it must have seemed even more important for him to be there. Otherwise he would be one of only two or three close Jackson men not at the inauguration, an event that he had helped bring about and had so longed for. But Sam Houston did not travel to Washington for one of the great events in American history.

Was there not enough time? Sam and Eliza had almost seven weeks after the wedding to make a trip that ordinarily took about three weeks.

Had the weather turned bad and made river travel impossible after Jackson and his party had left? It seems not. Jackson and his party were still en route and apparently experienced no difficulties. They arrived in Washington on February 11.

Did Eliza refuse to travel with him to the inauguration, and was he loath to leave her alone? His jealousy was a serious problem, but considering that she would have stayed with her family in his absence and that every move of the governor's wife was noted he had nothing to worry about.

Was his campaign against Billy Carroll lagging and his reelection so threatened that he was apprehensive about leaving the state? The real campaign would not begin until late in March and the election was not until August. As for public opinion, the people of Tennessee would have celebrated their governor going to see Old Hickory sworn in. More important, Jackson himself would be back in the state in the summer to help him out.

The most probable reason Houston did not go to Washington, which was not only a desire but a duty, was because his marriage was in trouble and he was desperately trying to prevent his new wife from leaving him. Otherwise there is no explanation for the precipitate, even irrational, behavior of Sam and Eliza in April. Everything did not just fall apart in a calamitous two or three days.

Eliza Allen had a good mind and some degree of curiosity, but she had been happy in her plantation world, the pastoral, seamless life at Allenwood. Now, in a small set of rooms in the Nashville Inn, that recent life seemed to her a succession of uninterrupted golden days.

On March 18, her infant brother Charles died. An agitated Eliza returned home to comfort and be comforted by her family. After the funeral she must have yearned to stay at Allenwood, but she dutifully returned to the lonely rooms on the second floor of the Nashville Inn. The future presented a bleak and dismal prospect to this fragile young woman just out of her teens.

On Wednesday night, April 8, Houston confronted Eliza with his growing suspicions that she had been in love with someone else before their marriage. Her coldness to him only proved this. Eliza protested her innocence and at her urging Sam went to talk to an old friend, probably Dr. John Shelby.

Houston later that night assured his wife of his faith in her, but the damage had been done. The next morning, the quarrel had not abated and Houston again assured Eliza of his love and confidence. Eliza, no doubt sensing that she had been finally provided with the means to end this charade, paid no attention to his entreaties.

Houston was faced with total ruin. His marriage and his political career were so intertwined that there was no way to separate them. But perhaps the scandal could be contained. No one knew of it yet. And there was one person who could reason with Eliza. Houston sat in the cheerless rooms of the Nashville Inn and wrote to his father-in-law at Allenwood.

> Mr. Allen The most unpleasant & unhappy circumstance has just taken place in the family, & one that was entirely unnecessary at this time. Whatever had been my feelings or opinions in relation to Eliza at one time, I have been satisfied & it is now unfit that anything should be averted to. Eliza will do me the justice to say that she believes I was really unhappy That I was satisfied & believed her virtuous, I had assured her on last night & this morning. This should have prevented the facts ever coming to your knowledge, & that of Mrs. Allen. I would not for millions it had ever been known to you. But one human being knew anything of it from me, & that was by Eliza's consent & wish. I would have perished first, & if mortal man had dared to charge my wife or say ought against her virtue I would have slain him. That I have & do love Eliza none can doubt,—that she is the only earthly object dear to me God will witness.
>
> The only way this matter can now be overcome will for be for us all to meet as tho it had never occurred, & this will keep the world, as it should ever be, ignorant that such thoughts ever were. Eliza stands acquitted by me. I have received her as a virtuous wife, & as such I pray God I may ever regard her, & trust I ever shall.
>
> She was cold to me, & I thought did not love me. She owns that such was one cause of my unhappiness. You can judge how unhappy I was to think I was united to a woman that did not love me. This time is now past, & my future happiness can only exist in the assurance that Eliza & myself can be happy & that Mrs. Allen and you can forget the past,—forgive all & find your lost peace & you may rest assured that nothing on my part shall be wanting to restore it. Let me know what is to be done
>
> SAM HOUSTON

Houston later told Andrew Jackson that this letter was written before Eliza left him. If that is so, then how could Allen have known about their problems, which it is clear from the letter he must have. Eliza probably left the Nashville Inn for Allenwood the day after the quarrel.

There was no response from Allenwood, and on Saturday the candidate went ahead with a scheduled debate with Billy Carroll at Cockrell's Spring. The debate went well, and he was much encouraged by the response of the large and friendly crowd, which clearly had not heard the news. In the rough and tumble of Tennessee politics if they had heard anything of his wife's defection they would have made it known. The recent presidential campaign had proved that.

Riding back into Nashville later that Saturday, Sam was pleased with himself. He could handle Carroll in debate and he looked forward to their next encounter. But he knew that the campaign was not going to be decided on issues. The two candidates were both Jacksonians and Governor Houston's program for the state differed little if at all from former governor Carroll's. This election would be decided by which candidate had the endorsement of Andrew Jackson.

As Sam climbed the stairs to his rooms at the Nashville Inn, buoyed by his success in the debate, the old confidence returned. Political confrontation fired him up. He had few rivals on the stump. Why, he wondered, could not marriage be as simple as politics and yield as easily to debate?

The euphoria was short-lived. The governor was informed that he had been burned in effigy by the outraged citizens of Gallatin. The scandal had been served up to the public. Houston decided to confront Eliza and her family directly. He rode out to Allenwood and demanded to see his wife.

On his knees and in tears he begged her "with all his dramatic force" to return to him, reported an aunt of Eliza's who was a witness. Eliza refused and the defeated man returned to Nashville.

Eliza's rejection was the beginning of a week of the most humiliating degradations for a proud man. Further effigy burnings and near-riots in Nashville added to his anguish. Some people claimed to have seen the governor roaming the streets of Nashville dressed in a calf skin.

Houston even tried to turn to religion. He asked the Reverend Hume to baptize him, but even that request was refused. It may have been so because the Allens were too much offended by what had taken place, but Houston clearly was in no proper mental condition for a meaningful baptism. Besides, he must have been baptized as a boy back in Virginia. His family was too devout to have overlooked this most important rite of passage for all Presbyterians.

On April 16, Sam Houston resigned as governor of Tennessee. The letter of resignation was addressed to William Hall, speaker of the senate and his constitutional successor. Houston's mental state and public humiliation had not lessened his eloquence.

"In dissolving the political connexion which has so long, & in such a variety of forms existed between the people of Tennessee and myself, no private afflictions however deep or incurable, can forbid an expression of the grateful recollections so eminently due to the kind partialities of an indulgent public," he said. "In reviewing the past, I can only regret that my capacity for being useful was so unequal to the devotion of my heart."

Houston remained cloistered at the Nashville Inn for another week, brooding in his rooms and drinking heavily. He recalled that on the way to his wedding he had seen a raven fluttering and crying in the road. That omen was now all too clear.

Some of his old friends, Crockett, Overton, McGregor, and Dr. Shelby, attended him, but he was abandoned by most of the others. The president in Washington, unaware of what had happened, had moved to get Carroll out of the governor's race by offering him a diplomatic post. When Jackson's offer reached Carroll, events had already overtaken everyone. He declined. He did not have to go anywhere. Billy Carroll was going to stay right there in Tennessee, and in the governor's office.

Finally the ordeal was over. On April 23, three months and one day after his marriage, Sam Houston left the Nashville Inn and walked down the steep hill to the steamboat landing on the Cumberland. He was accompanied by Sheriff Willoughby Williams, Dr. Shelby, and Colonel McGregor, who had lent him the money for his voyage into exile.

The farewells were brief. Sam boarded the steamboat, and the small vessel then pushed out into the river and headed northwest up the Cumberland, to the Ohio, and then on to the Mississippi. Fourteen years before, a young army officer full of hope for a brilliant career had boarded a little skiff right here on the Cumberland and also headed toward the Mississippi. That future had been realized. That twenty-two-year-old officer had gone far, farther than anyone could ever have imagined. Now there seemed to be no future at all.

At Clarksville, about fifty miles downriver, two armed men from the Allen family boarded the boat. They demanded that Houston either return and prove his rumored libel of Eliza or sign a paper denying it. Houston refused to do either. He told the Allens that they could put a notice in the papers that if "any wretch ever dares to utter a word against the purity of Mrs. Houston I will come back and write the libel in his heart's blood."

After the confrontation with the Allens, Houston's despair increased. He lapsed into a black and suicidal depression. He seriously considered putting an end to it by leaping from the boat and drowning himself in the Cumberland. Another avian talisman now intervened, however. An eagle swooped down low over the river and, with a great cry, rose up and flew toward the west.

6

The Wigwam
Neosho

WHILE SAM HOUSTON waited at the Nashville Inn for a reply to the letter to his father-in-law, John Allen, a peripatetic lawyer, filibusterer, and land speculator was busy with his own correspondence in Cincinnati, Ohio. David Governeur Burnet had been in and out of the Southwest since 1813. He had become increasingly concerned that the federal government was not sufficiently knowledgeable of the importance of the area, and he had decided to address his concerns directly to Secretary of State Martin Van Buren.

The country lying between the Colorado and Trinity rivers in Texas, "although not excelled probably by any section of the globe in point of soil and other natural resources" was valuable "only according to its intrinsic worth," he said. It was not vital to American interests.

"The fact is very different with respect to the country between the *Trinity* and the *Sabine*," said Burnet. "The acquisition of that district seems absolutely necessary to the compleat rounding-off of the southwestern frontier." The area referred to, "that district," was of course contiguous to the United States and had long been considered by many as part of the original Louisiana Purchase.

Burnet was at the house of his half brother, Senator William Burnet of Ohio, and this connection was of great help in reaching high government officials and powerful business figures. On April 13, 1829, a few days after writing to the secretary of state, Burnet wrote to John Jacob Astor to ask him to use his influence with Van Buren.

Van Buren replied to Burnet's letter on April 30. He thanked him for his "sensible remarks upon the subject of the boundary between the U. States and Mexico" and invited Burnet to call on him when he was next in Washington.

———

At Cairo, Illinois, Sam Houston disembarked from the steamboat on which he had left Nashville. He and a newfound traveling companion, an Irishman named H. Haralson, transferred their belongings to a flatboat for the trip down the Mississippi. These raftlike vessels were a primary means of transportation on the river, but they were limited. A flatboat could be steered when it was carried by the current, but it could go only downstream.

Haralson may have been at the Nashville Inn when Houston resigned the governorship. More likely they joined up with each other at one of the river towns. In any event, at this juncture, he was just the right companion for Sam.

The two had a merry time drinking and gambling on the water, camping out on the shore, or stopping over in the trading posts on the Mississippi. In one of them, Helena, Houston is supposed to have first met James Bowie, who had recently settled in Texas after a career as farmer, duelist, and slave trader.

Houston and Haralson abandoned their flatboat at the mouth of the Arkansas River to await a steamboat to take them upstream to Little Rock, the capital of the Arkansas Territory, where they landed on May 8, fifteen days after leaving Nashville.

A young Virginian named Charles Noland, the son of an old friend of Houston's, witnessed Sam's arrival. "Governor Houston arrived here three days since on his way to join the Indians," wrote Noland to his father in Virginia. "Merciful God! is it possible that society can be deprived of one of its greatest ornaments, and the United States of one of her most valiant sons, through the dishonor and baseness of a woman?"

Houston appeared to be in a cheerful and expansive mood and he confided to Noland that he planned to spend the winter with the Cherokees and then go on to the Rocky Mountains and the "country between the mouth of the Oregon and California Bay." Noland, however, had no doubt that "General Jackson will certainly persuade him to come back from the woods."

Andrew Jackson had received word of what had happened to Houston and where he was headed in a remarkably short time—less than two weeks after his resignation—and he was as disturbed as everyone else by his friend's behavior. "I have this moment heard of poor Houston's disgrace," Jackson wrote to his nephew-in-law, John McLemore. "My God is the man *mad*?"

At Little Rock, Houston was able at last to write directly to the president. The letter was not prompted by a desire to explain his actions in Tennessee to Old Hickory. Houston never did. Rather, he wrote to defend himself against the charge that he was scheming to separate Texas from Mexico and set himself up as head of a new country.

Jackson would have understandably been upset by these rumors. He himself had been accused of being a party to Aaron Burr's machinations to do precisely the same thing.

Sam swore to the Old Chief that there was no such plan afoot. How could there be? "What am I? an Exile from my home; and my country, a houseless unshelter'd wanderer, among the Indians! Who has met, or who has sustained, such sad and unexpected reverses?" protested Houston. He did volunteer to send along to Washington any information about the Indians and the government agents that he thought might be of interest.

Houston was clearly in a great hurry to move on. He had regained his equilibrium, but he was still in full flight to rejoin the Cherokees who had sheltered him before, when he was a confused boy. He posted the letter to Andrew Jackson and then boarded Captain Phillip Pennywit's steamboat *Facility* to travel up the Arkansas to the Indian country.

Steamboats had been traversing the river as far as Fort Gibson, at the Three Forks, since 1827. The greatest obstacle was Webber's Falls, the rapids that took their name from the nearby trading post of a Cherokee chief, Walter Webber.

If a smaller, less powerful boat could not negotiate the swift water, a long rope was strung from the boat to a team of oxen on the shore and the boat was towed upriver through the rapids.

Another river captain "jumped" sandbars by repeatedly backing up his sternwheeler and charging forward until he cleared the obstacle. This maneuver was generally accompanied by the sound of screaming passengers and breaking glass.

Sometime during this journey from Tennessee occurred one of the more drunken and bacchanalian of Houston's many colorful escapades. Houston, Haralson, and a man named Linton played a drinking game that closely resembled strip poker. In order to get a drink a player had to throw a piece of his clothing into the campfire.

The more naked they became, the higher the fire rose, the drunker they became—until the predictable end, when a player was either too drunk or too naked to continue.

Houston and Haralson were the first to wake up the next morning. After some hair of the dog, they rummaged through their baggage and managed to get themselves dressed. The unfortunate Linton had no extra clothes. Houston and Haralson quietly went on their way, leaving the naked man asleep by the dead fire.

The *Facility* arrived at Webber's Falls, near the mouth of the Illinois River, at dusk. A mile or so below the landing the whistle was sounded and a gun was fired to signal the approach of the steamboat.

The old chief Ooleteka, his way lighted by torches, came down to the river to greet Kalanu, the adopted son whom he had not seen in eleven years. The Raven had returned to his people and "when he laid himself down to sleep that night, after the gloom and sorrows of the past few weeks, he felt like a weary wanderer, returned at last to his father's house."

————

Ooleteka had left the Cherokee Nation in the east in February 1818, while his son was away in Washington with the Indian delegation. He and his followers from Hiwassee first settled in north central Arkansas on a vast tract guaranteed to them in perpetuity by the United States.

Within ten years, however, pressure from white settlers for the Cherokee land was again brought to bear on the helpless native population. Yet another iron-clad agreement was negotiated as the Adams administration forced the tribe to move even farther west.

In spite of the dislocations, Ooleteka was still a prosperous man. Wigwam was the term often applied to the Indian dwellings, but it does not do justice to the substantial houses of the wealthier Cherokees. Ooleteka's house in Tennessee was described by Return J. Meigs as one of the finest houses in the South. It can be presumed that the principal chief attempted to replicate this in the West.

He had a dozen slaves to look after the plantation and his guests, and he slaughtered at least one beef a week to keep meat on the table. He could certainly afford one beef a week. He had a herd of over five hundred cattle.

Ooleteka's wealth and relative sophistication did not guarantee him protection of the laws, however. Houston encountered yet another scheme of the whites to defraud the Indians. The Cherokees had agreed to move farther west in exchange for an annual cash payment for every member of the tribe. Unscrupulous agents paid these claims to the Indians in promissory notes instead of gold.

The Cherokee did not understand the value of paper, and the agents and traders persuaded them to trade the notes for a blanket or a bottle of whiskey or a cheap trinket. Houston had often witnessed the venality of the Indian agents and the victimization of their charges but nothing this extensive.

> I care not what dreamers, and politicians, and travellers, and writers say to the contrary, I know the Indian character, and I confidently avow, that if one-third of the many millions of dollars our government has appropriated within the last twenty-five years, for the benefit of the Indian population, had been honestly and judiciously applied, there would not have been at this time a single tribe within the limits of our States and Territories, but what would have been in the complete enjoyment of all the arts and all the comforts of civilized life.
>
> The President should be careful to whom Indian agencies are given. If there are trusts under our government where honest and just men are needed, they are needed in such places; where peculation and fraud can be more easily perpetrated than anywhere else. For in the far-off forests beyond the Mississippi, where we have exiled those unfortunate tribes, they can perpetrate their crimes and their outrages, and no eye but the Almighty's sees them.

Houston succeeded in having several of the agents removed from their posts, but his championing of the Indians inevitably involved him in controversy with old enemies, particularly those of Andrew Jackson.

Unfortunately the Cherokees had other antagonists besides the United States government. They had been settled on the ancient hunting lands of the Osage, Pawnees, and Comanches, who, of course, contested their right to be there. The ensuing conflict between the tribes threatened not only the Indians. Whites were often the victims as well. Nevertheless many of the government officials seemed content to let the Indians settle matters among themselves, hoping no doubt that they would exterminate each other.

Houston did not tarry long at Ooleteka's wigwam. He and his Sancho Panza, Haralson, soon left for the famous Indian trader Auguste P. Chouteau's outpost in the Osage country. The Chouteau family had been associates of John Jacob Astor in the fur trade, and Auguste presided over a large and rather messy trading establishment on the Neosho River.

His slaves, two Indian wives, and several mixed-blood children were all crowded together in a typical dog-trot building—two large downstairs rooms separated by an open porch, or breezeway, that ran through the building. There were more rooms upstairs.

Chouteau provided further evidence of the perfidy of the Indian agents as they traveled with him to the settlement at the Three Forks, the confluence of the Verdigras, the Arkansas, and the Neosho rivers.

Here also was the westernmost garrison of the United States Army, Fort Gibson. In April 1824, the post at Fort Smith, Arkansas, had been abandoned and the garrison moved 135 miles up the Arkansas to the Three Forks. The new fort was established to protect the Indian tribes from each other, to prevent whites from moving onto the Indian lands, and to prevent illegal trade with the Indians. But the fort is famous for another, less creditable mission. It became the western terminus of the Indian removal route known as the Trail of Tears.

The commander at Fort Gibson, Colonel Matthew Arbuckle, welcomed Houston, but he wondered what in the world a former major general, congressman, and governor was doing in the Indian Territory. Houston surely had to be there for some larger purpose than refuge from a failed marriage.

Houston fanned the flames by immediately meddling in Indian affairs.

In late June, he wrote to Secretary of War John Eaton. He had heard the United States was going to provide military escorts for trading companies traveling between St. Louis and Santa Fe. He warned Eaton that the western Indians had never made treaties with the United States and that the traders and soldiers faced considerable danger and even war.

Houston, the old Indian subagent, recommended that Chouteau be sent to pacify the fierce Plains Indians and that he accompany him. As for his own role, he did not want "any compensation for my services as the duty would recreate my mind." He obviously was casting about for some sort of vocation. Perhaps it lay in the far west. In any event, nothing came of this scheme. Neither Chouteau nor Houston ever traveled the Santa Fe Trail.

———

The western Cherokee still observed the greatest of the tribal rituals, the Green Corn Dance, and on July 7, they gathered at Bayou Manard to celebrate. Chief Ooleteka was ill and sent Houston as his representative. Thousands of Cherokees spent days feasting and dancing in this yearly celebration of renewal and rebirth.

Following the festival, the Cherokee elders met with a delegation of warriors from the Creek Nation. Houston listened as the young Creek braves, who had been stirred up by an unscrupulous white named B. H. Smith, urged the Cherokees to join them in a war against the Pawnees and Comanches. Houston called for calm and his intervention did at least delay the hostilities. In early 1830, however, the Cherokees joined up with other tribes and raided the Pawnees in Texas.

Another great source of friction for the Cherokees came from within the tribe itself. Those who had already removed to the West were not anxious to share their land with their brothers in the East who would eventually be forced to relocate. There were still some twelve thousand Cherokees in the old homeland in the South—about two-thirds of the tribe—so the potential for trouble was enormous.

As far as most of the white settlers were concerned, the Indians had no rights to property or legal protection. White families were known to move into an Indian's house and declare themselves the new owners, and the Indians could do nothing.

Houston zealously defended the Cherokees. As the confidant of

Ooleteka, he was a sort of ombudsman for the Indians. He not only took their complaints to Colonel Arbuckle, but much to the commander's annoyance he often bypassed him and wrote directly to Washington.

Houston by now was exhausted from his travels and his increasingly dissolute life. His general health had so deteriorated by early August that an attack of malaria nearly carried him off. He was very near death for weeks, but by September 19 he had sufficiently recovered to write to Jackson about what he might do.

The president had suggested to Sam that perhaps his future lay in Arkansas. Houston, however, felt that no one could succeed there without fraud, perjury, and cheating. "To become a missionary among the Indians, is rendered impossible," he said, "for a want of that Evangelical change of heart, so absolutely necessary, to a man who assumes the all important character, of proclaiming to a lost world, the mediation of a blessed Savior!"

Instead, Houston asked Jackson's advice about his relocating to Natchez and starting over in politics. His isolation had only increased his interest in public life. "It is hard for an old Trooper, to forget the *note* of the *Bugle!*" he confided to the Old Chief.

Sam did not remove to Natchez. Indeed, events of the next month seemed to indicate that he had decided to stay on in the Arkansas Territory and become a trader. On October 21, Houston became a citizen of the Cherokee Nation.

> We do . . . Solemnly, firmly, and unrecoverably grant to him for ever all the rights, privileges, and Immunities of a citizen of the Cherokee Nation and do as fully impower him with all rights and liberties as tho he was a native Cherokee, while at the Same time the Said Houston will be required to yield obedience to all laws and regulations made for the government of the Native Citizens of the Cherokee Nation.

Was accepting Cherokee citizenship just a gambit to enable him to open a trading post in the Cherokee Nation without government approval? It certainly seemed so to the other traders. He had already taken up Indian ways, but was he now abandoning his American citizenship? Or could he legally have dual citizenship?

Whatever his adopted son's legal status, Chief Ooleteka certainly considered Kalanu a Cherokee—and had done so since Sam first showed up on Hiwassee Island, a sixteen-year-old runaway. In December he dispatched Houston to Washington as an ambassador from the Cherokee Nation.

At the mouth of the Arkansas, Sam boarded the steamboat *Amazon* for the journey up the Mississippi and the Ohio. Given his love of words and gift for manipulating language, traveling these American rivers on the *Amazon* must have appealed to him greatly. He saw the New Year in on the river, looking back on a year of personal failure, public disgrace, and a near fatal illness.

Sam arrived in Washington on January 12, 1830, and went directly to Brown's Indian Queen Hotel, his old capital haunt. He felt resurrected and this was made clear to the public in just a few days' time at a White House diplomatic reception. Old Hickory affectionately, even effusively, embraced him and welcomed him back into the family circle.

Houston became a regular visitor to the White House, even though Andrew Jackson, a man of innate dignity and propriety, never got used to his friend's new eccentric style of dress. Houston often appeared in buckskin leggings, moccasins, and a brilliant Indian hunting shirt, with his head wrapped in the distinctive Cherokee turban.

Jackson had long since made up his mind as to what the proper solution was to the Indian question. He wanted all the southeastern tribes removed to the West, to the other side of the Mississippi. He never doubted the rightness of his course or manifested any ambiguities.

The president was in complete agreement with the southern governors. No independent or separate nation should be allowed to exist within the borders of a sovereign state. Further, given the greed of the whites, it was not possible—perhaps not even desirable—to keep them off the Indian lands.

Jackson also was not going to be pushed into a confrontation with the governors of the southern states over who had jurisdiction over the Indians. The tariff had already brought the issue of states' rights to the boiling point.

The year 1829 was a watershed year in Indian-white relations. Georgia had decreed that by mid-year all Indian residents were to be subject to Georgia law but not protected by it. Jackson knew that the other states would soon follow this course, and he sent John Coffee and William

Carroll to the Cherokees to convince them of the wisdom of their moving voluntarily. The Cherokee chiefs refused categorically to leave. They reminded Jackson's ambassadors that according to the Cherokee constitution it was an act of treason, punishable by death, for any Cherokee to sell land to the whites without the approval of the tribal council.

Jackson would have to go to Congress for legislation authorizing removal. He bought some time and peace with the Indians until Congress convened by sending in troops and removing white squatters from the Indian lands.

The president addressed the Indian removal issue in his usual direct fashion in his first State of the Union message, December 8, 1829. He asked Congress to set aside an area in the West, outside any existing organized state or territory, for the Indians.

Jackson stressed the importance of voluntary removal, but there was also the threat that if the Indians chose to remain they would be subject to the laws of the individual states—which everyone knew meant that they would have no protection whatsoever.

The federal government, Jackson argued, had erred in allowing the Indian nations to operate as sovereign nations inside the United States. Both the Cherokees and the Creeks had aligned themselves with foreign powers in the past. Might they not do the same again? Could the United States run the risk?

In addition to eliminating a potential threat to the security of the nation, Andrew Jackson no doubt was sincere in his belief that his policy guaranteed survival of the American Indians as a distinct people. However, given his own expansionist bent, how could he not have realized that the Indians in the West would soon be surrounded by immigrating whites and the cycle would begin again. Indeed it was already happening in Arkansas.

Houston's love and compassion for his Indian brothers blinded him to the inevitability of their destruction by the whites. Like Jackson he also believed that removal was their only option and that a protective national government would watch over them forever.

The old racist dichotomy was at work here. Americans could, at the same time, believe that all men were created equal and had inalienable rights but that some groups, most notably Indians and Negroes, were inherently inferior and not worthy of basic human rights. They must be cared for by a paternalistic government or kept in eternal bondage for their own good. It is no surprise that the ill-educated, naturally bigoted ordinary citizen could not recognize, much less reconcile, this philosophical split. Their leaders could not either.

The Jackson administration introduced bills in both the House and the Senate in February 1830 authorizing an exchange of land with the Indians and their removal to the West. Jackson brilliantly manipulated Congress and packed the committees to ensure passage, but he still faced serious opposition, even in his own party. For example, Congressman David Crockett of Tennessee voted against the bill. Nevertheless after one of the most bitter and divisive debates in congressional history the Indian Removal Act of 1830 passed both houses.

Houston had already embarked on a questionable scheme that involved another dichotomy that has dogged American political life. Should privileged information and access to policymakers be used for private gain? Jackson had made it clear to everyone in his inner circle that the Indians would be removed, by force if necessary. Houston, as a friend of the Indian—as a citizen of the Cherokee Nation—tried to minimize the damage.

Even before the removal bills were introduced, the War Department announced that bids were being accepted for supplying rations to immigrating Indians. The administration was clearly confident of success.

In March 1830 Houston traveled to New York to meet with financier John Van Fossen and Congressman Robert Selden Rose of New York to discuss bidding on the contract for the provision of rations for the Indians.

Houston was attempting to combine philanthropy, altruism, and business. In a letter to Van Fossen he reminded him of the importance of giving the Indians full rations of good quality. That must be the "sine qua non," said Sam to his partner. No matter, Houston was skirting the limits of propriety, and he would be called to account for it.

Secretary of War Eaton rejected all the bids as too high. The army could feed the Indians for a fraction of even the lowest bid. There had clearly been profiteering and collusion in the bidding, and the Indian rations would become a full-blown scandal in 1832.

While in Washington at this time, Houston met David G. Burnet, who in association with Lorenzo de Zavala, a Mexican national, had by then acquired a sizable land grant in Texas. Burnet and Zavala were unable to fulfill the contract and were looking for a buyer. Houston helped the financially strapped empresarios to dispose of their grant to the Galveston Bay and Texas Land Company, which was based in New York.

The mistrustful and impatient Burnet fired off at least one testy letter to Houston at the City Hotel in New York before the deal was consummated. These early dealings colored his opinion of Houston from the very beginning. He remained resentful of the sale and Houston's role in it for the rest of his life.

On April 13, 1830, the annual celebration of Thomas Jefferson's birthday was held at Brown's Indian Queen Hotel. Houston was in residence at the hotel and even in his reduced circumstances would hardly have been overlooked by Jackson, Eaton, Lewis, Polk, and the other Tennesseans of the administration.

The long celebration—the president was there for more than five hours—was the scene of Jackson's famous confrontation with Calhoun and the nullifiers. The southern states must obey all the laws of the land, argued Jackson. They could not pick and choose—enforcing the laws they liked, nullifying those they did not, and seceding from the union of states if they chose.

When asked to give a toast the president rose and said simply, "Our Union: It must be preserved." The effect could not have been stronger if he had slapped the vice-president. The battle had been joined.

Within a few days, Old Hickory had an opportunity to underscore his point. A young congressman from South Carolina was returning to his home and he called at the White House. The president was cordial and polite until the final leave-taking.

At the door he instructed the young man to "give my compliments to my friends in your State, and say to them, that if a single drop of blood shall be shed there in opposition to the laws of the United States, I will hang the first man I can lay my hand on engaged in such treasonable conduct, upon the first tree I can reach."

———

Houston's stay in Washington was a first step back into society. He returned to the Jacksonian fold and he made some powerful friends among the businessmen of New York. There was still a way to go, however, before he would be anywhere near his earlier eminence and there would be steps backward.

He now took one of those steps. He had decided to open a trading post in Arkansas, and after three months in the capital he left for home. His journey was not made in any great haste, however. He did not arrive at the Three Forks until almost mid-June.

Houston returned by way of Tennessee. At Baker's Creek, he found Elizabeth Houston in poor health and much discouraged by the fates of her children. Paxton and Isabella had died long ago. Robert had committed suicide. Mary was mentally ill. But it was Sam who had fallen the lowest and who was the most bitter of her disappointments. However, he was still her son and her favorite, and their reunion was a happy one.

Houston's trip across Tennessee was a survey of the political landscape. The "note of the Bugle" was indeed still resonating, and he probably heard more than a note while he was in Washington consorting with the Tennessee-based Jackson administration. The success of his old friends made him acutely aware of what he had lost.

He wrote to Jackson that the Eliza Allen–Sam Houston scandal still engaged the people of Tennessee, particularly the Allen family. They had even gone so far as to hold a public hearing to clear Eliza's name and much to Houston's embarrassment had published his rambling and distraught letter to her father of last April.

The family was so fearful that Eliza would try to effect a reconciliation when she heard that Houston was in Nashville that they sent her away to Carthage. And Eliza Allen Houston would have been humiliated. Sam had determined not to receive her and he so informed his friends in Nashville as soon as he arrived in the city. This cold attitude toward the woman who was still his wife and for whose return he was pleading only a year before only adds another layer of contradiction to the story.

Otherwise, Houston's reception in Tennessee led him to think that he could be returned to the governorship if he chose to run. "The affections of the people of Tennessee are with me," he wrote to Jackson, "and if I would present myself to them again, they would shew the world that they have confidence in me, and care nothing about my private matters, which they cannot understand."

A common failing of politicians had come to the fore. Ambition was coupled with wishful thinking to ride roughshod over common sense. It would not have been possible for Sam Houston to be elected to anything in Tennessee in 1830. In two years Tennessee had been sub-jected to the Rachel Donelson affair, the Peggy Eaton affair, and the Eliza Allen affair. The people were still reeling from the scandals, and too many of them believed the worst of all the parties involved.

Houston was obliged to remain in Nashville longer than he intended. Once again he was struck down by malaria. He was not able to travel until the third week in May, when he boarded the steamboat *Nashville* and headed back to Fort Gibson and a new career as a full-time Indian trader.

On the Arkansas, at the mouth of the White River, Sam transferred his stores and goods to a keelboat to be carried upriver to the Three Forks. He then waited for a steamboat. He passed the time by writing letters—with his gloves on because of the dense clouds of mosquitoes.

The keelboat was one of the most useful vessels developed for the river traffic. The boats were fifty to seventy feet long and fifteen to twenty feet wide, but they drew only about two feet of water. Some of them could carry up to twenty tons of cargo. The main form of propul-sion was a back-breaking process that involved the use of a thousand-foot length of rope called a cordelle. The rope was attached upstream to a rock or tree, and then the crew reeled it in. The boats could also be pushed along against the current with twenty-foot poles.

Houston set up his home and his trading post—the Wigwam Neo-sho—across the river from the stockaded Fort Gibson. There has been much speculation about the site of the wigwam and no one has deter-mined the exact coordinates, but the speculation has been far from idle. The best evidence is that the wigwam was about two-and-a-half miles inland, on a hill overlooking the military road called the Texas Road. The surrounding countryside is relatively flat with a few other low hills.

Since all lands in the Indian Territory were held in common, and Houston was a full-fledged citizen of the Cherokee Nation he could presumably build where he pleased. It also helped that he was the adopted son of the principal chief, Ooleteka. These advantages were brought to bear on July 20, when his supplies arrived.

Among the goods for the new store at the Wigwam Neosho were nine barrels of whiskey, brandy, gin, rum, and wine. If these were trade goods, another, even more serious contradiction is presented. Who were the prospective buyers of these spirits? For years Houston had fought against selling whiskey to the Indians, and it was illegal for the soldiers at Fort Gibson to have liquor on the military base.

But here he was, a white man, setting up shop without a trader's license in the Indian Territory, with nine barrels of spirits. Colonel Arbuckle was understandably suspicious. Houston allowed him to inspect the stores but he insisted that he could trade at will since he was a Cherokee citizen.

Sam also promised, somewhat hedgingly, not to sell whiskey to unauthorized persons without permission of the Indian agent or Arbuckle. Further, he was willing to store the whiskey at the fort except for one barrel—for his own use. This concession is a telling admission that Houston was drinking heavily. Although he had not yet become known to his Indian friends as Big Drunk, he was well on his way.

———

In the summer of 1830, Houston took a step that has charmed his admirers, embarrassed many of his descendants, provided ammunition to his enemies, and added immeasurably to his legend. He married Tiana Rogers Gentry. Whether the ceremony was with or without the benefit of Christian clergy is unknown, but it almost certainly followed Cherokee custom.

Tiana, or Diana—or Talahina as many of the Cherokees call her—was the widow of a white blacksmith named David Gentry. Her father was the Scottish trader John Rogers and her mother was seven-eighths white, which made Tiana one-sixteenth Cherokee. The proportion of Cherokee blood made little difference. Diana was Cherokee royalty. Her uncle, Ooleteka, was principal chief, as had been his brother, Tahlontusky.

By all accounts she was a striking woman, intelligent and educated. Her father had sent her to a missionary school in Tennessee and there had been a private tutor at home. She also was prosperous. She had property, livestock, and slaves.

Houston and Tiana were together at the Wigwam Neosho for the remainder of the time he was in the Cherokee Nation. In spite of his happiness with her, she did not, or could not, stop him from drinking any more than she could keep his temper in check. Houston did rouse himself from time to time, however, and nowhere is this more evident than in his brilliant and eloquent articles for the *Arkansas Gazette*. There were five of them, written under the name Tah-Lohn-Tus-Ky, and they appeared between June and December 1830.

Houston's pieces were an indictment of the Indian agents and their chicanery, a history of the removal of the tribes, and a defense of his actions in bidding on the Indian rations contract. Their publication created a storm in the territory and in Washington because he directly attacked the policies of the government, in particular the War Department.

Houston had forced his views on both Eaton and the president while he was in Washington the previous winter and spring. On February 16, Eaton issued a directive that all payments to the Indians were to be in cash—no more certificates or goods—and debts were not to be subtracted.

Perhaps another result of the visit of Houston and his Indian delegation was Eaton's announcement that there would be no further payments to Indians for trips to Washington unless authorized in advance by the secretary of war. Indian delegations had been a nuisance to every administration since George Washington. They sometimes stayed for months at government expense and then expected large presents before they left the capital.

As secretary of war, Eaton was ultimately responsible for Indian policy, but Houston's chief targets were Thomas McKenney, the head of the Bureau of Indian Affairs, and the agents who served under him.

Rumors of collusion in high places had reached Arkansas before Sam had returned from Washington. He took his anger out on Eaton, warning him on June 13 that he was going to write the articles. "The innocent will not suffer, the guilty ought not to escape," he said. It was clear that he was itching for a fight with his old friend.

Eaton did not receive Houston's letter until late in the summer, after he had returned to Tennessee. His chastening but civil reply tells much about the man and what he had gone through himself.

"In future when you shall hear such reports as these," Eaton said calmly, "I must ask you to treat them as a man of sense and reflection should; before you give credit to it, & act upon them, afford me an opportunity of informing you correctly. In high party times a man

should be quite slow to believe even a portion of what he hears—
certainly not the whole."

Thomas McKenney was a holdover from the Adams administration
and in spite of Houston's charges Jackson had kept him on for blatant
political reasons. He needed this "Adams man" to get the Indian
Removal Act through Congress. Jackson then dismissed him.

The Indian agents fought back, and their letters were published in the
Gazette. But Houston's invective was masterful and of course as the
originator of the feud he always had the last word in the press. When one
correspondent admitted that he was "no writer" Houston advised him
to get someone "to *help* him, and aid in pruning off the luxuriant suckers
of his too fertile imagination."

To another agent who warned him that "the worm will turn when
trampled on," Houston replied that "the worm shall not again be
molested by me, until a *pair* of tongs can be procured to handle him
daintily."

Houston's campaign against the corrupt agents, these "bright links in
a chain of the most *hellish corruption,*" was successful. They were sacked
and the entire program reorganized. But the exploitation of the American Indians by whites was too deeply ingrained. It would take more than
one man crying in the wilderness of Arkansas to change the thinking of
the Congress, the president, the courts, and the people.

Houston's defense of the Indians was compelling because it was
truthful. His defense of his own behavior during the bidding to supply
the Indian rations does not pass this test. He denied that he had been
a partner or made a bid with Van Fossen, which, of course, was not true.

In the letter to Van Fossen in April, Houston clearly stated, "When
I advised you to put in your *bid,* I did expect to be equally concerned
with you in the business." And if they won the contract, "I will be happy
to unite with you jointly, and will furnish the capital necessary for the
next six or nine months."

Even while his series of articles was appearing in the *Arkansas Gazette,*
Houston wrote to Van Fossen advising him how best to pursue contracts to supply the Indians.

Sam Houston had once had a distinguished public career, like few other men in the United States. Now he was scrambling to make a living. No one, even a person given to the wildest imaginings, could have foreseen his fall from grace. The man who in 1809 had run away to the Indians to avoid working in a store was now running a store in the Indian Territory.

Speculation in western lands had made many of Houston's friends rich, including the president of the United States. Perhaps such speculation could ensure his own fortune. On September 1, Houston and two partners bought a 640-acre tract from Auguste Chouteau's Indian children, about twenty-five miles northwest of Fort Gibson, on the east bank of the Neosho. The property contained a large salt spring called the Grand Saline and since salt was a rare and valuable commodity a salt works promised economic salvation.

It was a promise soon fulfilled. In Nashville the following summer Houston sold his one-third interest for $6,500. This was a very large sum for the time, but the buyer was John McLemore, Jackson's nephew-in-law. Was Old Hickory's fine hand at work here?

In spite of Houston's defense of the Cherokees and his prominence as a spokesman for them in Washington, he was rejected by the tribe when he ran for a place on the Cherokee Tribal Council in May 1831. He was devastated—and not just because he had never lost an election in his life, whether for attorney general, major general, congressman, or governor. He had been betrayed by his Indian friends and relations.

It was a bitter rejection and undoubtedly reflected what many of the younger Cherokees thought of him. He was just another interloper, a drunken and arrogant white man. While he might mean well they could not accept him as one of them.

Houston's defeat in the election for the Cherokee Council was particularly galling after his success in helping negotiate treaties of friendship between the Creek and the Osage and the Cherokee and the Osage. He witnessed the signing of the treaties at Fort Gibson.

Houston's disappointment and anger led to a nasty confrontation with Ooleteka. When the gentle patriarch presumed to lecture his adopted son on his drinking, Sam became abusive and violent. The old chief was saved from serious injury by the young braves who had to restrain Big Drunk after he had struck the principal chief of the Cherokee Nation. Houston's degradation was complete.

The *Cherokee Phoenix* reported on May 28 that Sam Houston was planning to move to the Choctaw Nation. By that time, however, Houston had already left the Wigwam Neosho. But he was not heading west to the Choctaw. He was traveling east, toward Nashville.

Houston had considered returning to white society many times before. The abortive attempt to enter Cherokee politics and his behavior toward his Indian father now hastened his departure.

Kalanu packed a few items of clothing in buffalo skin sacks, put a bowie knife in his belt, picked up his hunting rifle, and left his home and trading post. He dressed in his usual calico shirt, deerskin leggings, moccasins, and a dilapidated straw hat. His hair was in the Indian fashion, in a long queue. Trotting along beside him were two faithful dogs. His withdrawal from the Cherokee Nation and the end of his exile had begun.

A week or so later, near the mouth of the Arkansas, a steamboat came to a halt in midstream. The passengers leaned against the rail and watched as a small boat brought out a tall, roughly dressed man from the White River Landing. Although their new shipmate appeared to be an Indian, the captain welcomed him aboard. The astounded passengers soon learned why. This bizarre figure from out of the woods was none other than General Sam Houston, the former governor of Tennessee.

After dinner, Houston spent some time with a young man named Matthew Maury, who kept a journal of his trip through the West. Maury was appalled that a system of suffrage could elevate a man like Houston to public office. The former governor, he said, "gave no symptoms of that general knowledge & information which the imagination would consider indispensable in a Governor of a State." Houston added to his dissolute image by drunkenly ranting about setting up an independent colony in the Pacific Northwest.

Houston's behavior on the steamboat was only the prelude to a disastrous visit to Nashville. Old friends and relatives were shocked by his appearance. Both Jackson and William Lewis had remained in Washington for the summer. Perhaps they could have exercised some of their

old influence on Houston, but if his treatment of Ooleteka is any index
of his mental condition their presence in Nashville might have had the
opposite effect.

Andrew Jackson was beset by his own demons in the capital. The
Eaton affair was supposed to have been resolved by the resignation of
the entire cabinet, but the press had exposed the public to "Eaton fever"
and would not let the epidemic play itself out.

Old Hickory himself had one of the worst cases of the fever. He
became so obsessed with the scandal that he was like a dog with a bone.
He could not let go of it. He spent months trying simultaneously to
protect Eaton, defend Peggy Eaton's reputation, and govern the country. Unfortunately, government lost. Eventually the scandal did play
itself out, but as Jackson biographer Robert Remeni said, "Jackson's
behavior during this period borders on madness."

In Nashville, Houston exhibited some rather bizarre behavior himself.
The papers of the time regularly reprinted notices and articles from
around the country so that the reading public even in the most out-of-
the-way places was often well informed about public events and personalities.

The *National Banner and Nashville Whig* reprinted an article from
Arkansas that was yet another attack on Houston's personal life and his
professional dealings. Houston responded by running an announcement
that while it may have embarrassed his friends—it bears more than a hint
of drunken paranoia—is a splendid example of the Houston wit and his
talent for invective.

A Proclamation

Whereas, I have recently seen a publication originating in the
Cherokee Nation, east of the Mississippi, dated "18th May 1831,"
and signed "J.S." which said publication, or letter, has been repub-
lished in several newspapers, such as the Kentucky Reporter,
United States Telegraph, &c.; and as I presume it will find a
general circulation, notwithstanding the absurd personalities which
it contains—and as it is not the first which has found its way into
public prints, containing ridiculous and unfounded abuse of me:—

Now, know all men by these presents, that I, Sam Houston, "late Governor of the State of Tennessee," do hereby declare to all *scoundrels whomsoever,* that they are authorized to accuse, defame, calumniate, slander, vilify, and libel me to any extent, in *personal* or *private* abuse. And I do further proclaim, to whomsoever it may concern, that they are hereby *permitted* and *authorized* to write, indite, print, publish and circulate the same; and that I will in *no wise* hold them responsible to me in law, or honor, for either the use of the "*raw material,*" or the *fabrication* of *any,* or *all* of the above named articles, connected with the "American System;" nor will I have recourse to *nullification,* in any case whatsoever, where a conviction would not secure to the culprit the dignity of a penitentiary residence. And as some ingenuity has already been displayed in the *exhibition* of specimens, and others may be induced to invest a *small capital* in the business, from feelings of emulation and an itching after experiment—Be it known for the especial encouragement of all scoundrels hereafter, as well as those who have already been engaged, that I do solemnly propose, on the first day of April next, to give to the author of the most *elegant, refined and ingenious lie or calumny,* a handsome gilt copy (Bound in sheep) of the Kentucky Reporter, or a snug plain copy of the United States Telegraph, (bound in dog) since its commencement.

Given under my hand and private seal, (*having no seal of office*) at Nashville, in the State of Tennessee.

SAM HOUSTON,
13th July, 1831

The announcement in the paper was the most public display of Houston's bad behavior in Tennessee. He also was drinking heavily, but at least most of it was behind closed doors. At last the disastrous and humiliating visit ended and he headed back to the Wigwam Neosho. His friends may have been dismayed by his visit, but the Allens were happy that he had reappeared in Tennessee and disgraced himself. Any reconciliation between Eliza and this wreck of a man was clearly out of the question. She could now proceed with forgetting him.

Houston had barely resettled in at the Wigwam when word came that he must return to Tennessee. Elizabeth Houston was dying. Sam left immediately for his old home on Baker's Creek and arrived in time to bid his mother farewell.

Elizabeth Houston had raised her children and kept her faith in the face of adversity and loss. She had persevered as her hopes and dreams had died. No disappointment was as bitter to her as the fall of her son Sam, who wept as he knelt by her bed to receive her final blessing.

She died in the farmhouse that she had helped build with her own hands. They placed her body in a pine coffin, and after the simple Presbyterian service Sam helped carry it down the hill and across the creek to the cemetery behind the church.

Elizabeth Houston's death made Sam Houston profoundly aware of his terrible failure. He must now redeem himself and try to fulfill the destiny that had seemed to be his only two years before. He knew that his future lay elsewhere than the Indian country, but new habits can be harder to break than old ones. He returned to the Wigwam Neosho.

In December 1831 yet another Cherokee delegation made its way to Washington to try to get the government to honor its commitments and treaty obligations. It also expected, of course, to come away with as many gifts as possible. The corruption was complete.

Houston was not officially part of this group, but he traveled with them. He was penniless and this was a way of getting a free ride. He had business in the East, which he hoped would help him get back on track.

Other groups of Indians were also on the move that winter, but they were not part of any delegation to the center of power in the nation's capital. They were the new immigrants from the East to the western lands. A young French nobleman encountered such a group, a band of Choctaws from Tennessee, as he boarded a steamboat at Memphis on Christmas Day.

Alexis de Tocqueville had originally planned to travel down the Ohio and Mississippi to New Orleans, but the winter of 1831 was one of the coldest in memory. The northern waterways were blocked by ice and he had to travel overland to Memphis.

Tocqueville was thus able to observe firsthand the charade of voluntary immigration of the Indian tribes. These miserable, ragged, and destitute Indians huddled on the windy deck of the boat were living proof of the cruelty of the removal. The Choctaws disembarked at the

White River Landing on the Arkansas to proceed to their new homes in the Indian Territory.

Waiting for the boat was Sam Houston, colorfully attired as ever and riding a magnificent stallion. The inquisitive Frenchman, whose ostensible reason for visiting the United States was to study the penal system, occupied himself with every issue. On the way downriver, he questioned Houston at great length on the American Indians. Houston's observations served as the basis of Tocqueville's treatise on the native Americans.

The younger man—Tocqueville was only twenty-six—also questioned a system that could have produced someone like a Sam Houston. Tocqueville called him one of the "unpleasant consequences of popular sovereignty."

Tocqueville arrived in America at a particularly good time to assess the slavery question. During the dog days of the summer of 1831 those southern whites who led the campaign for removal of the Indians were diverted from their appointed task by a chilling reminder of their vulnerability to a greater social problem.

On August 21 and 22, Nat Turner, a thirty-one-year-old slave preacher in Southampton County, Virginia, led his followers in a rebellion against their white masters. The rampage was quickly suppressed but not before fifty-one whites had been killed.

Southerners blamed the whole affair on northern abolitionists, and Nat Turner's rebellion ended any talk of abolitionism in the South. The states' rightists had been given more ammunition in their war and they would use the threat of slave revolts to stir up the whites for the next thirty years.

Tocqueville saw the enormity of the problem and how intransigent the southern whites were even to those people who were only part black or were freemen. He constructed an imaginary conversation based on a real experience.

"Don't you intend to make these white black men your equal one day?"

"Never."

"Then I truly fear they will one day make themselves your masters."

Sam Houston and Alexis de Tocqueville's encounter on the Mississippi was a classic case of two men misreading each other. Houston had no idea that he had met one of the nineteenth century's most original thinkers. Tocqueville was just another tourist and a good listener. Tocqueville regarded Houston as just a washed-up politician with no firm grounding in politics or philosophy.

After the briefest of stays in New Orleans, Sam and the Cherokees left by boat for Washington, by the coastal route around Florida and up the East Coast. Houston left his Indian companions at Brown's Indian Queen Hotel. He had important business in New York. Another scheme was afoot.

Gold fever had struck in the South, and Houston hoped to interest New York speculator James Prentiss in the 10,000 acres that he owned in Tennessee. How Houston got hold of so many acres, which "inspire lively hopes of great success in obtaining Gold," is not at all clear. Considering his connections, however, it can easily be imagined.

Gold had been found in the Southeast as early as 1799 but it was not until 1828 that large commercial quantities began to be exploited in north Georgia, not far from Houston's holdings in southeast Tennessee. Houston was not as successful with gold as he had been with salt. His lands did not turn out to be El Dorado. However, Prentiss and his New York friends did serve another, and much more historic purpose. They directed Houston's attention to Texas.

The Galveston Bay and Texas Land Company had continued to expand its holdings in Texas, and Prentiss was one of the chief promoters. He and another promoter, Samuel Swartwout, sought to enlist Houston as an agent for the company.

Gold, salt, a colony on the Pacific Coast, Tennessee politics, a trading post, land grants in Texas—all this could either connote a prodigious appetite for work, a talent for multifarious business enterprises, or a renaissance man in full cry. Alas, no such coloring can be put on the sad truth. Houston was still a desperate man wrestling with an increasingly bleak future, his problems aggravated by heavy drinking.

Sam was drawn to speculation in Texas land, but nothing was settled by the time he returned to Washington from New York at the end of March. In any event on April 2, 1832, his life changed dramatically. It always did. There were never any smooth transitions.

The day began calmly enough at Brown's Hotel as Houston reflected on the various plans afoot that might just possibly redirect his life. He regularly read the reports of the congressional debates in the rabidly anti-Jackson *National Intelligencer.* It was always a good thing to keep up with the enemy. However, that day's news was not the usual attack on the Jackson administration and its Democratic policies.

Houston had been mentioned in debate on the floor of the House of Representatives by one William Stanbery, congressman from Ohio. "Was the late Secretary of War removed in Consequence of his attempt fraudulently to give to governor *Houston* the contract for Indian rations!" asked Representative Stanbery, who then went on to implicate the president. It was an old charge but Houston exploded.

The Indian rations mess had been stirred up again. Houston was certainly not blameless. Indeed he had tried to use his influence. But being accused of outright fraud was another matter.

The next day, Houston wrote to Stanbery, demanding to know if what he had read was true. The congressman immediately wrapped himself in legislative privilege. "I cannot recognize the right of Mr Houston to make this request," he airily replied. To make matters worse the response was to a third party, Cave Johnson, and not to Houston.

Stanbery realized that Houston's letter constituted a challenge and that he was regularly attending the sessions of the House, but he did not shrink. He began that day to carry two pistols and a dirk to the Capitol. "I expected every time I went out of, or came into this Hall, to meet him, and I was always prepared for such an event," he recalled.

Ten days later "such an event" occurred. Houston, Francis P. Blair, and Alexander Buckner were walking down Pennsylvania Avenue at about eight o'clock in the evening. In front of a Mr. Eliot's, Blair suddenly excused himself and began to walk rapidly in the opposite direction. He had spotted Stanbery crossing the avenue from Mrs. Queen's boardinghouse, and he knew a confrontation was imminent. As Stanbery recalled it, Blair was wise to retreat.

"At the moment of stepping on the side walk," said Stanbery, "Mr. Houston stood before me. I think he called me by my name, and instantly struck me with the bludgeon he had in his hand with great violence, and he repeated the blow while I was down; he struck me repeatedly with great violence."

Houston's "bludgeon" was reportedly a walking stick he had fashioned from a hickory sapling cut on the grounds of The Hermitage. If so, it was an appropriate touch.

Stanbery was carrying one of the pistols—"in the right pocket of my pantaloons"—and he drew the gun and shoved the barrel against Houston's chest. The weapon misfired. Houston maintained that he hit Stanbery only after he realized that he had pulled the gun. He was acting in self-defense.

Whoever started the fight, Houston certainly ended it. Stanbery suffered a severe concussion, a fractured left hand, a bruised left arm and right elbow, and "other marks of violence on difference parts of my person." Houston also ripped Stanbery's shirtfront and tore the buttons off his waiscoat.

Much satisfied, Houston returned to his hotel. The battered congressman limped back across the street to his boardinghouse, no doubt regretful that he had ventured out on Friday the thirteenth.

The next day, Stanbery wrote to the Speaker of the House from his sick bed, charging Houston with assaulting a congressman for remarks made in debate in the House. Theoretically congressmen were immune from prosecution, no matter how critical or libelous their speeches. Otherwise, said Thomas Hart Benton, the members would have to legislate "with pistols in their belt."

Houston was arrested and brought before Congress on April 17 and formally charged. The case engaged the attention of the country for the next three months. It was, after all, a presidential election year, and every issue was seized upon if it reflected badly on the other party.

Jackson knew that Houston's trial was a contest between his administration and its enemies, and he did not shrink from his accustomed habit of protecting and defending his friends. He wished, he said, that there were a "dozen Houstons to beat and cudgel the members of Congress." He also allowed that "after a few more examples of the same kind, members of Congress would learn to keep civil tongues in their heads." One paper regretted that the "tactics of the Nashville school were to be transferred to Washington."

Houston's trial before the House of Representatives began on April 19. Each day a huge crowd of Washington society and a sprinkling of famous people came to the Capitol. The great actor Junius Brutus Booth was there to hear his friend Sam defend himself. As *Niles' Weekly*

Register reported, "The crowd in the gallery, of ladies as well as gentlemen, being excessive, and a great many ladies being in the lobbies, it was
. . . ordered that the ladies be permitted to occupy the privileged seats
in the hall of the House."

The newspapers complained that very little legislative business was
conducted in the House, and the proceedings even spilled over into the
Senate. A special resolution was necessary to enable four senators to
cross over and testify for the defense.

Houston's lawyer was the Washington attorney Francis Scott Key.
Not surprisingly, the author of "The Star Spangled Banner" was an
ardent Jacksonian. He argued that of course private citizens had the
right to defend themselves against attacks made on them by congressmen. Besides, Houston's anger was directed not at the Congress and
what was said in debate but at what was reported in the press. Key was
splitting hairs to be sure. The main issues were assault and battery and
contempt of Congress.

Jackson had Houston to the White House regularly during the trial.
He even bought Sam a fashionable new suit of clothes for his appearance
before the House. No member of Old Hickory's family should confront
his enemies in buckskin leggings and a hunting shirt.

Key's summation for the defense lasted over three hours, but Houston insisted that he be allowed to speak also. He appeared before the
House of Representatives on May 7, nursing a fearful hangover from a
late-night debauch.

Among his fellow Sunday revelers were James K. Polk, Judge Felix
Grundy, and Speaker of the House Andrew Stevenson. Reveler is not
quite the word for the abstemious Polk, whom Houston called a "victim
of the use of water as a beverage." He went home early.

At precisely twelve noon, Houston, resplendent in his Jacksonian dark
suit, rose to defend himself in the chamber where he had once been a
respected member. There was a stir in the galleries, particularly among
a group of young women who had come regularly to see their handsome
ne'er-do-well.

Straight off Houston committed perjury. "Arraigned for the first time
in my life on a charge of violating the laws of my country," he began—
ignoring or brushing aside the indictment by the state of Kentucky for
shooting a man in 1826. He then delivered a grandiloquent and impassioned address—not to the House but to the nation.

Houston's main line of defense was that the House of Representatives had no constitutional right to try a private citizen for what it deemed a transgression of its privileges. He questioned the very existence of such privileges. No one has "been able to lay their hand on any part of the constitution which authorizes their claim to such an extraordinary prerogative," he said.

He made his trial the cause of the people. The accusers became the accused. He warned of the dangers of a corrupt and entrenched legislature. Were not frequent elections designed to guard against this threat to liberty? All tyrants had been elevated by a servile senate or parliament, said Sam. One had only to look at Caesar, Bonaparte, and Cromwell to see that this was so.

Houston said he was only defending his reputation when he attacked Stanbery, who was hiding behind so-called congressional immunity from prosecution for libel. "But it will ever be found that men have an inherent love of liberty, and an inborn sense of the value of reputation, which never can be made to yield to any authority," he insisted.

"Whatever gentlemen may have imagined, so long as that proud emblem of my country's liberties, with its stripes and its stars, shall wave in this Hall of American legislators, so long shall it cast its sacred protection over the personal rights of every American citizen. Sir, when you shall have destroyed the pride of American character, you will have destroyed the brightest jewel that Heaven ever made. You will have drained the purest and the holiest drop which visits the heart of your sages in council, and your heroes in the field. You will have annihilated the principle that must sustain that emblem of the nation's glory and elevate that emblem above your own exalted seat. These massy columns, with yonder lofty dome, shall sink into one crumbling ruin. Yes, sir, though corruption may have done something, and luxury may have added her seductive powers in endangering the perpetuity of our nation's fair fame, it is these privileges which still induce every American citizen to cling to the institutions of his country, and to look to the assembled representatives of his native land as their best and only safeguard.

"But sir, so long as that flag shall bear aloft its glittering stars— bearing them amidst the din of battle, and waving them triumphantly above the storms of the ocean, so long, I trust, shall the rights of

American citizens be preserved safe and unimpaired, and transmitted as a sacred legacy from one generation to another, till discord shall wreck the spheres—the grand march of time shall cease—and not one fragment of all creation be left to chafe on the bosom of eternity's waves."

Houston ended with his right arm outstretched, pointing to the American flag over the portrait of Lafayette. The great voice reverberated through the chamber. The effect was electrifying. The audience erupted in a chorus of bravos and hurrahs. One young woman tossed a bouquet of flowers from the balcony to Houston who bowed elegantly to her. Junius Brutus Booth ran down the aisle to embrace him. "Houston, take my laurels!" cried the actor.

It was a great speech, and if the public had been the judge the whole affair would have ended right there. The House, of course, had to look to its own, and after four days of debate voted a guilty verdict 106 to 89. Houston's friends, led by Polk, made sure the sentence would be nothing more serious than a reprimand from the Speaker of the House.

Houston returned to the House chamber on May 14. The reprimand from his old friend Stevenson was more commendation than punishment, and Houston was allowed to file a protest. He again questioned the constitutionality of the proceedings, but he accepted the sentence. *Niles' Weekly Register,* which had become thoroughly sick of the whole affair, commented, "The case of Samuel Houston is concluded—*somehow.*"

Stanbery, however, would not let the matter die. His cause became a vendetta. He engineered the appointment of a congressional committee to investigate the rations issue. He tried to have Houston barred from the House. And he brought charges against him in civil court.

"Nothing but the blackest malignity can justify the perverseness and vindictiveness of this man!" said Sam wearily. "Insensible to every manly emotion, he is incapable of an attempt to rise in the scale of being, and seeks only to drag others to his own loathsome degradation. His vices are too odious to merit pity, and his spirit too mean to deserve contempt."

The special committee exonerated Houston of the fraud charges, and the House voted not to deny the former member access to the House chamber. The court case was another matter. On June 28, Houston appeared before Judge William Cranch, a cousin of John Quincy Adams.

He was found guilty, and, said Sam, "the old sinner fined me $500."
He was given six months to pay it, but when the deadline came Houston
had long since returned to the West.

Sam Houston had risen like Lazarus. The public forum provided by
the House of Representatives had brought him back from the politically
dead. "I was dying out and had they taken me before a justice of the
peace and fined me ten dollars it would have killed me; but they gave
me a national tribunal for a theatre, and that set me up again," he said.

No one was happier than Andrew Jackson at this rebirth of his great
friend. The president's support had been total. Throughout most of this
litigious spring of 1832, Houston had lived at the White House. Jackson
even discussed with him a place in his administration, but Houston
declined. He was still a political liability and with the election in the fall
and the coming battle over the Bank of the United States, Jackson had
no need of further distractions.

Houston did accept with alacrity another offer from the Old Chief.
Jackson asked him to visit the Indians of the Southwest on his behalf.
With the two trials finally behind him, Houston was able to extricate
himself from Washington and return to the Wigwam Neosho to prepare
for his journey into Texas.

He tried to leave Washington on July 12, but that morning he "had
a very severe *chill,* & fever" and "it is possible that I may not be able
to sit in the stage today." Once again he had been felled by the malaria
that plagued him, no doubt exacerbated by his old wounds and the heat
and humidity of Washington in July.

He soon recovered and boarded the stage for western Virginia, where
he would take a steamboat down the Ohio. His decision not only to stop
over in Cincinnati but to attend the theater was a typical example of
Houston's thumbing his nose at convention. Sometimes he invited
trouble. Congressman Stanbery's constituents caused such a commotion
when Houston was spotted in the audience that the management had
to ring down the curtain and stop the play.

———

The Stanbery affair consumed four months of valuable time. Houston
had been on the verge of contractually committing himself to the Galveston Bay and Texas Land Company, and he had asked Charles F. Noland

to accompany him to Texas. Houston was rightly worried about his health and saw the wisdom of having a young energetic person along to carry on if he fell ill. He had been much impressed with Noland in Little Rock and saw him as the perfect companion. Houston wrote to him on June 10 that "if we should live, our wealth must be boundless."

Events in Texas, however, were threatening to overtake him and his prospective partners. Texas had been the focus, or target, of much political speculation and intrigue since the Louisiana Purchase. There was the bizarre conspiracy of Aaron Burr who had planned to wrest it from Spain. Andrew Jackson had always considered it part of the Purchase. There were now thousands of Americans settled there under the auspices of various empresarios, who had negotiated vast land grants from the Mexican government.

———

Mexico had first raised the banner of revolution against Spain in 1810, and after a decade of bloody fighting independence became a reality in 1821. The military leader Agustín de Iturbide had led the successful revolt of the people, but he soon succumbed to the idea that it was easier to rule Mexico alone, and he had himself crowned Emperor Agustín I. However, in 1823 he was overthrown by two of his subordinates, Guadalupe Victoria and Antonio López de Santa Anna.

A republic was proclaimed, and in 1824 a liberal constitution was promulgated. Santa Anna remained a powerful behind the scenes figure who from time to time would emerge from his farm at Manga de Clavo to set things right. By 1833, he finally decided that he might as well run the country directly. He was unanimously elected president by the legislature, "despite the fact," he said, "I had not reached the age required by law."

During these turbulent times, American empresarios alternately profited and suffered from the political instability. Stephen F. Austin did his best to accommodate first the Spanish and then the Mexican authorities, no easy task. Soon after he received his land grant, however, Mexico became independent and changed the rules.

The new republic preferred a general colonization law that would benefit everyone, but in April 1823 Austin's grant was recognized by the Mexican government and the colonization efforts that he had begun in late 1821 proceeded. Mexico continued its generous policies toward immigration and colonization.

Although new settlers might have resented the requirement that they convert to Catholicism, most of them felt that a 640-acre tract was worth a mass. The Anglos were also allowed to bring their slaves, even though slavery had been abolished in the other states of Mexico. All children born of slaves were to be freed at age fourteen, however.

Immigration proceeded unabated until 1830, when the Mexican government became alarmed at the increasing number of Americans entering its territory. Mexican nationals were encouraged to immigrate north into the state of Coahuila y Tejas in the hope that they would eventually outnumber the gringos.

The new policy failed and a restrictive immigration law, the Law of April 6, 1830, was passed. The infamous Article 11 of the law has been called the Stamp Act of the Texas Revolution. Further immigration from the United States was forbidden. Austin was able to get an exemption for his colony, but the law effectively halted the activities of the Texas Association and the Galveston Bay and Texas Land Company, which had invested in millions of acres of land.

The first revolutionary actions by the colonists took place at the port and garrison of Anahuac, at the head of Galveston Bay. This settlement was also the headquarters of the Galveston Bay and Texas Land Company.

The colonists were angered by customs duties, title delays, and the impressment of their slaves to work at the Mexican garrison. The high-handed commander, Juan Davis Bradburn, a mercenary from Kentucky, consistently meddled in civilian affairs.

Two recent immigrants from Alabama, Patrick Churchill Jack and William Barrett Travis, were particularly annoying to the commander and he had them arrested. The outraged settlers marched on the fort and forced Bradburn to free the prisoners.

The Anahuac disturbance was bloodless, but the arrests convinced the Texans of the perfidy of the authorities and they set about arming themselves. The Mexicans were quick to react. Their attempted detention of a vessel carrying a cannon for the Texans further aroused the insurgents.

On June 26, 1832, the first serious engagement between Mexicans and Texans was fought at Velasco. Ten Texans died in the ten-hour battle—the first martyrs to the cause of Texas independence. The Mexican force, under Domingo de Ugartechea, surrendered to John Austin.

———

Houston's negotiations with Prentiss and the Galveston Bay and Texas Land Company to act as agent finally came to naught. The immigration restrictions and the civil unrest in the Mexican state played a part certainly. Another reason had to do with money. Prentiss could not raise the money to pay Houston his fee. The cholera epidemic had created chaos in the New York business community.

Americans had watched with a horrible fascination as the disease advanced around the world. Never before had the progress of an epidemic been so well charted. In April, thirteen thousand people died in Paris. By June it had reached North America and started its trek south. In July and August three thousand people died in New York City. There were more than four thousand deaths in three weeks in New Orleans.

Prentiss may also have gotten wind of some of the dubious Texas schemes associated with Houston's name—stories that have appealed to believers in conspiracy theories ever since. Houston was planning to drive out the Mexicans with the aid of the Cherokees and to set himself up as a king. Houston was going to Texas to foment a revolution and call for intervention and annexation by the United States. Houston had engineered his failed marriage so that he could leave the country with no questions asked and be free to intrigue in Texas.

Historian Llerena Friend examined each theory in turn and demolished them all with great good sense. "What the devil was Sam Houston doing in Texas?" she asked. "He was there to make a living and a name for himself."

By early 1832, Houston had decided to go to Texas, either as a company agent, as the personal representative of the president of the United States, or—true to form—both at the same time. The land agency had collapsed; he would have to travel under the aegis of the president.

Houston was back in Tennessee when he was issued a passport on August 6. It called on all tribes of Indians, whether they were bound by treaty or not, to allow General Sam Houston safe passage through their territories. There is no mention of Texas or Mexico so it is not at all clear what the ultimate function of this passport was. Who would have paid any attention to it? Certainly not the illiterate and warlike tribes of the Southwest.

The passport does supply a good physical description of Houston, which effectively refutes at least one of the Houston myths. He was six feet, two inches tall—not six feet, six. He also had brown hair and a light complexion. But the passport, which bears the seal of the War Department and Houston's endorsement, also gives his age as thirty-eight years old. He was thirty-nine.

Houston left Nashville for Fort Gibson and the Wigwam Neosho in the middle of September. He arrived on Monday, October 8. On that same day, around noon, the sentries at the fort were alerted by a party that had dismounted on the opposite shore of the river and was boarding a scow to cross the narrow stream.

The most noticeable man in the group was dark-haired, middle-aged, and very small and slight. He must have looked a bit odd there on the frontier surrounded by rough soldiers and painted and feathered Indians. He did not think so. He had been to too many other strange places. His insatiable curiosity and interest must have been more than a little pricked as he was rowed across the river to the army post with its "neat look of white fortifications" in this "land of the *bloody hand*."

This was none other than America's most famous man of letters and indefatigable traveler—Washington Irving—who had come to see the West for himself. For weeks he had been traveling by steamboat, horseback, carriage, and on foot on his tour of the prairies. His companions were Charles Joseph Latrobe and a Count Pourtales. En route they met up with the party of Henry L. Ellsworth, who had been sent by President Jackson to oversee the settlement of the Indians south and west of the Arkansas.

Ellsworth was the son of Oliver Ellsworth, a chief justice of the Supreme Court during the Washington administration. His twin brother was the governor of Connecticut. He was both a shrewd businessman and a dedicated public servant. His career ranged from president of the Aetna Insurance Company, to land speculator, to Indian agent, to director of the Patents Office.

On this trip west, Ellsworth saw at once the great agricultural value of the prairie land. He also saw a way to combine private and public business, as custom dictated. In fairly short order he was one of the largest landholders in what had once been the Northwest Territory.

Ellsworth and Irving had stopped a few days before at Chouteau's agency north of Fort Gibson and then pushed on to the Union Indian Mission run by a courageous and dedicated couple from Connecticut, William S. Vail and his wife. From the mission they had come south to Fort Gibson.

They spent two convivial nights at the frontier fort, where they were entertained by the officers. The appearance of any group, especially one as distinguished as this, was always a reason to socialize, and Houston joined them at the fort.

Irving amused his dinner companions with the story of a fight he had once watched between two Galápagos turtles. One turtle raised its head and went "Foo, foo, foo!" The other turtle then raised its head a little higher and also went "Foo, foo, foo!" The turtles never made bodily contact, but these movements continued until one of the turtles had an advantage in height. The advantage was imperceptible to the observer but it was apparently very perceptible to the other turtle, which immediately retreated.

Houston later used Irving's anecdote in a Senate debate, which he said was like the turtle fight. "A little blowing and little tip-toeing was all that was done," he said.

Irving and Houston were in accord in their opinions of the Indians. "The Indians that I have had an opportunity of seeing in real life," said Irving, "are quite different from those described in poetry. They are by no means the stoics that they are represented; taciturn, unbending, without a tear or a smile."

Irving rightly attributed the Indians' shyness around whites to the language barrier. Did not whites behave the same way in a group of Indians? But, he said, observe the Indians in a group by themselves, where "they give full scope to criticism, satire, mimicry, and mirth. . . . There cannot be greater gossips."

On October 10, Ellsworth's party left Fort Gibson to continue the journey to the Indian tribes. Houston rode with them as far as the Creek Agency on the Verdigris, even though he had been home only two days and away from Tiana since December of the year before.

After a few days, Houston returned to the Wigwam and his Indian wife, and he remained there until mid-November. Autumn was a good time to start south. Houston left his past among the dead leaves in Arkansas and headed down the Texas Road to Fort Towson on the Red River.

Some friends in Tennessee had announced his name for governor and he considered returning there to run, although he later said that his intention in 1832 was "to become a herdsman, and spend the rest of his life in the tranquility of the prairie solitudes." He wrote to his cousin John, "My health and spirits are both good, my habits sober, and my heart straight."

On December 1, Houston sent a report to Ellsworth at Fort Gibson on what he had learned thus far about the southwestern tribes. Sam was at Fort Towson, about 125 miles south of the Wigwam Neosho, and about 5 miles north of the Red River, the border between the United States and Texas.

This report bears out what Houston always maintained was the purpose of his journey. It was a simple fact-finding mission. How many Indians were there out there? Where were they? Did they pose any threat to the United States? Could they be persuaded to attend a peace conference at Fort Gibson?

The plan for removal of all the eastern Indians to the West was being drawn up by the Jackson administration and a place must be found for them. Was there room for them in the West and how would they be received by the western Indians?

The Comanches and the Pawnees were the largest tribes in the Southwest. Houston estimated the number of Comanche warriors at about eight thousand, much too high, but they were nevertheless a very large and very dangerous army for any nation to confront.

These so-called wild Indians were always on the move following the immense herds of buffalo. Going north in the spring, they trailed behind the buffalo herds. Grass was plentiful and there was enough for the game and the hundreds, even thousands of Comanche horses. In the fall, when the grass was sparser, the Indians stayed well ahead of the buffalo on their return journey. There was little left for horses after the buffalo moved across the land.

It is sometimes difficult for late twentieth-century sensibilities to understand the importance of the horse in the nineteenth century. Horses were the primary means of transport and transportation. In warfare it was the general practice to shoot a man's horse out from under him before shooting the man. The horse was more important.

Horses, oxen, and all pack animals thus had to be provided with a more than adequate supply of grass and forage. Every journey or campaign was therefore planned around the proximity of grassland.

By December 1832, the Comanches and the other Plains Indians had ended their great return migration. They were already hundreds of miles to the south and west. Houston would have to journey deep into Texas to find them.

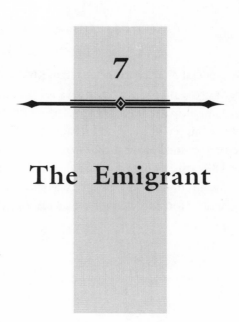

7

The Emigrant

SAM HOUSTON did not splash across the muddy Red River on horse-back and clamber up its south bank onto the prairies of Texas—except in fiction and poetry. The major crossing of the Red River below Fort Towson was by ferry, and so Sam Houston floated into Texas history.

He stepped ashore at the trading post of Jonesborough, about December 10, 1832. Although it was nominally Mexican, the town was the first Anglo settlement in Texas. Americans were living in the area as early as 1815. A Virginian named Henry Jones arrived two years later and began operating a ferry across the Red River. His ferry landing evolved into Jonesborough. Jones stayed around until 1824, when he moved on to Austin's colony, where he became one of the Old Three Hundred.

Jonesborough was a rough river town, with a population of over two thousand. It was home to hunters, trappers, traders, fugitives from the law, and squatters who had been driven off the Indian lands across the river by the federal troops at Fort Towson.

The Red River is low in December, but the generally placid Texas rivers are deceptive. In a few hours they can become raging torrents, quickly drowning the very tops of the cottonwoods along their banks and spreading out for miles across the flood plains. Fort Towson was situated five miles back for good reason.

A few years after Houston's historic crossing, a great flood diverted the channel of the Red River a mile to the north. The cut in the old riverbank where boats were tied up is still discernible, but nothing remains of Jonesborough.

For the past weeks Houston had traveled "thro' the least inviting country, that I have ever seen." A more inviting country lay to the south, however, as he would soon find out. After a few days in the river town, where he stayed with friends from Tennessee and attended the Masonic lodge, he turned his horse toward the Mexican capital of East Texas, Nacogdoches.

His route lay through a land of astounding fertility. Lush green meadows and fields rolled away to the horizon. There were scattered farms and settlements, but for the most part the land was empty. He was in Indian country.

Sam Houston had nothing to fear from the Indians in East Texas. They were a branch of the eastern Cherokees, led by Chief Duwali, known to the whites as Chief Bowles, or The Bowl. Duwali and his band peacefully immigrated from the Cherokee Nation in 1810, finally settling near Nacogdoches about 1818.

Houston and the Cherokee chief might very well have met back in Tennessee. The Bowl was living on the Hiwassee River when Houston ran away to Ooleteka's island. The Bowl would certainly have heard of Kalanu, the adopted son of the principal chief, Ooleteka. He welcomed him as a friend and ally. Houston could be useful in The Bowl's negotiations with the Mexican authorities for lands for his tribe.

———

Nacogdoches, the second-largest town in Texas, had become the center of revolutionary agitation against the Mexican government. Throughout the year there had been confrontations with the military authorities at Anahuac and Velasco.

The high-handed commander at the port of Anahuac, Juan Davis Bradburn, a mercenary from Kentucky, had angered the colonists by enforcing the unreasonable customs regulations, impressing their slaves, and arbitrarily arresting the citizenry.

When the Mexican commander at Velasco attempted to halt the delivery of a cannon to the Texans at Anahuac, he was attacked and defeated by a Texan force on June 26. Here occurred the first deaths in the struggle with Mexico.

The garrisons at Velasco and Anahuac withdrew from Texas, but the Mexican commander at Nacogdoches, José de las Piedras, was more stubborn. He ordered all residents to surrender their arms. The Texans refused and in the Battle of Nacogdoches, August 2–3, they overwhelmed the Mexican force of four hundred men.

Outright independence from Mexico was not yet a goal, at least not by a majority of the citizenry. Antonio López de Santa Anna, the president of Mexico, was presenting himself as a liberal democrat and the Anglos in Texas were willing to believe him. They were content when the chastened Mexican soldiers swore allegiance to the liberal and democratic Mexican Constitution of 1824.

Houston settled in at one of the primitive inns in Nacogdoches and then called on the Mexican commandant, where he presented his credentials as an emissary from President Andrew Jackson. He also renewed his acquaintance with Adolphus Sterne.

Although Sterne was an ardent revolutionary—who did want total independence—he had not taken part in the August disturbances. He was still on parole for supplying guns and ammunition for an even earlier uprising, the 1826 Fredonian Rebellion.

The empresario Hayden Edwards's attempt to break away from Mexico and set up the state of Fredonia was quickly put down by Mexico—with considerable help from unsympathetic Anglo settlers. Edwards fled to Louisiana but Sterne was captured and sentenced to death. At the last minute, his sentence was commuted, and he was freed. But his every step was watched by the suspicious authorities.

After the Anahuac, Velasco, and Nacogdoches confrontations, a convention was called to meet at San Felipe de Austin to discuss the crisis. Delegates from sixteen of the Texas municipalities assembled during the first week in October.

This Convention of 1832 pledged itself to support Santa Anna and the central government in Mexico City, but it also petitioned the government to institute reforms. The Texans asked that Texas be separated from the larger Mexican state of Coahuila y Tejas. They wanted an autonomous state, which, of course, would be predominantly Anglo. They also asked for renewal of immigration from the United States, exemption of tariffs for three years, and land for primary schools.

William H. Wharton was appointed to present the petition to the political chief in San Antonio, Ramón Músquiz. The wily Músquiz knew that there was a secessionist movement in Texas, no matter how much the colonists protested their loyalty to Santa Anna and the Constitution of 1824. He declared the convention and its proceedings illegal.

The bugle was sounding again, and Houston was listening. Wharton and Sterne, among others, realized that Houston was someone who could lead the movement, and they began their efforts to convince him to settle permanently in Texas. There was to be another convention the following April, and Houston was asked to offer himself as a candidate in the election to choose the delegates.

For the present, however, Sam Houston had business to conduct for the president of the United States. He set out on the Camino Real, the Old San Antonio Road, across Texas to San Antonio de Bexar, three hundred miles away. El Camino Real, the King's Highway, was first laid out in 1691 to connect Mexico with the missions in the northeast. It was a well-traveled route of traders, soldiers, pilgrims, officials, and settlers, so Houston did not lack for company.

On Christmas Eve, Houston was in Stephen Austin's San Felipe de Austin, the de facto capital of Anglo Texas. Austin's colony had grown quickly as new immigrants flocked to join him. "We have weddings so fast and numerous that it will take up too much room to give a list," Austin wrote to David Burnet, "an old bachelor who hates *baby musick* has no business *here*, for he would be beset with squalling brats at every turn."

But there was more going on at San Felipe than marriages and burgeoning families. There was serious political talk, and it was so urgent that Houston now had little doubt that there was a future for him in Texas. He applied for a headright, or grant, in Austin's colony. The price for his league of land, 4,428.4 acres, was $375—about eight and a half cents per acre. Austin immediately approved Houston's application.

Governor Juan Martin Veramendi welcomed Houston to San Antonio. As an emissary of the president of the United States and a former governor of Tennessee, Houston would have had no trouble gaining an audience, but it was probably James Bowie who introduced him to Veramendi. Bowie was married to the governor's daughter, Ursula.

Andrew Jackson's plan to remove the Indians from the Southeast depended on the friendship of the western Indians. Inevitably some of the Indians who had already been relocated would move even farther west, where they would run up against the fierce Plains Indians.

In winter, the Comanches were accustomed to spending a good deal of time in San Antonio de Bexar. These sorties to the local capital in many ways resembled the delegations to Washington of their eastern brothers. The Comanches were more blatantly extortionist than the more civilized Easterners, however. They were also more dangerous. In addition to outright tribute from the Mexican authorities, they collected ransom for any unfortunates who had been captured by the tribe.

The Comanche chiefs, speaking through Mexican interpreters, agreed to travel to Fort Gibson for a peace conference but it could not be before April or May. They had to wait for the spring grass to rise. Winter kill and the burning off of the land reduced the forage, and their horses could not survive on grain.

Houston presented the Comanche chiefs a large silver medal engraved with President Jackson's portrait to take to their principal chief. He then headed back up the Camino Real, retracing his route to San Felipe and Nacogdoches. He planned to return to Fort Gibson by a water route. The arduous travel overland had opened his old wound, which soon became "worse than it has been for years."

Great floods throughout the Southwest made river travel impossible in early 1833. Sam halted at Natchitoches, Louisiana, on his way back to the Three Forks and the Wigwam Neosho, and on February 13 sent reports to the president at the White House and to Jackson's commissioner to the Indians, Henry L. Ellsworth, at Fort Gibson.

While the Comanches had agreed to be at Fort Gibson sometime between May 15 and 20, Houston planned to go back to Texas and make sure they were on their way. "For they are a dilatory people," he told Ellsworth.

Jackson no doubt was pleased to hear that Texas was "the finest country to its extent upon the Globe," but he was probably happier to be told that it was almost in a state of rebellion and that "nineteen twentieths of the population desire annexation by the United States."

The president was even more delighted by Houston's prediction that "Texas will by her members in convention by the 1st April, declare all that country as Texas proper, and form a State Constitution."

Jackson was not so pleased to have Houston's opinions of his representative to Mexico, Anthony Butler. He warned Jackson that Butler was not only disloyal to his country but probably in the service of England. Houston had known Butler in the East and disliked and distrusted him. His outrages in Mexico could only cause distress to the Anglo community in Texas.

Jackson hoped to acquire Texas peacefully, by purchase, and toward that end he had authorized Butler to offer $5 million to Mexico for the province. When the Mexicans would not even discuss it with him, Butler tried bribery.

Jackson, always steadfast as far as his friends were concerned, ignored Houston and stuck by Butler, even though he realized Butler was unreliable. Indeed, the president once endorsed a letter, "A. Butler. What a scamp." He kept Butler on in Mexico until he eventually was forced to recall him.

In his letter from Louisiana, Houston also confessed important personal plans, although he phrased the news to the Old Chief with lawyerly circumspection. "It is probable that I may make Texas my abiding place!" he said.

———

But Andrew Jackson had more serious concerns that winter of 1832–33 than Texas or Mexico. Calhoun and his cohorts were trying to wreck the Union. South Carolina had passed an Ordinance of Nullification in November. Federal tariffs were declared null and void and it would be illegal to collect duties in South Carolina after February 1, 1833.

Jackson struck back at once. His declaration that he would crush treason and rebellion was backed up with the threat of arms. He placed the United States military on alert. The nullifiers backed down, but Jackson knew his victory was temporary. He predicted that the next great issue and pretext for dismembering the Union would be slavery.

The colonists in Texas had stayed abreast of the crisis. Austin wrote that "a most gloomy cloud hangs over our native land—South Carolina has passed the rubicon—it is said that Virginia will join her, also N. Carolina & Georgia. If so the union is at an end, & it is not very improbable that it may split into three parts. God help them—they are all mad."

Events in the United States were bearing out what Austin had gloomily predicted to David Burnet. "The men of '76' are sinking into the grave," he said in 1829, "and I do seriously fear that the bonds of national union will decay and rot with them."

Houston was in complete agreement with Austin, and he sent unreserved support to his Old Chief. He saluted Jackson for his condemnation of nullification and the nullifiers, in particular Calhoun. "God grant that you may save the Union! It does seem to me that it is reserved for you; and you alone, to render millions so great a blessing."

On his way back to San Antonio to hurry along the Indians, Houston stopped off at Nacogdoches and found that he had won an election. He was to be a delegate to the meeting that was scheduled to convene at San Felipe on April 1—the Convention of 1833.

His reception at Bexar was less gratifying. The Mexicans had become suspicious of his mission to the Indians on behalf of the president of the United States. They understandably presumed that there was an ulterior motive. What, after all, was the United States doing trying to make a peace treaty with people who were subject to the laws of another nation? Was Jackson trying to incite the wild Indians against the Mexicans?

———

Stephen F. Austin was punctilious in his dealings with the Mexican authorities, and he was always absolutely open with them. However, in the winter of 1832–33 he found himself trapped between his Anglo compatriots and the government of Mexico.

Although Austin had come to feel that the Convention of 1832 had been a mistake, or at least misguided, he agreed that another was probably in order. First, however, he wanted to try to reason with the political chief. Austin believed that any movement for true reform must begin with the Mexican population. He thus began a tour of the settlements to gauge the depth of feeling. Inspired by Austin, the ayuntamiento, the governing council of San Antonio, produced the Bexar Remonstrance.

The Texans asked for complete separation of Texas from Coahuila y Tejas, increased representation in the national legislature, and repeal of the Law of April 6, 1830, restricting immigration from the United States. The Bexar Remonstrance also called for better schools, more protection from the Indians, and support for local industry.

The immigration law was particularly odious to the Anglo population.

Common criminals, with nothing to lose, entered Texas illegally, while North Americans with skills and investment capital were barred.

The political chief in Bexar forwarded the remonstrance to the governor. He knew that there was a deadline for redress of the grievances, April 1, and he informed his superior that the purpose of the remonstrance was to avoid a revolution.

The Bexar Remonstrance was endorsed by other ayuntamientos, but, unknown to Austin, plans were going full speed for a convention. "Bowie raised a mob and the people would have a convention," he said. Austin felt that he had betrayed the Mexicans. He had, after all, persuaded them to take a reasonable approach and he felt that the Texans should now wait for a response from Mexico City.

Although he had agreed, in principle, to the calling of a convention, "I did not think it would have been done in my absence," he said. "I went there to consult with the authorities of that place. I considered that very great respect and deference was justly due to them as native Mexicans, as the capital of Texas, and as the oldest and most populous town in the country, and I knew the importance of getting them to take the lead in all the politics of Texas."

If there was to be a convention Austin wanted it to be in Bexar, "but at that time it was death to any man's popularity to speak in favor of the Mexicans." He wrote to Burnet, who was living on his plantation near Lynchburg, that he must be a delegate to the convention. "*You* must be elected from the Liberty Municipality—you *must be* in—we need ballast for our wild boys."

Austin was a man clearly committed to a peaceful solution when there really was not any. "My object & wish is now, what it always was," he said, "to keep the country quiet, & protect the interests of the honest & hard working part of the community—they are the real bone and sinew of Texas—our jump up *big folks* are all smoke, but they serve as an ignis fatuus to lead others astray—we must never loose sight of our duty, or *moral obligation* to mexico & to Coahuila."

His friendship for the Mexicans and opposition to violence was used by his opponents—whom he called the real enemies of Texas—"to set the flame of discord and confusion ablazing." Austin had naively "thought it best to deprive them of the kindling matter by a passive course. I mistook the means, and committed a great error, but I have learned this lesson in politics, that there is no medium with envy and party spirit between victory and defeat." Austin's sad summation of the order of events is a lesson in realpolitik.

His honorable intentions were even misread by his Mexican friends and by many of those whom he worked so hard to protect. As he rufully admitted later, "I was a mere *passive actor* when I ought to have been a firm and unbending *director*."

Houston had allowed his name to be put forth as a candidate to the convention well in advance of any reply to the Bexar Remonstrance. But now he had observed firsthand how opinion was running. He was in Bexar not many days after the ayuntamiento had drafted the remonstrance and in Nacogdoches when it was endorsed.

Some efforts were made to have the convention held in Bexar, but the political chief refused. The colonists should first ask the government's permission to hold the convention, he said. They would thus demonstrate that they were acting in good faith. The political chief was stalling for time.

The colonists went ahead without government approval and chose San Felipe as the site. The delegates labored from April 1 to April 13—many of them, like Austin, still believing that they were working toward recognition of Texas as a separate state but one within the Republic of Mexico.

There were others, however, who believed no such thing. This latest convention was only one step toward total independence and then annexation by the United States. Those bold steps lay in the future, however. The delegates, for now at least, had to recognize the power of the Mexican government, no matter how fragmented and corrupt it was.

Houston was no longer just a delegate to the convention. The constitution was written by a committee chaired by him, and his stamp is all over it—in no section more so than in the article forbidding the establishment of a bank. Andrew Jackson would have been proud of his man. Sam was exultant that he was able to sign the constitution "just one day short of the anniversary of my flogging Stanbery!"

The second task of the convention was to draft an appeal to the Mexican government asking that the constitution be approved by the Mexican congress, that the state government be reorganized, and that Texas be recognized as a state independent of Coahuila. David G. Burnet was the author. Santa Anna was clearly the man of the hour in

Mexico. He had presented himself as a liberal, so the convention addressed its appeal directly to him.

Most of the players who would be instrumental in bringing independence to Texas had now assembled. But other than the fact that everyone wanted a leading role no one really knew what their parts were. It was an extraordinary grouping of individuals, although Houston did not think much of his colleagues.

"All new States are infested, more or less, by a class of noisy, second-rate men who are always in favor of rash and extreme measures," he said. "But Texas was absolutely overrun by such men."

Austin was chosen to carry the appeal and the new constitution to Mexico City. He left San Felipe on April 22. He would not return to Texas for over two years, much wiser, more militant, and a confirmed *independentista*.

————

Sam Houston had reentered public life, but attending conventions, however noble, and writing constitutions, however eloquent, were no means of support nor were they a career. As soon as the convention adjourned, he returned to Nacogdoches, and before the month was out he had again taken up what he did best, the practice of law.

He set up his practice in a log building just off the muddy town plaza. He was an immediate success. In one two-week period, he wrote to his cousin John, he had been retained by clients who guaranteed him $2,000 per year and was paid fees totaling $750.

Houston had as many clients as he could handle. After all he was the most famous man in Texas. Indeed, he was almost bound to be the most famous man wherever he went. If nothing else, a great scandal ensures such attention.

While the law was good for day-to-day sustenance, land speculation was the route by which Houston hoped to become rich. In a very short time his holdings comprised 140,000 acres that he bought "with two other Gentlemen, (who furnish the capital)" and 10,000 acres that he paid for himself. In a usual burst of enthusiasm he wrote to his cousin John, "Jack! Texas is the finest portion of the Globe that has ever blessed my vision!"

In May, Houston again traveled north to present his report to the Indian commissioners at Fort Gibson. He arrived there at the end of the month. The commissioners were absent, but Sam was able to settle up his affairs at the Wigwam Neosho, whatever there was left to straighten out.

Tiana Rogers had long since realized that Sam was lost to her. Indeed she was probably surprised that he had come back at all. In any event, the man who returned to Arkansas this May was much changed from the derelict who had arrived there in 1829.

Houston was back in public life. He had returned to his profession. And he owned or controlled vast amounts of land. The buckskin leggings, colorful hunting shirts, and old straw hat had been replaced by a sombrero, a silver belt buckle and spurs, and a Mexican sarape.

He did not stay long at Fort Gibson. The old wound in his right shoulder had opened up again, and fragments of bone were working their way out. Perhaps the soothing mineral waters of Hot Springs would restore him.

In the highly colored, romantic version of their final parting, Houston supposedly asked Tiana to return with him to Texas but she refused, choosing to remain with her own people. Houston probably did no such thing. His ambition had been rekindled, and he realized that there was no place for Tiana Rogers in his new life. He wanted no repeat of the Eliza Allen, Peggy O'Neill, or Rachel Robards scandals. He would marry again, certainly, but it would have to be a perfect marriage.

Before he left the Wigwam Neosho for Hot Springs and its soothing waters, he did, however, make sure that his favorite dog had a good home. And he ordered a new stock to be made for his hunting rifle.

Sam stayed at Hot Springs until July, and the long rest and the waters restored him. Even sores not connected with war were healed. As he wrote to his cousin John, "The *tetter* on my head seems cured entirely!"

Houston never shrank from discussing his aches, pains, fevers, chills, agues, wounds, or any other discomfort. For such a robust man, who had a magnificent physique and was known to get off his horse and swim rivers if he had to, he suffered from an amazing variety of ills.

There is no question that his wounds were terrible and a constant worry and that like most people of his time he had some life-threatening moments with disease. But there also are sure signs that he suffered from serious hypochondria.

Houston's health was much affected by another factor as well. He had never given up liquor. In spite of his new life and reentry into civilized society, Sam had continued to drink heavily. He was still a splendid specimen of manhood, as one observer at the Convention of 1833 remarked, but he was dissipated and looked years older than he was. From time to time friends attempted to reason with him, but their good advice was ignored.

————

As Sam had said, the Texas Indians were a "dilatory people." In fact, they never did go to Fort Gibson to take part in the negotiations supervised by Governor Montfort Stokes of North Carolina. Stokes, the father-in-law of William Lewis and a staunch supporter of Jackson, had been appointed by the president to attempt to reconcile the differences between the native tribes in the West and the immigrating Indians from the East.

The seventy-year-old governor now underwent a change in career as radical as Houston's had been. He resigned from the governorship in the fall of 1832 and abandoned his wife, who was eighteen years younger, and his eleven children, the youngest of whom was only five. By February 1833 he was in the Arkansas Territory.

The Stokes Commission was not successful. Intermittent warfare between the various tribes continued for years. After the commission expired, Stokes stayed in the Indian Territory, working on behalf of the various tribes. He had become besotted by the Indians, and he never returned to the East. He died in 1842, at the age of eighty, and was buried with full military honors at Fort Gibson.

————

Houston was in and out of Texas and Louisiana the remainder of 1833. He had settled at Nacogdoches, but he was often at Natchitoches, San Felipe, and the Ayish Bayou District (San Augustine). The political situation was relatively quiet. The colonists were still awaiting word from Austin in Mexico City. Santa Anna was now in control of Mexico, but he too was reasonably quiescent. Another, more deadly enemy threatened, however. Cholera, which had so devastated New York the previous summer, had steadly advanced down the East Coast. Many of the Texas settlements suffered enormous numbers of deaths from the disease. Stephen Austin, who almost died of cholera himself, estimated that between eighteen thousand and twenty thousand died in six weeks in Mexico City. Smaller towns, such as Monclava, especially suffered. In just eighteen days six hundred people died, including Jim Bowie's wife, his children, and his father-in-law.

Many of Houston's friends and associates died during the epidemic, but he escaped. His behavior, however, was characteristic of a fevered mind. He simultaneously filed for divorce and joined the Catholic church. It is hard to imagine two things more diametrically opposed.

The divorce petition, which Llerena Friend perceptively called a "strange medley of ideas," was filed on November 30 in the Ayish Bayou District. And strange it certainly was. Houston was not at all content, as he said, "to rest his application mainly on the length of time that has elapsed since the separation, all conclusively showing the impossibility of reunion."

Sam Houston also felt it was his duty to share his views on marriage, law, and the Catholic religion. He was appalled that most civilized countries followed canon law. Its "mysterious reverence for the nuptial tie" had been a "never ending source of domestic strife in all countries that have followed its precepts," he said. He then let loose with an indictment of the church's "fopperies and conceits" and the "nauseious and repulsive practice of taking confessions." Perhaps he had his Cherokee marriage in mind when he said of church-sanctioned traditional marriage, "and thus the sanctuary of Hymen had been polluted by the carnival of rant and jargon."

The divorce petition was pure Houston. Who else would incorporate an attack on the church and an ode to the brave settlers and the glorious future of Texas into a petition for a divorce? Texas must look to the genius of her people and not rely on the "antiquated, unpopular and preposterous doctrines of trans-Atlantic judges," he said.

There is a good chance that the real provenance of the divorce petition was a bottle of Tennessee whiskey or Mexican tequila. In any event, nothing came of it at this time. Perhaps the Anglo alcalde of the district, William McFarland, felt it was too inflammatory.

Certainly no member of the clergy saw the petition, for soon afterward Houston was baptized a Catholic. A profession of the Catholic faith was required of all landholders, and Houston had put it off long enough.

Adolphus and Eva Stern acted as his godfather and godmother. Eva Sterne was a good Catholic and Adolphus Sterne had, as the law required, converted years before from Judaism. The baptismal service was held in the living room of the Sterne house, where Houston had become a permanent paying guest.

Sam was now both a Roman Catholic and, nominally at least, a citizen of the Republic of Mexico. Henceforth he was Don Samuel Pablo Houston. His Presbyterian forebears who had held off the forces of his Catholic majesty James II at Londonderry must have turned in their graves. It was a business arrangement and nothing more, however—a baptism of convenience. Don Samuel Pablo never set foot in a Catholic church, and rarely in any other church for that matter. Only three years before, a missionary to the Cherokees had said, "He is vicious to a fearful extent, and hostile to Christians and Christianity."

Meanwhile Austin had pressed on in Mexico City, even though he often felt frustrated. In fact he had become so discouraged by the end of September that he had despaired of success. On October 2, 1833, he wrote to the ayuntamiento of San Antonio that it should take the lead in organizing a government for Texas separate from Coahuila. It had become clear to him that the Mexican congress was not going to grant separate statehood. Therefore everything should be in readiness for the people to act on their own.

He enjoined the ayuntamiento of San Antonio not to "lose a moment in urging all the ayuntamientos of Texas to unite in organizing a local government independent of Coahuila even though the general government refuses its consent."

The letter was not typical of Stephen Austin, who was neither rash nor impulsive. But he was human. The negotiations were not going well and the news from Texas was devastating. At San Felipe his close friend and associate John Austin and his wife and two children had died of cholera. The Austins were not related, but they had become closer than his own family to the shy bachelor empresario.

Civil War in Mexico had also threatened Austin's mission, but Santa Anna had put down the rebellion and he was now undisputed dictator.

There were still reasonable men in the Mexican government who recognized the necessity of granting the requests Austin carried, and his quiet diplomacy began to meet with success. The Law of April 6, 1830, was amended to allow immigration, and the Mexican congress promised real reform in the judiciary and in the organization of the territorial government.

Statehood was another matter. Austin stood his ground in his meetings with Santa Anna, but he recognized that separation from Coahuila was a dead issue. And, after all, he had achieved much. He wrote home to say that more had been done for Texas in ten days than in the previous ten years. Besides, Santa Anna had assured him that when a new Mexican constitution was drafted, he would use his influence to give Texans a special organization suitable to their education, habits, and situation.

With a great sense of relief Stephen Austin left Mexico City on December 10. He had been away almost eight months and he would be another month or more on the journey home to San Felipe.

Unfortunately Austin's inflammatory and seditious October 2 letter to the ayuntamiento of San Antonio had found its way back to Mexico. A courier was dispatched from the capital with special orders to the commandant at Saltillo, where Austin planned to stop over. On January 3, 1834, Austin was arrested and taken back to Mexico City.

The news, while it certainly upset the colonists, did not impel them to revolt. Austin, fearing the consequences of any uprising, urged caution. "I hope there will be no excitement about my arrest," he said. And, truth to tell, there was none.

Austin had his enemies and his detractors, many of whom felt that he stood in the way of independence. Some of them were actually accused of conspiring to keep him in jail in Mexico. Houston was thought to be inimical to Austin, and he did speak deprecatingly of him on occasion, calling him "the little Gentleman" and saying he had "the disposition of the viper without its fangs."

But Houston did not want Austin kept locked away in a Mexican prison. The two great Texans were much closer in their philosophy and politics than is commonly thought. Of course, in almost every other thing they were poles apart.

The Galveston Bay and Texas Land Company, smelling blood and back in business as a result of the repeal of the anti-immigration law, reentered Houston's life in March 1834. The company again dangled in front of Houston the possibility of his being its Texas representative. Once again he set out for New York.

Houston's murky connection with Galveston Bay has never been satisfactorially explained or completely documented. He maintained an off-again, but mostly on-again, relationship with the company until it went out of business in 1848.

Galveston Bay represented various Texas empresarios in the United States and sold scrip that entitled the holders to land in Texas. Much of the scrip was redeemed and the settlers happily settled. However, a great deal of the scrip was traded illegally and the purchasers were defrauded.

The Indian rations scandal should have taught Houston a lesson about trying to reconcile public life and private gain, but he intervened on behalf of the company no matter what his position.

In New York he met with James Prentiss at the City Hotel. Houston asked for $2,000 in advance and a payment of $1,000 every six months until he had received a total of $5,000. He then got so drunk at the hotel bar that he left the city without first picking up an important survey map that he had entrusted to the barman for safekeeping.

Back in Washington, Houston thought better of his offer, especially when it became increasingly clear that Prentiss and the company were not going to meet it. He came up with a more modest request.

"As money is scarce, and I have some small demands that I should like to meet," he wrote to Prentiss, "I have concluded for you to make any arrangement, not under $2,000 *part* down, and the balance to be paid in twelve months." He would take the remainder in lands. Sam then asked somewhat sheepishly if Prentiss would retrieve the map from Willard the bartender at the City Hotel.

Houston also made some predictions to Prentiss about the future of Texas. Within one year, he said, Texas would be a sovereign state. Within three years it would be separated completely and forever from Mexico.

Houston's fee was still too high for the directors of the company, and they hired someone else. There was therefore no money forthcoming for Houston's "small demands," one of which was the unpaid fine imposed for caning William Stanbery on Pennsylvania Avenue in 1832.

Houston, however, hit on a surefire way of discharging that obligation. In late April 1834, he sent a note to Andrew Jackson at the White House. "He prays that the *fine and costs of suit* may be remitted by *your* PARDON," he said in his appeal to Old Hickory. Jackson did not fail his old friend. He picked up his pen and wrote across the letter, "Fine remitted." The Stanbery affair was finally laid to rest.

Houston looked forward to returning to Nacogdoches. In addition to his law practice, there was a more personal reason for wanting to go home. Her name was Anna Raguet.

Sam had met Anna's father, Henry Raguet, the previous year in New Orleans. Raguet's life had also been one of boom and bust. The Raguets were a prominent Pennsylvania family, and Henry had become a successful businessman in Ohio and a director of the Bank of the United States.

A series of business reversals culminated in a humiliating bankruptcy, and he had gone to New Orleans in pursuit of new ventures. Houston's descriptions of Texas had convinced Henry Raguet to go have a look. Like Houston, he was quickly persuaded after a brief visit that his future too lay in Texas. He moved his family from Cincinnati to Nacogdoches, where he opened a mercantile business.

Raguet's background, education, and breeding set him apart, and he quickly became a leader in the growing Anglo community. His warm friendship with Houston lasted until Houston's death, and he encouraged Houston's attentions to his charming daughter in spite of their great age difference. Anna was eighteen. Houston was forty.

Anna Raguet was pretty and flirtatious, but she was more New England Yankee than southern belle. She was well educated, spoke several languages, and had more than a passing interest in politics.

Nacogdoches was a world away from Cincinnati, where Anna Raguet grew up, or Philadelphia, where she went to school. According to the census of 1833, there were 319 single men in a town of 1,272. The figures do not tell us much of their eligibility, which cannot have been too great. There were also, strangely enough, 291 single women, but Miss Anna gave them little credit.

The social heap of Nacogdoches was not very high, but the Raguets were at the very top. Anna perforce had to devote herself to the handsome and attentive Governor Houston, but to be on the safe side she left some time for a good-looking, twenty-seven-year-old physician turned land speculator named Robert Irion.

For the next seven years, Sam Houston paid court to Anna Raguet, but as a medieval knight to an unattainable lady. He sent her flowery letters—so restrained that they seem exercises in politeness—poems of his own composition, and pressed flowers. She wrote him letters that were alternately coy, intelligent, and flirtatious and she made for him a woven silk sash for his sword.

Houston concentrated on his law practice in Nacogdoches and in the municipality of San Augustine, which had been created from the Ayish Bayou District as part of the reforms promised by the central government. All the while he was also wheeling and dealing in Texas land with his law partner and fellow speculator Philip Sublett, who lived just outside San Augustine on the Camino Real. Houston, Sublett, and a third partner, John R. Dunn, accumulated large tracts of land, particularly in present-day Liberty and Jefferson counties, where the partnership had almost thirty thousand acres, acquired from Manuel de los Santos Coy.

––––––––

In the fall of 1834, Houston traveled once more to New York to confer with Prentiss and then to Washington to see the president. King Andrew was now firmly in control not only of the Democratic party but of just about everything else. Jackson had crushed the Nullifiers and his veto of the bill to recharter the Bank of the United States had been sustained in the Congress.

A particularly sweet victory, however, was more personal than political, and it came on the home turf of the despised Adams. Almost over the Brahmin former president's dead body, Harvard University awarded his proletarian successor an honorary doctor of laws.

Adams declined to attend the ceremony since he could not witness his alma mater's "disgrace in conferring her highest literary honors upon a barbarian who could not write a sentence of grammar and hardly spell his own name."

Criticism from Adams was almost a badge of honor. After all, he had said of Jefferson that "insincerity and duplicity were his besetting sins throughout life" and that he was "a rare mixture of infidel philosophy and epicurean morals."

Not only Adams was unhappy with the Old Chief, however, and

Jackson paid a high price for his high-handed, albeit high-minded policies—the rise of the Whig Party. Disaffected Democrats, the Nullifiers
and other states' rightists, advocates for the Bank of the United States,
all came together to oppose Jackson.

Nowhere was the split as great as in Jackson's home state. Tennesseans were particularly angered by Jackson's choice of Van Buren over
Hugh L. White of Tennessee as his successor. John Bell became a
leading Whig and defeated fellow Tennessean and Jackson loyalist James
K. Polk for the speakership of the House of Representatives in 1834.

Houston could only observe the controversy and perhaps wonder at
what might have been. He had once been a part of the grand Jacksonian
scheme that was now unraveling. No matter. Sam's destiny lay elsewhere.

———

While on this 1834 trip, Houston ran into Junius Brutus Booth on
Pennsylvania Avenue. The great Shakespearean from England and the
actor manqué from Texas repaired to Brown's Indian Queen Hotel,
where after many toasts and responses a competition began. Booth
would recite the great classical speeches and Houston would echo them.

Carried away by Booth's forceful rendering of a tale of Pizarro and the
Conquest, Houston leapt to his feet. "Yes! Yes!" he cried. "I am made
to revel in the Halls of the Montezumas!"

This anecdote has been used for years as evidence of Houston's
complicity in a plot to annex not only Texas but all of Mexico, and
another tale from the same period added to the legend that Houston was
at the center of a web of conspiracies. G. W. Featherstonhaugh, a young
English traveler, encountered Houston at the village of Washington, in
the Arkansas Territory, near the Texas border. In his *Excursion Through
the Slave States,* he recalled the scene.

> I was not desirous of remaining long at this place. General Hous-
> ton was here, leading a mysterious sort of life, shut up in a small
> tavern, seeing nobody by day and sitting up all night. The world
> gave him credit for passing these, his waking hours, in the study of
> *trente et quarante* and *sept à lever;* but I had seen too much passing
> before my eyes, to be ignorant that this little place was the rendez-

vous where a much deeper game than faro or *rouge et noir* was playing. There were many persons at this time in the village from the States lying adjacent to the Mississippi, under the pretence of purchasing government lands, but whose real object was to encourage the settlers in Texas to throw off their allegiance to the Mexican government.

This lurid picture is certainly an arresting one, filled as it is with those stock images of the Old West—whiskey-soaked frontiersmen and all-night card games played in rooms illuminated by firelight. There is also the delicious taste of desperate men conspiring for empire.

Whiskey and card games were always available in every tavern worthy of the name, and Houston's daytime absences and early evening appearances sound about right. He had not given up his old habits, which involved drinking all night and sleeping all day.

Sam Houston was not conspiring in anything except the collusion necessary to add to his holdings and make some money. He had by then determined on a careful but always circumspect path for Texas—statehood within the Mexican federation, total independence, and then annexation by the United States.

He was sure that each of these stages would come in its own good time. Irresistible revolutionary forces had been set in motion, but they must be allowed to proceed at their own obviously quickening pace. Care must be taken to guard against rash acts by impetuous men.

Stephen Austin agreed and from his various Mexican prisons he urged the citizenry to remain calm. To do otherwise "will do me harm, and great harm to Texas," he said. "Keep quiet and let me perish if such is to be my fate."

Self-denial understandably gave way to self-pity when Austin began to suspect that nothing was being done by his friends and neighbors to effect his release. He was wrong, of course, but martyrdom has it limits, particularly if no one seems to be paying attention.

Texans were particularly hard-pressed in 1834. Money was so scarce that even the well-to-do had no ready cash. Large landholders might not see more than five dollars in hard money in a year's time. Austin's friends and supporters, no matter how willing, were unable to raise money for bail, or for bribes, or even for ransom to free him from his Mexican prison.

The Aztec capital Tenochtitlan was already two hundred years old and had a population of well over 200,000 when Hernán Cortés arrived in November 1519. In less than two years the emperor Montezuma was dead and the city in ruins. On these sad foundations the Spanish conquerors built Mexico City.

In the 1830s, La Capital was the largest and most cosmopolitan city in the western hemisphere. It was a city of churches, parks, an opera house, and theaters. The upper classes lived lives of splendid indolence in their palaces. There were no slaves, but the Indians and peasants were bound to their white masters as tightly and as cruelly as any field hand in the American South. For these eternal poor, the revolution had only increased the uncertainty of life.

Few of the aristocracy had any concerns about the faraway province of Tejas. Indeed, it is unlikely that many of them could have located it on a map. Who cared about this northern province where there were more than four times as many Indians as native Mexicans and where the thirty-five thousand immigrants included more than five thousand slaves.

However, the more enlightened leaders of the government had some inkling of the importance of the rebellious province, but they had no information on which to formulate policy. An American-educated Mexican officer, Colonel Juan Nepomuceno Almonte, was sent north to have a look around.

He began at Nacogdoches in May and traveled about the province until the middle of July. Austin's plight did not much affect his journey across Texas. The charming Almonte was received everywhere with great civility and hospitality.

Almonte was a prescient and astute observer. New colonists were pouring into the province by the thousands and it was clear that their primary allegiance was to the United States, not Mexico. Only the most dim-witted could fail to discern what eventually would happen.

Almonte's *Statistical Report* was a revelation. Texas was a prosperous and fertile country that was clearly of vital economic, political, and strategic importance to Mexico. Santa Anna forthwith determined to hold on to it. But was this possible?

While countercolonization by Mexican nationals was still the most desirable avenue, it had been impossible to persuade people in sufficient numbers to move north. Mexico would have to send in troops if it hoped to hold on to Texas. Force was therefore a necessary option. This did not trouble Santa Anna, for whom force was often the first option.

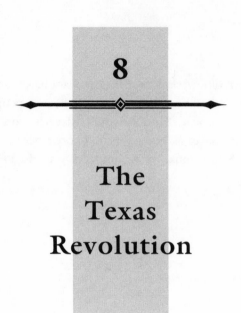

8

The
Texas
Revolution

M ANY EVENTS have been put forward as marking the beginning of the Texas Revolution. The independence of Mexico from Spain in 1821. The Constitution of 1824. The Fredonian Rebellion. The Anahuac disturbances. The battles of Nacogdoches, Velasco, or Gonzales. Each has its partisans, particularly among those who like their history packaged and neat, a string of beads rather than a ribbon.

Certainly everything that happened began with the arrival of the first of the Old Three Hundred in Stephen Austin's colony. Sworn to observe the laws of a land for which they had contempt and the tenets of a religion that they despised, many of these first Texans immediately began to look forward to the day when they would be joined to their native land and Protestantism.

———

Stephen Austin languished in the prisons of Mexico from January until Christmas of 1834, when he was set free on bail. He was allowed to move around Mexico City, but he could not leave the country. Austin had been away since April 1833, and while he was by no means a forgotten man, new leaders had come to the fore. Largely from the southern states, they were convinced of Anglo-Saxon supremacy. They were also more bellicose and not at all open to compromise with their Mexican masters.

As for Houston, he was content in early 1835 to continue to practice law and to add to his land holdings. In addition to the nearly thirty thousand acres on the Trinity River, he had acquired a third of a league of land, about fifteen hundred acres, in David G. Burnet's colony. "Samuel Pablo Houston es un hombre de muy buena moralidad," said his sponsor, Juan M. Dor. Burnet was, of course, only titularly involved in the colony, for he had sold his land contract to the Galveston Bay and Texas Land Company five years before.

At about this time also, another New York investor entered the picture. James Auchincloss wrote that he had begun speculating in Texas lands with that shadowy New York company. Houston and Auchincloss developed a high regard for each other and remained friends for years.

Houston also continued the platonic relationship with Anna Raguet, but there was no serious move toward marriage. Besides, he was still a married man and the scandal had not died. One night during dinner at the house of an old friend, Hugh Johnston, his host began to press Houston about his marriage to Eliza Allen. Each time Houston changed the subject, Johnston returned to it. Finally Sam leaned forward and in a hushed and conspiratorial tone asked Johnston, "Can you keep a secret?"

"Of course I can," Johnston replied.

"So can I," said Sam.

Houston did not always respond to indiscreet inquiries with such grace. One evening during a driving Texas rainstorm he arrived exhausted at Sublett's plantation. He was so tired that he bedded down on the floor in front of the fire. In spite of his fatigue, he was in a more than usually voluble mood so his friend thought this might be a good time to find out what had really happened in Tennessee in April 1829. At the first mention of his failed marriage and Eliza Allen, Houston stormed from the house, called for his horse, and rode off into the rainy night toward San Augustine.

Houston kept a sharp eye on the political situation—he was congenitally incapable of not becoming involved in politics—but he had adopted a wait-and-see approach to the problems with Mexico. He knew first-hand that Andrew Jackson was doing everything in his power to acquire

Texas. At least Jackson thought he was doing everything in his power.

Unfortunately, affairs in Mexico were still entrusted to Anthony But-ler, whose modus operandi was limited to intrigue and bribery. Few American ministers have created such problems with a sovereign state at such a sensitive time.

Butler had unconcealed contempt for Mexico and he considered that all of its citizens were open to bribery if only the right amount of money could be applied. Jackson himself was never a party to Butler's wild schemes, but neither did he stop them.

As had happened so many times before, the president was the last to realize what a liability a trusted subordinate had become. Soon, however, he could no longer ignore the indiscretions of the "scamp," especially when Butler began to send dispatches from Mexico City in uncoded or barely encoded letters. There could be serious diplomatic consequences.

Butler was removed, but the unrepentant scoundrel threatened to remain in Mexico and represent private interests, most notably the Galveston Bay and Texas Land Company. On behalf of the company, Butler offered Mexico $10 million for all of Texas—double the offer he had made on behalf of the United States! And thinking that a revolution in Texas might prompt the Mexican government to want to get rid of the place, he wrote the O.P.Q Letters, exhorting the Texans to rise up over Austin's imprisonment. The letters were as foolish as the man, and the colonists ignored them. The days of the Robber Barons were still in the future, but clearly America was getting ready.

Butler had seriously exacerbated the problems between Mexico and the United States, and his actions translated directly into repressive measures against the Anglos in Texas. Santa Anna had no intention of selling the province to his northern neighbor and he began to tighten the screws.

In January 1835, the Mexican authorities, in an effort to halt the smuggling on the eastern border, reopened the customshouse at Ana-huac. In June, the commander, Antonio Tenorio, arrested Andrew Briscoe and DeWitt Clinton Harris for trading in goods on which no duty had been paid.

In a nice twist, Briscoe and Harris were rescued by William B. Travis, who had precipitated the first of the Anahuac disturbances when he was confined in the same fort in 1832. On June 30, 1835, the outmanned and outgunned Mexican garrison marched out of Anahuac toward Bexar.

Travis and the war hawks were condemned for their rash action by those citizens who purportedly still wanted peace with the central government. However, opinion soon shifted in their favor when Travis and his companions became the issue. Mexico demanded their arrest and extradition.

A chief target of the Mexican government was the defector Lorenzo de Zavala. After various high government posts and an ambassadorship to France, the great liberal gave up all hope of Santa Anna ever implementing the promised reforms and left Mexico. He was settled permanently in Texas by the middle of 1835.

The peace party and the war party differed precisely as much as their names suggest, although their ultimate goal was the same. The one wanted immediate and complete independence while the other called for a separate state of Texas within the Mexican confederation with actual independence somewhere in the near future. The war party called for a consultation to be held at Washington on the Brazos on October 15.

But what of Stephen Austin? Word had come that he had finally been freed in July and he was on his way home. On September 1, 1835, he landed at Velasco, where he was received as both a hero and a potential savior. Everyone seemed to realize that perhaps only he could head off a war that seemed all too certain.

Austin's new demeanor surprised his enemies and delighted his friends. The perfidy of his captors and the hopeless political instability in Mexico had stiffened his spine. At the welcoming dinner on September 8 in Brazoria, he endorsed the planned October consultation. He apprised the crowd of his discussions with Santa Anna, in which he had maintained his loyalty to Mexico but had warned the dictator that he could expect a war if he sent troops into Texas.

If anyone still doubted that Santa Anna planned to establish military rule in Texas they were soon set right. Within days, the dictator's brother-in-law, General Martín Perfecto Cós, landed five hundred men at Copano, on the Gulf of Mexico. The Mexican commander then began the march overland to Bexar to set up his headquarters from which to put down the rebellious colonists.

On September 19, Austin issued a call for each municipality to send delegates to the consultation and also to form a militia and hold regular musters. "WAR is our only resource," said the former dove. "There is no other remedy."

Stephen Austin had matured politically to that fine point where you say one thing to gain support and then do another. He was calling for war while maintaining that Texans should remain good Mexican citizens within the framework of the liberal Constitution of 1824. He knew perfectly well that these two goals were irreconcilable.

"No more doubts—no submission," he wrote to David Burnet on October 5, 1835. "*I hope to see Texas forever free from Mexican domination of any kind.* It is yet too soon to say this publicly, but that is the point we shall end at—and it is the one I am aiming at. But we must arrive at it by steps and not all at one jump."

Three days before, just up the Guadalupe River from the little village of Gonzales, the "first shots" of the revolution had been fired. Mexican troops under Francisco Castañeda had attempted to retrieve a small brass cannon given to the citizens of Gonzales for protection against the Indians.

From the west bank of the river the Texans, among whom was James W. Fannin, taunted the Mexican troops on the opposite shore. They raised a white banner with the famous legend *Come and Take It* over their little cannon. After a few rounds were exchanged and one death occurred, the Mexicans withdrew to San Antonio.

Houston, who had been made commander of the troops of the Nacogdoches Department, issued a stirring proclamation on October 8.

> The morning of glory is dawning upon us. The work of liberty has begun. . . . Let your valor proclaim to the world that liberty is your birthright. We cannot be conquered by all the arts of anarchy and despotism combined. In heaven and in valorous hearts we repose our confidence.
>
> Union and courage can achieve every thing, while reason combined with intelligence, can regulate all things necessary to human happiness.

On October 10, the mission and fort at Goliad fell to a Texan force under George Collinsworth and Ben Milam. They had raced across the country to intercept General Cós, but he had slipped away and was safely at San Antonio de Bexar.

Within a few days hundreds of unruly volunteers had responded to the call to battle and had descended on Gonzales, which was now the military center of Texas. Bowie and Fannin were both there, but no one could agree on a commander. Order was restored only after Austin agreed to take over.

Stephen Austin had come full circle—empresario, diplomat, peacemaker, political prisoner, and now commander in chief. On October 13, General Austin led his army out of Gonzales north toward San Antonio and the Mexican army, seventy miles away. That night a great comet blazed across the heavens above the little army.

———

General Austin. He was much too sensible and good humored not to have been aware of the irony. He was the most unlikely of choices. He had no military experience, but at that moment he was the only man who could unite the warring parties.

The most likely choice, militarily, was back in Nacogdoches. Sam Houston still hoped that the United States would settle the whole matter with outright purchase and annexation. Besides, Texas had no real army, only a ragtag rabble, and the seasoned Mexican troops were a deadly adversary. But Houston was also a realist and he wrote to a friend that "*War in defence of our rights, our oaths, and our constitutions is inevitable, in Texas!*" And, he continued, "Our war-cry is 'Liberty or death.' "

The site of the consultation was changed from Washington on the Brazos to San Felipe de Austin because of the new printing press that had been installed there. Stephen Austin's town now boasted a newspaper, the *Telegraph and Texas Register,* which began publication on October 10.

The editor, Gail Borden, Jr., said that the newspaper was originally to be called the *Telegraph and Texas Planter* and its "engrossing object was the accumulation of wealth and consequent aggrandizement of the country." However, "affairs have assumed an entirely different aspect, and the all-absorbing question is how to protect ourselves and what we already possess." Its mission had changed from celebrating Texans and their accomplishments to calling them to arms.

After fits and starts and utter confusion, the consultation finally got

down to business on November 3. Austin did not attend—he remained
with the army—but he was very much a presence.

The consultation took great care that its actions not antagonize and
scare off the friendly Mexican Federalists and unite them with the
Centralists of Santa Anna against Texas. An invasion by a united Mexico
could put an end to the independence movement. The Declaration of
November 7, 1835, was therefore purposely ambiguous. It stressed the
restoration of the Constitution of 1824 and the fact that Texas was the
victim of a despot.

Actually the war was already under way. It had been a month since
Austin had announced that "our fellow citizens at Gonzales *have been
attacked—the war has commenced!*" And while the consultation was in
session, word arrived that Mission Concepción, outside Bexar, had fallen
to Austin and his Texans on October 28. More than fifty Mexican
soldiers had been killed in this first large engagement of the war.

While it was clear that Texas was by now firmly on the road to
independence from Mexico, that final step was deferred by the consultation. Instead, a provisional government was set up under a device called
the Organic Law. The law was imperfect but it did provide the basis for
effective government if men of good will so desired.

The legislative branch of this provisional government was the General
Council, made up of one member from each of the municipalities.
Executive power was in the hands of a governor. In an attempt to pacify
the war party, the colorful Henry Smith, a firebrand who was in favor
of immediate independence, was given the job.

The delegates at Washington on the Brazos were well aware that their
plans could succeed only with the political and financial support of the
citizens of the United States. To that end the consultation appointed
Stephen Austin, Branch T. Archer, and William H. Wharton as commissioners to drum up American support for the struggle and, of course,
to solicit volunteers to come fight for Texas.

Austin, ever conscious of his duty, but no doubt relieved also to give
up the command of the army, returned to San Felipe on November 29.
Soon after, he and the other commissioners left for the United States.

Another action taken by the consultation had more fateful consequences. On November 12, 1835, Sam Houston was made commander
in chief of the Texan forces and ordered to raise a regular army. The

irregulars and volunteers at San Antonio were not placed under his command, however. The government thus created problems for the new commander at the outset.

Austin was now out of Texas entirely and Houston was ordered to set up his headquarters fifty miles away in Washington on the Brazos. The General Council was free to run the revolution without the interference of the two most charismatic figures in Texas.

Houston's service in the regular United States Army and his generalship of the Tennessee State Militia were a direct contradiction to his enemies' charge that he had not enough experience to take over the command. His comments in 1821, when he had sought the major generalship of the Tennessee Militia, were still relevant.

> If I have claims to the office of *Major General*, I trust my countrymen will duly consider them. I have been long and intimately acquainted with the duties of a soldier and an officer; I have risen from the rank of a private in the regular army; I have experienced a soldier's feelings; I have learned to respect them; I have done my duty, and I will be always proud to do it, in return for the confidence of my countrymen.

On November 13, the day before adjournment, the consultation approved a "solemn declaration" that the Cherokee Indians of East Texas had legitimate land claims against Mexico and that an independent Texas would honor those claims. Houston was determined to look after his friends.

Houston began immediately to build his army. There had been three engagements thus far—Gonzales, Goliad, and Concepción—and the Texans had been victorious in all three. But Houston knew there had been no real test. Besides, luck, not skill, had carried the day. Undisciplined volunteers were no match for trained professional soldiers.

Andrew Jackson had been faced with the same challenge in the backwoods of Alabama in 1814. Houston had been there. The job now at hand was even more daunting, but it could be done.

On November 13, Houston offered James W. Fannin the post of inspector general of the army. The thirty-two-year-old Fannin had attended West Point for two years, he clearly had some military administrative ability, which Houston desperately needed, and he had already seen action at Gonzales and Concepción. His patriotism was unquestioned and he was a rabid revolutionary.

Fannin's private life was not so idealistic or elevated, however. He had come to Texas from his native Georgia the year before and settled at Velasco, where he became involved in the slave trade. On just one voyage from Cuba he had transported 153 of those sad creatures to Texas.

In a confidential letter to Fannin, Houston revealed his practical strategy for prosecuting a defensive war. Artillery was expected from New Orleans but it could not possibly arrive until March. And there were no tents, provisions, arms, and ammunition to keep a large force in the field. Until supplies and artillery arrived, Houston planned to retain only enough troops to man the defenses at Goliad and Gonzales. The others were to be furloughed.

Houston was concerned about the western frontier, but he believed that there would be no invasion from there. For the present the strategy should be defensive until the Texan force was strong enough to take San Antonio de Bexar.

First, Texas must prepare. Houston's philosophy, he told Fannin, was that it is better to do well even though it might take some time, than never to do well at all.

Fannin wanted action immediately and he declined the offer to be inspector general. The events of the next three weeks did give some support to those who felt that Texas should not wait but strike.

Edward Burleson succeeded Austin in command at San Antonio and he began the withdrawal to Goliad as ordered by Houston. But Ben Milam, in the rapidly evolving tradition of military insubordination that characterized the Texas Revolution, disobeyed Burleson.

Milam had no trouble in rounding up a contingent of volunteers. "Who'll go into Bexar with old Ben Milam," he asked, and three hundred men responded. Miraculously the Texans prevailed, and on December 10 San Antonio was in Texas hands, well in advance of Houston's planned March offensive. And the Texans now had artillery—ten cannon altogether, including four twelve-pounders.

It was another victory, but the Mexicans had been defeated by their own poor generalship, not by the superior arms and strategies of the

Texans. Milam, the hero of the battle, was shot dead by a Mexican sharpshooter as he stood in the open plaza in front of the Veramendi house in broad daylight.

Houston's strategy was still the correct one, but few people recog- — nized that this was so. The majority were now convinced not only that right makes might but that Texans were invincible. Indeed, this "mob nicknamed an army," in Henry Smith's dismissive phrase, was a group of undisciplined volunteers who relentlessly pursued their own agenda, which ranged from patriotism to plunder.

While the volunteers were undisciplined, they were colorful and romantic. Two of the groups, the Mobile Greys and the New Orleans Greys, did indeed wear nondescript grey denim outfits. The members were mostly young men of various backgrounds and places, and even various nationalities. They were also completely inexperienced in warfare. The Texas Revolution was a great, exciting, chivalric outing.

One of the founders of the Mobile Greys was James Butler Bonham, an old friend of Travis's from South Carolina. Like Travis, he had settled in Alabama, where he was practicing law in 1835. The similarities to Travis and most everyone else end there. Bonham was unblemished unless one is predisposed to find selflessness suspect. He had no overriding ambition, he was not a land speculator, nor did he trade in slaves. And he was blessed with noticeable good looks.

Bonham was at San Felipe by at least December 1, when he wrote to "S. Houston Generalissimo of the Texas forces." "Permit me," he said, "through you to volunteer my services in the present struggle of Texas without conditions. I shall receive nothing, either in the form of service pay, or lands, or rations."

Here was the ideal soldier. Intelligent, deferential, dedicated, and he had served with honor in the South Carolina Militia. Houston was impressed and immediately took him into the Texas Army. Little more than a month later, on January 11, 1836, he recommended Bonham's promotion from major to colonel. "His influence in the army is great— more so than some who 'would be Generals,' " said Houston.

The commander in chief was generalissimo in title only. Houston had but very little overall authority. Petty jealousies and rivalries undermined him, but of more importance was the ignorance of many in the government as to just how an army must be organized. Those who "would be

Generals" did not hesitate to break off from their commanders and start up their own little armies, often with the approval of the General Council.

There was a very small pool of military talent in Texas, which much delayed the first order of business, the appointment of officers to command the ranks. It was a hard principal for the provisional government to grasp—that armies are built from the top down. While the revolution was about democracy, there could be no such thing in a properly run army.

And as if that were not enough, the experienced and talented did not readily flock to Houston's banner. In no instance is this better illustrated than the refusal of his old friend and colleague Philip Sublett to join the command. "I would be proud to hold the situation were it not for my private business which would be neglected were I compelled to attend to military matters, without leisure to attend to my farm," wrote Sublett.

Houston had a similar letter from Robert C. Morris, the commander of one troop of New Orleans Greys. He too declined a commission. His men would have nothing to do with the regular army, "the name of which is a perfect Bugbear to them," he said. Morris and his 225 men had no interest in chains of command, discipline, or training. They had come to Texas to fight and now they wanted to carry the war into Mexico. Otherwise they would return to the United States. Morris also felt compelled to tax Houston for tarrying at headquarters instead of being with the troops, where he belonged.

The difficulties of building a military organization were not the only reasons for delay in putting an army into the field. When Houston announced on December 28, 1835, "Say to our friends that, by the rise of grass, we will be on the March," it was not just a neat turn of phrase. No army could move across the land without grazing for the horses. In fact, he begged the volunteers from the United States "to bring NO HORSES, unless for teams, or for packing."

Houston attempted to set up recruiting stations, supply depots, and training camps for a regular army. He asked friends in the United States to send him manuals of military procedures and rules, books of illustrations of military uniforms, and even copies of the forms used by the United States Army. And, in one of his sartorial fits, he ordered a proper commander in chief's uniform from a New Orleans tailor.

He also asked that his personal effects in Nacogdoches be packed up and sent to him at army headquarters. Included in the three trunks were four dress coats, a frock coat, pantaloons, a red shawl, and other fancy dress items. More important to Houston, however, were his fifteen-volume history of England and editions of Livy, Tacitus, Milton, Pindar, Robert Burns, and Thucydides. Other titles included a Bible, a work on family medicine, a classical dictionary, a history of Texas, a book of army regulations, and the *Renunciation of Popery*. The trunks of clothes and books became a permanent part of the campaign.

The other volunteer commanders agreed with Morris. There was not just little sense in elaborate preparations. It made no sense to them at all. They did not believe in a defensive war. They had come to fight Mexicans, and, by God, that is what they would do—which meant that they would have to go across the Rio Grande. After the fall of San Antonio and the withdrawal of Cós's army, there were no more Mexican troops in Texas.

They could, of course, prepare and train and wait for an invading force. And it would not be a long wait. Mexican forces were already on the march. After the defeat of Cós, Santa Anna had reorganized his forces for the invasion, and he had over six thousand men and a dozen pieces of artillery. El Presidente joined up with his troops at Leona Vicario on January 26, 1836.

Santa Anna drove his troops mercilessly over a route that ranged from dry and dusty plains to freezing mountain passes blocked by deep winter snow. The intimidated officers and staff offered no opposition to his strategy or his tactics.

Meanwhile in Texas, discussions went on and on about carrying the war into Mexico. Both Governor Henry Smith and Houston were initially in favor of sending troops across the Rio Grande. If such a campaign served no other purpose, it would help to keep the army together to fight off the expected invasion.

Their enthusiasm for an expedition against the Mexican town of Matamoros quickly waned and the commander in chief and the governor became openly hostile to the idea when they realized that its purpose was for spoils and to protect land claims in other states of Mexico. Others, most notably Morris, Francis W. Johnson, Dr. James Grant, and Fannin, pressed on with the plan.

Houston had already heard from Dr. Grant. The truculent and belli-cose physician turned land speculator had demanded to know why

Houston did not hurry to the troops and take command. Was he going to wait until everyone had wearied of the inaction and decamped for the United States? Grant still had interests in Coahuila and was anxious to carry the war south and revolutionize all of Mexico.

Other letters were more encouraging and sympathetic, particularly those from the United States, where the Texas Revolution was being fervently taken up by liberals, patriots, and, of course, zealots.

William P. Duval of Bardstown, Kentucky, wrote Houston that while he was poor he so believed in the Texan cause that he was sending two of his three sons to fight for it. "May God prosper your efforts in justice and Liberty," he said. Burr H. Duval was killed at Goliad. His brother, John Crittenden Duval, escaped the massacre and later became known as Texas John, the first Texas man of letters.

Hugh McLeod, an officer in the U.S. Army across the border at Fort Jesup, Louisiana, wrote that he was resigning his commission to join the Texas Army. But "I do not come to your country as 'a summer soldier or a sunshine patriot,'" he said.

Houston's control over military affairs was little better than marginal. Overlapping commands, egos, and rivalries were sapping the revolution of its strength, and the chairman of the military committee of the provisional government "interposed every possible obstacle to the organization of the army." Indeed the chairman had made remarks of a personal nature about Houston that were "so indecorous that they were stricken out of the report" of the General Council.

In early January, Houston's despair was almost as great as that of the day he resigned as governor of Tennessee. "No language can express my anguish of soul," he wrote to Henry Smith. "Oh, save our poor country!"

On January 8, Houston left Washington on the Brazos for Goliad. When he arrived at the fort a week later he found the troops there deprived of the most basic necessities. Dr. Grant had commandeered the horses and supplies for the expedition against Matamoros.

The treacherous physician, whose filibustering had the approval of influential members of the General Council, had even begun calling himself acting commander in chief. He and his men were ready to leave for the rendezvous of the Texan forces at Refugio when Houston arrived.

On January 15, Houston delivered a stirring address to the troops.

Total and complete independence from Mexico was the only viable choice for Texas, he said, and to that end there was to be a convention in March.

His racist attack on all those Texans of Mexican descent, the Tejanos, who had not joined in the revolution helped rally the troops, but even allowing for the prejudices of the times, it detracts from Houston's Jacksonian image.

The news from Bexar was unsettling. Colonel James Clinton Neill, the commander at San Antonio, wrote that he expected an attack from Mexico at any time and begged for help. Neill had only about eighty men to defend the abandoned mission that had been turned into a fortress, the Alamo. On January 17, Houston wrote to Governor Smith from Goliad.

> Colonel Bowie will leave here in a few hours for Bexar with a detachment of from thirty to fifty men. . . . I have ordered the fortifications in the town of Bexar to be demolished, and, if you should think well of it, I will remove all the cannon and other munitions of war to Gonzales and Copano, blow up the Alamo and abandon the place, as it will be impossible to keep up the Station with volunteers, the sooner I can be authorized the better it will be for the country.

Houston then set out for Refugio with Grant's little army. Throughout the journey the commander in chief of the nonexistent regular army rode back and forth along the line talking to the volunteers in an effort to convince them of the folly of the expedition. They listened carefully to the general.

On Thursday evening, January 20, F. W. Johnson arrived from San Felipe and was shown into Houston's quarters at Refugio. He brought stunning and sickening news. The General Council in San Felipe had deposed Governor Smith and placed Fannin in overall charge of the Matamoros Expedition, giving him powers as great as those of the despot in Mexico. The council was completely under the thrall of the adventurers.

Houston and his aide, George Washington Hockley, left immediately for Washington on the Brazos. He had little choice. His command had been taken from him.

The long journey back across Texas gave him much time to reflect with the trusted Hockley on the proper course of action. Under the Organic Law, the commander in chief was subject only to the governor. The old argument over separation of powers between the executive and the legislative had boiled up. Houston, the Jacksonian, had no ambivalence about the need for a strong executive and he blasted away at the usurpers at San Felipe.

Henry Smith, of course, agreed, and did not go gently into the good night of political oblivion. He refused to resign, to vacate his office, or to turn over any government documents to his successor or to the General Council. Further he threatened to send the whole General Council to Bexar to be tried by court-martial. As a result of the standoff, Texas was essentially without a government.

Just as Governor Smith refused to submit to the provisional government, so did Commander in Chief Houston "regard all their acts as void." As he said, "I am not prepared to violate either my duty or my oath, by yielding obedience to an act manifestly unlawful, as it is, in my opinion, prejudicial to the welfare of Texas." Henceforth Houston applied this simple test whenever he was confronted with a great problem. Was a particular course of action "prejudicial to the welfare of Texas"?

Houston was particularly dismayed by the actions of the ambitious Fannin, who was not a volunteer but a colonel in the regular army and subject to the orders of his commander in chief. By accepting the appointment to head the army, Fannin had betrayed not only his oath but his country.

And as for the Matamoros Expedition, Houston sneeringly remarked that "a city containing twelve thousand souls will not be taken by a handful of men who have marched twenty-two days without bread-stuffs, or necessary supplies for an army."

James Bowie and James Bonham arrived in San Antonio de Bexar on January 18. After conferring with Commander Neill, Bowie decided that the Alamo was crucial to the defense of Texas and he determined to hold it at all costs.

The cannon and other weapons in the fortress were important, and

since they could not be moved to Goliad and Copano as ordered—
Grant had taken the horses and wagons from the Alamo as well—
perhaps Bowie felt that he was justified in protecting these vital
armaments. Otherwise his decision was without any military merit.

Bowie's defenders have maintained that he was given wide latitude
and discretionary authority by his commander in chief. Houston, of
course, denied this all his life. He felt betrayed by the man he had
described as someone who always carried out orders "with his usual
promptitude and manliness." The only important fortification, and the
only really defensible one, was at Goliad.

Colonel Neill never had to answer for his insubordination, at least not
with his life. He left the Alamo on February 11 for a twenty-day leave.
With Neill's departure a real Texas row erupted over who was in command. William Barrett Travis had arrived and he insisted that he outranked Bowie.

The two antagonists split the command between them—Travis over
the regulars and Bowie over the volunteers—but bad blood continued
until Bowie was stricken with typhoid and Travis assumed sole command.

After reporting to Smith, whom he still considered in charge of the
government, Houston went on to Nacogdoches. In late December,
Governor Smith had charged him with negotiating a treaty of friendship
with the Indian tribes on the frontier and Houston now prepared to
carry out the commission.

The large band of Cherokees under Chief Bowl occupied the area near
the isolated and completely unprotected white settlements in East Texas.
There were some fifteen thousand Indians in all of Texas, and it did not
take a great deal of imagination to figure out what would happen if these
tribes allied themselves with Mexico and opened a two-front war. The
thought of thousands of Indian warriors attacking from the west and
large Mexican armies attacking from the south was enough to scare even
the toughest of frontiersmen.

Months earlier Houston had become alarmed about Indian immigration into Texas, and he wrote to Jackson on September 11, 1835,
pleading with him to prevent five thousand Creek Indians from buying

land and moving into Texas. He wanted them sent to the territory reserved for them on the Arkansas. Texans already had enough trouble with the Indians, and there was no Jackson in Texas to control them as he had done when he was "controlling the chivalry of Tennessee and Georgia." This action was no doubt necessary given the situation, but it was a blatant betrayal of his old friends the "children of the forest."

Houston also recruited the friendly Indians to help protect the frontier from the marauding wild Indians. He offered the Cherokees and some of the other tribes cash payments and half of all the property they seized.

The Indian treaty took two weeks of negotiations, but it was signed in Chief Bowl's village on February 23, 1836. The Cherokees and twelve associated tribes signed the agreement, which reaffirmed lasting peace and friendship between the Indians and the provisional government and guaranteed to the Indians a huge tract of land as a permanent home for the thirteen tribes.

Houston was much praised for what he had done, and it was a diplomatic triumph. He had eliminated a formidable threat. He was an old Indian agent, however, and he knew that conditions at the seat of government are very much different from those at the conference table or the wigwam—no matter how much power is vested in a negotiator by his government. Agreements are never binding until ratified.

The successful conclusion to the negotiations with the Indians was about the only bright spot for Houston in February. In a field of seventeen candidates competing for the four seats from Nacogdoches for the March constitutional convention, he finished next to last.

All was not lost, however. Houston's name had also been entered in the election for delegates from Refugio, and the army vote ensured that he would attend the convention at Washington on the Brazos.

———

The Republic of Texas was born in a village that was little more than a collection of rough log buildings scattered on a bluff about half a mile back from the Brazos River. Colonel William Fairfax Gray, a lawyer–land agent from Virginia, called it a "disgusting place."

Representative Houston arrived at Washington on the Brazos on Monday, February 29, and his appearance, Gray noted in his diary, "created more sensation than any other man." The colonel also remarked that Houston was "much broken in appearance, but has still a fine person and courtly manners."

The convention opened the next day. For the first session, forty-four delegates crowded into the freezing Convention Hall, an unfinished structure with animal skins nailed over the windows to keep out the drafts.

Although ever mindful of their duty—the declaration of Texas independence—the delegates were much distracted by the news from Bexar. Three days earlier, on a Saturday, a horseman had galloped into San Felipe with a dispatch from Travis addressed "To the People of Texas & all Americans in the world."

> Commandancy of the Alamo
> Bejar, F'by 24th 1836
>
> Fellow citizens and compatriots—
>
> I am besieged, by a thousand or more of the Mexicans under Santa Anna—I have sustained a continual Bombardment & cannonade for 24 hours & have not lost a man—The enemy has demanded a surrender at discretion, otherwise, the garrison are to be put to the sword, if the fort is taken—I have answered the demand with a cannon shot, & our flag still waves proudly from the walls—*I shall never surrender or retreat*. Then, I call on you in the name of Liberty, of patriotism & everything dear to the American character, to come to our aid, with all dispatch—The enemy is receiving reinforcements daily & will no doubt increase to three or four thousand in four or five days. If this call is neglected, I am determined to sustain myself as long as possible & die like a soldier who never forgets what is due to his own honor & that of his country—
> **VICTORY OR DEATH.**
>
> William Barret Travis
> Lt. Col. Comdt.

Houston reflected with both anger and sadness on his order of January 17. If he had been obeyed, as he should have been, Travis and his men would not be holed up in an indefensible fort and faced with almost certain annihilation. He would do what he could, but the signs were ominous. The affairs of the convention must therefore be settled with great dispatch, as indeed they were.

The very next day, a recent arrival in Texas, George C. Childress of Nashville, produced the Declaration of Independence, written in his own hand. The document was adopted almost unchanged by the convention. Just a few weeks earlier Childress had harangued a pro-Texas meeting in Tennessee—calling on the young men of the United States to go and free their Anglo cousins from the Mexicans, "a cowardly, treacherous, semi-civilized people, without enterprise, workmanship, or discipline."

There is no record of Childress's reaction on meeting Lorenzo de Zavala at the convention or if he had any second thoughts about his rascist diatribe after he met the great Mexican-born Texas patriot.

This somewhat unstable nephew of Sterling C. Robertson—he killed himself in 1841—not only wanted Texan independence but believed that all of Mexico should be conquered. The United States should end by placing the "eagles of freedom even on the glittering domes of Mexico," he said. Childress apparently was not troubled about how a people without enterprise, workmanship, or discipline had managed to build the largest city in the Western Hemisphere, complete with glittering domes.

The vote on the declaration supposedly was delayed one day to honor Sam Houston. He was riding high at the convention, and he might very well have been extended the courtesy of having the adoption of the Texas Declaration of Independence delayed until March 2, 1836, his forty-third birthday.

The convention now had to face the military crisis that had been caused by the weak government set up by the consultation of 1835. They had no choice but once again to call on Houston to take command of the armed forces. He issued a stirring "Proclamation Concerning the Enemy's Occupation of Bexar." Texas "must and shall be defended," he said. "The patriots of Texas are *appealed to in behalf of their bleeding country.*"

Houston then set forth the terms under which he would accept a second commission as commander in chief. He left nothing to chance or the whims of politicians. Every vaquero knew that if you were kicked once it was the horse's fault. If the horse kicked you a second time it was your own fault.

At 9 o'clock in the morning on March 4 the convention was called to order. Houston's demands were met. It was agreed unanimously that there would be "one superior head or commander in chief" and it was to be Sam Houston. Further, there would be "due degrees of subordination defined, established and strictly observed." The command was to comprise all the land forces, including regular army, volunteers, and militia. And Houston was to be "endowed with all the rights, privileges and powers due to a Commander in Chief in the United States of America."

Houston moved quickly to take command. On the afternoon of March 11, he arrived in Gonzales to a tumultuous reception from the troops. No army needed a charismatic leader more than the frightened band gathered in the camp on the Guadalupe, where two Mexicans had just arrived from Bexar. After listening to their story, Houston sent an urgent dispatch to James Fannin at Goliad.

Head Quarters
Gonzales 11 March 1836

Col. J W Fannin
Commanding at Goliad

Sir

Upon my arrival here this afternoon, the following intelligence was received through a Mexican supposed to be friendly, which however has been contradicted in some parts by another who arrived with him—it is therefore only given to you as rumor, though I fear a melancholy portion of it will be found true.—Anselmo Borgara states that he left the Alamo on Sunday 6th inst. and is three days from Arroches Rancho.—That the Alamo was attacked on Sunday morning at the dawn of day, by about 2300 men—and carried a short time before sunrise, with the loss of 521 Mexicans killed and as many wounded. Colonel Travis had but 150 effective men out of his whole force of 187.—After the fort was carried, *seven* Men surrendered, and called for Genl St Anna and for quarter.—They were *murdered by his order*. Col. Bowie was sick in bed and also murdered.—The enemy expect reinforcements of 1500 men under General Condelle, and 1500 reserve to follow them.—he also informs that Ugartechea had arrived with two millions of dollars for the pay of the troops.—The bodies of the Americans were burned after the massacre, an alternate layer of wood and bodies were laid and set on fire. Lieut. Dickinson who had a wife and child in the fort after having fought with desperate courage tied his child to his back and leaped from the top of a two story building—both were killed by the fall. I have little doubt but that the Alamo has fallen—whether above *particulars* are all true may be questionable. You are therefore referred to the enclosed order.

I am, sir, &c., Sam Houston

The wife of Lt. Dickinson is now in the possession of one of the officers of S Anna. The men as you will perceive fought gallantly— In corroboration of the truth of the *fall* of the Alamo, I have ascertained that Col Travis intended firing signal guns at three different periods each day until succor should arrive—No signal guns have been heard since Sunday and a scouting party have just returned who approached within 12 miles of it & remained there for 48 hours.

The "enclosed order" from the commander in chief to Colonel Fannin contained clear and explicit instructions as to what course of action Houston expected Fannin to take.

You will, as soon as practicable after the receipt of this order, fall back upon Guadalupe Victoria, with your command, and such artillery as can be brought with expedition. The remainder will be sunk in the river. You will take the necessary measures for the defence of Victoria, and forward one third the number of your effective men to this point, and remain in command until further orders.

Every facility is to be afforded to women and children who may be desirous of leaving that place. Previous to abandoning Goliad, you will take the necessary measures to blow up the fortress; and do so before leaving its vicinity. The immediate advance of the enemy may be confidently expected, as well as a rise of water. Prompt movements are therefore highly important.

———

With the exception of the fatal leap of Lieutenant Almaron Dickinson with his child strapped to his back, the account of the Mexicans was accurate. Two days later, on Sunday, March 13, Dickinson's widow, Suzannah, arrived in Gonzales with the child, a little girl named Angelina. Suzannah Dickinson was accompanied by Travis's slave, Joe, and Colonel Juan Almonte's manservant, Ben.

Ben carried a message from Santa Anna calling on all Tejanos to return to the Mexican fold. The real message from the Mexican president, however, was in the person of the widow and child. The Texans could expect nothing but death if they persisted with their revolution. Terror was not a new weapon by any means, but these Anglo-Saxons had never heard of warfare like this.

The arrival of the widow and her child on that early Sunday evening silenced all doubts of the fall of the Alamo and the advance of the Mexican Army, which could not be more than two days away. Panic swept through the town, where there were thirty new widows.

Every inhabitant, soldier, and civilian alike, hastily gathered up a few belongings and a little food and fled toward the east. Gonzales was completely deserted by midnight.

The great retreat across Texas had begun. The rush to escape was frenzied, but the disorderly rout that became known as the Runaway Scrape—that headlong dash for safety back toward the eastern settlements—took a few days to materialize.

As the hundreds of Texans straggled across the prairie on that cold March night, the western sky behind them began to glow a brilliant orange and red. Then came the sound of the explosions. This was no fire to warm refugees from Mexican terror. The flames were from their abandoned houses and barns. Houston had ordered Gonzales put to the torch.

9

Retreat
to Glory

T RAVIS AND BOWIE's disobedience of Houston's direct orders to abandon and then blow up the Alamo not only cost them their lives. Another 187 brave men were lost with them. But the gallant band's defense against the superior Mexican force that besieged them for thirteen days has become America's greatest example of military bravado. It was rash and foolish, yes, but it was grandly heroic.

Bonham, Crockett, Travis, Bowie, and their comrades have been eulogized and celebrated and their actions have been debated endlessly since that Sunday morning when they were cut down by Santa Anna's troops and their bodies stacked like so much cordwood and burned in San Antonio.

Houston throughout his life was always careful to praise the courage of the defenders at the Alamo, but he had no respect for them militarily. Travis and his men had let themselves become "forted up." Sam had learned this lesson well at Horseshoe Bend, where the Creeks had committed the same folly and met the same fate.

"Our forces must not be shut up in forts, where they can neither be supplied with men nor provisions," he said. "Long aware of this fact, I directed, on the 16th of January last, that the artillery should be

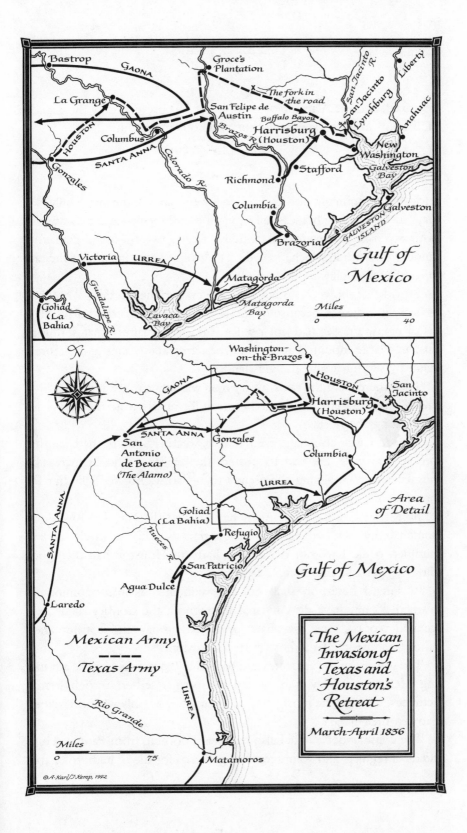

Bastrop
GAONA
Groce's
Plantation
La Grange
San Felipe de
Austin
HOUSTON
Columbus
Harrisburg
(Houston)
SANTA ANNA
Buffalo Bayou
Brazos R.
New
Washington
Gonzales
Colorado R.
Stafford
Galveston
Bay
Richmond
Columbia
Galveston
Brazoria
GALVESTON
ISLAND
Gulf of
Mexico
Victoria
URREA
Goliad
(La
Bahia)
Guadalupe R.
Lavaca
Bay
Matagorda
Matagorda
Bay
Miles
0   40
San Felipe de Austin
The fork in
the road
San Jacinto R.
San Jacinto R.
Lynchburg
Anahuac
Liberty

Washington-
on-the-Brazos
N
GAONA
HOUSTON
San
Jacinto
Harrisburg
(Houston)
SANTA ANNA
Gonzales
San
Antonio
de Bexar
(The Alamo)
Columbia
URREA
Area
of Detail
SANTA ANNA
Goliad
(La Bahia)
Refugio
Nueces R.
San Patricio
Gulf of Mexico
Agua Dulce
Laredo
Mexican Army
Texas Army
Rio Grande
URREA
Miles
0   75
Matamoros

The Mexican
Invasion of
Texas and
Houston's
Retreat

March–April 1836

©A·Karl/J·Kemp, 1992

removed, and the Alamo blown up; but it was prevented by the expedition upon Matamoras, the author of all our misfortunes."

————

Houston's command now comprised fewer than 375 men with only two days' rations, a few horses—all very poor specimens—and two wagons with two yoke of oxen to pull them. He faced a two-thousand-man army under Santa Anna, which, according to his spies, was moving at the rate of twenty-five miles a day.

Providence, however, was with the Texans. The Mexican Army had to slow its advance because of the lack of grazing for the horses. The usual prairie grasses had not risen in sufficient quantity that spring to sustain a large mounted army. And the retreating Texans gave nature a hand by setting fire to the grasslands.

Then there were the rains. Every road was a quagmire and every little creek a torrent. The flood waters spread for miles across the low plains lying along the rivers.

Houston was also hampered by the weather, but he had another problem as well. He had to protect the civilians, who in increasing numbers were attaching themselves to his army, not to fight but for protection.

By March 15, the Texas Army had reached the Navidad River, and some twenty men had deserted. These traitors, while relatively small in number, could have not done more harm to Houston had they gone directly over to Santa Anna's army.

"I intend desertion shall not be frequent," Houston ominously warned. "They have disseminated throughout the frontier such exaggerated reports, that they have produced dismay and consternation among the people to a most distressing extent."

The rumors of the atrocities and barbarities committed by the advancing Mexicans quickly transformed prosperous settlers into hysterical refugees, who for the most part had brought away only what they could carry in their hands.

The commander in chief also had heard nothing from Fannin. Hundreds of regulars and volunteers had gathered for the Matamoros Expedition, but they would be no match for the thousands of Mexican troops who were rumored to be advancing into Texas from the south.

———

Colonel James W. Fannin had landed his force at Copano on February 4 and marched the twenty-five miles inland to the rendezvous at Refugio in preparation for a march on Matamoros, which lay two hundred miles further South. His disillusionment was immediate. It was not only the lack of supplies and the pitifully too few men that doomed the expedition, however. A large Mexican army under General José Urrea was already at Matamoros and preparing to move north.

Fannin retired to the presidio at Goliad, twenty-five miles northwest of Refugio, and began to repair the rundown fortress. In a moving letter to the provisional government, begun at ten o'clock in the evening on February 7 and finished up at seven o'clock the next morning, he berated his fellow Texans for their "indifference" and "criminal apathy" toward the defense of their country.

Fannin now sat in his fort at Goliad, still dreaming of military glory. He had asked that he be allowed to serve only in "the posts of danger and honor," and he had been accommodated. But this presidio was not a castle in a Sir Walter Scott novel to be defended against knights of like-minded chivalry. It had in fact become a prison.

James Fannin's fortunes had declined steadily since January when he had issued the stirring call to carry the war into Mexico. "Attention, Volunteers! To the west, face: March!" The Matamoros Expedition had been a fiasco.

Others would take up Fannin's indictment, what the government itself called the "unpardonable and almost criminal indifference of the people of Texas." And it was true. The actual fighting and dying in the Texas Revolution was done by a very small group—fewer than two thousand people, out of a population of thirty-five thousand. The great pride of their descendants in these heroic early Texans is justified.

But the dissolution of Fannin's romantic dream was by no means complete, nowhere near so. His boast to the government that he had forwarded orders to Bexar "to place that post in a state of defence, which if attended to will make it safe" escaped being mocked only because of the great tragedy.

But Fannin had not reached his Golgotha yet. Urrea's army left Matamoros on February 18 and by February 27 they were at San Patricio, only about sixty miles from Goliad. There they met Francis W. Johnson's volunteers. Johnson barely escaped with his life when his small troop was overwhelmed.

James Grant and Richard Morris met a worse fate at Agua Dulce on March 2. Morris was killed in the fight and Grant was captured. When the Mexicans discovered that Grant was a doctor he was promised a passport and his freedom if he would attend to the wounded Mexican troops.

Dr. Grant obliged his captors, but the promised "passport" turned out to be a wild mustang. Grant's feet were tied to its hind legs and his hands tied to its tail. The horse was then set free to kick him to death.

Houston was no doubt upset by the Mexicans' brutality and Grant's grisly murder, but he cannot have shed too many tears over the death of this man who had caused so many of his troubles.

The Texan Army was now at Burnam's Ferry on the Colorado. Houston had confidence in himself and his men and he felt that the army had grown sufficiently in strength to make a stand. But the threat of being surrounded by Mexican troops and cut off forced him to change his mind and to continue the retreat. On March 17, he crossed the river and turned south. By March 19, the army had set up camp at Beason's, on the east bank. His army had grown to about six hundred men, but he continued to plead with the government and his fellow Texans to come and join them, using the massacre at the Alamo as a rallying cry. "Let the men of Texas avenge their deaths!" he said.

Houston was up against a ruthless but able opponent. Santa Anna may not have been the Napoleon of the West, as he styled himself, but he was a canny military leader. He had marched a large army a thousand miles over impossible terrain and had achieved a stunning succession of victories. The Texan forces were divided, and his campaign of terror had achieved its purpose. The panicked civilians were disrupting the army even further.

But Santa Anna could be stopped. Houston estimated that just 1,500 men could do the job, and as Santa Anna moved deeper into Texas it would become increasingly easier. However, every man who could be rounded up was needed, and he again appealed to Fannin to abandon Goliad and moved his men and munitions to the coast. They could thus protect the lines of supply from the east and be ready to join up with the main army when needed.

Fannin meanwhile had sent an expedition under Amon King to rescue several families in the area around Refugio. King could not be content with his rescue, however. Instead of returning to the relative safety of Goliad, he insisted on first punishing some local Tejanos who had taken the side of the invaders. When he returned to Refugio, he found the mission surrounded by Urrea's troops.

When King and his men were forced to take refuge in the Refugio mission, Fannin sent Col. William Ward and his Georgia Battalion to their aid. In the ensuing confusion, King attempted to escape but was captured. Ward and his men, under cover of darkness, managed to escape from the mission, but they left their wounded behind. King and the other Texas survivors, thirty-four altogether, were executed in the plaza at Refugio on March 16.

Few had believed the Mexican declaration of December 30, 1835. "All foreigners who may land in any port of the republic or who enter it armed and for the purpose of attacking our territory shall be treated and punished as pirates, since they are not subjects of any nation at war with the republic nor do they militate under any recognized flag."

If there were still any doubts as to Santa Anna's policy, they were quickly being dispelled. All Texans bearing arms were to be treated as rebels and executed.

The disaster at Refugio spurred Fannin's efforts to withdraw from Goliad toward Victoria as Houston had ordered. But he had delayed too long. Urrea's army overtook the retreating Texans on the open prairie near Coleto Creek, about ten miles from Goliad.

The Texans were more than a match for their pursuers, and they held them off gallantly until nightfall. Fannin was wounded, but he could easily have escaped with the bulk of his army in the darkness. He would not abandon his wounded, however.

The next day, March 20, Mexican reinforcements arrived with artillery. The Texans were unable to withstand the bombardment in their exposed position, and Fannin surrendered unconditionally to General Urrea. There was an unstated, but nevertheless implicit, understanding that Urrea would intercede on the Texans' behalf with Santa Anna and they would be treated as prisoners of war. Fannin and the Texans were then marched back into the presidio at Goliad.

The Mexicans now had over 300 prisoners at Goliad, including William Ward and his Georgia Battalion, who had been captured after their escape from Refugio, the New Orleans Grays, the Red Rovers, the Mobile Grays, and various other volunteer groups. In addition, they had captured nine field pieces, a thousand rifles, and large amounts of ammunition.

———

Houston was still at Beason's Ferry when he received word on March 23 of Fannin's retreat and the fight at Coleto Creek. The final outcome was unknown, but the commander in chief had long since lost confidence in unruly and independent subordinates. He rightly assumed the worst. "If what I have heard from Fannin be true," he said, "I deplore it, and can only attribute the ill luck to his attempting to retreat in daylight in the face of a superior force. He is an ill-fated man."

A few days before, Houston had sent a stinging rebuke to Fannin. "You have received my orders sir repeatedly and have not obeyed them," said Houston angrily, "my last directed you & your command to join the main army—a sufficient time elapsed for you to do so—the Special order was not obeyed—Your general conduct meets with my decided disapprobation." The "ill-fated man" at Goliad never received this final message.

As the Texas Army moved east it found only abandoned farms and houses. Houston believed that if he could have sent an express ahead of the deserters he could have stopped the flight but "all who saw them breathed the poison and fled." But how could he have expected the civilians calmly to watch the retreating army pass by their farms with the bloodstained Mexican troops only about fifteen miles behind?

Noah Smithwick, a member of the rangers who were dispatched by the government to protect the settlers against the depredations of the Indians, described the scene.

> The desolation of the country through which we passed beggars description. Houses were standing open, the beds unmade, the breakfast things still on the tables, pans of milk moulding in the

dairies. There were cribs full of corn, smoke houses full of bacon, yards full of chickens that ran after us for food, nests of eggs in every fence corner, young corn and garden truck rejoicing in the rain, cattle cropping the luxuriant grass, hogs, fat and lazy, wallowing in the mud, all abandoned.

The commander in chief was also having trouble with a government that was itself becoming increasingly restive and fearful. On March 17 the Texas Constitution was ratified and a provisional government installed. David G. Burnet was elected president and Lorenzo de Zavala vice-president. Unfortunately, one of the first official acts of the new government was to move east to Harrisburg. Burnet and his cabinet had become part of the headlong flight to escape the advancing Mexicans.

At San Felipe, Houston turned his army up the west bank of the Brazos, and after another march of twenty-five miles they set up their camp near Mill Creek, about a mile from Groce's Ferry. The decision was his to make and he did so unilaterally. "I consulted none—I held no councils of war," he said. "If I err, the blame is mine."

The citizens of San Felipe had watched helplessly as the Texas Army marched out of town. When they received the news that the pursuing Mexican forces had also crossed the Colorado, only thirty-five miles away, they reduced Stephen Austin's town to ashes and fled east.

Houston was enraged at the craven removal of the government to Harrisburg. He wrote to Secretary of War Thomas J. Rusk on March 29 from his headquarters at Mill Creek. "For Heaven's sake, do not drop back again with the seat of government! Your removal to Harrisburg has done more to increase the panic in the country than anything else that has occurred in Texas, except the fall of the Alamo."

If the commander in chief had any worries that the secretary of war might be upset by his letter, Rusk soon put his mind at rest. On April 1, he too left Harrisburg—not to flee with the government but to join the army.

Houston at this juncture had become inordinately suspicious, which is perhaps understandable considering the great handicaps he was working under. He did not even have a tent, for example. He ordered D. C. Barrett and Edward Gritten arrested as spies and traitors when neither man was any such thing.

His suspicions were in some cases justified, but they did not entitle him to open sealed letters written by his officers. One such letter, written by James Hazard Perry, caused him to fly into a rage. Perry was extremely critical of the army. "Indeed," he said, "in an election riot in the United States I have seen the contrasting parties better organized."

And "the general," he said, "either for want of his customary excitement (for he has entirely discontinued the use of ardent spirits) or as some say from the effect of opium is in a condition between sleeping and waking, which amounts nearly to a state of insanity." Perry was nevertheless "sanguine of our success." He counted on the "cowardice of the enemy."

Houston forwarded the letter to Burnet and later had Perry arrested for insubordination. Although Houston did allow him to return to the army, he and Perry remained bitter enemies for life.

Houston might also have been suspicious of Rusk if he had heard the rumors. Burnet was alleged to have sent Rusk to spy on Houston and report on his drinking. Rusk also supposedly reported that while the drinking seemed to be under control Houston was smoking opium.

———

At Goliad, General Urrea had kept his word and it did look as if the captives would be paroled to the United States. Spirits were so high on the night of March 26 that some of the young men could be heard playing "Home Sweet Home" on their flutes.

In the early evening a courier arrived from the headquarters of the Mexican president. All the prisoners were to be executed immediately. Urrea was away in Victoria, and the acting commander, Lieutenant Colonel Nicholas de la Portilla, had made no promises to the rebels. He was all too anxious to carry out Santa Anna's decree. These adventurers were, indeed, pirates and must die for their crimes against Mexico.

The prisoners, including the Duval brothers of Kentucky, were divided into three groups and marched out of Goliad in different directions on Palm Sunday, March 27. Fannin and the other wounded remained in the courtyard. Until the Mexican soldiers suddenly turned on them with guns blazing, the prisoners suspected nothing. A handful managed to escape into the tall grass and the trees along the river.

The wounded men in the courtyard of the presidio heard the gunfire beyond the walls and realized what their own fate was to be. They met it bravely. When ordered to kneel before their executioners they refused and were shot to death where they stood.

Fannin was the last to die. He was allowed to write a letter to his wife and when he had finished he asked Captain Carolino Huerta to send the letter and his gold watch to her in Velasco. He then gave Captain Huerta ten pesos and made a touching, almost Byronic request. He asked that the firing squad stand far enough back so that he would not be marred by powder burns and that they not shoot him in the head.

This quixotic, brave man was then seated on a chair and blindfolded. The perfidious captain pocketed the watch and the money and gave the order to fire. The lead musket balls tore into Fannin's head and destroyed the handsome face. He was then stripped and his naked body carried a quarter mile outside the fort and dumped in a pile with the others. Brush and logs were brought and the corpses were burned.

The men executed outside the fort were also stripped by the Mexicans, but they were left where they fell. Great flocks of vultures soon began to circle the blood-soaked sites and at dusk packs of wolves and coyotes began to move in. Their ghastly feast lasted for days.

Months later, the burned remains and scattered bones of the 332 Texas soldiers killed at Goliad on Palm Sunday, 1836, were gathered up and buried.

————

José Enrique de la Peña and many other Mexican officers were appalled by the carnage at Bexar, Refugio, and Goliad. Peña's firsthand account, while self-absolving, makes this clear. But they did nothing to stop it. There were some, however, such as Colonel Francisco Garay and Francisca Alvarez, the heroic wife of an officer, who risked their lives to save several of the prisoners.

Colonel Garay moved Dr. J. H. Barnard and several Texans outside the walls or hid them in his quarters. Señora Alvarez supplied food and drink to the prisoners and smuggled a few out of the fort before the massacre. In his journal, Dr. Barnard said, "Her name deserves to be recorded in letters of gold."

————

Travis at the Alamo, Fannin at Goliad, Dr. Grant and the other adventurers on the Matamoros Expedition had all cost the revolution dearly. Their debacles had resulted in the loss of nearly a thousand good fighting men, along with rifles, sidearms, and artillery.

Houston now had a struggle on his hands to keep his men in order and in the army. He raged and stormed as he marched his army eastward through a landscape that was more a lake than a prairie and where even small creeks were impassable. The rains were unrelenting.

The atrocity at Goliad further inflamed the settlements. Santa Anna's policy was clear. No one was safe. All rebels were to be treated as common criminals and could expect no quarter. The flight of the civilians now became the headlong rush to safety known as the Runaway Scrape.

The men were understandably concerned about their families, and as the bad news spread there were more desertions. Nevertheless Houston reported that he had between seven hundred and eight hundred "effective men." But, he said, "the fame of Jackson could never compensate me for my anxiety and mental pain."

On April 2, the general of the army acquired a navy. The steamboat *Yellow Stone* was at Groce's Ferry on the Brazos. Houston had been worried about how he would be able to cross the swollen river, should that become necessary. He now, at least, had one less worry.

Captain John E. Ross had agreed to help out the army. He assured Houston that he could take five hundred men on board with ease. The *Yellow Stone* would stand by, but there was a price—sizable land grants for the captain and the crew. Engineer Lewis C. Ferguson, for instance, was given 1,500 acres of land and the assurance that he would not have to take up arms.

Houston gladly gave his word, but almost twenty years later the obligation had still not been honored by an ungrateful government, which had forgotten Ross's great service to the republic. He and his ship had, in fact, saved Texas by getting the army across the flood-swollen Brazos. In 1855, Senator Houston endorsed the appeal from Ross's widow, saying, "Poor Widow: Hope deferred maketh the Heart sick."

The steamboat *Yellow Stone* belongs among the elite ships of American maritime history. Houston had long known of it. The Chouteaus had built it for the fur trade. When Houston dined with Washington

Irving at Fort Gibson, the writer had only recently been in a collision involving the *Yellow Stone* on the Mississippi. Houston himself doubtless traveled on it during his time with the Cherokees.

On April 3, Houston wrote to Rusk. "You may rest easy at Harrisburg; the enemy will never cross the Brazos, and I hope the panic will soon subside." He was particularly encouraged because, as he said, "People are planting corn on the east side of the river."

He had also arrested two more suspected spies. "I have nothing pointed against them," he said, "but suspicion has fallen upon them, and they are to be secured." Treasonous activity seems to occur most often in revolutionary wars, which are always times of great suspicion, even paranoia.

Texas was under martial law and Houston was behaving like most wartime commanders who see the enemy under every bed, but he often went too far. He even had "a list of men obnoxious to our cause" drawn up.

Houston was, of course, like Jackson in this regard. Old Hickory had a very clear notion of loyalty. If you were not with him, you were against him. If you were not for a cause, then you were against it.

While Houston was confronting his demons in the form of imagined spies, a rather stupid young deserter, Private Abraham Scales, was condemned to death. The whole affair may have been stirred up by Houston's proclamation of April 3. "All men are now required to join the army and do duty—and those who do not . . . are liable to the pains & penalties of desertion."

The company surgeon diagnosed Scales as suffering from "Mono Mania," but Sam was not moved and the execution was scheduled. The grave was dug and the firing squad chosen. Houston asked to be called five minutes before the execution was to take place. After a lecture on God, country, duty, and patriotism, he pardoned Scales.

Scales may have suffered from monomania, but if so, it was for civilian life. He deserted again less than a week later. His war record was not held against him, however. Two years later he was given 1,500 acres of land, and in 1850 he was working as a carpenter in, appropriately, Liberty.

In the April 3 proclamation, Houston also enjoined the troops to protect private property—it was a soldier's duty. A soldier did indeed have his duty, but a commander in chief also had to ride and a superb gray stallion on a nearby plantation had caught Houston's eye. He requisitioned the horse.

———

While the commander of the Texan forces brooded outdoors at his camp on the Brazos, another commander fidgeted in his headquarters at Fort Jesup, Louisiana, a day's march from the Sabine and the crossing into Texas.

General Edmund Pendleton Gaines had been transferred from Florida by Andrew Jackson, supposedly to prevent hostile Indians from siding with Mexico and attacking the whites in Texas. If Jackson's move was meant to intimidate Mexico, as has been claimed, it failed. Santa Anna did not stop his advance.

The official correspondence gives no hint that Gaines's troops were placed at Jesup in case they were needed to invade Texas. On the contrary, Gaines was told not to exceed his authority. However, he had served in Florida with Jackson when Old Hickory had answered to nobody and he could read between the lines. In another of those historical ironies, the officer who had arrested Aaron Burr in 1807 was now itching to be part of another scheme to separate Texas from Mexico.

Gaines was bombarded with inflammatory propaganda from the west—pillage, rape, and arson by the Mexicans; thousands of fleeing refugees; an imminent strike against defenseless white settlers by blood-thirsty Indians stirred up by Mexican provocateurs. He moved troops to the Sabine, but there they stayed. Andrew Jackson drew back from the brink and declared strict neutrality.

Was Houston drawing Santa Anna and his armies into a trap that would be sprung when their supply lines had been exhausted and they were completely surrounded by hostile forces? There was no question of it. East Texas was the only likely place for the final battle to be fought. Almost the entire population of the province was there as well as supplies for an army. If more manpower were to be raised it would have to be in the east.

Indeed, on April 6, the citizens of Nacogdoches—only 150 miles to the north—in a wonderful display of civic pride and boosterism—appealed to the government at Harrisburg to move the capital there. Their logical argument that Burnet and his cabinet must maintain communications with the army in the field and the government of the United States was ignored.

The government had already made its cowardly plans to flee to Galveston Island, and Acting Secretary of War David Thomas admitted that all the public stores and two field pieces from Brazoria had already been shipped to Galveston. He would do his best to get them back to the army, however.

Communications between the civilian authorities and the military were not good even in the best of times. Houston complained to Rusk on April 4 that he had heard nothing from Harrisburg—only fifty-five miles away—for five days. He was not reassured when Thomas wrote that Houston's last dispatches had been dropped in a bayou by the courier.

Within a few hours another dispatch arrived. The "documents lost last evening have been recovered from their watery expedition," it was flippantly reported. Sam was in no mood for humor, however.

One welcome letter did get through. A friend, Captain John Stuart, wrote from Fort Coffee that the stock on Sam's gun had been repaired and that he would keep it safe until he could send it on. Sam's dog was at Fort Gibson. And, Stuart added, "your particular friend near Fort Gibson was well the last account I had from there."

This discreet reference to Tiana Rogers brought back memories of a far simpler life, but Houston had little time for reminiscences. The army was still ill-trained and badly in need of discipline.

Houston used the advantage of the respite at the camp on the Brazos to restore order and morale. The day began with reveille and roll call at 5:00 A.M. and ended with retreat at sunset and tattoo at 9:00 P.M. The camp was near a lake, and the men were able to wash their clothes when they were not drilling.

Illness was a constant threat and any epidemic could destroy an army in a few days. A threatened measles epidemic was averted by moving the sick men across to the east bank of the river.

"The advance of the enemy is at San Felipe," Houston announced to his troops on April 7, "the moment for which we have waited with

anxiety and interest is fast approaching—the victims of the Alamo and
. . . those who were murdered at Goliad call for *cool deliberate* vengeance."

Two days earlier, Houston had reaffirmed his intention not to retreat
further—"I don't intend to leave the Brazos," he said. However, now
that Santa Anna had reached the river, the situation had changed. On
April 8, Houston modified his earlier resolve. "The army will not cross
the Brazos unless to act with more effect against the enemy," he said.

Santa Anna soon forced an even greater change in the Texans' stategy.
On April 10, a scout, J. B. Dexter, reported in. "After a satisfactory
survey of the enemy's camp from a lofty tree, I am persuaded that a very
large portion of his force has been withdrawn from San Felipe." He
signed the note, "In haste."

The next day, Lt. Col. J. L. Bennett wrote from his camp opposite
San Felipe that the enemy was crossing the Brazos. In a daring maneuver, Santa Anna personally led a small group of troops and captured the
ferry at Fort Bend, near Richmond, about fifty miles downriver from
Houston's headquarters. Juan Almonte, who spoke perfect English, had
tricked the slave who manned the ferry into coming across the swollen
stream to pick him up.

By the following day, Santa Anna had moved his army of six hundred
across the Brazos and was marching east towards Harrisburg, where he
hoped to capture Burnet and the entire government. Understandably
the cabinet feared for their lives, but their headlong flight forever condemned them.

Riders raced overland to headquarters with the dispatches from the
scouts. Houston was shaken by the suddeness and the speed of the
dictator's advance. He had expected Santa Anna to cross at San Felipe.
The Mexicans had bombarded the shore opposite the town until the
morning of April 12, and Houston had fallen for their deception. But
he was quick to recover.

"The enemy have crossed the Brazos," he said, "but they are treading
the soil on which they are to be conquered. . . . Those who do not aid
Texas in her present struggle, but flee and forfeit all the rights of citizens,
will deserve their fate."

Brave words from the man who had promised to fight at the Colorado
and had assured his countrymen that he would never let the enemy cross
the Brazos. A response was not long in coming—but it was from the

frightened president at Harrisburg. Burnet had bombarded Houston with orders to stand and fight, even as he and his government fled.

"Sir, The enemy are laughing you to scorn. You must fight them. You must *retreat* no farther. The country expects you to fight: The salvation of the country expects you to do so," said the president.

By the time Houston received this hysterical message, Burnet and the cabinet had already left Harrisburg, escaping capture by just a few hours. The government first fled to New Washington, now Morgan's Point, where they anxiously awaited a vessel to carry them to Galveston Island.

Houston, angered beyond measure by the "taunts and suggestions . . . gratuitously tendered to me," fired back at Acting Secretary of War David Thomas.

> When I assured the department that the enemy should not pass the Brasos, I did not intend to convey the idea that either the army or myself possessed the powers of ubiquity; but that they should not pass through my encampment. I do hope that my last envelope to his excellency the president, will show you on *whom* to rely, and on *whom*, for awhile, the burden must rest.

Captain Ross kept his promise and Houston's army began the crossing of the Brazos on the *Yellow Stone*, at ten o'clock in the morning on April 12. When the army was safely on the opposite shore, the gallant captain felt it was time to get his vessel out of harm's way. He headed downstream to the Gulf of Mexico and safety.

Above Fort Bend he had to run a gauntlet of Mexican troops who lined each side of the river. The *Yellow Stone* was wrapped from stem to stern in cotton bales, which protected it from the gunfire from the shore. Several of the soldiers even tried to lasso the boat as it passed them by unscathed and proceeded down the narrow stream. As Peña reported, "Few in the camp were acquainted with steamboats, so all was in confusion."

The Army of Texas was now east of the Brazos and rapidly running out of room to retreat further. It was clear that Santa Anna had more in mind than capturing the feckless government of Texas at Harrisburg. A few miles beyond the temporary capital lay Lynch's Ferry across the San Jacinto River, the only available crossing left to a retreating army. If Santa Anna got there first, Houston would be completely trapped.

More than five thousand refugees were rumored to be on the other side of the San Jacinto River at Lynchburg. They were waiting to see what would happen but they were poised to continue their dash to the Trinity and even the Sabine and the United States if necessary.

The April rains had continued and the low land east of the Brazos was now one great swamp to be negotiated. But negotiate it the Army of Texas did. No one had a greater sense of noblesse oblige than their commander in chief who did not hesitate to get in the muddy ditches with his men to help them move the wagons. Their lifelong fealty was pledged here on this muddy path.

Two days after the crossing of the Brazos, at a fork in the road, the hour of reckoning came. To the left lay Nacogdoches and continued retreat and to the right lay Harrisburg and Lynch's Ferry—and Santa Anna's army. Houston had informed a handful of his men what direction he would take, and without a word the advance guard turned onto the Harrisburg Road. The momentous decision spread back through the ranks like lightning. A great cheer rose from the troops.

The reaction from the refugees, who would, of course, take the Nacogdoches Road, was much less laudatory. Their only interest was their own safety and they demanded protection. Houston agreed to send a hundred men along with them—but another two or three hundred disgracefully went along also, men Houston would badly need.

One of the refugees, Mrs. Pamela Mann, demanded that her yoke of oxen, which she had lent to the army, be returned to her forthwith. Instead of impressing the beasts, as was his right as commander in chief, Houston, ever the gentleman, returned the oxen. Unaccountably Mrs. Mann is considered not an unpatriotic virago but a folk hero.

The Army of Texas was now reduced to fewer than a thousand men but they were of the very best. These were men to whom the battle cries "Victory or Death!" and "Remember the Alamo!" were not just slogans but true calls to arms.

In less than three days of marching, covering fifty-five miles under the most difficult conditions, the army reached the north bank of Buffalo Bayou, opposite the blackened ruins of Harrisburg, on the evening of April 18. The town had been partially destroyed by its fleeing inhabitants and then finished off by the Mexicans.

Here, near Harrisburg, the Texan Army took delivery of the two field pieces promised by Thomas. They had been brought up to New Washington from Galveston on the steamboat *Flash* and then transferred to the *Opie* for the trip up the Buffalo Bayou.

A captured Mexican courier revealed that Santa Anna was marching in the direction of Lynch's Ferry, about fifteen miles to the east, with five hundred men. Another thousand Mexican troops were about forty miles away on the Brazos.

Although every captive in the narratives of the time is represented as having, or so it seems, willingly passed on vital and often damaging intelligence, it is hard not to believe that the most frightful coercion must have been employed. Indeed, this poor man was later chained to a tree and tormented by the army.

Santa Anna was pushing his troops even harder than Houston. The Texas government had escaped to New Washington but he was determined to round them up there. He would then turn north and capture the ferry at Lynch's.

Burnet and his party avoided capture and certain death by just minutes on April 17. They had embarked in a rowboat and were moving away to a waiting ship, the *Flash*, when the Mexican cavalry, under the ubiquitous Colonel Juan Almonte, rode up. Fortunately, Mrs. Burnet was in the boat, and the gallant Almonte held his fire.

Houston, when he heard that the government had sailed away on the same vessel that had brought the two little cannons, the "Twin Sisters," no doubt considered the exchange a good trade.

On Tuesday, April 19, Sam Houston and the Army of Texas began crossing Buffalo Bayou just below Harrisburg. While he waited in his makeshift camp on the south bank of the bayou, Houston wrote to Henry Raguet in Nacogdoches.

Sir: This morning we are in preparation to meet Santa Anna. It is the only chance of saving Texas. From time to time I have looked for reinforcements in vain. The Convention adjourning to Harrisburg struck *panic* throughout the country. Texas could have started at least four thousand men. We will only have about seven hundred to march with, besides the camp-guard. We go to conquer. It is wisdom growing out of necessity to meet the enemy now; every consideration enforces it. No previous occasion would justify it. The troops are in fine spirits, and now is the time for action. . . .

We shall use our best efforts to fight the enemy to such advantages as will insure victory, though the odds are greatly against us. I leave the result in the hands of a wise God, and rely upon his providence.

My country will do justice to those who serve her. The rights for which we fight will be secured and Texas free.

The campaign had undergone a profound change. Houston was now on the trail of Santa Anna. The pursued had become the pursuer.

The commander in chief and the secretary of war issued joint proclamations to the people of Texas as the army turned east to meet the enemy on April 19. Their appeals are a terrible indictment of the more than three-quarters of the men of Texas who did not serve in the army during the revolution.

A few hours more will decide the fate of our army: and what an astonishing fact it is, that, at the very moment when the fate of your wives, your children, your homes, your country, and all that is dear to a freeman, are suspended upon the issue of one battle, not one-fourth of the [men] of Texas are in the army! Are you Americans? are you freemen? If you are, prove your blood and your birth by rallying at once to your country's standard!

THOMAS J. RUSK, *Secretary-of-War*

Houston then added his own rhetorical flourishes, which owe much to the speeches of Shakespeare's warrior kings at Agincourt or Bosworth Field and to Homer's warrior kings at Troy.

We view ourselves on the eve of battle. We are nerved for the contest, and must conquer or perish. It is vain to look for present aid: none is at hand. We must now act or abandon all hope! Rally to the standard, and be no longer the scoff of mercenary tongues! Be men, be freemen, that your children may bless their fathers' names!

Colonel Rusk is with me, and I rejoice at it. The country will be the gainer, and myself the beneficiary. Liberty and our country!

SAM HOUSTON, *Commander-in-Chief*

Everything now depended on Houston's moving his army with dispatch. He had to head off Santa Anna before he captured the ferry and before he was reinforced by the Mexican army advancing from the Brazos. He left a camp guard behind with the baggage and the sick, and with about seven hundred men headed for Lynch's Ferry.

Except for a brief rest, the Army of Texas marched all day and all that next night. At sunrise, on April 20, they looked out over the small plain lying on the peninsula bounded by Buffalo Bayou and the Rio de San Jacinto.

There was little time for contemplation, however. Mexican scouts could already be seen. Houston hurried on and encamped in a grove of trees a half mile from the ferry landing. Santa Anna had tarried too long at New Washington in his futile attempt at capturing President Burnet, and the Texans won the race to Lynch's by just three hours.

Since they had not eaten in two days, Houston's men set about slaughtering cattle and roasting the meat for their breakfast. Their feast was soon interrupted by the sudden appearance, not a mile away, of the Mexican Army in full battle formation. Was the long awaited battle now finally to be joined?

The Texans quickly fell into line as the Mexicans opened up a bombardment with their one piece of artillery, a brass twelve-pounder. The Mexican infantry began to advance toward the Texas camp. The air was filled with the blood-chilling *Degüello*, the "no quarter" signal from the Mexican bugles.

Houston replied with the "Twin Sisters." The grape and canister from the two six-pounders tore into the advancing Mexicans, who retreated back into a small wood. There was only sporadic small arms fire throughout the rest of the day.

Santa Anna looked over the field and arbitrarily ordered the camp set up without giving it much thought or consulting with his general staff. His officers and aides disagreed with the site and the deployment of the troops, but as usual they grumbled only to each other. Meanwhile the troops busied themselves with erecting a breastwork of packs and baggage forward of the camp. In the center they left an opening for the single cannon.

Santa Anna had Houston trapped, with his back to the bayou. He could attack and destroy the Texans at will. El Presidente was also expecting General Cós and five hundred more troops to arrive the next morning. *Mañana* would be soon enough to take care of the rebels.

Near sunset, eighty-five Texan cavalry rode out to reconnoiter the enemy lines and attempt to capture the Mexican cannon. Their commander, Sidney Sherman, in direct defiance of Houston's orders, led a charge, which resulted in two men being severely wounded and the loss of several horses.

Houston later praised Sherman's efforts but his real opinion of his actions, which were reminiscent of the other disasters caused by such foolhardiness, is shown by his removing Sherman from command of the cavalry. He replaced Sherman with a recent addition to his army who had demonstrated great courage in rescuing two wounded men and killing one Mexican during the brief engagement—Mirabeau Buonaparte Lamar.

The Texans had still had nothing substantial to eat for over forty-eight hours and as soon as it was quiet they went back to roasting slabs of beef over their open fires. The day ended quietly with the two armies facing each other across the Plain of St. Hyacinth.

Sitting under an oak, at the place he had named Camp Safety, Houston wrote to Burnet in Galveston. He reported on the skirmish but he could not resist expressing his bitterness. "There would be no difficulty in securing the rights of the people and the liberties of Texas," he said, "if men would march to their duty, and not fly like recreants from danger."

———

Thursday, April 21, 1836, dawned clear. It was warm, but a slight breeze from the bay and the marshes fluttered the ensigns of the two armies under a bright blue sky. Understandably the Texans had spent a sleepless night in spite of their exhausting march, and the four o'clock reveille found most of them already awake.

Sam Houston slept late—or at least pretended to—for the first time in months. It was a brilliant display of nonchalance staged for the benefit of his men. He had passed the night on a blanket under his oak tree, using his saddle for a pillow, and did not rouse himself until long after sunrise. High in the sky over the bayou an eagle soared. "The sun of Austerlitz has risen again," Houston cried.

At nine o'clock there was a flurry of activity in the Mexican camp. General Cós and his five hundred fresh troops had arrived. Houston's army was now outnumbered by almost two to one. He now began to move among his troops to reassure them. There were no reinforcements. It was a ruse on the part of the Mexicans. Santa Anna was marching the same men around and around the camp to make it appear that there were more of them.

The scout Deaf Smith, whom Houston called "my stay in darkest hour," was enlisted to aid in the subterfuge. Houston sent Smith to check on the enemy movements and to destroy the rough log bridge, over which Cós and his men had just crossed nearby Vince's Bayou. Houston could thus prevent any more Mexican reinforcements from arriving.

If this was Houston's reason for burning the bridge, it is a mystery as to why it was not done the day before. However, as historian Eugene Baker has pointed out, the bridge was not that important. Vince's Bayou is only about three miles in length. It could easily have been headed with little loss of time by an army.

Smith returned to the camp and assured the Texans that what their commander in chief said was true. There had been no reinforcement of Santa Anna's army. The Texans were reassured, but there was still uneasiness over their precarious position. They had no means of escape. Although they held the ferry landing there was no hope of transporting hundreds of men across the San Jacinto while holding off an attacking army.

A war council, of sorts, was held at the request of the field commanders. Houston, after asking their opinion as to whether they should attack or wait to be attacked, had nothing further to say. The two junior officers voted to attack, but the four senior officers were in favor of a defensive battle. Houston remained withdrawn and noncommittal.

By three o'clock, he had measured the war temperature of the troops and decided to attack. Within a half hour all was ready. "Our troops paraded with alacrity and spirit, and were ready for the contest," said Houston, who received their salute with personal pride. He had been with many of these men since March 11 at Gonzales. Together they had suffered the humiliation of retreat and the betrayal of their fellow countrymen and their government. But victory surely was now to be their reward.

The large stand of live oaks enabled Houston to hide his preparations from the Mexicans so that his entire force could form up undetected. But Houston's great care in concealing his troop movements was probably unnecessary. The Mexicans had decided that there would be no attack from the Texans that day and their own offensive could be carried out whenever they chose.

Consequently, the enemy arms were stacked and the troops were either enjoying a siesta or going about the routine chores of an army in the field—carrying water, washing clothes, or gathering firewood. Santa Anna himself was supposedly passing the siesta with his mulatto mistress. True or not, the supremely confident Mexican general was certainly guilty of neglecting the most routine task when one army faces another—placing pickets forward of the lines.

At about four o'clock, Houston mounted his white stallion Saracen. He drew his sword and, pointing it toward the Mexican lines, cried to his troops, "Remember the Alamo." The retreat was over at last. The long-awaited advance began.

On the extreme left flank, Houston had placed the 2nd Infantry Regiment under the former leader of cavalry Sidney Sherman. On Sherman's right was the 1st Infantry under Edward Burleson. Next came the artillery—the "Twin Sisters"—commanded by the estimable George Washington Hockley. To his right were four companies of regular infantry. The right flank was assigned to Lamar's sixty-one horsemen, whose charge would provide distraction and cover for the ground troops.

The Texans quietly moved out from under the protective grove of trees in double-quick time. Halfway across the plain a little band of three fifes and a drum began to play "Will You Come to the Bower" and the army picked up the cadence.

Houston rode back and forth in front of the line urging his men on, shouting, "Hold your fire, God damn you, hold your fire!" When they were within six hundred feet of the Mexican lines, the "Twin Sisters"

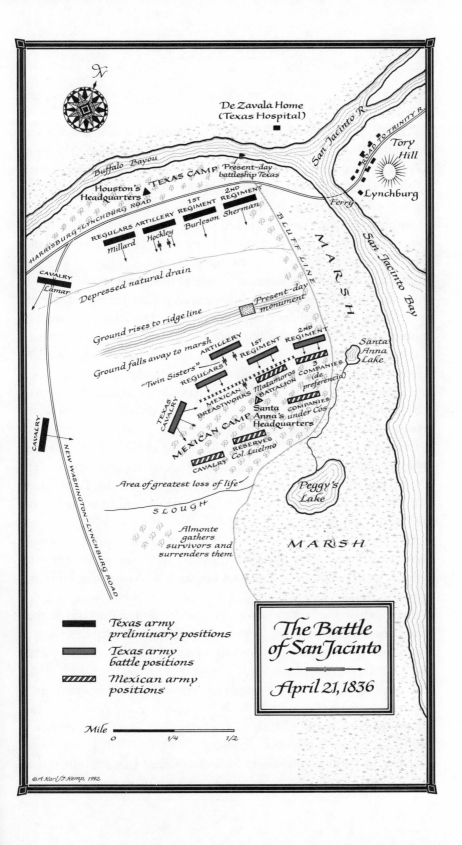

The Battle of San Jacinto

April 21, 1836

Texas army preliminary positions

Texas army battle positions

Mexican army positions

Mile   0   1/4   1/2

De Zavala Home (Texas Hospital)

San Jacinto R.

ROAD TO TRINITY R.

Tory Hill

Buffalo Bayou

TEXAS CAMP

Present-day battleship Texas

Ferry

Lynchburg

Houston's Headquarters

HARRISBURG-LYNCHBURG ROAD

REGULARS ARTILLERY REGIMENT

1ST REGIMENT Burleson

2ND REGIMENT Sherman

Millard   Hockley

San Jacinto Bay

BLUFF LINE

MARSH

CAVALRY Lamar

Depressed natural drain

Present-day monument

Ground rises to ridge line

Ground falls away to marsh

Santa Anna Lake

"Twin Sisters" ARTILLERY

REGULARS

1ST REGIMENT

2ND REGIMENT

3 COMPANIES (de preferencia)

CAVALRY

NEW WASHINGTON-LYNCHBURG ROAD

TEXAS CAVALRY

MEXICAN BREASTWORKS

Mexican Matamoros BATTALION COMPANIES

Santa Anna's under Cós Headquarters

MEXICAN CAMP

RESERVES Col. Guelmo

CAVALRY

Area of greatest loss of life

SLOUGH

Peggy's Lake

Almonte gathers survivors and surrenders them

MARSH

©A. Karl / J. Kemp, 1992

abruptly began to rain grape and canister on the hapless and unprepared Mexicans.

The Texans now took up the cry "Remember the Alamo—Remember Goliad" and it resounded throughout their formation. The firing increased and they advanced without a halt until they were almost on top of the enemy lines. The smoke from the black powder covered the battlefield and reduced visibility to only a few yards.

Suddenly Saracen sank to his knees, his white coat stained with five great crimson blotches. The Mexican cannon had fired only a few rounds but the deadly shot had found the great horse.

Houston immediately mounted another horse but it too was shot out from under him. As he went down, he felt an unbearable pain in his right ankle. It had been shattered by a musket ball. Ignoring the wound he mounted yet another horse and rode on, his boot filling with blood.

The breastwork was quickly overrun and the cannon silenced. The Texans found themselves in control of the enemy encampment only eighteen minutes after the engagement had begun. The battle was over. The killing had only started, however. It went on into the night as the troops ignored all moral or official restraint.

Houston had remained in the saddle in spite of his wound. Towering over his men, he ordered them to stop the slaughter and regroup. The victory was theirs, but there was still great danger to the Texas Army. If the Mexicans could be rallied or reinforced they could easily overcome this undisciplined rabble.

But Houston had lost control, and Rusk, Burleson, and Lamar were just as ineffective. The Army of Texas, which had performed with control and precision only minutes before, was now a wild mob in a killing frenzy.

Even though the Mexican soldiers threw down their arms and on their knees begged for mercy, the Texans shot, clubbed, and stabbed them to death—even the wounded. Those who fled into the marsh were picked off from the bank.

One of the greatest of the crimes was the murder of General Manuel Castrillon, who had intervened with Santa Anna at the Alamo in a vain atttempt to save the captive David Crockett's life. Castrillon was shot at point-blank range after surrendering.

The ever-resourceful Colonel Almonte realized that the only way to save his life was to gather together enough men to surrender as a body.

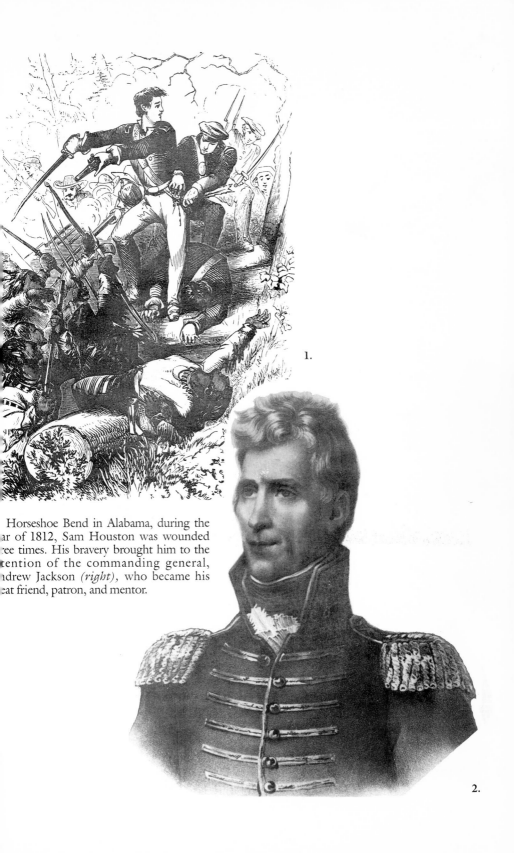

1.

Horseshoe Bend in Alabama, during the
ar of 1812, Sam Houston was wounded
ee times. His bravery brought him to the
tention of the commanding general,
ndrew Jackson *(right)*, who became his
eat friend, patron, and mentor.

2.

3.

Artists were drawn to Houston throughout his life. Thomas Sully painted him when Houston was a U.S. congressman from Tennessee (1823–1827). Joseph Wood's miniature *(facing page, top)* is the earliest known likeness of Houston.

In 1830, during his exile among the Cherokees, Houston was in Washington as a tribal ambassador. He habitually wore full Indian regalia, even to the White House to visit President Jackson. A year later, he was in Nashville, where he had himself painted as Marius among the ruins—a pointed reference to the scandal that had wrecked his Tennessee political career in 1829.

4.

5.

6.

7.

George Washington Hockley was only one of Houston's devoted inner circle, but he was a particular favorite. He served as aide, friend, and confidant. During the great retreat across Texas (March–April 1836), Hockley also acted as the general's secretary.

"HOUSTON, WHO WAS COMPLETELY EXHAUSTED FROM FATIGUE AND LOSS OF BLOOD, FELL FROM HIS HORSE."   page 134.

8.

Houston's horse was shot out from under him and he was wounded during the charge across the field at San Jacinto, but he quickly commandeered another mount and led the Texans on to victory.

fter the battle, the commander in ief distributed the legendary "San cinto corn," enjoining his men to turn to the planting of crops and her peaceful pursuits.

9.

While General Santa Anna *(left)* proceeded unchecked across Texas, Houston was mocked by his countrymen. Opinion quickly changed, however, after San Jacinto. Even Houston's friendship with the Indians was celebrated, as in this drawing, where he is depicted as 10. a victorious Cherokee chieftain.

13.

Santa Anna was captured on April 22, 1836, and brought to Houston's camp on Buffalo Bayou. "That man may consider himself born to no common destiny, who has conquered the Napoleon of the West," he proudly said to Houston. Later the Mexican dictator was imprisoned in a heavily guarded house *(below)* at Orozimbo Plantation, near Columbia, Texas.

14.

TEXAS!!

Emigrants who are desirious of assisting Texas at this important crisis of her affairs may have a free passage and equipments, by applying at the

NEW-YORK and PHILADELPHIA HOTEL,

On the Old Levee, near the Blue Stores.

Now is the time to ensure a fortune in Land: To all who remain in Texas during the War will be allowed 1280 Acres.

To all who remain Six Months, 640 Acres.
To all who remain Three Months, 320 Acres.
And as Colonists, 4600 Acres for a family and 1470 Acres for a Single Man.

New Orleans, April 23d, 1836.

17.

Agents in the United States circulated broadsides, soliciting volunteers to fight for Texas. The date on this one is two days after Houston's victory at San Jacinto. The news did not reach New Orleans until early May.

16.

15.

On a visit to Alabama in 1839, Sam Houston fell in love with twenty-year-old Margaret Moffette Lea. The forty-six-year-old general gave her an Italian cameo of himself. The following May, he returned to Alabama to marry the beautiful young woman.

18.

he wounded Texan commander in chief
s taken to New Orleans, where the
ouston legend began. There he was
inted by George Catlin *(15, opposite)*,
t hero worship took other forms as
ell—for example, a song called "The
xian Grand March."

19.

President Houston's first Official Residence at Houston 1837

20.

Houston served twice as president of the Republic of Texas. He lived in this two-room cabin—the Executive Mansion.

21.

2

In early 1846, Houston went to Washington as a senator from the new state of Texas. He was in the capital for most of the next thirteen years, and once again he was able to indulge his penchant for being painted *(by Martin-Johnson Heade, left)* or photographed *(by Matthew Brady, above)*.

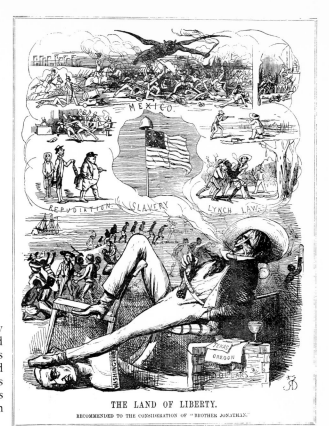

THE LAND OF LIBERTY.

RECOMMENDED TO THE CONSIDERATION OF "BROTHER JONATHAN."

artoonists were often relentlessly
d virulently anti-annexation and
ti-Texas *(below)*. Even after Texas
as admitted to the Union, the old
imosities would not die. *Punch*'s
ew of the new state *(right)* was
pical of public opinion in both
ngland and America.

24.

MATTY MEETING THE TEXAS QUESTION.

23.

Gen'. Sam Houston
of Texas.

no 4

W. E. ARMSTRONG.   NASHVILLE, TENN.

25.

Houston's delight in costumes a
in changing his appearance last
throughout his lifetime. He cou
be the stern father of the Repub
(left), a rugged frontiersman *(bel
right)*, the elder statesman *(bel
left)*, or a pillar of the United Sta
Senate *(facing page, top left)*.

SAM HOUSTON

27.

28.

ouston's pro-Union views aroused
e hatred of his enemies, but he was
rticularly derided for his member-
ip in the Know-Nothing Party
ight).

is friends and admirers, particu-
rly in the North, saw him much
fferently—the heroic Southern
atesman steering the Union
rough the secessionist storm.

29.

BRAVING THE STORM!!!

"I REGARD THE CONSTITUTION OF MY COUNTRY, AND I AM DETERMINED TO STAND BY IT."—*Extract from Gen. Houston's Letter of Nov. 1*

. (*From "Vanity Fair," New York*)

30.

Although rejected by the Texas L
islature and not returned to
Senate in 1859, "Sam Jacin
nevertheless retained the loyalty
the people, who elected him go
nor. Characteristically, he celebra
with an elaborate inaugural ball
the Capitol in Austin.

31.

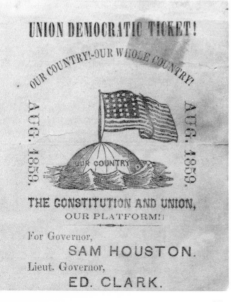

UNION DEMOCRATIC TICKET!

OUR COUNTRY!-OUR WHOLE COUNTRY!

AUG. 1859.

AUG. 1859.

OUR COUNTRY

THE CONSTITUTION AND UNION,

OUR PLATFORM!

For Governor,

SAM HOUSTON.

Lieut. Governor,

ED. CLARK.

32.

INAUGURAL BALL
OF

Gov. Sam Houston

To be given at the Capitol in the City of Austin
DECEMBER 21, 1859.

Your company is respectfully solicited

MANAGERS

S. A. MAVERICK,   ELI H. BAXTER,   FRANK R. LUBBOCK,
R. B. HUBBARD,   JOHN HANCOCK,   C. S. MELLETTE,
JAS. H. RAYMOND,   BEN. H. EPPERSON,   N. H. DARNELL,
WM. CLARK, JR.,   W. L. MANEY,   JUSTUS DAVIDSON,
JAS. W. HENDERSON,   E. M. PEASE,   D. M. WHALEY,
W. D. CARRINGTON,   G. SCHLEICHER,   A. T. RAINEY,
H. H. CUMBY,   N. O. SHELLY,   O. W. PASCHAL,
J. B WILSON,   R. H. TAYLOR,   FORBES BRITTON,
BLACK. D. DAVIS,   W. L. CHALMERS,   A. H. GENTRY,
BEN. HENRICKS,   C. W. BUCKLEY,   JAS. R. JACKSON,
D. C. DICKSON,   AMOS MORRILL,   R. P. HOLLINGSWORTH,
B. BENEVIDES,   A. M. BRANCH,   J. H. HERNDON,
             R. M. ELGIN,   A. W. CRAWFORD.

TWO BANDS OF MUSIC IN ATTENDANCE

SUPPER BY J. K. JOHNSTON.

Austin, December 3, 1859.   Intelligencer Prin. Asso.

THE NOBLEST ROMAN OF THEM ALL.

Houston—"What should the people do with these bald tribunes?
On whom depending, their obedience fails
To the greater bench : in a rebellion,
When what's not meet, but what must be, was law,
Then were they chosen ; in a better hour,
Let what is meet, be said it must be meet,
And throw their power i' the dust."—*Coriolanus, act. 3, scene 1.*

34.

Houston's stand against secession, which led to his being deposed from the governorship of Texas, made him a hero in the North. *Vanity Fair* likened him to Shakespeare's Coriolanus.

36.

The old warrior retired to Huntsville, where he lived in the eccentric Steamboat House. He died in the downstairs bedroom, beneath the outside stairway. The simple gravestone *(above)* was later replaced with a more heroic monument.

An individual had no chance of surviving. Amazingly he was able to round up almost four hundred men, who surrendered en masse. His stratagem worked and they were spared.

Houston, although faint from loss of blood, rode back across the field to his campsite, acknowledging the cheers of the men. Almost on command—of his imagination perhaps—two ravens appeared above the enemy cannon.

As he reached the oak under which he had slept the night before, he collapsed and tumbled from his horse. He was placed on a blanket under the tree and the surgeon, Dr. Alexander W. Ewing, was called.

As Houston was being attended by the doctor, the large, seemingly organized group of Mexican soldiers under Almonte appeared. His worst fears had become a reality. Reinforcements had arrived. "My God," he cried. "All is lost."

He soon realized what was actually happening, but his brief panic was used for years by his enemies as a sign that Houston lost his nerve during the battle. This was not the cry of a coward, however. He later said that a hundred disciplined men could have wiped out the Texans at that moment.

Over six hundred Mexicans lay dead or dying on the field at San Jacinto. Santa Anna's secretary, Ramon Martínez Caro, described the scene. "Where are our six hundred victims?" he had skeptically asked an aide.

> Wishing to satisfy my doubts, he led me to the entrance of the road taken by our troops in their flight, and there I saw, both to the right and to the left, as far as the eye could see, a double file of corpses, all men from our force. Moved by this sad spectacle— would that it had been the last—I still had the more bitter sorrow of being conducted a short distance to the left, where there was a small creek, at the edge of the woods, where the bodies were so thickly piled upon each other that they formed a bridge across it.

There were some seven hundred prisoners, but the greatest prize had made his escape in the first minutes of the battle. Santa Anna dashed from his tent, mounted a horse, and fled to the west—toward the army of General Vicente Filisola, only a day or two away.

Santa Anna outran his pursuers as far as Vince's Bayou. Finding the bridge destroyed, he jumped from his horse and hid in a pine thicket. After dark he waded across the bayou, in water up to his chest, and escaped.

In an abandoned farmhouse he found a disguise, some civilian clothing. The story that Santa Anna donned a woman's dress is only another of those imaginative twists that are often used to further humiliate a hated enemy and destroy his reputation.

On the morning of April 22, Captain James Austin Sylvester and six enlisted men, including Joel W. Robison, were searching the area. At about eleven o'clock they overtook a fleeing Mexican out on the open plain. They had no idea that the man they ordered to march ahead of them back to the battlefield was the Mexican president.

In a short time, the exhausted prisoner pleaded that he could not go on. They could kill him, he said, but he could walk no farther. Some of the men wanted to shoot him on the spot, but Sylvester instead let him climb up and ride behind Private Joel Robison.

According to Robison, Santa Anna was so grateful that he gave him the gold braided vest he was still wearing underneath his civilian shirt. For years afterward young men in Fayette County, Texas, borrowed the "Santa Anna vest" from Robison to wear at their weddings.

As they entered the camp, the scouting party was about to turn Santa Anna out with the other prisoners when the Mexican officers and men rose and began to shout, *"El Presidente! El Presidente!"* The captive then asked to be taken to General Houston.

Santa Anna's conqueror was lying on his blanket under the oak. His wound had been probed and some of the numerous bone splinters removed. He was in great pain, but he did not lose any of the sense of the occasion. Almonte was summoned to act as interpreter.

The Mexican dictator was extremely agitated and asked if perhaps there were some opium in the Texan camp. Houston ordered some of the drug for him, and Santa Anna was soon calm enough to talk.

"That man may consider himself born to no common destiny, who has conquered the Napoleon of the West," he said, "and now it remains for him to be generous to the vanquished."

"You should have remembered that at the Alamo," replied Houston.

When Santa Anna defended his actions on the ground that he was only obeying the orders of his government, Houston angrily cut him off.

· "Why, you are the Government of Mexico," he said. "A dictator, sir, has no superior."

As for Goliad, the Mexican president denied that he had ordered the execution of prisoners and blamed everything on General Urrea. Then, turning logic on its head, Santa Anna swore that he would execute Urrea when he got the opportunity because he should never have accepted the surrender of Fannin and his men in the first place.

The army was, to a man, calling for Santa Anna's head, but Houston realized the value of keeping him alive. Filisola and Urrea were rumored to have seven thousand men still in the field, and Houston had no idea where they were. In exchange for his life Santa Anna agreed to order all Mexican forces in Texas to withdraw beyond the Rio Grande. An express rider left the Texas camp at once with the order, and the Mexican withdrawal began.

That night, the defeated Antonio López de Santa Anna, the Napoleon of the West, slept on his own camp bed, watched over by his aides and guarded by soldiers of the Texan Army. His sleep was deep and calm and uninterrupted. A small, long-stemmed pipe, now cold, lay on the campaign chest beside the bed. The sweet smell of the soothing smoke of opium scented the air in the silken tent.

General Sam Houston lay just a few feet away on his blanket beneath the oak tree and regarded the stars in the brilliant heavens over the Plain of San Jacinto. The old wounds from the War of 1812 and the terrible damage done to his body in the charge across the field the day before kept him from sleep, but he rested easy. Texas was free.

———

The Battle of San Jacinto lasted perhaps twenty minutes. Houston lost only a handful of men and victory was total. There was no grand battle plan, he brought no great armaments to bear on the enemy, and his army had been outmanned. But Sam Houston had used the oldest and most effective of military weapons—daring and surprise.

10

Sam Jacinto—
President of
the Republic
of Texas

A FEW DAYS AFTER the great battle, a sweat-stained and exhausted soldier rode into Nacogdoches. He reined in at the house of Henry Raguet and asked the slave who answered the door to summon her master. In a few moments Henry Raguet and his family had surrounded the rider and were listening to his astounding news.

While they talked, Anna Raguet opened a small package wrapped in oilskin that the express rider had brought for her. A broad smile lighted up her pretty face as she held up a small wreath, its leaves slightly wilted but still a clear pale green. She handed her father the note that had been enclosed.

To Miss Raguet   Nacogdoches, Texas

These are laurels I send you from the battlefield of San Jacinto.

Thine,

HOUSTON

On Galveston Island, two hundred miles to the south, President David G. Burnet and his cabinet read Houston's "Official Report of the Battle of San Jacinto," dated April 25, 1836, four days after the battle. The first news had reached them earlier—they were only fifty miles from the battlefield—but it was not until the courier arrived with Houston's own message did they dare believe it.

Houston attributed the delay only to "my situation." The government, quite naturally given their state of mind and their opinion of the commander in chief, suspected he was guilty of his usual dilatoriness or, even worse, perhaps negotiating on his own with the defeated Mexican president.

Burnet and his shamefaced coterie of escapees immediately set about to leave for the battlefield. More humiliation ensued. There was no wood for the steamboat, again the intrepid *Yellow Stone*, which was to carry them to Buffalo Bayou. They did not arrive at the battlefield until May 4.

By then Houston had moved the camp three miles farther up the bayou. The stench from rotting Mexican corpses and dead horses was overpowering. In yet another disgraceful episode illustrating the barbarity of the war on both sides, the bodies had not been buried or burned.

In spite of his great victory and the freeing of his countrymen from subjugation or even death, Houston was not immune to the rantings of ungrateful citizens. He was now subjected to an outpouring of ingratitude and selfishness that would have even taken aback Mrs. Mann.

Another one of those harpies who unaccountably become celebrated for their ill-humor descended on him, in the person of Mrs. Peggy McCormick. This widow of one of Stephen Austin's Old Three Hundred owned the land on which the great battle had been fought.

In a perfect fury she sought out Houston on his sickbed and demanded that "them stinking Mexicans" be removed from her property. When Houston tried to mollify her, pointing out that the spot would be celebrated in history, she cried, "To the *devil* with your glorious history! Take off your stinking Mexicans."

Mrs. McCormick's demands did lead to a halfhearted attempt to bury the dead, but visitors to the site for years afterward reported that human bones scattered all around were a common sight.

In spite of the victory, Burnet and the cabinet were in an equally bad humor. Houston should have pressed on and destroyed Filisola'a army, they argued. Instead he had taken several days to divide up the spoils while the Mexican Army fled to the southwest. "Hannibal distributed spoils at Cannae and Rome was saved," Burnet sarcastically remarked later.

The spoils of battle were slim pickings. The $12,000 in silver in Santa Anna's baggage had been doled out—a few dollars per man. Even Lamar said it was a "gratuity, which but feebly expressed the gratitude of their countrymen." Houston had also kept Santa Anna's saddle, but he eventually gave it away, to a relative in Tennessee, to stop the criticism.

Two treaties, one public and one secret, were negotiated with the dictator. Burnet always maintained that Houston had already negotiated an agreement with Santa Anna before he and the government had arrived at San Jacinto. Houston, of course, declared that his role was exclusively military and that negotiation was a civilian prerogative.

Houston's suggestions were followed, however, and President Burnet, for his part, was in complete agreement with Houston as to the importance of keeping Santa Anna alive. They differed only as to where. Houston felt he should be kept in Texas as a hostage until all matters were settled.

In the public treaty it was agreed that Santa Anna would cease all hostilities, that he would never take up arms against Texas, and that all Mexican forces would withdraw from Texas forthwith. Santa Anna was to be allowed to return to Mexico as soon as possible.

The secret treaty provided that Santa Anna would be freed immediately to return to Mexico and work to secure the recognition of the independence of Texas and that the permanent boundary would be the Rio Grande.

On May 9, Burnet and his cabinet, Santa Anna and his entourage, and Houston and two aides boarded the *Yellow Stone* for Galveston. Houston's shattered ankle had worsened and Dr. Ewing recommended that he be taken by ship to New Orleans, where he could be treated properly.

Burnet is supposed to have denied Houston permission to leave the army. The faithful Captain Ross refused to sail without him, however, and Houston was carried aboard by General Rusk and his brother David.

As the *Yellow Stone* descended Buffalo Bayou, Santa Anna and his entourage received perhaps their first lesson in what constitutes true honor. When the Plain of San Jacinto came into view off to the right, the Texans came to attention. They stood silently thus, paying tribute to their dead and wounded comrades, until the little vessel had rounded the point and the battlefield lay far behind.

Houston had said his farewell a few days before to his victorious San Jacinto soldiers. His address was brief, full of affection, and guaranteed to bind them to him forever. When liberty is firmly established, he said, "it will be fame enough to say, 'I was a member of the army of San Jacinto.' "

At Galveston, another argument broke out over whether Houston was to be allowed passage on a Texas navy vessel, the *Liberty*, which was leaving for New Orleans for repairs. Whether or not it was Burnet who prevented his sailing on the *Liberty* is unknown. Almost certainly someone did, for Houston had to sail on a commercial schooner, the *Flora*, which left Galveston on May 11.

Houston was accompanied to New Orleans by his new private secretary, Henry P. Brewster, and Dr. Ewing. Brewster was a twenty-year-old South Carolinian who had arrived in Texas just in time to join the revolution and fight at San Jacinto. Dr. Ewing, a roving twenty-seven-year-old graduate of Trinity College, Dublin, and the University of Edinburgh, had settled in Texas in 1830. Burnet had been responsible for his appointment as chief surgeon of the Texan Army, but the president was quick to dismiss him from this post when he insisted on accompanying Houston to New Orleans.

The trip around the Gulf Coast and up the Mississippi was frightful for the wounded man. He was half-delirious throughout the voyage. When the *Flora* docked at New Orleans on May 22, 1836, Houston was barely conscious.

It had been a month since the great battle. The news had spread throughout the country, but nowhere was there more excitement than in New Orleans. Hundreds of Texas refugees had fled there to wait out the war and they crowded the wharf to get a glimpse of the hero.

Among this great throng that gathered to greet the wounded warrior was a seventeen-year-old girl named Margaret Lea, who was visiting New Orleans from her home in Marion, Alabama.

How like the greeting Houston had witnessed when Old Hickory had arrived in 1828 for the anniversary celebrations of the Battle of New Orleans! In emulation of his idol, the ravaged hero staggered to his feet to acknowledge the tribute of the crowd. It was a thrilling moment, and when the general fainted into the arms of his companions the drama could not have been greater. Sam Houston captured New Orleans and the public imagination without firing a shot.

Sam Houston was now forty-three years old, and he was still handsome and had retained his remarkable physique. But the destruction caused by disease, debauchery, and three serious wounds—from shot, shell, and Indian arrows—was unmistakable.

Houston used his war-damaged appearance to great effect, however. For the arrival in New Orleans he could have worn the elaborate uniform, befitting a commander in chief, that he had ordered back in October 1835 from a fashionable New Orleans tailor. Instead, he shamelessly, but dramatically, appeared on the deck of the *Flora* in tatters and bandages as if he had just staggered in from the battlefield.

For weeks Houston lay in pain at the mansion of William Christy, being attended to by the surgeons, one of them the same Dr. Kerr who had treated him in New Orleans in 1815. More than twenty splinters of bone were removed from the shattered ankle, but he rallied quickly.

There was an exhausting stream of visitors to Christy's house on Girod Street and letters, messages, gifts, and greetings arrived throughout each day. The most eagerly anticipated—and certainly the most welcome—was the message from the Old Chief at the White House. The president praised Houston's victory at San Jacinto as being far greater than his own at New Orleans. Jackson had only defended himself. Houston had attacked.

A surprise, but also welcome, visitor to Christy's was Houston's old associate from the Texas and Galveston Bay Land Company, John T. Mason. He advanced the hero $2,000 to act as an advocate and agent for the company's land business when he returned to Texas. Mason reported to the inveterate speculator Samuel Swartwout in New York that Houston's "power in Texas will be very great, & he has now a double motive in interest & friendship to give us."

———

Andrew Jackson was correct in his assessment of the relative importance of the two battles. San Jacinto was not only a remarkable feat of arms in which a small army from a province of some thirty-five thousand people had defeated a superior force from a nation of eight million. The battle altered the politics and geography of America in the most profound ways.

The role of the United States as the great power in the western hemisphere was solidified, and all or part of six states was carved out of the vast amount of territory that was soon gained from Mexico, nearly a million square miles.

Mexico's loss of its most valuable territories also led to social ramifications that have became a permanent part of Mexican-American relations. Much of the racism, xenophobia, poverty, and distrust between the two countries can be traced directly to the Texas Revolution.

———

The adulation and praise of Houston by the citizens of New Orleans and, in particular, the refugees were unstinting and had a profound effect in Texas. These Texas expatriates in New Orleans were the initial instrument for spreading the Houston message, and they became a strong and fiercely loyal power base for the man they embraced as their savior. His journey to New Orleans made Sam Houston a national hero.

The adulation of the public, however, did not keep Houston from chafing at his convalescence in New Orleans. The news from Texas was not good. Burnet's government had a tenuous control at best, and volunteers, many of them little better than outlaws, had continued to arrive by the thousands in the republic. A total breakdown of civil order appeared inevitable.

Houston decided he must return, and he left New Orleans the second week in June for his old stomping grounds of San Augustine and Nacogdoches. The former congressman, governor, and now conquering hero might have had a great deal of Texas land but he had no place he could call home. In fact, he had not had a permanent residence since he left his mother's house to join the army in 1813. But even there he only stopped off between stays with the Indians. Houston had been more or less a person with no fixed address since he was fifteen.

But there was no lack of hospitality. His old friend Sublett was at San Augustine, and the Sternes, where he had lived before, were still at Nacogdoches. He was welcome anywhere he chose to go. He could regale his hosts for hours with his stories, most of them about himself.

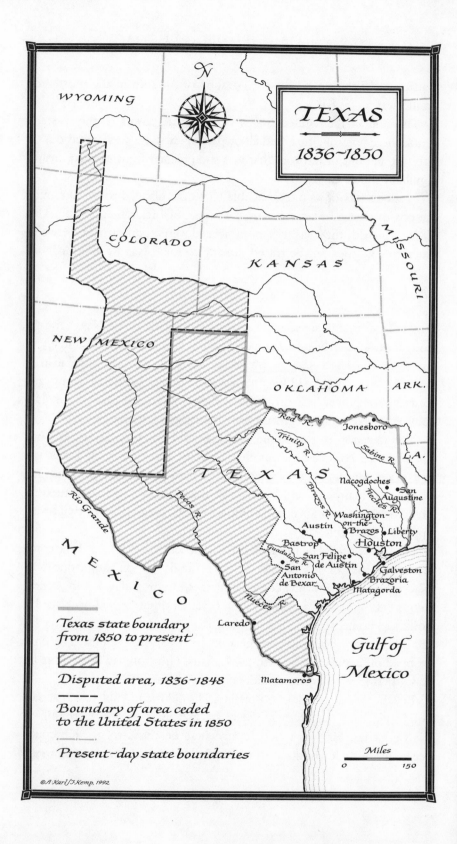

WYOMING

COLORADO

KANSAS

MISSOURI

N

TEXAS
1836~1850

NEW MEXICO

OKLAHOMA   ARK.

Red R.   Jonesboro

Trinity R.   Sabine R.   LA.

T E X A S

Nacogdoches   San
Augustine

Neches R.

Brazos R.   Washington-
on-the-
Pecos R.   Austin   Brazos   Liberty

Rio Grande   Bastrop   Houston

Guadalupe R.   San Felipe
de Austin

San
Antonio   Galveston
M E X I C O   de Bexar   Brazoria
Matagorda

Nueces R.

Laredo

Gulf of

Mexico

Matamoros

Texas state boundary
from 1850 to present

Disputed area, 1836~1848

Boundary of area ceded
to the United States in 1850

Present~day state boundaries

Miles
0   150

©A·Karl/J·Kemp, 1992

But he was always interesting. He had already had half a dozen careers and it seemed that there was nobody he had not met.

During one meal his fellow diners were amazed when Houston suddenly spewed hot soup all over them. He had been telling one of his amusing but long stories, and his hostess, fearing that his soup had become cold, quietly signaled to the servant to replace it with a fresh bowl. The replacement was not just hot, it was boiling. Houston did not notice the switch, and when he paused to help himself to some soup, he found his mouth on fire. He looked calmly around the table at the stained guests and the soiled tablecloth. "A damned fool would have swallowed that," he said.

Houston was still commander in chief of the army, and although Burnet and his cabinet were impatient with him for not returning to his command they would not dare replace him and stir up the army and the people.

His wound was by no means healed, but he did not want it known that he was still disabled, so he enjoined his friends to keep it quiet and give it out that he was detained in East Texas by business.

Burnet, finally exasperated by Houston's absence from the army, appointed Lamar as commander in chief. It was a characteristic action, which meant that Burnet ignored public opinion and political realities. The army, predictably, would have none of it and refused to recognize Lamar as commander. Burnet thus weakened himself even further and embarrassed the loyal Lamar.

Santa Anna signed both of the treaties at Velasco on May 14 and two weeks later boarded a Texas warship, the *Invincible*, for the voyage to Mexico. Unfortunately for the general and his staff, which included Almonte, an American steamboat with over a hundred new recruits and volunteers from the United States pulled into Velasco while the *Invincible* waited for favorable winds.

Under the command of Thomas Jefferson Green, who had been sent to the United States to raise volunteers, and Memucan Hunt, who had signed on in Mississippi, these wild adventurers had come to Texas looking for a war. But the war was over. The enemy, however, was sitting out in the harbor. The situation quickly deteriorated.

The late-arriving filibusterers ordered the Mexicans to be brought ashore. Fortunately, their escort, perhaps on Burnet's orders, landed them across the Brazos at Quintana—out of reach of the mob. Burnet placed a guard troop around them, but Santa Anna narrowly escaped lynching when four of the soldiers turned out to be survivors of the Goliad Massacre.

Clearly if Santa Anna and his party were not going to be allowed to leave the country they would have to be moved to a more secure location. As the dictator said, "The exaltation that caused my being brought ashore continued to increase to such an extent that every private felt himself called to assassinate me."

Burnet moved Santa Anna up the Brazos to Columbia, but he was still subject to harassment and threats. Finally, in July, he was transferred to Orozimbo, the plantation of Dr. James Phelps, twelve miles north of the town.

Santa Anna's predicament meant little to the Mexican government, which repudiated any agreements he might have made. But a larger issue was at stake, and Houston continued to insist that the dictator not be harmed.

"Santa Anna living and secured beyond all danger of escape (in the Eastern section of Texas as I first suggested) may be of incalculable advantage to Texas in her present crisis," he said. "In cool blood to offer up the living to the names of the departed, only finds an example in the religion and warfare of Savages." If Santa Anna were killed what would happen to the Texan prisoners being held in Mexico? And what of the North Americans who lived there?

"The affairs of Texas connected with Genl Santa Anna as President of the Republic of Mexico have become matters of consideration to which the attention of the United States has been called," Houston reminded the people, "and for Texas at this moment to proceed to extreme measures . . . would be treating that Government with high disrespect."

In other words, if the government of the United States perceived Texas as barbaric—a place that did not observe the rules of civilized warfare—there was no chance of diplomatic recognition, military and economic aid, and, of course, annexation.

But Houston did more than write what he believed. He paid a pointed tribute to Captain James A. Sylvester, who had led the group that captured Santa Anna the day after the battle—and had spared his life. The commander in chief saluted Sylvester for his gallantry in the battle, but it is clear from the timing of this accolade how important it was to Houston to impress on the army the necessity of Santa Anna's remaining alive.

All that summer Houston worried over the rumors that Texas was about to be invaded by Mexico—the "present crisis." The estimate that the Mexican force was somewhere between eight thousand and twelve thousand men was, of course, inflated, but Houston did believe that an invasion was imminent and he called for more recruitment of volunteers in the United States to come to the defense of Texas.

The rumors of invasion worried others as well, in particular General Edmund P. Gaines and the American troops at Fort Jesup. In late July, a detachment of the United States Army crossed the Sabine and occupied Nacogdoches, supposedly to provide protection for the Anglos against the Indians. It was interpreted, however, particularly in Mexico, that Gaines had acted to ensure Texan independence.

There was also another view. Gaines was in Texas to enforce the American claim that the boundary between the United States and Mexico was the Neches River and not the Sabine—which would have put a great chunk of Texas in the United States. Although Stephen Austin had advocated Gaines's incursion into Texas, he too became suspicious that more than protection was involved.

The invasion threat remained only that, a threat, and had evaporated by autumn. The issue of American troops in Texas was also resolved with Gaines's withdrawal to Fort Jesup.

Another invasion, which Houston thought had been put to rest, was given new life in the summer of 1836. Indeed, if proof is needed that the more idiotic a project is the longer it takes to kill it, the scheme to invade Mexico and capture Matamoros is a prime example.

While he was recuperating at Nacogdoches, Houston received word that Thomas Jefferson Green had proposed yet another Matamoros Expedition. He wrote to Rusk, who was now in command, and lectured him sternly on the foolishness of the army having anything to do with the plan. He repeated almost verbatim his earlier reasons for opposing the original Matamoros Expedition—except that he now had history on his side.

At a former period of our war it was a favorite project. I was then opposed to it. Its partial prosecution reduced Texas to the very verge of ruin. The slaughter of the Alamo, the massacre of Goliad and the desolation of the greater portion of Texas were the fruits of it; and I am frank in saying that I apprehend consequences no less disastrous.

Even if the invasion by Mexico never materialized, Texas still faced disaster, and Houston's enforced inactivity left him preoccupied with the crisis and what his role was to be. The thin-skinned, envious Burnet clearly was not capable of running a government, although his ancestry and connections certainly recommended him for high position. His father had been a member of the Continental Congress and a close friend of Lafayette, and a half brother was a distinguished senator from Ohio.

But David Burnet was orphaned when he was very small so he did not receive the rigorous indoctrination of the older children, although the brothers who raised him gave him a good education and every advantage. As one biographer observed, Burnet was done in because "his inflexible honesty and high sense of self-respect made it impossible for him to cultivate the arts of popularity." In short, he was the exact opposite of the man he hated with an intensity that never slackened for the rest of his life—Sam Houston.

Both Wharton and Austin were in Washington when news came of the great victory. They were of one mind, and their opinion was shared by Andrew Jackson, that Burnet's subsequent actions—or, more properly, inaction—had cost the new republic immediate recognition by the United States.

All that Washington needed were assurances from Texas that there was a de facto government in existence and that it could perform all the functions required of an independent nation. Burnet failed to do either and the opportunity was lost.

Indeed, the first communication that Austin received from the Burnet government was also the last—a message summoning him back to Texas. He arrived home on June 27, and he immediately called on Burnet to lecture him on the proper way to deal with his ministers abroad.

Austin also took time to remind his family of their responsibilities.

The great, like everyone else, cannot choose their relatives, and the Austins were having a difficult time with noblesse oblige. Austin's cousin Henry had sat out the war in New Orleans and now with the threat of invasion from Mexico his sister was about leave for there herself.

Austin wrote to Henry to return to Texas at once. As for Emily Austin, "I shall advise her to stay at home and abide the fate of Texas," he said. The Runaway Scrape had almost lost Texas, and if his own sister now left the country it might trigger another such reaction in the public. "I wish all of my name or connection to stay in Texas and abide the issue be it what it may," said Austin.

Burnet was ineffectual as a leader, but he realized that the sorry state of affairs had to end. By law, he could not succeed himself, which was out of the question anyway given his unpopularity. But it hardly mattered. David G. Burnet had become thoroughly sick of the whole business of government. He set elections for September 5. The republic would elect a president and also vote on the Constitution and annexation by the United States.

Austin was an obvious candidate, of course, and in late July he announced he would run, but for one reason only—to ensure the annexation of Texas to the United States. His stern enjoinder to his relatives to behave like Austins was issued a full month before his announcement, but he no doubt was already considering the presidency.

Henry Smith, who always enjoyed a good brawl, also decided that he wanted another go at running the country. His brief, combative tenure as provisional governor had only whetted his appetite for ruling.

Houston had spent the summer playing Coriolanus, but he finally gave in to the urging of his supporters and only eleven days before the election he too announced his candidacy.

"You will learn that I have yielded to the wishes of my friends in allowing my name to be run for President," he wrote to a friend. "The crisis requires it or I would not have yielded. Duty, I hope, will not always require this sacrifice of my repose and quiet."

The election was really decided the moment the victor of San Jacinto announced. But the niceties had to be observed, and on Monday, September 5, 1836, Sam Houston became the first popularly elected president of the Republic of Texas.

There were 6,449 Texans who voted that day and 5,119 voted for Sam Houston—79 percent of the total. Smith received 743 votes and

Austin a disappointing 587. There was only one small cloud on the horizon, but it would grow and cast a considerable shadow. Mirabeau Buonaparte Lamar was elected vice-president.

The electorate approved the Constitution drawn up at Washington on the Brazos in March, but they denied the Congress authority to amend it. The vote for annexation to the United States was almost unanimous.

The inauguration was to be the second Monday in December, as set out in the Constitution, but Burnet suddenly resigned on October 22 and Houston was inaugurated that afternoon at four o'clock. Burnet's action was praised by many as a selfless, even graceful act inspired by his realization that the crisis was indeed acute. A less charitable interpretation was that Vice-President Lorenzo de Zavala, by resigning on October 21, had forced Burnet unwillingly to follow suit. Lamar, of course, insisted that it was a Houston-engineered power grab for early control of the government.

Whatever the reasons for Burnet's act, the crisis demanded it, to borrow Houston's felicitous phrase. The republic was close to disintegration and six weeks of further paralysis could have been fatal.

———

Houston took the oath of office in Columbia, where the government had moved in September. For the ceremony both houses of the First Congress, which comprised forty-three men, crowded into the small chamber of the lower house. William Christy of New Orleans, the great benefactor of the revolution, was a special guest. The oath of office was administered by the Speaker of the House, Ira Ingram.

Like Napoleon, who took the crown from the pope's hands and crowned himself, Houston took the oath of office *as* president of the republic—not as Sam Houston being sworn in as president. "I, Sam Houston, President of the Republic of Texas, do solemnly swear that I will execute the duties of my office . . . ," he said.

Since he had been informed scarcely four hours before that he was to be sworn in as president that very day, Houston could not give his inaugural address the attention he most certainly would have. Speaking more or less extemporaneously, and briefly, he nevertheless managed an almost spontaneous eloquence.

As is required on all such occasions, he first professed the expected false modesty. "I have never been emulous of the civic wreath—when merited it crowns a happy destiny," he said. He then quietly began to deal with the immediate problems that concerned him most. First was the matter of the Indians—whose cause he always made his own—and a clear reference to the treaty that he had negotiated in February.

> Treaties of peace and amity, and the maintenance of good faith with the Indians, present themselves to my mind as the most rational grounds on which to obtain their friendship. Let us abstain on our part from aggressions, establish commerce with the different tribes, supply their useful and necessary wants, maintain even-handed justice with them, and natural reason will teach them the utility of our friendship.

Next he praised the volunteers from the United States who had come to the aid of Texas—a political but sincere gesture—and he reminded his listeners that the danger from Mexico was still real. As for annexation, the people of Texas had, on September 5, ringingly endorsed that course.

> They have with a unanimity unparalleled, declared that they will be reunited to the great Republican family of the North. . . . We are cheered by the hope that they will receive us to a participancy of their civil, political, and religious rights, and hail us welcome into the great family of freemen.

Houston then dramatically drew from its scabbard the sword he had worn at San Jacinto and held it before him with both hands. Every eye in the room followed the brilliant steel blade. The crowded room became silent. Houston himself was so overcome that he continued only with difficulty.

> It now, Sir, becomes my duty to make a presentation of this sword—this emblem of my past office! I have worn it with some humble pretensions in defence of my country; and should the danger of my country again call for my services, I expect to resume it, and respond to that call, if needful, with my blood and life.

The man of war had turned himself into a man of peace. His supporters were deeply moved and applauded vigorously. His detractors had seen no good in his election and this dramatic action appeared as just another of Houston's calculated displays, no matter how well timed and effective it was. They did not understand that Houston used this melodramatic gesture, this stratagem straight out of antiquity, to help turn the people away from war.

He had recently witnessed the carnage of war and the mindless emotions it sometimes inspires, and it was now time to turn to peaceful pursuits. Texas should be strong and watchful, but it should commit itself only to defense.

————

The republic Burnet handed over to Houston was bankrupt—if that term can be applied to an enterprise that had little money to begin with—war damaged, almost paralyzed by invasion threats, and was close to anarchy. The public debt was $500,000. The army was running on a two days' supply of food. And two of the four vessels of the Texas Navy were impounded in New York because there was no money to pay their repair and outfitting bills. Little wonder Burnet stepped aside early and retired, at least for awhile, to his farm near Lynchburg.

Houston's first appointments signaled that his was to be a government of amity and conciliation. His two opponents in the election were immediately brought into the administration, Austin as secretary of state and Smith as secretary of the treasury. However, he really had no great choice in the men he appointed, as he admitted. There were talented men in Texas, to be sure, and the number was out of proportion to the population. But the population in 1836 was minuscule—only about thirty-five thousand men, women, children, and slaves.

————

There was one thing Houston knew he had to do immediately: resolve the crisis caused by Santa Anna's continued presence in the country. He and the other Mexican prisoners were an increasing liability. They were not only in perpetual danger of being murdered, but the government did not have the funds to provide for even their most minimal needs.

Lamar and the army continually pressed for Santa Anna's execution, which Houston and other right-thinking men knew would destroy any hope of recognition by the United States or, indeed, any other power. If there was any doubt about this, Jackson himself communicated his feelings to Houston in the strongest terms. "Nothing *now* could tarnish the character of Texas more than such an act at this late period," said the president on September 4.

The decision was finally up to the Senate, and Houston personally set about to convince them, in secret meetings, that it was vital to the future of Texas that Santa Anna be released and allowed to travel to the United States to meet with Jackson.

In Washington, Santa Anna could reiterate his support of Texas independence—directly to the president and members of the Congress. Although Mexico would no longer be held accountable for anything Santa Anna said, he would have considerable influence when he returned home. And there was hardly anyone with a feel for politics who did not believe that Santa Anna's return to power was inevitable. Even if he did not take over the government, his very presence would so destabilize Mexico that any further adventure in Texas would be impossible.

Houston prevailed and it was agreed that Santa Anna would be freed. The president of the republic rode the twelve miles out to the farmhouse prison at Orozimbo, carrying a letter of introduction to Andrew Jackson for Santa Anna and also a gift—a great woolen cloak for the journey to the United States. Houston knew that the Mexican would suffer in the northern winter.

Santa Anna left Orozimbo under cover of darkness on Sunday, November 20, 1836. His escort included George W. Hockley, William H. Patton, Barnard E. Bee, and Almonte. They traveled overland to the Mississippi, where they boarded the steamboat *Tennessee* for the trip upriver. The weather turned out to be unusually severe. Above Louisville the Ohio was blocked by ice and the vessel had to turn back.

On Christmas Eve the party set out in hired carriages for Washington. They arrived in the capital on Tuesday evening January 17, after "a most fatiguing and unpleasant ride—the weather was uncommonly inclement and bore hard upon Genl. Santa Anna," Hockley said.

The dictator was lodged at a Mrs. Ulrick's opposite the State Department. Patton stayed with him in a small adjoining room. The others put up at Gadsby's. Santa Anna and Patton had developed racking coughs on the journey and in their small suite "they bark a duet together," as Santa Anna said.

Santa Anna "never looks from the window, (the streets are covered with snow)—never ventures out,—or returns home, but he is grateful to *Sam* Houston—such is the name he has given to the cloak with which you presented him," reported Hockley.

The man who not even a year before had been reviled by the people of the United States as a tyrant and murderer was now the object of ghoulish curiosity. He was feted and made much of by official Washington. The culmination of his visit was a dinner given by the president of the United States, with the full cabinet, on January 26.

The Old Chief chuckled over Houston's letter of introduction. "The distinction, and character of Genl Santa Anna, will supersede the necessity of my saying anything in his favor, so far as his reputation is a portion of the history of mankind!" wrote Houston.

Santa Anna had also written to Jackson in July, at Austin's suggestion, but Jackson made it clear then and he made it clear in Washington that the United States could not negotiate with him since he no longer headed the government of Mexico.

Nobody was fooling anybody, however, and the president told him that the United States would pay three and half million dollars for Texas. Santa Anna later said that Jackson had offered to pay six million pesos if Mexico would recognize the independence of Texas, but that he had replied that only the Mexican congress could decide that question.

In addition to being lionized, Santa Anna sat for his portrait with the Jackson court painter, Ralph E. W. Earle. True to form he insisted on going to Earle's White House studio. That way it would appear to the public as if he were calling on the president regularly.

Houston was almost as vain about his picture as he was about his clothing, and he had instructed Hockley to have Earle do a portrait of him. Hockley informed the victor of San Jacinto that he would have to wait until the painting of the Napoleon of the West was finished. Houston had to make do with a portrait that William Christy had commissioned of him. He sent Sam fifty copies, but the original remained on Christy's mantel in New Orleans.

Everyone took to Santa Anna. Even the hardheaded William Lewis admitted to being charmed by his manners, intelligence, and good looks. But Washington eventually tired of its exotic visitor, and Jackson sent him home—in style, however. The president ordered up a battleship and Santa Anna sailed away. He landed at Vera Cruz on February 21, 1837.

Santa Anna was not received in Mexico as he expected he would be, and he retired to his farm at Manga de Clavo. He busied himself for the next few weeks drafting his *Manifesto,* which explained all the disasters as the fault of others, in particular General Vicente Filisola. His betrayal in Texas had disillusioned him about political life and he wanted no more of it, he said. "But," he asked, "how does one escape one's destiny? And what a fatal destiny and what bitter days to come!"

Along with the letter of introduction for Santa Anna, President Houston also sent a more personal letter to Jackson. He was candid with his old mentor. Texas, he wrote, was close to collapse. "My great desire is that our country Texas shall be annexed to the United States," he said forthrightly, but added that it must be "on a footing of Justice and reciprocity to the parties."

It was being bruited about in the new republic that perhaps Texas should remain an independent nation. They had won the war. Could they not also maintain their independence? Houston was disturbed and he felt obliged to confide in Jackson. "I am free to say *to you* that we cannot do it," he said. "I look to you as the friend and patron of my youth and the benefactor of mankind to interpose in our behalf and save us."

In these two letters, written the same day to the same man, Houston revealed those traits that raised him so far above the ordinary. Benevolence toward a defeated enemy. Bravery. Political acumen. A profound patriotism. Loyalty and respect for an old friend and ally. And an ironic sense of humor mixed with wit.

Houston's letter bore out what Jackson's secret agent to Texas, Henry R. Morfit, had reported back to the chief. Texas could not defend itself from another massive attack from Mexico. But political realities dictated a slow course, no matter that the president still burned to possess Texas.

Nevertheless Jackson realized that he must heed his adviser Amos Kendall, who bluntly told him that "as guardians of the peace and interests of the United States we are not permitted to go to war through philanthropy or a design to conquer other nations for their own good."

Kendall's advice is appropriate for all presidents at all times, but it was particularly so during this troublesome period. Jackson's enemies remained convinced that the Texas Revolution was nothing but a plot hatched with Houston to wrest Texas from Mexico. The abolitionists saw annexation as only another barefaced attempt to extend slavery into new territories.

And when General Gaines crossed the Sabine, supposedly to protect the settlers against the Indians, the opponents of expansion and annexation interpreted it as a repeat of Jackson's own high-handedness twenty years before in Florida, which it was.

But that was then. Jackson was still capable of the old fire, but he was by and large more equable, more even tempered, and more conscious of his place in history now that he was seventy years old.

At The Hermitage, in the summer of 1836, Old Hickory had decided on the proper course. He could not alienate England or France by appearing to seize part of Mexico. At the same time, both the abolitionists and the slaveocracy must be kept at bay until after the presidential election. Nothing must be allowed to endanger the candidacy of his handpicked successor, Martin Van Buren.

———

Houston's choice as minister plenipotentiary to the United States was William H. Wharton. He was given carte blanche to reach any agreement that he felt could be beneficial to Texas—diplomatic recognition, trade, confederation, alliances, or boundaries—with annexation at the top of the list. Any treaty had to be ratified by the Texas Senate, of course, but seldom has a minister enjoyed such broad powers.

Wharton was the right man for the job certainly. True, he was the leader of the war party in the early days of the revolution, but he and Stephen Austin had reconciled their differences while they were serving as commissioners to the United States and, indeed, had become close friends. The secretary of state now spent days with Wharton discussing his embassy to the United States.

Wharton was later joined by Memucan Hunt, filibusterer turned diplomat, and they represented their country brilliantly, lobbying the Congress and Old Hickory relentlessly. When Jackson mentioned the possibility of outright purchase by the United States or a Mexican-American treaty guaranteeing Texan independence, Wharton proudly rejected both. Texas already had its independence, he reminded the president. His country sought only recognition—and eventual annexation—by the United States.

On George Washington's birthday, 1837, the Texas ministers were invited to the White House. The centerpiece at the reception was a giant cheese that had been sent to the president by the citizens of Genesee County, New York. Jackson, ever the politician, made much of this homely gift from simple farmers.

When he learned that an officer from the Texas Navy was at the reception, he personally cut off a slice of cheese and had it put in a metal box to be carried to his friend Houston. Francis P. Wright arrived in Galveston with the presidential cheese on May 24.

Jackson limited himself to cheese paring for Texas, however. He would not be pushed into recognition of its independence. That must come through the Congress. Although there was a strong and organized opposition, the majority of the country was in favor of recognition of Texas. This was also true of most members of Congress—John Quincy Adams being the most notable exception.

The president went to work on the leadership and the individual members. The House voted favorably on February 28. The Senate was more of a problem, but on March 1 it too recommended recognition— by a margin of only four votes, 23 to 19. Jackson immediately sent Alcée La Branche's name to the Senate for confirmation as chargé d'affaires to Texas.

On Friday evening, March 3, 1837, William Lewis hurried through Washington to round up Wharton and Hunt and bring them to the White House—to celebrate with the president and the president-elect the Senate's confirmation of La Branche. Lewis roused the indisposed Wharton from a sound sleep and the two went to collect Hunt, who was not at home and therefore missed the great event.

A jubilant Jackson, Wharton, and Lewis raised their glasses in a toast. Van Buren joined them but with considerably less enthusiasm. He still had to deal with this after he was sworn in the next day. The Little Magician's reticence did not dampen the spirits of the occasion. Texas was recognized.

The narrow vote in the Senate, however, signaled that annexation was going to be a long and difficult battle, but for now Old Hickory exulted over this last official act of his administration. A dream of many years had at least been partially fulfilled and there was the added joy of one last blow at Adams before he left for retirement at The Hermitage.

The man who had labored so long and hard for recognition did not see it come to pass. Stephen F. Austin had died on a pallet on the floor of his two-room cabin at Columbia on December 27, 1836. His fragile health weakened by malaria, he had contracted pneumonia.

As he lay dying, Austin dreamed that the United States had recognized the independence of Texas. About half past noon he awoke and said, "Texas recognized. Archer told me so. Did you see it in the papers?" He then peacefully died. He was forty-three years old.

Houston's differences with Austin had been more of style than goals. He was genuinely grieved by the death of his fellow statesman. "The Father of Texas is no more!" he announced to the nation. "The first pioneer of the wilderness has departed." He ordered all army installations and navy ships to fire a twenty-three gun salute, one for each county in Texas, with intervals of five minutes between each firing. The *Yellow Stone* was dispatched to take Austin's body down the Brazos for burial near his sister Emily Austin Perry's plantation at Peach Point.

The salute and the mourning were in order. No other Texan did as much as Austin to make a nation. But this gentle and great man has never seized the popular imagination. It is the nature of people to look to larger-than-life characters instead. As Santa Anna's troops advanced across Texas and the country seemed to be coming apart, Austin was dismayed by the actions of his Texans, but he never despaired and he never abandoned them. "No man in Texas has yet taken a step which he may not retrace with honor," he said.

His was ever the voice of calm. "Come. Let us reason together," said Stephen Austin. That admonition might well have served as his epitaph.

In Washington, William Wharton's task was finished. He had labored diligently for his country and he could expect to return to a hero's welcome. He said good-bye to Hunt and sailed for home. At New Orleans he transferred to the *Independence* for the final leg of the journey.

Within sight of the landing at Velasco, two Mexican warships appeared. The crowd that had gathered to welcome the *Independence* watched as the Texas vessel tried to fight off the attackers. The battle went on for four hours, but the outgunned *Independence* finally had to surrender. Wharton spent the next year in prison at Matamoros.

Hunt's journey home was much less eventful, and he was able to return to Washington in June. The prospects for annexation had improved. Van Buren had barely carried the South in 1836, and he needed all the southern support he could muster.

The president invited Hunt to dine with him at the White House a full week before the Texas minister was officially scheduled to submit his credentials. If Texas were annexed, Hunt told the president, he could count on the support of the leading men of the state in his bid for reelection in 1840.

There was also talk in Washington of Houston running for vice-president with Van Buren in 1840. Hunt was opposed. He did not want Sam to run for a second-place office. Houston should certainly support Van Buren in the next election but then run on his own for president in 1844. Hunt was certain that Houston had only to be prudent and the presidency was his. These plans, of course, depended on annexation by the United States.

Hunt also proposed, only half in jest, that Houston send a secret agent to Washington with 100,000 acres of Texas land—to be disposed of on easy terms to "members of Congress and others of influence." Annexation would then be assured.

———

Recognition by the United States was, of course, the high point of Houston's first presidential administration, but there were other almost equally important issues and successes. His experience in Congress and the Tennessee state house during the Monroe, Adams, and Jackson administrations proved invaluable in organizing a national government for Texas.

For one thing he did not hesitate to exert the power of the executive branch. It was vital to set an example for successive administrations regarding the role of the executive vis-à-vis the Congress and the judiciary. The last presented relatively few problems. Houston for some time had understood that "a well organized judiciary, composed of enlightened and honest members, is the palladium of civil liberty."

The House and Senate were another matter entirely, but Houston quickly served notice that he would brook no interference from the Congress in the constitutional duties of the president. He was clearly determined to establish the primacy of the executive. Andrew Jackson would have been proud and no doubt was.

In one week in December 1836 he sent to Congress a brilliant series of veto messages filled with legal insight, knowledge of the Constitution, and often dripping with sarcasm. He was surrounded by dangerous amateurs and he did not bother to hide his scorn.

Houston vetoed the bill establishing a Post Office Department because the postmaster general was to be elected by both houses of Congress instead of appointed by the president. The Congress was clearly up to mischief, setting up an independent department to be headed by someone of their own choosing.

The bill was "unsafe to the interests of the country," he wrote in his message, and "an encroachment on his rights, and a prostitution of the powers of the senate." Houston's veto was sustained and five days later he nominated Robert Barr as postmaster general. Barr was then confirmed by the Senate as the Constitution provided.

But the lawmakers were not always so easily bested. Houston was also determined that the Senate ratify the treaty that he and the other commissioners had negotiated with the Cherokees in February. The Indians had kept their part of the bargain and remained neutral in the war, and Houston now called on the people of Texas to honor their word.

The arguments made in favor of negotiating with the Indians the previous spring were still valid. Texas was again faced with the possibility of an invasion and there were rumors that the Mexicans were again stirring up the Indians. It was in the best interest of the republic to have them as friends. He reminded the Senate that the Indians were not being given the land but only its use. Texas "does not part with the right of soil, which is in this Government."

Nevertheless, the Senate tabled the treaty on December 29, 1836. Houston was too perceptive not to realize that the treaty was doomed but he pressed on. The following summer he summoned Chief Bowl and the leaders of other tribes to Nacogdoches. In a rather touching letter to his old friend he said, "I want you to bring in with you the copy of the Treaty which I last sent to you. Don't forget to bring it. It has Ribbons and a seal on it."

In his annual message to Congress, in the fall of 1837, Houston argued that the Indians living in the midst of the white settlements might be persuaded to move if land were appropriated for them farther west. Even this tack did not work. In December 1837, the Senate declared all provisions of the treaty of February 23, 1836, null and void.

Another important confrontation with Congress came over Houston's veto of the General Land Office Bill. Any bill should, he said, "be full, clear, and embrace the whole subject; and also be equal in its operation. I cannot believe that the bill now before me, is of this character."

He urged the Congress to examine the issue more carefully and defer the question until the next session. There was no reason for haste and some attempt should be made to reconcile all the previous, present, and overlapping land claims, in particular the land bounties paid to the army.

Here Houston's obligations to his eastern friends who had speculated in hundreds of thousands of acres of Texas land possibly influenced his position. The issue certainly cannot be ignored, since not six months before he had been paid a $2,000 retainer to ensure his cooperation. In any event, his veto was overridden the very next day, December 22, 1836. The General Land Office, under John P. Borden's direction, opened on October 1, 1837.

————

But as the new year began Sam was in an expansive mood, and why not? He had been victorious in battle and in politics. Only one thing remained. On January 1, 1837, he sent New Year's greetings to Anna Raguet in Nacogdoches. "I did intend to send you a few stanzas for criticism," he said, "but as it would be taking liberty with the brain of a friend, I feel some hesitancy." He overcame his shyness, however, and enclosed the poem.

MARCH, CHIEFTAIN

March, Chieftain, to the battle fly
And wear thy falcon on thy thigh
To meet a ruthless enemy
And strike for victory!

The day will come when it shall be
Thy fate to meet the enemy
And see the base invader flee
From Anglo-Saxon chivalry.

This armor on thy person placed
Was made to shield a warrior's breast
Who guards the weak that are oppressed,
His due from chivalry!

When in the battle van you move
Thy thoughts in other scenes may rove
Nor meet a corresponding love
Of her who arms thee now.

But still the heart must e'er admire
The deeds that flash from valor's fire
To blast the base invader's ire.
Such deeds shall be adorned.

Adieu! Nor cease the hero's toil
While foes pollute our sacred soil
Go, mingle in the deathly broil
And make a nation free!

Lady, thy mandate I'll obey
And make it good in mortal fray
Or ne'er survive the battle day
To greet thy smile again.

Should I return from well-fought fields
I'll bring again thy warrior's shield
And at thy feet I'll proudly yield
The laurels won for thee.

Houston then left to deal with a crisis in the army at Camp Independence on the Lavaca, twenty-five miles east of Victoria. The new commander, the firebrand brigadier general Felix Huston, was out of control. He had ordered Juan Seguin, the commander at Bexar, to raze the city, which he felt could not be defended, and to move all the inhabitants to the east. And of course, he was advocating—once more—an expedition against Matamoros, that Jerusalem of all Texan Crusaders.

The president quickly saw that Huston must be replaced and on January 31 he appointed Albert Sidney Johnston commander of the army. Huston not only refused to surrender his command to Johnston but challenged him to a duel. A week later Johnston was seriously wounded in their showdown at Camp Independence and could not assume the command.

The army was no longer a body that defended the citizenry. It had become their enemy, seizing their horses, cattle, and supplies at will. Civilian complaints poured into the capital. John W. Smith pleaded from Bexar for Houston to stop Seguin's men from pillaging the countryside. Seguin had requisitioned all the horses and slaughtered hundreds of cattle to feed his men.

The president had to act. He had a large army on his hands—over seventeen hundred men—but there was no money to support it, there was no war, and no invasion had materialized. Worse, at least 500 of the men had no weapons.

Algernon S. Thruston, the new quartermaster general, was dispatched to New Orleans to arrange for supplies but he had little success. He did, however, have news of the old schemer Anthony Butler who was passing through the city on his way to take up residence in Texas. True to form, Butler's intelligence was worthless. He told Thruston that Anastacio Bustamente, Santa Anna's chief rival, would "prostrate Santa Anna." Said Thruston, "If he does I'll give my head for a football."

Butler also predicted that Mexico intended to invade Texas and reoccupy and fortify Bexar, Goliad, and Copano. Thruston was equally blunt. "I would not credit the Angel Gabriel were he to tell me that within nine months Texas would be invaded."

The quartermaster general did not confine himself to military and political matters, however. But his more personal news was not as welcome.

"I on yesterday visited Miss R[aguet]," he said. "She is a clever and a pretty lady but I think overrated. . . . forget her sir She will not suit you. . . . She seemed to claim a sort of presumption. Twill not do."

Butler's prognostications, however flimsy their foundation, received wide circulation and volunteers continued to pour into Texas. Angrily, Houston wrote to the Texas agent in New Orleans, Thomas Toby, that no more volunteers were needed. "We do not want naked men nor men unarmed nor starving," he said. The army was difficult enough now to deal with.

The situation further deteriorated when Colonel Henry Teal was murdered in his tent at Camp Independence on May 5. That very day he had written to the war department, "We have not one mouthful of bread stuffs nor haven't had for ten days."

Beyond the suffering of his own army, the president also tried to respond to the pleas of the Mexican prisoners still being held at Velasco. By now they were in desperate want and they could do nothing but appeal directly to the president of Texas. Remarkably their petition got through to Houston, and he had clothing and food sent to the poor wretches. His act of compassion did not set well with the Texans, who were in almost as bad shape as their prisoners.

Bad shape or not, Felix Huston, still nominally in command of the army, lobbied the Congress on behalf of his plan to gather a force of several thousand men for an invasion of Mexico. The president had now had enough. If he could not get rid of his commander, he could get rid of his army.

He dispatched the secretary of war in the middle of the night on May 19 to the rebellious army with orders to the commanders to furlough all but six hundred men, until further notice. The army was divided up into several sections and marched to posts on the coast, where they were furloughed.

After writing the orders for the dissolution of the army, Houston calmly sat down and wrote to Anna Raguet. "It is past midnight," he said. "The toils of the day have passed by, and all the recollections of friendship and affection recur." He was playing Benedick to Anna's Beatrice. He had heard that there was to be a wedding. "I cou'd play the part of a God Father, you know," he said, "and this among other matters wou'd eke out a scanty tradition, and tell to other times that I had once existed." Then he slyly added, "You know that men love fame!"

He may or may not have spent two and a half hours on the letter but he said, "It is half past two in the morning, and this is Sunday! Shou'd I remain longer from repose, I cou'd not look well at church tomorrow."

By the time the news of Houston's plan to disband the army got back to the capital, the deed had long since been done. The large army was no more and would never be reconstituted. He later confided to Anna Raguet, "We will never have another *Volunteer Army.*" Congress was in a dither, but could do nothing. Houston had bet on the traditional fear of a large standing army and gotten away with it. "Economy is the mother of comfort and safety," he said by way of explanation.

The legislators were not through with the president, however, and they thought they had found a way to deal with some of their frustrations. They passed a resolution instructing him to send the only two available Texas warships, the *Invincible* and the *Brutus,* to Brazos Santiago, near Matamoros, to force the release of the schooner *Independence.*

In a stinging veto message on May 31, Houston again lectured the Congress on the separation of powers. He also reminded them of the superior firepower of the Mexican Navy and what would happen to Texas if the two ships, which were the only means to defend the coast, were captured or sunk. Congress and the secretary of the navy backed down and Felix Huston, now the former commanding general of the army, left Texas.

But after the furloughing of the army, the president's problems with the military were by no means ended. New animosities were aroused. Many Texans did not want to be told the truth, just as later many Southerners did not want to be told the truth. It was a short step from "One Texan can whip ten Mexicans" to "One Southerner can whip ten Yankees." A conceit soon became dogma.

Houston was faced with mutinies at both Galveston and Velasco, and there was justified fear of a conspiracy to overthrow the government and perhaps even an attempt on Houston's life.

The anti-Houston faction in Texas was still led by Burnet and Lamar, but they, for the moment at least, left the dirty work to Colonel Robert M. Coleman and Houston's former secretary, Algernon P. Thompson. Their scurrilous pamphlet *Houston Displayed or Who Won the Battle of San Jacinto,* which accused Houston of cowardice and betrayal, was printed at Velasco on the press of the Velasco *Herald* in the spring of 1837.

Coleman was rather an unsavory character whose depredations against the Indians as head of his own regiment of rangers had seriously aggravated their hostile attitude toward the white settlers. One of Houston's negotiators with the Indians said that if Coleman could be shot and the Indians could witness it their grievances would be less severe. Coleman's seditious career was soon ended, however. On July 1, he drowned while swimming in the Brazos near Velasco.

Secretary of State Robert Irion was one of those most concerned about Houston's safety and he wrote to him on July 2 of his fears that "the hand of an assassin will be brought into requisition." He was pleased when the president left the capital for the friendlier atmosphere of Nacogdoches that summer. As for Houston, he was always happy to be on the road. "Confinement always impairs my health and exercise never fails to restore it," he said.

————

Sam Houston, as president of a nation, had the power finally to resolve a problem that had been hanging over his head since 1829—a divorce from Eliza Allen. To that end, he wrote to Judge Shelby Corzine, an old friend who had also been wounded at Horseshoe Bend. Houston had appointed Corzine judge of the First Judicial District, which automatically made him a member of the Texas Supreme Court.

William McFarland, the alcalde who had received the original petition in 1833, had also been elevated by the president. He was now chief justice of San Augustine County. President Houston was thus assured a friendly hearing.

Houston was represented by W. G. Anderson of Nacogdoches. When the new petition was heard in April, it was suggested that the proper course was to take no action until the court could correspond with Eliza Allen Houston in Tennessee. The judge sustained Anderson when he objected to any delay and the court appointed a local attorney to represent Mrs. Houston. The hearing proceeded. In just a few minutes Sam Houston was single again.

Eliza Allen, who had been, at least in name, first lady of Texas since the previous October, doubtless was also in favor of finally putting an end to the awkward relationship. It had been eight years since she had last seen Sam. However, neither she nor her family could have approved of the manner in which the divorce had been engineered. But, true to her nature, she accepted it with equanimity, at least outwardly, when sometime that summer she was informed that she was a divorced woman. She was twenty-seven years old.

During this first year, Houston often reflected on the untimely death of Austin. If ever any country needed a few honest men it was Texas. "Texas seems to be subject of Robbery and sport," he wrote to Thruston whom he had charged to get a full accounting from the agents in New Orleans. "I have lost all confidence in them," said Houston.

Houston had already heard from his private secretary, John Ricord, who visited New Orleans in January. "I have ascertained," said Ricord, "that the Agent is personally little esteemed in New Orleans, where many look with suspicion upon the movements of men who belong to the sect of Jews." Houston's view of agents, however, was based on the general avarice affecting men of every persuasion.

Thruston collected much of the outstanding land scrip that had been entrusted to the agents for sale, but records were so spotty that it was impossible to get a true picture of what sales had been. When Thruston had to press Toby over and over for an accounting, the agent huffily said that he was not answerable even to the president of Texas.

No one matched the venality and avarice of the men in high places better than S. Rhodes Fisher, the secretary of the navy. However, any one of the land agents or registrars or the hundreds of people who applied for those jobs—with their promise of quick graft—might serve just as well.

In January 1837 Fisher wrote to Thomas Toby. "I feel disposed to make a proposition to you which may result in a very handsome profit." Tobacco was selling for the huge sum of $150 a bale in Mexico and Fisher suggested that they transport a shipment from Texas through the Mexican blockade. They would sell some for cash, but the preferred payment would be in horses and mules.

Fisher would then sell the horses and mules to the Texas government, which was so desperately in need of them. The speculators could even afford to accept the heavily discounted government paper because their profits would be so high.

Toby was told not to worry about the shipment getting through. "I shall have a government vessel on the coast, watching the movements of the enemy so that the Tobacco vessel will have nothing to fear from Mexican cruisers," promised the secretary of the navy.

But Fisher had more in mind than smuggling and profiteering. In June, he asked to be furloughed and Houston granted his request. Henry Smith was appointed acting secretary, but Fisher continued to interfere in the running of the department. The president wrote to Fisher to inform him that a leave of absence or a furlough from service meant that he had no more power than an enlisted man. Fisher responded that he was withdrawing the request for furlough, but he still did not return to duty.

Smith and Houston were soon astounded to receive a message that Fisher was aboard the *Invincible* cruising the coastline looking for prizes. The secretary turned smuggler had now turned privateer, but he assured Smith that he was not interfering in any way with the command of the vessel.

The rest of the message was even more alarming. The *Invincible* had captured a British schooner, the *Eliza Russell,* and they were now going to try and free Wharton from his prison at Matamoros. Houston was appalled. This fool had not only created an international incident by capturing a British vessel but he had the temerity to go against the president's express orders not to attempt a rescue at Matamoros. Houston ordered the British vessel released immediately to avert a crisis with the British government.

In early September, Fisher returned from his "voyage" and blithely reported for duty. But Houston had finally had enough of Fisher's troublemaking and suspended him.

The anti-Houston faction in the Senate refused to recognize that the president had such authority and demanded that Houston reinstate the secretary. A special commission was appointed to call on Houston, whose actions were labeled "disrespectful dictatorial and evincive of a disposition on the part of the Executive to annihilate those coordinate powers conferred upon the Senate by the Constitution."

Houston was not intimidated. The delegation complained that they were greeted with "unheeded abuse." Fisher himself wrote an insulting letter to Houston in which he made reference to "illness and mental aberration" and "peculiar diseases." Houston's answer was so dripping with scorn that even Fisher must have been shocked. "That you ever were connected with the Cabinet has to be deplored," said Houston. "My motives for the selection are the only apology, which I can offer for it to my country. I believed you capable and thought you honest."

The Senate held hearings on the matter. Houston refused to appear, but his private secretary, Alexander Henriques, testified on November 16. Henriques was more than just an official stenographer, however. He was the president's loyal confidant. During the Fisher controversy one of the principals asked him not to tell Houston what he had said. It was off the record. Henriques, putting *"duty before decency,"* immediately passed on the information to his chief.

Henriques answered the criticism that Houston had delayed in responding to Fisher's appeal because he was too ill to write. The old wound from Horseshoe Bend had reopened and for six weeks Houston was confined. He had declined to dictate his reply because he felt the secretary of the navy deserved a completely confidential letter and one in his own hand. Eventually, however, he had to give in and let Henriques take down the letter.

With Houston under scrutiny, the anti-Houstonites decided to press the attack. Houston was requested to forward any treaties he may have made with the Indians and the relevant documents. The president declined to turn over his own papers on the grounds that they were privileged. Instead he sent a twenty-page message outlining his charges against the deposed secretary of the navy.

In the end, the Fisher controversy resulted in another victory in his ongoing war to establish presidential authority. On November 28, the Senate "on the grounds of harmony and expediency advise and consent to the removal" of S. Rhodes Fisher. However, in a fine example of legislative waffling and continued sniping, the statement also said that "the President has not adduced sufficient evidence that proves him guilty of dishonorable conduct."

———

During the third week in April 1837, the government had moved from Columbia to the new town of Houston, a few miles up Buffalo Bayou from the San Jacinto battlefield and near the charred ruins of Harrisburg. The president was no doubt gratified by the name of the new capital, but the living conditions were only marginally better than at Columbia. The ratty collection of tents and log cabins was so unprepossessing that the first boatload of government officials went right by the town without seeing it and had to back up. By the end of the year, the population had grown to over twelve hundred.

One of the new residents was Pamela Mann. After the Runaway Scrape, she decided to settle in the Harrisburg area. She abandoned farm life, and the famous oxen, when the new capital was founded. Society beckoned. She opened a hotel on the northeast corner of Congress and Milam streets. Considering the hostess, the Mansion House quickly acquired a notorious reputation for its drinkers, carousers, and brawlers. But things rarely got so out of hand that Mrs. Mann could not soon reestablish order.

The president, the cabinet, and members of Congress were regulars, and even Houston could laugh about the incident with the oxen. In what Marquis James called the "Bachelor Republic," good times were had by nearly all. Sam's drinking was no longer a sometime thing. He was drinking steadily and heavily, and he was often seen reeling from the Mansion House to his residence.

There was also a darker rumor of a more serious addiction. Given the times and the availability of opium it could have been true. Santa Anna had asked for opium to calm his nerves after his capture, and it was immediately supplied. The druggists in Texas ran advertisements in the newspapers whenever a new shipment of Turkish opium arrived, so it was readily available.

One incident gives special credence to the stories. In June 1838 an old congressional friend, Rufus K. Goodenow, came to visit and was stricken "very sick at Floyd Tavern up stairs to the left hand." Sam dispatched Dr. Anson Jones to care for his friend, adding in the note, "You will find out that he has used *opium* to excess." And he enjoined Jones to keep the affair "Private." His request and the explicit directions seem to indicate that he himself had been in the room at the tavern, and arouses suspicion that he was more than just a concerned friend.

The churches condemned the use of alcohol and drugs, but their use was not regulated by government until the twentieth century in most of the United States. Indeed, it is almost certain that a larger percentage of the population was addicted to drugs in the nineteenth century than today.

Houston suffered throughout his life from his many wounds and the recurring attacks of malaria, jaundice, and dysentery. Perhaps he did seek relief through opium and become addicted, although there is no direct evidence of this. Alcoholism was another matter. There the record is clear.

His friends worried constantly that liquor would get the best of him. William Christy wrote from New Orleans that Houston's "health and reputation would soon sink under the influence of liquor. . . . May an alwise Providence chain you down to Sobriety and prudence." Later that summer Christy wrote again, warning Houston that "you are losing your friends and popularity faster than ever you gained them."

Christy was no bluenosed Baptist, and Houston respected his opinions and tried to oblige him. "In great haste and long sober," he ended one letter to his friend. And to Anna Raguet, Sam said jokingly, "I never drinks nothing." On January 7, 1838, he bet A. C. Allen a five-hundred dollar suit of clothes that he could get through the entire year drinking nothing but beer or ale. Judging from the gossip he lost the bet.

Houston's namesake town might have gained some of its energy from opium and "ardent spirits," but it was an exciting place even for the sober. It was also a rough place—the so-called governor's mansion was just two rooms with a dog trot between them—but there was a lively society. The bachelor president's remark about annexation—"We must be up and doing, to the last moment!"—also applied to his social life.

Much of the comment about Houston—as usual—involved his clothing. Sometimes he wore a velvet coat and trousers trimmed in gold lace. Or he would affect a black velvet coat, a scarlet waistcoat, and a ruffled shirt. For the San Jacinto Ball on April 21, celebrating the first anniversary of the battle, he showed up in a black velvet suit lined with white satin and a hat with egret plumes. Because of his ankle injury he could not wear the prescribed dancing slippers, but instead wore black boots with red tops and silver spurs.

The president regularly reported on Houston society to Anna Raguet, who never set foot in the capital while he was president. Her absence certainly fits the theory that theirs was no more than a strong friendship.

There has been speculation that Anna Raguet spurned Houston because she discovered that he had been courting her while he was still a married man. Houston, however, maintained that he petitioned the Tennessee legislature for a divorce as early as 1829 and he sent Anna a copy of the petition. However, no records exist in any of the Tennessee archives of the petition or any action of the legislature concerning a divorce by either Sam Houston or Eliza Allen Houston. Did Houston manufacture a petition as late as 1837 to cover himself?

He also gave Anna Raguet affidavits testifying to the legality of the 1837 decree at San Augustine. "The question was solemnly argued in court for the adverse party, and the judge on calm deliberation rendered his decision to be recorded—which was done," Houston told her. But San Augustine is only thirty-five miles from Nacogdoches and perhaps the spirited and independent Anna Raguet learned what really went on in that courtroom.

In any event whatever was going on between Sam Houston and Anna Raguet continued, and his courtly, flowery, and often witty letters to her are one of the best keys to his complex personality. They remained the best of friends even after they married other people.

———

While Houston fervently pursued annexation by the United States, he also had to proceed with building a nation. All plans had to be made as if Texas would continue to be an independent republic, which it was for almost ten years.

To create international respect for Texas—and to impress Washington—he appointed Pinckney Henderson minister to Great Britain. George S. McIntosh was named secretary of the legation. The two left for England in June 1837, but poor Henderson had a terrible time getting to his post because there was no money. In mid-August he was still in Charleston trying to raise the funds. He finally sailed from New York on September 1.

Henderson's most important charge was obtaining recognition of Texas, but he was also authorized to negotiate any treaty he felt could be beneficial to the republic.

The British foreign secretary, Lord Palmerston, was in no hurry about Texas. Henderson cooled his heels for weeks before he saw the great man. The *Eliza Russell* incident had annoyed the British, but there were two larger—perhaps insurmountable—obstacles to recognition.

Many British citizens had invested in Mexican bonds and the only possible form of payment was in Texas lands. If Texas were permanently separated from Mexico, they could not be paid. The other obstacle was even more serious. Texans owned slaves, at least ten thousand of them in 1837. While the African slave trade was forbidden in Texas, slavery flourished and slaves could be brought in from the United States and sold within the country.

Joseph T. Crawford, the British consul at Vera Cruz, often visited in Texas and he had become a friend of Houston's. He had submitted a reasonably favorable report to the British foreign office, but he was uneasy. "I have placed the infernal Slave concern on as good a footing as such a misfortune can be represented," he wrote to Houston, "but I wish from my heart that Slavery had never been a blot on your charter of freedom—You, I know think as I do on that subject."

Crawford suggested that Houston institute a regular census of the slave population in Texas. In that way, any slaves smuggled into the country could be easily identified.

The British people would not countenance recognition as long as slavery was allowed in Texas, but a trade agreement was worked out. All trade was to appear as if it were with Mexico and therefore fall under the existing treaties with that country. No matter that Texas was independent and its vessels carried Texas papers, this diplomatic figleaf would hide that fact and harbor masters were instructed to look the other way.

Houston was delighted with Henderson's achievement. Foreign trade was essential to the survival of the republic. It not only provided markets for Texas products, but the customs duties were a significant source of revenue. The trade agreement was also a first step toward full recognition by Great Britain. He conveniently ignored the words in the agreement that seemed to say that Texas was still part of Mexico, rephrasing it for his less sophisticated colleagues—or subjects, as Lamar might have put it.

It was hoped that an increase in trade would help offset the decline in the other great source of revenue for Houston's government, land sales. The Panic of 1837 had ruined land sales in the United States and speculators and investors were not inclined to look abroad.

Christy wrote from New Orleans that the only money available was at 18 to 20 percent interest and even then the very best security was necessary. Two of the biggest financial houses were in danger of failing.

Even the price of slaves had fallen to five hundred dollars. Panic or not, Christy also reported that "we have had a very gay winter (many private balls etc.) but the sudden change of things has made us all *Hewers of Wood*." Christy lamented that he spent "*all all all;* will I ever learn the art of keeping as well as making money?"

Houston was not able to control the mounting national debt, which had increased by 20 percent to over $600,000 in spite of his economies. Even the president was broke. He had to ask his friend Ashbel Smith to pay off a note for him. "My cash is exhausted!!!" he said.

The land market was further depressed because of the continuing government policy of land grants to new settlers and bounties for veterans. To add to the problem, the New Orleans agent was selling land on long-range terms, which made the sale for immediate cash impossible, and the veterans were unloading their 640-acre bounties for as little as twelve and a half cents an acre.

An attempt was made to overcome the shortfall in revenue by falling back on the oldest of economic remedies, printing paper money. But within a year it depreciated to sixty-five cents on the dollar.

Much worse than the shortage of cash was the shortage of food. The planting season had been completely lost because of the war for independence, and it would take several seasons to recover. The president even went so far as to ban cattle from being taken out of the country.

Ironically, the Indians, who had not gone to war, had surplus food, which they gladly traded to the whites for whiskey, which only created another problem. Hardly a week went by that there was not a report of trouble between the Indians and the whites. When Congressman John G. Robinson and his brother were murdered a half mile from their house, the residents of Cummins Creek and Mill Creek petitioned the president to send rangers to protect them.

———

Texas was at peace, or at least not at war, but a true rule of law had yet to be established and the infant republic reeled from one economic crisis to the next. Lack of money and shortages of even the most basic items seemed endemic and likely to remain so. Immigrants were pouring in, but the population was still only about fifty thousand, including Indians and slaves. How could such a small republic hope to develop viability.

Annexation and assumption of the public debt by the United States offered the only solution.

Toward this end on June 25, 1838, Houston announced Anson Jones's appointment as minister to the United States. He then wrote to Martin van Buren, recommending Jones to him as the representative of Texas and someone whom the president of the United States could rely on to best see to the interests of both nations.

The brilliant forty-year-old Jones was a native of Massachusetts. After studying medicine in New York, he had begun a disordered, peripatetic existence, in which he failed at both medicine and business. He ended up in Texas in 1833, where he was more successful. He established a profitable medical practice in Brazoria and became a leader in revolutionary politics.

The Texas Constitution limited Houston to one presidential term, so in July he announced that an election for president and vice-president would be held on Monday, September 3. Vice-President Lamar, of course, was a candidate. He was opposed by Peter W. Grayson and James W. Collinsworth.

On his way to take up his post in Washington, Anson Jones stopped over in New Orleans, where he received the devastating news that Grayson and Collinsworth were dead—both of them suicides.

Grayson, despondent over illness, had shot himself to death in east Tennessee. Jones felt his death keenly and felt it was a national calamity, comparable, he said, to the combined deaths of any twelve of his friends.

The unstable Collinsworth's death did not surprise Jones. "I knew him to be deranged & when excited by liquor almost mad," Jones said, when he learned that Collinsworth had jumped from a ship into Galveston Bay.

———

Houston left the capital at the end of June and headed north to Nacogdoches, where civil disturbances involving both the Anglos and the Mexicans and troubles with the Indians demanded his presence. He was accompanied by John R. Ross, the newly appointed first clerk of the Indian Department. They stopped to take part in the July Fourth celebration in Liberty, as Houston had done the year before, and then went on to meet with the Indian tribes.

Three days later, young Ross was stricken with dysentery so severe that Houston feared for his life. The president himself treated him, bleeding him twice, but Ross remained critical. Worried, he summoned Dr. Ashbel Smith to ride as quickly as he could from Houston, and Smith covered the great distance in less than three days' time.

Ross seemed to rally under Smith's ministrations, and the president postponed his journey for another week to stay and look after his young friend. Houston then left him with Dr. Smith and proceeded on to Nacogdoches. He was so confident of Ross's recovery that he lightly commented in a note to Dr. Irion from Menard's Mill that "I am most effectually broken down as a medicine man, and feel the want of science and skill. I am the fifth but not the seventh son in the family."

The illness that had felled Ross spread. The wife of Houston's host, Pierre J. Menard, died while he was there, and Dr. Smith became ill on the return trip to the capital. Houston himself was confined to his bed in Nacogdoches when the news came that Ross had died on August 9. He was still so weak that he had to dictate a letter to the young man's mother.

"I would never have left him had it not been for the anticipated revolution which I had barely time to meet, and the effects of which are not yet passed by," he wrote to Mrs. Ross in Virginia.

> You may be assured, Madame, that while you are bereaved of a noble son, I am deprived of a valued friend—one whom I had marked as an associate in my retirement, where his situation would have been that of a son. His fine intelligence, his nice sense of honor, his manly pride, and excellent discretion, as well as the purity of his habits had endeared Mr. Ross beyond all others who have stood in the same relation of life to me.

The crisis in the summer of 1838 was the threat of an armed uprising by dissatisfied Mexican citizens and the fear that they would be joined by the Indians against the Anglo Texans. Houston had come to Nacogdoches to try to calm the situation.

Vicente Cordova, a former alcalde of Nacogdoches and a leader in the uprising of 1832, had remained loyal to Mexico as had many of the Mexican citizens of Texas. They had not looked for total separation from Mexico but only for redress of their legitimate grievances. Cordova and his followers enlisted the support of about three hundred Indians who had their own complaints against the Anglo government.

The white settlers began violent reprisals against the Mexican community and the Indians for a series of murders and thefts against the outlying settlers, which may or may not have been committed by Cordova's men and their Indian allies. By the time Houston arrived, the situation was out of control. "The violence of the American character was one cause," he wrote to Andrew Jackson.

Old Hickory had only to go down to the road that passed by The Hermitage to see firsthand that "American character." The overland route of the Indians who were being forceably removed to the West ran by the gate of his plantation. The ragged and pathetic bands of Cherokees passed by The Hermitage all that summer and into the fall and winter.

The violence against the Indians in Texas was the logical extension of Jackson's own beliefs. While he perhaps truly believed that his policies were designed to save the tribes and preserve them from the white man, in effect they played on white fears and greed. The transplanted Southerners had taken all their hatred of the Indians and their desire for the Indian lands with them to Texas. And they had Jackson's removal plan for a blueprint.

Houston appealed to the Indian chiefs to abide by the treaty he had made with them in spite of the fact that it had been rejected by the Texas government. To Chief Bowl, he wrote, "Do not be disturbed by the troubles which are around you, but be at peace—Remember my words, and listen to no bad talks of any one! I have never told you a lie, nor do I intend it."

But Houston too had gone along with Jackson's removal policy as a way of saving the tribes and he felt it could work in Texas. In good faith, he was trying to set up the equivalent of the Indian Territory in his new nation. His countrymen wanted none of it. When they had lived in Georgia, they had not been content with being given the Indian lands. They wanted to be rid of the Indians altogether.

"No man living can so well appreciate the difficulties which have beset me as yourself," he said to Jackson. "But thank God they always arise from pure and ardent patriotism. The man who would save his country must pass the ordeal of fire.

"My soul now burns, for matters were not worse previous to the day of San Jacinto," he said. "I have for myself one only alternative. You can readily imagine what that must be." This last must have chilled Jackson, especially when Houston added that "you will do me the Justice to vindicate me to the world."

> You, General, have left monuments of Glory to your country, such as no man ever did before you. But you had an organized Government, and men who were accustomed to civil rule, while I had to command a Government from chaos, with men who had never been accustomed as a community, to any rule, but their passions, nor to any government, but their will. You had experience with mature wisdom. I lacked experience and could not render that assurance, which give largeness of promise to my country.

Houston here revealed that despair and sense of hopelessness that can affect only men with great public responsibilities. He also, in opening up his heart and his mind in this most revealing of letters, showed the great trust and love that the old soldier in Tennessee commanded from him.

> The principles of holy patriotism which you inculcated upon me, in my early life have never ceased to abide, nor can they ever cease to remain with me while life lasts. I feel proud in offering you this assurance, while I am happy, that it is rendered one who will confide in it.

In spite of his depression, Houston pressed on with his peacekeeping efforts. He dispatched troops under Rusk to put down the Mexican rebels and their Indian allies, which was done with relative ease, but his main concern was the friendly Indians. They must do nothing to arouse the whites.

He promised the Cherokee chiefs, The Bowl and Gatunwali, or Big Mush, that an official boundary line would be run between the lands claimed by the Cherokees and the whites—a first step in guaranteeing to the Indians possession of their lands. "I will never lie to that treaty while I live, and it must stand as long as good man lives and water runs," said the Raven to his Indian brothers.

On October 10, Houston ordered Rusk to run the boundary line, warning him that "if it is not done, all future calamities must be attributed to its omission. I am satisfied if it is not done there will be another runaway scrape and Eastern Texas will be desolated." The Indians were prepared to go to war to protect their lands.

He said to The Bowl, "Genl Rusk will protect you. Look to him as to a great friend." To the other Indian tribes he promised, "You must not take up the Tomahawk, nor will I allow other men to raise it against you." He exhorted them to keep the young warriors under control. "Old men speak Wisdom, and Young Men should pursue their counsel."

Houston still hoped for a miracle—that the Texas Senate would ratify the Indian treaty. He had only a very brief time left in office, however. Lamar had been elected on September 3, without opposition. David G. Burnet was the new vice-president. The change in administrations was as abrupt as when Jackson succeeded John Quincy Adams. Everything was different. True, Lamar had been Houston's vice-president, but he played a very minor role and in fact spent most of 1837 at his family home in Georgia. It was just as well. He detested Houston and was still sulking over Santa Anna's release.

The outgoing president did not return to the capital until a month after the new Congress convened. With only three weeks remaining in his administration, he renewed the battle over the Indian treaty. His sincerity cannot be questioned, but his timing can. It is to be wondered why he did not return to Houston at the beginning of the session and join the issue.

In his message to the Congress in mid-November on the Indian question, Houston readily admitted that he had run the boundary line between the Indian lands and the white settlements even though the treaty had never been ratified.

As president he was justified in doing so based on the actions of the consultation of 1835 and the General Council set up in 1836. He had to do it also in order to save East Texas from ruin. Whites were moving into the Indian hunting grounds but not in sufficient numbers to protect themselves. They were therefore being attacked. The Indians had not yet attacked the eastern settlements but they might at any time unless the treaty were honored.

In some ways Houston was blaming the white victims for the Indians' crimes, but he was certainly on firm moral ground. The legal ground was a bit shakier. Any treaty had to be ratified, and his original instructions had so stated.

In this final message to Congress, Houston also chastised the members for usurping his constitutional power as commander in chief. They had taken an inordinate interest in military affairs and were in effect controlling the army directly. Once again Houston felt constrained, as all presidents have, to remind the Congress of the separation of powers set forth in the Constitution.

> A deliberative body, general in its character, varied and diversified, in the interest of its members, will necessarily yield to the impulse of circumstances. . . . The legislative is temporary, and has its intermissions; what Congress does is done by no one, and therefore no responsibility devolves upon it. The executive not being temporary to the same extent is responsible, and held so by the nation.

No action was taken on the treaty, nor could there be, even if the House and Senate had been sympathetic to the plight of the fourteen thousand Indians living in Texas. A new administration was to be sworn in soon, and no responsible legislative body would dare to act on such an important issue at such a moment. But Houston ended his term on a high moral plane. Kalanu had once again come to the defense of his defenseless old friends.

———

President Sam Houston arrived for Lamar's inaugural on December 10, wearing knee breeches, white stockings, an elaborate coat, and a powdered wig. Not content to steal the show visually, he underscored the Washingtonian analogy by delivering a farewell address—which was three hours long. Witnesses to the crime reported that Lamar was made so nervous by Houston's antics that he decided to have his own speech read by the secretary of the Senate.

———

Far removed from Texas, Tiana Rogers had gone about her life in the Cherokee Nation. She heard from her uncle, Chief Ooleteka, of the great victory of the Raven at San Jacinto, and she and the old chief knew that he had now gone forever. She remarried in 1836, to a ne'er-do-well named Samuel D. McGrady, but the unhappy marriage was a brief one.

Tiana Rogers died sometime in 1838, not far from the Wigwam Neosho. Tradition placed her grave at Wilson's Rock and it was so regarded until September 3, 1904, when the remains of a woman were exhumed. The next day there was a public viewing. The large tortoise-shell comb that had held her hair in place was still in good condition.

Hundreds of people attended the burial service in the Officer's Circle at the national cemetery at Fort Gibson. Her monument is the plain white marble, government-issue stone that marks hundreds of thousands of military graves. And the inscription is just as simple.

TALAHINA R.
—
WIFE OF GEN.
—
SAM
HOUSTON

11

A Disloyal Opposition

S AM HOUSTON was out of a job but he still had a profession, and in January 1839 he agreed to establish a law partnership in Houston with John Birdsall, who had immigrated to Texas from New York in late 1836. He and Houston had become fast friends almost immediately, and when James Collinsworth committed suicide, Houston nominated him to be chief justice of the Texas Supreme Court.

Birdsall was qualified—he had served as a judge in New York State and also in the New York State Senate—but the Texas Senate did not confirm him. There were only four months left in the Houston administration, and it was felt that Lamar should make the appointment.

The ex-president did not particularly want to remain in the capital. The town was no longer the lively place it had been as the center of the "Bachelor Republic." There was now a new chief—"Who is to give Texas character!" Sam scornfully remarked. Nacogdoches was still Houston's official residence, and he was finally having a house built there. The new house was promised for that summer and Sam looked forward to being reunited with his East Texas friends.

Houston's name on the law firm was apparently little more than that. He was more interested in another real estate scheme—specifically a new town, Sabine City, that was being laid out at the mouth of the Sabine

River. His partners included Sublett and Hockley, and the three old friends and long-time speculators spent much of that spring "town or city making."

They issued their prospectus at the beginning of May and the plan was a sound one, particularly their idea of opening up the Sabine to shipping. Sabine City would eventually grow to a population of over six thousand, but repeated hurricanes gradually made it seem less viable. The more protected areas farther up the river displaced it, and the original Sabine is today part of Port Arthur, Texas.

Since no one in Texas had any money it was obvious that lots in the new city would have to be sold in the United States, and partly to that end, Houston left for the East. He also had personal reasons for the journey. A brother had visited him in Houston, but otherwise he had not seen any of his family in five years. And he also wanted to visit Andrew Jackson at The Hermitage. Besides, Sam Houston had seldom stayed anyplace for very long in his entire life and he needed a change of scene. "I find a total change of habits causes a change of health," he said to Anna Raguet.

But there was no "total change of habits." During his journey through the United States that summer of 1839 vivid reports came back to Texas about his drunken behavior in New Orleans, Mobile, and Nashville. The Indian sobriquet Big Drunk had been picked up and used against Houston by his enemies while he was president, and he had begun to address the problem—but in a minor sort of way, to be sure.

He flirted with the temperance movement, even attending at least one temperance meeting in February 1839. But it was no more than that—a flirtation, not even an affair. A long-term relationship with sobriety was still impossible.

Lamar and Burnet were dismayed when they learned that the former president was not going to return to Nacogdoches but would be right down the street from the Capitol. They were much relieved when he left for the East. When they heard of his drunken shenanigans they were delighted. Perhaps Old Sam Jacinto was finally doing himself in.

From New Orleans, Houston went on to Mobile with his prospectus for selling lots in the new city on the Sabine. His New Orleans connections had recommended that he contact William Bledsoe, a Mobile merchant. Bledsoe was not only interested in the speculation but invited Houston out to his home at nearby Spring Hill.

Bledsoe's pretty eighteen-year-old wife, Emily Antoinette, was the daughter of Temple Lea, a deceased Baptist minister who had settled in Marion, Alabama, in 1818, soon after the Creek War. His widow, Nancy Moffette Lea, was also at Spring Hill, and Bledsoe encouraged Houston to present his plans to her as well. Mrs. Lea, who was both a hard-shelled Baptist and a good businesswoman, recognized the investment possibilities. She would go out to Texas and have a look round.

Spring Hill was a part of the South that Houston had once known fairly well, and Sam was reminded of that more genteel time when his life had revolved around visits to The Hermitage and Allenwood. This pleasurable sojourn was further reinforced when Antoinette Bledsoe introduced him to her older sister while they were walking in the garden.

Margaret Moffette Lea smiled as Houston, always the courtier, bowed over her hand. He was instantly taken with the twenty-year-old brown-haired beauty with the enormous violet eyes. She was much more than simply a beautiful young southern belle, however. She was educated, well-read, and intelligent, but thankfully, without the brittleness and cleverness of Anna Raguet.

She did, however, have a romantic nature, fed by the novels of Sir Walter Scott, which did much to soften the deeply rooted religiosity that had been instilled in her since birth by her pious Baptist family. And she was thrilled to meet, here in her sister's garden, the famous General Houston himself. Sam still wore his chestnut hair long and she was struck by the piercing blue eyes that were so pale they seemed gray at times.

Yes, she thought, he was a bit haggard to be sure and he looked even older than his forty-six years. No matter. To her, and to most other women, the afflictions he had suffered, and his rumored dissipation, only enhanced his looks. And Margaret had not forgotten that day in May three years before when she had been part of the crowd that welcomed the wounded hero to New Orleans.

For the remainder of the afternoon, Sam stayed by her side, doing his best to charm Margaret Moffette Lea. He decided to linger a while longer at the Bledsoes, and for the next week he and Margaret were together for most of every day.

In the afternoons, they sat on the porch out of the hot Alabama sun and he told her about Texas. They took walks together in the cool of the early evening, reciting poetry. Once he picked a pink from the garden and she wore it in her hair. He identified the stars and the constellations for her. One evening he pointed out a single star in the bright Alabama sky—the Lone Star?—and asked her to look for it each night when he was gone and to think on him.

———

Houston spent the rest of the summer in Tennessee with the Old Chief at The Hermitage. Jackson was in better health than he had been in years, thanks, he said, to "Dr. Flood's burnt brandy cure," which he forced on everyone, and no doubt Sam had to have a dose of it himself.

Old Hickory's nostrum was prepared by dissolving a forkful of loaf sugar over a cup of burning brandy. The brandy was then allowed to burn itself out. This sweetened burnt brandy elixir was drunk just before going to bed and again on rising. How much was not specified.

Jackson's health might also have been improved by the messy but successful legal fight he had just had with two of his nephews. They had not only abandoned the Democrats for the Whigs, but they had betrayed the family. At their urging four of Jackson's slaves were charged with killing the fiddler at a slave Christmas party. Jackson defended his slaves and got them off, which buoyed his spirits immensely. As for the wayward nephews, they were dismissed as "worthless Whig scamps."

Houston was delighted to find his old friend in such good form and his presence at The Hermitage seemed to improve Jackson's health and spirits even further. The others there were protégés and extended family, but Sam Houston reflected so many of the Old Chief's own traits of character and personality that their bond was indeed special.

Above all else, Sam had returned to Tennessee victorious in both war and politics. Jackson must be told every detail of the Alamo, Goliad, the march across Texas, and the great victory at San Jacinto. Then came politics, and in particular the politics of annexation. Jackson had always, of course, believed that Texas had been part of the Louisiana Purchase and already belonged to the United States. He was also aware of the political realities.

The opposition to the admission of a state in which 25 percent of the population were slaves had grown stronger. The abolitionists were no longer a fringe group to be dismissed as a bunch of do-gooders. There were now almost two thousand auxiliaries of the American Anti-Slavery Society.

They had been stymied by the passage of the infamous "gag rule" in 1836. All petitions to Congress having to do with slavery or its abolition were automatically tabled. In order to ensure party unity, even the northern Democrats had voted for it. Jackson had approved it, in spite of the fact that it clearly violated the First Amendment, in the hope of avoiding a crisis. The abolitionists and antislavery petitioners, by invoking the wrath of the old nullifiers and the new secessionists, could tear the Union apart.

Such an abrogation of the rights of others often and ironically serves a useful purpose. The abolitionists' cause became the cause of everyone who believed in civil liberties. The most eloquent spokesman, John Quincy Adams, was not a fire-breathing abolitionist, but he was antislavery and he was certainly a believer in the constitutional right of petition. He took up the cause and every session he persistently introduced antislavery petitions in direct defiance of the rule.

The antiannexation abolitionists were joined by the antiexpansionists who were content for the United States to remain within its present boundaries. Again the leader of this formidable opposition was Adams, who, while he pursued his goals for the most moral of reasons, no doubt rejoiced that he also was fighting his old enemies.

Then in 1839 a formidable political scandal, damaging to the cause of Texas, came to light. Samuel Swartwout had turned out to be one of the greatest scoundrels of the age. In January, investigators revealed that not only had he stolen over a million dollars of public funds as collector of the Port of New York but that he had probably used at least some of the money to speculate in land in Texas. Swartwout was now hiding out in England to avoid arrest.

Houston was concerned that he might be dragged into the scandal. The embezzler had once sent him a ring that was specially made for Sam in New York. "A thousand thanks for the Ring," he had written to Swartwout, "I will kiss it and wear it as long as I am 'a young man.' " Was it paid for with money stolen from customs revenues? Houston now wondered.

Swartwout's perfidy came to symbolize the spoils system that has become associated, however unfairly, with Jackson's administration.

Jackson had, however, trustingly given Swartwout the greatest of the patronage plums and, as it turned out, the most profitable one.

———

Another, even greater scandal also occurred in 1839, but it was quickly covered over. No one wanted to admit that such a thing could happen in a civilized country. During the winter of 1838–39, the last pitiful band of the eastern Cherokees arrived in the Indian Territory, at the end of the infamous "Trail of Tears." Their suffering had made even the soldiers who had been sent to carry out their forced removal weep for their unfortunate charges.

Houston himself had helped begin the removal over twenty years before, convinced that it was the only way to save the tribe from the white man. The removal of the eastern Cherokee was inevitable and he had tried to help his friends.

But it was not the loss of their lands that caused the greatest damage to the Cherokees. The new land in the Arkansas Territory was in many ways superior to the land in the east, as Houston's Cherokee father, Ooleteka, had found out. The soil was rich and well-watered. There was abundant grass for livestock. The tribe would not starve.

And while the deaths of thousands of innocent people on the "Trail of Tears" was one of the great crimes in American history, that too has to give way to a greater tragedy—the destruction of the social and hierarchical organization of the Cherokee Nation.

The Cherokee were rent with dissension. Feuds, the struggle for power, and the desire for revenge against those who had signed the treaty of removal led to murder and assassination. Many of the most prominent men of the tribe were killed. The great Cherokee Nation had fallen.

Houston's successor, Mirabeau Buonaparte Lamar, now called for the same policy to be applied in Texas—removal or annihilation of all Indians in the republic. Lamar had been a chief instigator of the expulsion of the Indians from Georgia, and it was predictable that he would continue his virulent hatred and genocidal policies in Texas. He was also overwhelmingly supported by the people and the Congress.

The Cordova Rebellion of the previous summer had inflamed the fear and distrust of the whites who continued to invade and occupy the Indian lands. The Texans were still afraid, or so they said, of a possible alliance between the Cherokees and Mexico—the chances of which in the summer of 1839 ranged from unlikely to impossible.

The Indians, however, were becoming more aggressive, and throughout late 1838 and into 1839 attacks on the whites increased. The Cherokees, who had been in Texas longer than their white tormenters, were ordered to leave Texas and join their brothers in the Indian Territory across the Red River.

To Chief Bowl and Big Mush the betrayal was complete. They had signed treaties, they had aided the Texans in their wars, and now they were being expelled. They saw no option but to fight for the land they had been promised.

Lamar sent his army against the Cherokees, and on July 16 the Indians were defeated at the Battle of the Neches. Both Bowl and Big Mush were killed. Bowl was wearing the sword and sash that his old friend Kalanu, The Raven, had presented to him. And tied to a cord around his neck was a small metal canister containing the treaty guaranteeing the Cherokees their lands. The surviving Indians fled to the north. One of them carried the blood-stained canister with the treaty signed by Houston. By the end of July the Cherokee War was over.

———

From The Hermitage, Sam wrote to Margaret Lea in Alabama. She missed him, she wrote back, and looked forward to his return. Clearly she had become infatuated with the older man. "I am in the midst of my childhood's friends, and greeted on every hand with gentle words and soft endearing epithets and I am happy," she said. "Quite happy? Ah no . . . there are those absent whose station within my heart remains unfilled."

She could not even look for solace to her beloved books. "I am in the midst of a band of heroes, ideal and real, and sages with their wisdom and philosophy . . . and orators and poets," she said, but her heart was not with them. "It is like a caged bird," said Margaret.

"Last night I gazed long upon our beauteous emblem the *star of destiny*, and my thoughts took the form of verse, but I will not inscribe them here, for then you might call me a romantic star-struck young lady," said the romantic and indeed star-struck young lady. Her poem was called "Lines to a Withered Pink."

Why have I sought thee out—loved flower?
To gaze upon thy radiant bloom?
Or doth some tranquilizing power
Breathe in thy rich perfume?

Ah no, thou art a withered thing
Thy perfume long since gone!
Say then what magic yet doth cling
Around thee, faded one!

Tis true, no beauty now doth dwell
With in thy leaflets sere
But ah for me a holy spell
Doth ever linger there.

He placed thee in my hand, that friend
Who now doth distant roam,
I took thee, little thinking then
How dear thou wouldst become.

That joyous eve, upon my brow
Thy fresh young leaves I wore
Thou wert beauteous then tis true, but now
Poor flower, I love thee more.

Although thou art a blighted thing
E'en in thy lone decay
Thy form doth recollections bring
Of bright hours passed away.

Time onward flies and swift advance
The years when friends are few
The years when I shall live perchance
Like thee, to wither too.

Thou sweet memento! Gentle flower!
Say will he cherish me.
And love me too in that dark hour
As now I cherish thee?

Somerville, Alabama
May 31, 1839

Sam forthwith decided to stop over in Alabama on his way back, but first he had to discharge his remaining family obligations, particularly with relatives in east Tennessee, where his appearance delighted his nieces and nephews.

Unfortunately, by the time he returned to Nashville, his inoculation with temperance had worn off again, and the rest of his stay was punctuated by drunken sprees. He always behaved himself at The Hermitage, however. Everybody did.

Houston had an interest in good horseflesh, and Old Hickory, America's greatest horse trader, rekindled this particular fire during the summer of 1839. On August 30, Sam completed an agreement with Hickman Lewis of Limestone County, Alabama, to buy seven blooded fillies. One of the Lewis horses, Proclamation, cost him $2,000. Here was the serious beginning of Houston's own string of horses, a grand passion that lasted throughout his life. Houston had no cash, of course. He paid Lewis in Sabine City land scrip. Indeed, he had had to borrow five hundred dollars from a friend, William G. Harding, while he was in Nashville.

Drinking and, perhaps, horse-trading aside, Houston's trip east had restored him. Jackson stiffened Houston's spine. The doubts of late 1838, the almost suicidal despair, had disappeared. Further, Houston's belief in a strong executive branch, the sanctity of the Union, and annexation by the United States were even more strongly fixed when he left Nashville in September.

A few days after he wound up his horse-trading, Houston presented himself at the house of Margaret Lea's brother, Henry Lea, on Green Street in Marion, Alabama. Margaret and her mother had returned from Mobile and were staying in that lovely town, with its tree-shaded streets and gracious white houses. Marion lies in the center of rich farm country, not unlike the prairies of East Texas. In 1839, the town had two colleges and had already become known as the Athens of Alabama, even though it was barely twenty years old.

Houston put up at the Eagle Hotel, across the street from the Lea house, and he behaved himself. Whatever his behavior in Nashville had been, it is certain that he was a picture of sobriety and rectitude in that Baptist Alabama town, where a cork being pulled from a bottle could be heard for half a mile.

However, the townspeople, indeed the whole county, were anxious to see the famous visitor, and Houston obliged them. He made a speech from the balcony of the hotel. The Leas listened to the impressive voice from their own balcony just across the way.

Mrs. Lea had tried to learn everything she could about this man with whom her daughter had become so infatuated. Like everyone else, she too responded to his easy charm and his splendid manners. His public life—his great fame—dazzled even her.

Houston's private life was something else. He was divorced, he was a drinker, and everyone had heard about the Indian wife and the rumored Indian children. Houston was also forty-six years old. By the time they married he would be forty-seven.

Her mother may have worried about the match, but Margaret had no doubts at all. She had decided to accept Sam Houston's offer of marriage and go with him to Texas. Nancy Lea consented, but first she and her son-in-law, William Bledsoe, would go ahead with their plans to visit Galveston and Sabine City in the spring. Margaret meanwhile would work on her trousseau and the wedding plans.

Houston was back in Nacogdoches by late September, in the house that had been built for him while he was away. It was a simple log structure, not more than two rooms, which had to serve as both residence and law office.

He now saw firsthand the enormity of Lamar's Indian policy, and he made a scathing speech denouncing the Cherokee War and the president. His outrage at the expulsion of the Indians was by no means shared by all of his friends—indeed, by very few of them. Henry Raguet had warned him not to push the Indian question. There were after all over two hundred white families now settled on the former Indian lands—"all voters."

And other good friends had gladly gone to war against the Cherokees. Burleson and Rusk were commanders and David Kaufmann and Adolphus Sterne were officers at the Battle of the Neches. Albert Sidney Johnston, even though he was secretary of war, was also there—perhaps in emulation of S. Rhodes Fisher's piratical adventures in the Gulf of Mexico.

Some of Houston's most bitter enemies were also present at the slaughter. Vice-President Burnet was cited for his exploits in the field. One may well ask what the vice-president was doing on the battlefield, when he had run across Texas to avoid a battle while president. To ask the question is to answer it. It was precisely because he had run away from war then that he had to run toward it now.

Houston could not have been surprised by Lamar's program. The president announced it in his message to Congress a week after his inauguration. All Indians had to leave Texas. The women and children were not to be harmed, but all warriors were to be driven out forcibly if necessary or killed outright. It was as simple as it was clear. Expulsion or extinction.

There has been considerable speculation that Houston left Texas before the Cherokee War to avoid having to stand by helplessly while his Indian friends were either killed or deported. There is equal speculation that Lamar waited until Houston had left the country before he dared start his program of annihilation of the Cherokees.

Whatever motivated Lamar's or Houston's actions, the use of force against the Indians did not begin until July 1839, while Sam was in Nashville, and he remained ignorant of the full scope of the disaster until he returned home.

———

Houston could not long ignore the notes of the bugle calling him back to government, and he was easily elected to represent Nacogdoches in the Texas House of Representatives. John Quincy Adams had led the way in the United States for a former president to serve in Congress, although Houston would have been appalled by the comparison.

The Fourth Congress assembled that fall in yet another capital city, the seventh since independence. President Lamar may have been inept at governing, but he was responsible for other things that would benefit the republic. High on his list was the permanent relocation of the capital from East Texas to the frontier. He sought thereby to ensure settlement of the west.

Lamar liked one particular area on the Colorado River, almost two hundred miles to the west of Houston, and the commission appointed to select the site for a new capital went along with the president's choice.

On May 17, 1839, Edwin Waller announced in the *Civilian and Galveston Gazette* that a new city, called Austin, was to be laid out at a hamlet called Waterloo, thirty-five miles north of Bastrop. A public sale of land was scheduled for August 1.

Lamar and his cabinet arrived in October, but the honorable representative from Nacogdoches delayed until November 13. From that day until he died, Houston never had a kind word to say about Austin. He called it "the most miserable place on the face of the Earth" and "the most unfortunate site upon earth for the Seat of Government." Within a month he made two speeches to the House urging his colleagues to move the capital at once to a more congenial spot nearer civilization. Austin might be visited by a "pious pilgrim" who would be willing to make the journey, but no one else—certainly not the "defrauded people of the east"—would ever come there.

The new capital was more primitive than Nacogdoches or Houston, and the Indians were a serious threat. One did not go about unprotected. In fact, thirteen men were killed by Indians while constructing the first buildings. However, there were some amenities. A newspaper, the *Austin City Gazette,* began publication in October, and there was a hotel, the Eberle House.

For Houston, however, worse even than the capital was the Lamar administration, which was destroying the nation with its disregard for budgetary restraints. "I might have been happy in ignorance at home had I known the full extent of Lamar's stupidity," Houston wrote to Anna Raguet.

Sam never hesitated to discuss politics with Anna Raguet or any other woman for that matter, which was another trait that endeared him to them. He had, after all, been brought up by a strong-willed and determined woman and he always enjoyed the company of women.

Pleased, and perhaps a bit smug, about his forthcoming marriage, Houston somewhat officiously advised Anna Raguet about romance. In a heavy-handed way he condescendingly suggested to her names of eligible young men. He never recommended the most eligible of all, however—Robert Irion. Remarkably, Houston was oblivious to his great friend's attraction to Anna. More likely it was the result of his egocentric view of the world. Irion was part of his court, after all. In any event, Anna Raguet made up her own mind. On March 29, 1840, she married Robert Irion in Nacogdoches.

Sam Houston's supporters suffered through the Lamar administration. Their own man was bound to be returned to power in the 1841 elections. Certainly, whatever popularity Lamar had was being dissipated. This was apparent when only ten members of Congress who had been elected with Lamar in 1838 were reelected in 1839. Public opinion was easily and quickly gauged in the early days of the republic. Representatives had to present themselves to the electorate every year.

Under the circumstances, however, three years was a long time to wait for a new president. The public supported Lamar's expulsion of the Indians, and some of them even applauded appropriating public lands for public schools. But they were critical of his building a new capital city, complete with a "mansion" for himself, and they were decidedly against his running the republic millions of dollars into debt.

Houston had failed to save his friends the Cherokees, but now that they had been driven off the land he was determined that the vast territory they once occupied did not fall prey to speculators and squatters. The position of these predators was that the Indians had never owned the land, and since they had invested in it, surveyed it, and in many cases occupied it, it was now theirs.

Houston insisted that the Cherokees had indeed owned the land, but through conquest, if nothing else, it was now part of the public lands of the nation. Accordingly, on December 22, he introduced a bill to divide all the former Cherokee land into sections of 640 acres and sell it for the use of the government. He spoke for an entire day in support of his bill. Hour after hour he harangued and lectured the House on Texas history, particularly the betrayal of the Indians, who had patiently awaited for their rights.

"Vain hope! Unnatural delusion! When did the white man ever respect the rights of the Indian—or avarice loose its grasp?" asked Houston of his fellow legislators. "When the Indian sat upon the rock at Plymouth, and saw the first sail upon the deep, though *white*, could he have removed the veil of futurity, he would have seen it crimsoned with their gore."

The Indian had made the white man welcome and fed and cared for him. What was his reward? "Too soon he found he had nursed a viper in his bosom, and gloomy and dark has been the history of the Red man since that unfortunate day."

It was a dangerous speech politically and one that could only anger his enemies and dismay his friends. Houston's dogged defense of the Indians, even though there were almost daily reports of depredations, so aroused his enemies that they contrived an insult so stinging that Houston flew into a rage on the floor of the House.

"Sir," wrote General Edward Burleson to Adjutant General Hugh McCleod, "I send by Lieutenant Moran the cocked hat of the distinguished friend of General Sam Houston, Colonel Bowles, and, as it first emanated from him, I specially request you to present it to him from me as a compliment."

The hat was not a gift from Houston. It was a Mexican hat that Bowles was given when he had been commissioned a colonel in the Mexican Army. No matter. Houston was livid and called for the dismissal of McCleod. He withdrew his resolution the next day after he calmed down a bit, but new battle lines were drawn and lifetime enmities born.

But Houston prevailed against the squatters and speculators. In the House, Speaker David S. Kaufman changed the wording from "owned and occupied" to "reserved for and occupied," which satisfied those who maintained that the Cherokees had never owned the land. The bill then passed almost unanimously.

Lamar used his veto, but Congress overrode him. Then in the 1840 session the whole controversy came up again because of an amendment to pay the mostly illegal settlers on the land over $1.3 million in compensation.

Predictably Houston again took the floor to defend the Indians and lambaste the speculators and their supporters for threatening this further drain on the treasury. Sam's listeners expected theatrical flair when he spoke and he did not disappoint them. When he advised the House that a subject should be handled with "gloves as soft as silk," he produced a pair of white silk gloves and dramatically drew them on.

On January 15, 1840, a second newspaper, the *Texas Sentinel,* began publication in Austin. The editor, George W. Bonnell, asked forebearance on the part of the public because, after all, they were in "a city.that is but six months old."

Bonnell did not hesitate, however, to sing the praises of Austin, which "with its mountains and hillocks, its river and rivulets, its luxuriant prairies, and its pure and delicious climate, occupies one of the most agreeably romantic spots that can be found throughout whole region of the south-west."

Bonnell loathed Sam Houston, and his paper was the official publisher of anti-Houston sentiment. Burnet was a regular contributor, and the paper supported him for the presidency. But the editor also had some integrity about educating the public and squelching foolishness.

For some time a rumor had persisted that Davy Crockett had survived the Alamo massacre and was being held prisoner in the mines of Mexico. The story had its attractions, and many people believed it. Bonnell unhesitatingly pronounced it a "humbug," a plot to persuade thousands of Tennessee volunteers to come south and invade Mexico.

Even though the Congress was still in session the prospective bridegroom left for Alabama in April. He asked his friend Ashbel Smith to accompany him and serve as his best man. Smith reluctantly declined. He had no money, and he couldn't borrow from the groom because Houston had none. Their plight was not unusual. Everyone had land, sometimes as much as hundreds of thousands of acres, but no one had any cash.

The story is told that Houston expected to meet Margaret Lea in Galveston, but when he boarded the vessel in the harbor he was met by the mother and not the bride. Mrs. Lea supposedly informed him that if he wanted to marry her daughter he would have to travel to Alabama. Considering the people involved and the customs of the times, it is unlikely that Nancy Lea would have behaved in such a manner. The wedding had been planned to take place in Henry Lea's house in Marion all along, and so it did.

Houston was able to travel by boat as far as Selma, Alabama. From there he went on to Marion on horseback. Once again he stayed at The Eagle on Green Street.

On May 9, a beautiful Saturday afternoon, Sam Houston married

Margaret Moffette Lea. There had been a slight delay caused by a member of Margaret's family, who was deputized to inquire into the reasons for the failure of Houston's first marriage. Houston declined to comment. When he was pressed, he said if they insisted on pursuing the issue, then "call off your fiddlers."

That was the end of the matter and the bridegroom left the hotel, crossed the street, and climbed the outside stairway to the upstairs veranda and the main entrance of the Lea house. He entered through the large double doors and then turned left into the beautiful upstairs parlor with its carved moldings and wainscotting.

The sun was streaming through the tall windows as the preacher from the Siloam Baptist Church, where Margaret's father had preached, pronounced them man and wife. So began a new life for the forty-seven-year-old bachelor. Eleven years had passed since his twelve-week marriage to Eliza Allen. It had been over seven years since he left Tiana Rogers in Arkansas. Except for these brief interludes, he had lived alone all of his life.

Many of Houston's old friends doubted that he was capable of sustaining a marriage, and they advised him against it. Their comments were not generous. They soon came round, however, when they met the new Mrs. Houston. She might possibly be capable of doing what no one had done before—reform their old friend. At the wedding banquet, a Major Townes raised his glass to "the conqueress of the conqueror," and how right he was.

Sam was concerned from the beginning about Margaret's health. How would she survive in the rigorous climate and the arduous life of Texas? The answer was not long in coming. Everyone wanted to see the "Conqueress," and she was subjected to an exhausting summer of visits and barbecues, speeches and celebrations. It was not long before she collapsed with a fever, probably malaria.

Margaret recuperated at the home of Antoinette and Will Bledsoe, who had also settled in Texas, at Grand Cane, on the Trinity River, north of Liberty. Houston's law practice kept him in Nacogdoches and San Augustine, but he wrote ardent and longing letters to his young wife.

"I cannot be happy but where you are!" he told her. But perhaps troubled by his outburst, he said, "The reiteration of my love will only annoy you, and I must learn to write something else than love letters."

He hoped that this educated and well-read woman might put up with effusive love letters while she was ill but as soon as she had recovered "you will wish me to write more on business."

He added a touching postscript. "'Tis late in the day and I will ride to pass the night with an old bachelor friend. He is very old and one of my first friends in Texas. He is the only Revolutionary soldier I know in the republic."

Five days later Houston received word that Margaret had suddenly become critically ill. He dispatched a message to Jesse Walling at the nearby Strickland Settlement. "Please bring my horses, saddle, bridle, Blanket and Curry Comb, or send them by Mr. Thomas Chumley, as I must start to the West—Come directly. My wife is very unwell."

Margaret did not fully recover until the following spring when they moved at last into their own house at Cedar Point, at the head of Galveston Bay, near present-day Baytown. Houston had bought the two-thousand-acre property during his first term as president, and this beautiful windswept spot was his and Margaret's first home in Texas.

The log house was only the usual two rooms with a dog trot running through the house between them, but Margaret romantically named it "Ben Lomond," from the novel *Rob Roy* by Sir Walter Scott. The servants lived in a small outbuilding, and she and Sam had their little log house to themselves.

The modest house was typical of the young Republic of Texas. Truly grand houses were few and far between, even in the old, settled parts of the South. The majority of Texans lived subsistence lives, and log houses, homemade furniture with hide seats, and glassless windows were the rule, not the exception. Food was cooked over an open fire, water came from wells or streams, and indoor plumbing was unknown.

However, the air at Cedar Point was not the miasma that hovered over much of the lowlands. It was salty, fresh, and healthy. The fevers, chills, and agues, those common afflictions elsewhere, seemed not to strike as often, if at all, there on the bay.

They returned to Cedar Point throughout their married life. For Margaret it always represented their greatest happiness together. If Margaret lacked for company she had Houston's great friends Ashbel Smith and George Hockley to amuse her. Both had farms nearby and were frequent visitors.

The two bachelors were good companions for the young Mrs. Houston, and they helped her to understand her husband and his ambitions. She might have come to understand it but she never liked politics. It was a rival she could never hope to overcome.

Margaret Houston was plagued by various illnesses throughout their married life, the most persistent being a religious melancholia. She clearly had a strong constitution, however, and one suspects most of her physical indispositions were of the Victorian variety—vapors, fainting spells, nervous attacks—expected, indulged, and overlooked.

Then, too, Margaret Houston had a child about every other year— eight in all—which meant that for the twenty-three years they were married there was almost no time that she was not pregnant or did not have a small infant to care for. When Sam Houston died, the oldest of his children was only twenty and the youngest was not yet three. Where there are gaps in this cycle, they are possibly explained by miscarriages.

Her faith was profound, and like her mother, who was a preacher's wife, she worked hard on behalf of the Baptist church. In every community in which they lived they wholeheartedly supported the church. If there wasn't one they founded a new one.

Margaret Houston's childbearing and child-rearing were often done alone. Sam and Margaret were apart fully half their married life. Sometimes he was away from home ten months out of the year on legal or government business.

———

If any reminders were needed as to how precarious life was on the Texas frontier, the Comanches provided them throughout 1840. These Indians had never settled down in villages but followed the buffalo on which they depended. The huge herds still made the great migrations across Texas, and as late as December 1841, Adolphus Sterne recorded in his diary seeing large numbers of the beasts east of Austin.

The Comanches paid no attention to land claims, nor did they respect boundary lines—sometimes they hunted the white settlers as well as buffalo. The Anglos, however, were not as forbearing or given to peace-making as their Mexican predecessors, who had paid off the Comanches to keep the peace.

Once a year a delegation of Comanches used to come to Bexar for what was in effect tribute. After abusing the Mexican citizenry for three or four days, they left town and everyone lived more or less at peace for another year. It was extortion, but it worked.

The Anglos were having none of it. On March 19, the Texans and the Comanches sat down to talk in San Antonio. Although the Comanches had agreed to bring in all their white captives, they brought in only one, a fifteen-year-old girl named Matilda Lockhart. The Texans informed the Indians that they would be held captive themselves until all their white prisoners were released.

The Comanches boldly insisted that Matilda Lockhart was their only captive, but she told a different story. The others were being held about sixty miles away and the Comanches intended to surrender them one at a time, dragging out the process in order to extract more and more ransom.

When the braves realized that the Texans were on to them and were serious about holding them prisoner, they tried to fight their way out of the building. Seven whites and thirty-five Indians were killed in the so-called Council House Fight. A few more whites were released, but the Comanches murdered most of their captives in retaliation.

In a separate incident, the Comanches gave up a little girl, about seven years old, but promised to surrender more. The whites at first went along, but when the Comanches did not release any more prisoners the Texans attacked, killing or capturing the entire band. Again it was the captives who suffered, however. Before they could be rescued, most of them were killed by the enraged Indians.

Although the inhumanity of the hostage-taking and the barbarous murders by the Comanches were appalling and indefensible, the incidents were handled abysmally by Lamar. Most of the unfortunate white captives were dead, and the Texans had an Indian war on their hands.

The Comanches wanted more revenge than the murder of a few captives for the deaths of the chiefs and warriors at the Council House. A few months later, in August 1840, over four hundred Comanches rampaged down the Guadalupe all the way to the Gulf of Mexico, where they burned Linnville and sacked Victoria. Twenty whites were killed in the raid, houses and barns were burned, and over two thousand horses and mules were taken.

A German couple, the Kuchens, found themselves besieged in their cabin by three hundred Indians. They held their fire in spite of the provocations of the raiders—waiting until the Indians were close enough so that every shot would count. The Comanches might overrun the cabin, but too many of them would die in the event. They finally withdrew and left the brave couple with their house and their scalps intact.

From Victoria, the Comanche force began its retreat to the west and safety. They were intercepted at Plum Creek, near, appropriately, Lockhart, and on August 12 were decisively defeated by the Texans and their allies, several bands of Lipan and Tonkawa Indians. A firsthand account of the carnage and atrocities after the battle gives a heartrending picture of how dangerous life was on the frontier, especially for women.

> Beneath the shade of some trees that formed a point of woods . . . we beheld a melancholy picture of distress. Mrs. Watts, a young and delicate bride, whose husband had been murdered at her side, during the bloody massacre at Linnville, lay wounded, paralized and almost fainting from the loss of blood. At the commencement of the action, to prevent her rescue or escape, an Indian warrior had sent a barbed arrow into her breast, and left her for dead. But a few yards off, and most dreadfully mangled, lay a negro woman her faithful servant, whose little daughter stood weeping at her side. . . .
>
> Further on, between two gigantic live oaks, which stood isolated on the prairie, was extended the lifeless, mutilated form of Mrs. Crosby, a young and interesting woman, who was beautiful even in death. . . . Lances and arrows had pierced her breast in many places, and the green earth where we buried her was red with the warm and generous current of her heart. But a few days before an Indian had snatched her infant from her arms, while she was bound by cords to her horse, and catching it upon the point of his spear, as it fell, after having been thrown high into the air, cast it from him and crushed it in pieces on the ground.

The defeated Comanches themselves suffered terrible atrocities. In accordance with tribal rituals, the Tonkawas carved up a Comanche chief and hung the hands and feet and the "choice pieces of flesh from his body" alongside the strips of buffalo and venison which they carried on the trail. The Tonkawas reportedly ate twenty-two Comanche braves.

Not all the Comanches were driven west, however. As Noah Smithwick commented, "enough for vengeance still remained." In December

1840, Judge James W. Smith was killed only three miles outside Austin and his ten-year-old son was abducted.

———

Most Texans on the frontier no doubt disagreed with the *Texas Sentinel* that "all of those idle reports about Indian murders and Mexican depredations, are mere stuff; and only serve to keep off the ennui," but the Indians had ceased to be a major problem for the republic. Isolated Indian attacks continued for years, but the Anglos were now calling attention to another minority that was threatening the republic.

The Fourth Congress turned its attention to an act "concerning free persons of Color." As a percentage of the total inhabitants, the number of slaves was growing at a rate faster than the white population. Abolitionism, which was rapidly increasing in strength in the North, also made Texans fearful. Free Negroes were seen as a potential source of unrest.

On February 5, the Congress passed a freed slave code so severe that it constituted actual renewal of bondage. When the law took effect in two years' time, any free Negroes who were still in the country had ten days in which to leave. After that, they were subject to immediate arrest.

A bond of a thousand dollars was required guaranteeing removal. Any free Negro who could not post bond was to be auctioned at the courthouse door to the highest bidder—for one year's service.

After the year's servitude, the Negro was to be returned to the sheriff of the county and given another opportunity to raise the thousand-dollar bail guaranteeing deportation. If the bail could not be raised, the poor wretch was again to be returned to the auction block and this time sold for a lifetime of slavery.

Actually, the Texas law differed little from the slave codes enacted all over the South and which had their origins in Jefferson's 1778 Virginia statute that forced emancipated slaves to leave Virginia or "be out of the protection of the law."

———

As soon as he left office in 1838, Houston's supporters began to lay plans to return him to the presidency in 1841. Otherwise they were certain that Texas would not survive. Lamar, however laudable his intellectual and cultural goals, had been a disaster for the republic.

He opposed annexation to the United States. He had a grander vision for Texas than mere statehood in another republic. Lamar dreamed of a Texas that stretched to the Pacific Ocean and incorporated parts of Mexico. He initially worked for recognition by Mexico, but when it was not forthcoming he asked for a declaration of war instead. The Congress seem disposed to go along with this madness, but it was averted by Houston's impassioned plea for peace.

It was Lamar's fiscal policies, however, that most threatened the republic. He did not hesitate to print more money as needed. There was so little faith in the economy that when the currency called "red backs" appeared they were valued at only thirty-seven and a half cents on the dollar. The country was so buried in debt that there was real danger of complete economic collapse.

In December 1840, Lamar became too ill to discharge his duties and had to take a leave of absence. The illness was unspecified, but nervous exhaustion was the favorite cause chosen by his enemies. The vice-president, David G. Burnet, assumed the duties of president of Texas.

Incredibly, the first order of business was an attempt to raise the acting president's salary, in spite of the fact that the country was broke. Lamar's salary was reportedly $10,000 per year with an additional $11,000 for a house and furnishings and $1,500 for a secretary. Houston killed the pay raise by vociferously pointing out that the constitution forbade a salary increase for a sitting president. The Congress circumvented this legal obstacle by voting a "donation" of $6,500 to Burnet.

Burnet and Lamar—unfortunately—were in accord over policy, so the direction of the government changed not at all. The plans for the Santa Fe Expedition, which was as foolish as any of the proposed expeditions to Matamoros, proceeded. Lamar was convinced that the citizens of New Mexico were anxious to be part of Texas and were only waiting for an invitation. He planned to send a mixed force of soldiers, traders, and the merely curious to open up the lucrative trade route to the West and press the citizenry to join with Texas.

Lamar was correct that new trading markets had to be opened up, but the Congress fortunately declined to authorize what was clearly an invasion of Mexican territory no matter how it was presented.

Houston knew what disastrous consequences could come from such an expedition. It would not only provoke Mexico, which had been relatively quiet since Texas independence, but it could create a full-blown diplomatic crisis with other nations—particularly the United States. Annexation was still the goal, at least to right-thinking people.

In the spring of 1841, Lamar, his health improved, returned to Austin and to his dreams of a great independent nation. Imperiously, he dispatched the expedition to Santa Fe without congressional approval. As far as he was concerned, the executive had almost unlimited power. The caravan set off in a flood of high spirits, which soon dried up in the arid reaches of West Texas. Worse than thirst and hunger awaited them as they neared their destination. Not only was Mexican Santa Fe not interested, but the pathetic group that finally straggled into New Mexico was captured and marched off to Mexico City in late 1841.

———

Houston's campaign for a second presidential term officially began in March. His opponent was Vice-President Burnet. For months acrimony, vitriol, and just plain nastiness became commonplace in Texas. In addition to their inflammatory speeches, the two candidates each wrote a series of newspaper articles attacking the other—Houston signing his "Truth" and Burnet using the nom de plume "Publius." For all their viciousness, the articles were never less than literate and always a special source of amusement to the candidates' supporters. They were political invective of a high order—slander raised to an art form.

Burnet had begun the newspaper war over a year before in the *Texas Sentinel.* He was an educated man, but his articles reveal a polish that was probably given them by the poet-president Lamar. In refuting Houston's argument that the Mexicans had provided for the Indians of Texas in their settlement decrees, he wrote that such a conclusion can only have come from Houston's "own fertile brain, which, in spite of long habitual inebriation, is still prolific of low devices, and of foul machinations to injure others, and cunning contrivances to benefit himself."

Burnet not only called Houston a drunk, but also allowed that he was a coward, a bad lawyer, and a worse general. A large proportion of the ravages of the war were perpetrated not by the Mexican invaders but by the Texas forces under Houston. The burning of San Felipe de Austin was the "stupid order of a frightened chief," he said.

Bonnell, in an editorial, also disparaged the events of 1836, even denigrating Houston's efforts to keep the wagons moving. "Travis held in check a mighty army with a handful of men, for weeks; while the prince of renegades was heaving and grunting at the hind wheel of a wagon, to create as much space between him and the enemy as possible."

Bonnell had other targets as well. He despised any sort of competition from other editors and impetuously attacked them and their newspapers. Bonnell said of A. M. Tomkins of the *Houston Daily Times,* that he was "destitute of truth, as he is of the common decencies of life." As for the Indians, Bonnell poured more pitch on that fire, as if it needed any. "An Indian has not one redeeming quality in his composition: the whole race are *thieves* and *murderers;* and the Cherokees, with all their boasted improvement, are not an exception to the rule."

Houston's first "Truth" article appeared in the *Houstonian* on August 16. He immediately attacked "Publius" by telling the public that the middle initial of David G. Burnet stood for "Grog" not Governeur. Sam also consistently and sneeringly called Burnet either Davy or Wetumpka.

He accused Burnet of delaying the departure from New Washington and risking capture by Almonte in order to retrieve a demijohn of brandy. And in Galveston, Burnet had women and children thrown off a ship to make room for himself and his family in case they had to flee again.

As for Houston's condemnation of Burnet's sale of his land grant to the Galveston Bay and Texas Land Company, Houston himself probably profited from this sale. He was, after all, an agent of the company and had helped set up the meeting between Burnet and the New York financiers. He chose to ignore this finer point, however.

"Truth" also accused Burnet of treason, fraud, cowardice, drunkenness, and hypocrisy. He ended one of his pieces with a polemical flourish—"You political brawler and canting hypocrite, whom the waters of Jordan could never cleanse from your political and moral leprosy."

Burnet continued to respond in kind, but when Houston called him, of all things, a "hog thief" he challenged him to a duel. Moral leper, coward, drunk, and common thief were apparently acceptable. Hog thief was not. Burnet sent Branch T. Archer to deliver the challenge to Houston. Dr. Archer said to Sam, "General Houston, do you remember the lie you told me in '36, soon after your inauguration? You told me that Judge Burnet had received two hundred and fifty thousand dollars for liberating Santa Anna."

Houston replied with his "peculiar emphasis," reported Burnet. "G-r-e-a-t G-o-d!! MY-dear-friend!! Didn't Judge Burnet charge me with being bribed too?" Houston's deliberate calm and good humor defused the situation.

One morning as he left the Eberle House in Austin and was walking down Congress Avenue, Houston ran into one of the meanest and most persistent of his many critics.

"Good morning," said Sam.

"I don't speak to scoundrels," replied the other.

"I do," said Houston.

The vindictiveness had little real effect on the election, other than provide entertainment for the electorate. The people realized that Burnet was not what the country needed. He, after all, had been allied with the Lamar administration for three years so he was at least partly responsible for the disarray of the country.

However such a campaign can only have an adverse effect on government, the political system, and society in general. The political mudslinging by the two principals also exacerbated animosities across the political spectrum. The early republic was always a volatile place, but the worst violence had come from invaders and hostile Indians.

Now some of the most respected citizens did not hesitate to attack each other. A bill was passed to suppress dueling, but not much could be done if people chose to assault each other in the halls of Congress. A favorite spot to get even was in the Capitol building itself, the hallway between the House and Senate.

While the Cherokee Land Bill was being debated, Representative Thomas Green from Fayette attacked Senator Kindred Muse from Nacogdoches with a dirk and Samuel W. Jordan threatened Houston with an an ax. Only the timely intervention of Adolphus Sterne prevented Houston from being hacked to death. The unstable Jordan committed suicide the following summer.

The bloodiest encounter was between David Kaufman and James S.

Mayfield in December 1841. After a bitter exchange on the floor of the House, Mayfield waited for Kaufman in the hallway outside and shot him. Kaufman survived and no one was prosecuted, but Mayfield continued his murderous ways. He challenged Burleson to a duel and then killed a man named Absolom Bostwich during an argument in La Grange.

Perhaps the lowest point in the election campaign was an editorial in the *Texas Sentinel* in May. "If our citizens, regardless of this reproach, should elect to the highest office within their gift, a confirmed sot and worn out debauchee, will they not fix this calumny like an indelible stain upon the fair escutcheon of their country's reputation?" asked the editorialist. What will the world think of Texas if "our chief magistrate is seen reeling in the chair of state, with his robes of office dappled in the vomit of intoxication."

Houston was elected president on September 6, 1841. He received 75 percent of the vote. Burleson became the new vice-president. After such a vitriolic campaign, the winner was not about to extend an olive branch. "The *result* has shown the contempt of a free people for the wicked and base orginators of falsehood," said Houston.

The president-elect moved immediately to project an image of austerity and belt-tightening by refusing invitations to public dinners. "I have no wish to add to the pressure of our circumstances, by incurring any unnecessary expenses, to those unavoidable outlays of money, which the citizens have been compelled to pay for the support of the Government," he said.

He did, however, accept speaking engagements. In Houston there was a great parade, with Sam on horseback and a seven-gun salute. The procession ended at the Presbyterian church, where he delivered a stem-winder—more sermon than speech—in praise of hearth and home, country, virtuous women, democratic ideals, fiscal responsibility, and temperance.

"For the want of the sweet attractions of the fireside, it has been too usual among us to have recourse to the grog shop," said the recent convert to sobriety and family bliss, "either for the purpose of exhiliration, or to while away the time; or, still more demoralizing, to resort to the faro bank."

The speech was not all religious piety just to make his wife happy, however. He blasted the Lamar administration, fiscal irresponsibility, and foolish expeditions like the one to Santa Fe. He was especially anxious to restore the rule of law—to stamp out the lawlessness that had become rampant. "I shall endeavor to sustain the judiciary of the country—the true palladium of civil, political and religious liberty," he said.

Houston arrived in Austin on Wednesday, December 8, for his inauguration. A large crowd went out to meet him on the road into town, led by the Travis Guards and accompanied by carriages filled with the ladies.

He was welcomed by the mayor and then the whole parade moved into town where the president-elect was greeted by an artillery salute. A "collation" at the Eberle House and a dance closed the day's festivities. The pro-Houston Austin *Daily Texian* extolled the triumphant entry of the hero.

> We stop the presses to announce the arrival of Gen. Sam. Houston, President elect. We are happy to state that he is in good health and fine spirits. We look forward, with pleasing anticipation, to Monday next as the great day of deliverance from profligacy and misrule, visionary and poetical effeminancy in the administration of the affairs of government.

The *Texian* like its archrival the *Bulletin* lasted only a few months, but the two editors managed to stir up the usual Texas journalistic blood feud in the first issues in spite of the fact that they were both Houston supporters. G. H. Harrison of the *Texian* said that the *Bulletin*'s editorial columns were "entirely destitute of intelligence." Samuel Whiting of the *Bulletin* said that Harrison was not only "an idiot" but was "a fellow as ignorant as a cart-horse."

He also wondered why no copies of the *Texian* had been seen in a while, although someone had reported seeing a seedy character heading into the trees behind the Capitol carrying a copy and "manifesting a nervous disposition of his fingers to interfere with the fastenings of his suspenders."

———

Margaret Houston did not come to Austin to attend her husband's inauguration. She very likely was pregnant and had remained in Houston. Sam was alone again, although not a bachelor, and he was sober. He ostentatiously refused to stay in Lamar's ostentatious presidential mansion. Instead he put up at the Eberle House.

Angelina Belle Eberle welcomed the president-elect, the hero of San Jacinto, although she did not think so well of him. She had grown up in Nashville and she had lived in Columbia during his first presidential administration. However, it was another association with Houston that rankled. She had lost her hotel in San Felipe when the town went up in flames during the retreat in 1836. As for President Houston, he soon would have cause to curse Angelina Eberle's name for the rest of his life.

12

A Second Term

MORE THAN a thousand people—the entire population of Austin, give or take a few die-hard anti-Houstonites—attended the swearing-in. The crowd was so large that the ceremony was moved outdoors to a covered platform behind the Capitol. The weather was sunny and warm and there was a perfect Texas blue sky.

Houston had left the nation in relatively good shape three years before, and he had delivered his farewell address done up as a well-to-do eighteenth-century gentleman. The people of Texas had come to expect almost anything of their hero, but when he appeared on the platform there was considerable murmuring in the audience. Houston was wearing a linsey-woolsey hunting shirt, pantaloons, an old hat, and his favorite footwear, doeskin Indian moccasins. The fastidious Adolphus Sterne was not impressed—"*too much Indian that*," he said.

The imagery was not lost on the crowd. Old Sam was dressed as a mendicant for good reason. The republic was millions of dollars in debt and there was not a penny in the till. The ceremony was not without color, however. Houston took the oath of office surrounded by battle flags from San Jacinto, and, by telegraphic arrangement, at precisely the moment he kissed the Bible, one of the famous "Twin Sisters" roared the news that Houston was back as president.

The inaugural ball that evening was a splendid affair. The Senate chamber was brightly lighted and decorated with a large picture of the hero of San Jacinto. The packed room was hot and uncomfortable, but no one minded. The revelers danced until one o'clock in the morning.

The vitriolic election campaign had been contested mainly on personality. Now the great issues had to be confronted—fiscal austerity, disputed land grants, security from hostile Indians, and the removal of the capital. The most important concern, annexation, was supported nearly unanimously by the people.

Congressman Houston had worked tirelessly to engineer the removal of the capital back to the east. Perhaps President Houston might have more success. Austin still had its proponents, however, mostly Lamar partisans but also that Texas perennial that is even hardier than the fabled bluebonnet or the tough mesquite—the land speculator.

When Margaret Houston did not show up for the inaugural, everyone's suspicions were aroused. Was she really indisposed or was she waiting in Houston for her husband's speedy return—with the government in tow?

———

The president's closest advisers were Secretary of State Anson Jones, Secretary of War George Washington Hockley, Treasurer Asa Brigham, Attorney General George W. Terrell, Comptroller Francis R. Lubbock, and Washington D. Miller, his private secretary.

The vice-president, Edward Burleson, was virtually ignored. He and Houston kept their distance. They communicated only a few times and then through an intermediary. During one entire congressional session, Houston saw the vice-president only twice, when they happened to run into each other in the street.

Texas fiscal affairs were in disorder bordering on insolvency. Land sales were stagnant. The Lamar paper currency, the redbacks, had sunk to two cents on the dollar. Inflation seemed uncontrollable. Texas could not look to the United States for either private or public funds. Things were not much better up north.

The Van Buren administration had been done in by the Panic of 1837, which still continued to depress the economy. Van Buren learned, as all politicians must, that any accomplishments, no matter how noble, are soon drowned in disaffection if the people are in a sorry economic plight.

Furthermore Van Buren opposed annexation. He was convinced it would cause war with Mexico, a split in the Democratic party, and inflamed sectionalism. As it turned out he was right on all three counts. Many old-line Democrats deserted Van Buren and joined William Henry Harrison and the Whigs in the election of 1840.

Old Tippecanoe died on April 4, exactly a month after his inauguration. John Tyler became the first vice-president to succeed to the presidency. "His Accidency" promised no good to anyone in the Jackson-Houston camp. He had run with White of Tennessee against Van Buren in 1836. Worse, he had resigned from the Senate in 1837 rather than vote to expunge from the record the Senate censure of Jackson. Clay, whose hatred of Jackson bordered on the pathological, had sponsored the censure resolution in 1834 after Jackson had removed the government deposits from the national bank.

However Tyler felt about Jackson and Houston, he was nevertheless a fervid annexationist and Houston looked to him now to lead the way in Washington. Sam was more convinced than ever that the only salvation for Texas lay in becoming part of the United States.

Houston's first message to the Congress on December 20 was an eloquent and straightforward diagnosis of the state of the republic.

> It seems that we have arrived at a crisis in our national progress, which is neither cheering for the present nor flattering for the future. I heartily regret that truth will not allow me to approach the Congress with the usual felicitations of the present and prospective happiness. The time has arrived when facts must be submitted in their simplest dress.

He chastised those who, ignoring recent history, still longed to involve themselves in the internal affairs of Mexico. Every such expedition had ended in disaster and Texans must abandon such folly.

Once more he advocated treaties with the Indians and the establishment of trading posts on the frontier. Not only would private business profit but the government would save over three quarters of the amount being spent on defense against the Indians.

His recommendation for a long-term suspension of debt payments was uniquely forthright. Few elected officials would dare say to the Congress and the people: "We have no money—we cannot redeem our liabilities. These facts are known, and we had as well avow them by our legislation as demonstrate them by every day's experience."

Houston also cordially chided the Congress for the "unfortunate and improvident legislation" that had removed control of the military from him in his previous administration. He tacitly warned them that he would not allow this to happen again.

Ultimately, however, Houston's strength, like that of Old Hickory and all great leaders in a democracy, lay in the people. He reminded his listeners that "the people hope much and expect much in our present calamitous condition." As for himself, "I should," he said, "be accountable for the motives of my heart as well as the exercise of my intellectual faculties."

Two days after Houston's message to the Congress, a farewell ball was given for Mirabeau B. Lamar in the Senate chamber. Lamar's friends made sure that their celebration was grander than the inaugural ball. Abundant evergreens and candles were used to transform the rustic room. Two large signs proclaimed "An honest man the noblest work of God" and "We hope for your return."

In response to a complaint from an Austin lady, who wanted to wear a silk dress, spittoons were strategically placed around the dance floor. She had written to the *Austin Daily Bulletin* that she did not mind if her dress were spotted systematically—but irregularly "is not to my fancy." Couples also were asked not to bring their children to the ball since they "will have little opportunity to enjoy themselves, and will be much in the way of older persons."

Robert Potter introduced Lamar. In what must be one of the few recorded incidents of an insect being used to praise a politician, he extolled the ex-president. "The caterpillar of calumny would devour the leaves of the wreath which glory has bound upon his brow," said Potter. "Vain task!"

———

While Lamar and his partisans were dancing in the Capitol, out on the prairie about ten miles south of town a lone rider added a few dry sticks to his small campfire. The hard ride up from Bexar had worn him and his horse out and he had decided not to press on to Austin with the mail but to bed down for the night by the San Antonio Road. Fatigue and the chill Texas air made him careless. Even a small fire was visible for miles across the prairie.

On December 27, the *Daily Bulletin* reported the ominous news that the San Antonio mail rider had been missing for five days and a posse had been sent out to look for him. As the posse headed down the San Antonio Road, a great St. John's Day procession of Masons moved through the dirt streets of Austin. It was led by the president, followed by the cabinet and most members of Congress. At the Capitol, Houston delivered an oration.

The posse found the mail rider lying by the ashes of the little fire that had led the Indians to him. He had been scalped and his body left to be fed on by wolves. The mutilated remains were buried in a shallow grave and the site covered with rocks. That same night Austin went back to dancing, at the Masonic ball at the Eberle House.

The day after Lamar's friends had bid him farewell, many of the tired revelers took their seats in Congress, where they were presented with a report from the president. With his unerring instinct of just where and when to insert the knife, Houston recommended that the Lamar-built "President's House" and all the furniture be sold and the money put in the Treasury. The house was in too great a state of disrepair to be livable and because there were no locks on the doors it was being pillaged. Better to get rid of the house altogether, said the president. The report did more than just puncture the revelers' balloon. There was an implicit and sly analogy between the state of the nation and the state of Lamar's presidential mansion.

The question of annexation by the United States hung over Houston's second term like a great cloud. The Houston administration and the Texas Congress had to go about the business of government, but the real business of government was in Washington, D.C., and everyone knew it.

The population of Texas was still under 100,000, and fully one quarter of that number were slaves. Only large-scale immigration could alleviate many of the problems facing the country. More settlers were not going to come, however, until the statehood question was settled and the Mexican threat permanently removed.

Santa Anna had risen up from the political dead and returned to power in Mexico. The charismatic demagogue had been called back to lead the army against the French, who had occupied Vera Cruz. His bravery cost him part of a leg, and the people of Mexico could not content themselves with just idolizing the wounded hero. In a few months he was their absolute master. Forgetting or casting aside the agreements he made in Texas to save his skin in 1836, he again began to look north at the lost province. Trouble was to be expected.

The full story of the ghastly fate of the Santa Fe Expedition now reached Austin. Even though it was a great blunder—Andrew Jackson said it had so damaged Texas that it would take three San Jacintos to make people forget it—the people still came to the defense of the victims.

The massacres at San Antonio and Goliad were still fresh in everyone's memory, and the atrocities committed against the Santa Fe survivors and the rumors of an impending invasion by Mexico had Texas in an uproar. Houston felt obliged to remind his countrymen of their brave heritage and thus give them courage. He declared March 2 a national holiday.

————

Houston's ongoing battle with the Texas Congress is no better illustrated than by his attempts to bring it to heel over its cavalier public land policies. No one argued with selling land cheaply to new settlers and thus ensuring the future of Texas. But the House and Senate had found it too tempting to use public lands to finance wars, pay off debts, reward heroes, and hire soldiers without much regard for the consequences. Flooding an already depressed land market with more land lowered the price even further. An important source of revenue was made liable to the wildest fluctuations.

In his zeal, Houston unfortunately vetoed a bill awarding land bounties to officers, seamen, and marines of the navy. The old soldier realized that a navy was important, but he also had the soldier's bias against his maritime colleagues. He argued that naval personnel received bounties and prize money from the ships captured and that was enough. However, it seems unlikely that many sailors in the Texas Navy ever matched their land-based compatriots dollar for dollar.

His veto message betrays an almost puritanical, even hypocritical, argument against the bill. Perhaps Margaret's religiosity was already beginning to take hold. "Generally, the seaman has had no interest (except a transitory one) on shore," Houston said. Therefore the only real beneficiaries of the government's largesse would be the "harpies that are usually found in sea-ports, and to whom seamen usually become indebted."

Other vetoes were motivated by a concern for the common good and the diplomatic image that Texas presented to the world. Nothing must be allowed to endanger recognition by other powers and annexation by the United States. Mischievous members of the House and Senate, of course, had other agendas and they willfully passed one piece of ill-advised legislation after another.

Houston's political leadership during this particularly difficult time for the republic was as important as his military leadership had been during the revolution. He used the veto power like a machete to hack away at the foolishness sprouting in the Congress. He also did not hesitate to write the newspapers in order to take his case directly to the people.

The most dangerous congressional measure he confronted was an act of war disguised as "an act to define the boundaries of Texas." In a breathtaking display of imperialism, the House of Representatives passed a bill extending the boundaries of Texas to include two thirds of Mexico. It was, of course, Lamar's old dream of extending the territorial limits all the way to the Pacific.

Houston returned the bill, reminding the legislators that Texas had a population of under 100,000 and the proposed annexed territories had over 2,000,000. How could Texas govern this vast domain with a population twenty times its own? Further, it would jeopardize diplomatic negotiations with Europe and the United States.

England, which was serving as an intermediary between the two still-hostile nations, could withdraw. In Mexico the opposition to Santa Anna would cease as everyone united to fight the common foe, Texas. Immigration from the United States and Europe, which was essential to the growth of the republic, would also be halted. Even the hint of a war scared off new settlers. And then there was the plight of the Santa Fe captives still held in Mexican prisons. They would be slaughtered in reprisal.

Finally, he could not resist a jab at the Congress itself. Perhaps worse than all the problems he had listed was the damage the act could inflict on the image of Texas as a nation able to govern itself. "I am inclined to believe," he said, "other nations would regard the measure as visionary—or as a legislative jest."

Houston also vetoed a bill that would have established a chain of sixteen military posts—forty to a hundred miles to the west of the current frontier. The purpose of the bill was to encourage the extension of settlement, but the new posts and settlements could only be located in the Indian hunting grounds.

Again here was a bill that in effect was a declaration of war—against the Indians. Houston's old military nightmare was reborn. Soldiers and rangers would find themselves "forted up" with no hope of reinforcement when the inevitable attack came from thousands of understandably vengeful warriors. The isolated settlers would be exposed to even greater danger.

Houston renewed his plea with Congress to pacify the wild Indians by trade and commerce, the way the English had pacified the Cherokees. He reminded the legislators that Texas would still be a wilderness if Stephen Austin had not done the same thing. He excoriated what he called the "policy of 'extermination' by war."

The last week in January and the first week in February of 1842 saw a blizzard of messages, vetoes, and proclamations. Houston was lonely in Austin. He missed his wife. He began rushing through his executive duties so he could leave for Houston and be reunited with her.

It had been two years since the draconian bill concerning free persons of color had been passed. The deadline for these innocent unfortunates to leave Texas or face renewed slavery was upon them. In a presidential proclamation, Houston extended the deadline and remitted all penalties for twelve months. He also lowered the bond to five hundred dollars. It was an imperfect solution, but once again he had come down on the side of right.

Sam left Austin on February 5. For the journey home, he chose an unusual but more serviceable mount than the stallions he usually favored—a riding mule named Bruin. He made the trip in just under four days, passing everyone else on the road and getting to Houston at the same time as friends who had left Austin a full day before he had—at least according to his account of the journey.

Margaret was surprised and delighted that Sam had returned from the capital early. He had kept his word. She had not had to go to the wild frontier and he had been away only two months. If his plan to bring the capital back east went as it should, he would never return to Austin.

As it happened his plan did not work out, but it was still many years before he again set foot in Lamar's city on the Colorado. This short-sightedness and stubbornness on the issue of the capital lost Houston many of his supporters. He actually lied to his friend Samuel Whiting when he told him that even though bills were introduced authorizing the removal of the seat of government as well as the national archives neither would actually take place.

In a rare, for him, lack of foresight, Houston never grasped the psychological and political importance to Texas of having the capital at the projected center of the country. It was certainly true that Austin was a dangerous place, as the murder of the mail rider reminded everyone. Indians sometimes came into the town itself and only the foolish went alone into the countryside.

While Congress wasin session a young deerhunter was killed and horribly mutilated just across the Colorado, not two miles from the Capitol. And each full moon—the so-called Comanche Moon—the residents kept close to home and walked a little more carefully. The bright moonlight lit the way for the Indians raiders who often came on foot. They could ride home—on stolen horses.

Houston's critics, of course, charged that his opposition to Austin as the capital had more to do with his large landholdings in the East than the threat of Indian raids. Nevertheless, it was the destiny of Texas to move west.

Sam and Margaret spent the rest of the month at Cedar Point and Galveston. Margaret's fragile health—or whatever it was that caused her indispositions—again interposed and prevented her from enjoying the sea air and her husband's company.

However, Sam's concerns over Margaret Houston's health were almost forgotten when on March 10 he heard the news that Texans had expected and feared the most. A Mexican invasion force had crossed the Rio Grande and captured Goliad, Refugio, Victoria, and Bexar.

All the old terrors now surfaced. Houston not only feared a repeat of the Runaway Scrape, but it was the planting season and he worried that farmers would not get their crops in the ground. Perhaps even worse than people fleeing to the east would be irregulars marching to the west, "without orders and in a tumultuous mass" to engage the Mexicans. He ordered that no army was to move until he returned to Houston to supervise directly the mobilization. He and Margaret arrived in Houston on March 14.

Houston thought that he had at last been given a compelling reason to order the removal of the country's archives to Houston, now the de facto capital. Austin was in the line of the enemy march. The citizens of Austin felt differently and guessed what was behind the order. They packed up the archives, set a guard over them, and there the records remained.

President Houston could not resist becoming General Houston in the emergency. The old military juices began flowing. He issued detailed orders to his commanders facing the Mexicans. His dispatches were only for the interim. He intended to join the army for the fight.

There was no war, however. The Mexican force turned out to be much smaller than reported—only about four hundred men—and it was not an invasion but an incursion. The Mexicans held San Antonio just two days and then withdrew—almost a week before the Texans arrived.

Houston was clearly disgusted with the feeble intelligence he had received. He wrote a sarcastic note to Ashbel Smith, his new minister to France, "You are right!—just right, Rodriquez!!! What a pity they did not reconnoiter the force at San Antonio—e're they hallowed wolf— This won't make a Major General.—My composure is not much startled. 1200 men can whip a Cavalliardo of Mexicans. 'Tis so!"

Of course, he was well aware of the dangers that Mexico still presented to the republic, but he also had to control the hotheads. He therefore publicly favored going on the offensive. "No one in Texas is more determined that Mexico shall be invaded than I am," he said, "but we must be prepared." He would see to it that the preparations took a very long time. Houston had no intention of taking the war south.

Privately he said that such an invasion could only be done in concert with "our 'Uncle Sam.' " But he knew that there was not a prayer of John Tyler's sending troops into Mexico.

The presence of any Mexican troops in Texas, no matter how few, was enough to rupture relations between Texas and Mexico. Texas had unsuccessfully tried various schemes to gain recognition of its independence by its former master. Eventually the Texas diplomats fell back on the usual Anglo solution to a diplomatic problem with a country to the south—bribery. Texas offered to deposit in London $5 million for Mexico and $200,000 for the agents of the government.

Santa Anna not only refused, he published the correspondence in the American press. He announced that the honor of Mexico demanded that Texas be reclaimed and that he intended to do just that. Houston responded directly to "the pompous declaration of the self-created potentate of Mexico." Writing to Santa Anna on March 21, 1842, he countered the threat with a promise to "march across the Rio Grande" and plant the "Texian standard of the single star" on the Isthmus of Darien.

He was posturing, however, because he still did not call the Congress into session. His natural contempt for the legislature played some part in his delay, but there was also some doubt as to whether the western delegates would show up in Houston. The executive branch might now look upon that eastern city as the capital, but many in the Congress still favored Austin.

By the summer Houston could avoid the confrontation no longer. Congress was convened in Houston on June 27, and the dissidents from the west showed up. The president asked for new laws to deal with "insurrection," a clear reference to the people in Austin who had now supposedly buried the national archives to keep them in town.

As for an offensive war against Mexico, the Congress was not long in exhibiting the sort of behavior that deservedly merited Houston's contempt. He was given a war but no means to fight it. The president was authorized to sell ten million acres of land to prosecute the war, which was impossible in the economic climate of Texas and the United States.

The other conditions were as frustrating. The war must be fought with volunteers, but the prescribed term of service was so short that Texas could have as many as five thousand unemployed men on the loose in six months' time. To Houston this was a greater danger than an invading army of Mexicans.

The president's chief complaint was much more serious. The Congress had invested him with "extraordinary powers and discretion." Houston would never misuse the powers, he said, but in some future emergency another leader "clothed with similar power, and deriving authority from this example alone," might not be so forbearing and crush the liberties of Texas. He rejected these new and unconstitutional powers. "I can never sanction the adoption of a principle at war with the convictions of my mind, the practice of my life and the liberties of my fellow men," he said at the end of his veto message.

The president was upholding higher constitutional principles, but the war party, which is to say the political opposition, was aroused. There were also misgivings among his own partisans who felt that Houston *should* exercise more power. Indeed, Hockley resigned from the government. Houston had to remind his friend that "the President's duty is to execute the laws, but not to enact them—nor is he to decide what laws ought to have been passed."

Still, in the long run, Houston's popularity was diminished not at all by his refusal to accept extraordinary powers and to prosecute an offensive war. On the contrary, the people remained bound to him. He was stronger than ever. From The Hermitage, Jackson wrote on August 17, "By your veto you have saved your country, and yourself from disgrace."

Santa Anna's threats were serious, but Houston nevertheless revoked the Texan blockade of Mexican ports and began to pursue a more peaceful course at the behest of the newly arrived British chargé d'affaires, Charles Elliot. The British diplomat was amazed when he was received by the president of Texas in a resplendent floor-length red silk robe, a gift of the Ottoman sultan, Abd al-Majid. The sultan had also sent a pair of baggy Turkish pants, with yellow shoes sewed to them, a silk sash, and a red fez with a black tassel. Houston balked at wearing the trousers, but he liked the robe and regularly wore it on hot days. In 1843, he dazzled the Indians when he showed up wearing it to a conference.

Houston's peace overtures to Mexico were repaid by another Mexican army marching into Texas. On September 16, a courier from Bexar galloped into Houston with the news that General Adrian Woll, the Belgian mercenary, had marched into San Antonio on September 11 with an army of thirteen hundred men. Woll captured the town without a shot being fired.

Although Houston was again seriously ill and obliged to dictate his correspondence to Miller, he issued mobilization orders to the country to expel the invaders and pursue them into Mexico if necessary so "that they should receive that chastisement which the injuries inflicted upon us imperiously demand." Interestingly, Jackson, in his letter of August 17, had used much the same wording and prescribed almost the same strategy.

Woll retreated after only ten days. Santa Anna's tactics clearly involved nothing more than harassment of the frontier and were designed to keep Texas off guard and in a constant state of anxiety. Houston had to respond, and on October 3 he dispatched Alexander Somervell to proceed with a volunteer force of seven hundred men to the southwest frontier. Somervell was authorized to advance into Mexico if there was any "prospect of success," but this was to assuage those who demanded invasion. Houston never really believed that Texas should go much beyond the threat he had set in motion.

Using the unrest on the western frontier as an excuse, Houston had kept the capital in the east, but by October the government of Texas had moved again—to Washington on the Brazos. That little town's citizens had enthusiastically offered various enticements, including free transportation, to lure the seat of government away from Houston.

As the caravan cleared Houston, the president climbed down from his carriage and while stomping the dust off his boots pronounced a curse on his namesake city, which presumably had not done enough to hold on to the government.

Whatever the drawbacks were with the town of Houston, Washington on the Brazos certainly had more of them. The largest building in town and the only one that could accommodate the Congress was Hatfield's Grocery, which was not what its name implied. Hatfield's was not a place to buy provisions. It was a saloon with a large upstairs gambling hall.

All saloons were euphemistically called "groceries" in republican Texas, but that still did not make them respectable. It was still considered unseemly for legislators to enter and exit through a saloon. So the stairway up to the gambling hall where Congress met was moved to the outside of the building and the interior stairwell covered over.

When the Congress was not in session, the room reverted to being a gambling den, social hall, or even church. Hatfield was not particular as long as he got his rent. On one memorable Sunday morning the sacred and profane were joined. An itinerant preacher named Robert Alexander arrived at Hatfield's to conduct church services and found the town gamblers had already assembled in the hall for their regular game. The Reverend Alexander was not inhibited in the least by the rough crowd and he railed away. The gamblers listened. The collection plate overflowed.

In his message to Congress in December, Houston again demonstrated that rare political candor that while it defines a nation's problems makes no friends among those who refuse to recognize that there are any problems. "Texas in truth presents an anomaly in the history of nations," he said, "for no country has ever existed without a currency, nor has any government ever been administered without means."

Houston once again called for the archives to be moved from Austin to the east, a regular force to patrol the frontier, and increased trade with the Indians. He was resolute on the Indian question, and placed the blame on the whites for the Council House Fight and the Comanche raid of 1840. As for treaties with the Indians, "God will ratify all the advantages which may arise to either party under equitable stipulations; for He hates fraud, imposition, oppression, and injustice." Little wonder that there were people who wanted to kill the president.

General Somervell pressed on to the Rio Grande with his enthusiastic army. It was another of those crowds that Henry Smith would have quickly condemned as a mob masquerading as an army. They did meet with some success—capturing Laredo and Guerrero—but it was soon evident that a full-scale crossing of the river and an invasion of Mexico proper were not feasible goals. The expedition, which by now comprised about five hundred men, faltered on the banks of the Rio Grande. Somervell and two hundred of the volunteers turned back into Texas.

The remainder, about three hundred men under the command of William S. Fisher, refused to retreat. The expedition crossed the Rio

Grande. It would soon become famous as the Mier Expedition, after the little town on the west bank of the Rio Grande which the Texan force attacked on Christmas Day, 1842.

A fierce battle ensued, and although the Texans inflicted fearful casualties on the Mexicans they had no chance of victory. Their surrender on December 27 marked the end of serious agitation for invasions of Mexico, or at least it would have if not for the malevolent Santa Anna.

During the overland march toward Mexico City, the Mier prisoners revolted and escaped near Salado, Mexico. Some made good their escape, but 176 were recaptured. Perhaps to enhance the image he had so carefully cultivated in 1836 or to repeat his great successes at the Alamo and Goliad, Santa Anna ordered all the recaptured Texans executed. After remonstrances from his marginally more humane subordinates, his orders were modifed so that only every tenth man was to die.

In the infamous Black Bean episode at Salado, 159 white beans and 17 black beans were placed in a jar and each man forced to draw. The seventeen unfortunate men who drew the black beans were immediately put to death. The leader of the escapees, Ewen Cameron, drew a white bean, but Santa Anna ordered him to be shot anyway.

On January 4, 1843, Houston sent a message worthy of Pontius Pilate to the Texas House of Representatives. It is illustrative of the enduring fact that even the greatest of leaders is subject to pique. He had become as monomaniacal on the subject of the capital and the archives as Jackson had been on John and Peggy Eaton.

"Whatever evil that may befall the Nation from the loss or destruction of its archives, must fall upon the people, but not by the agency of their President," he said. Houston complained that he had done everything he could to protect the archives, but he was now "discharged from all further agency and his hands are clear." He foresaw only calamities and, he added ominously, "they will be heavy and manifold!"

Houston's outburst was caused by a more or less spontaneous uprising in Austin the week before. The president had sent rangers to remove the archives and they had loaded them onto wagons and were heading out of town when Angelina Eberle discovered what was going on. She ran out of her hotel and set off the cannon that was kept loaded to warn the town against Indian attacks.

The ranger archivists made good their escape, but the next day, January 1, a vigilante force overtook the wagon train at Kenney's Fort near present-day Round Rock. The archives were returned to Austin to await a friendlier administration. The Archive War, General Sam Houston's only military defeat, was over.

———

On May 25 Margaret Lea Houston gave birth to her first child, Sam Houston, Jr., in Washington on the Brazos. According to Houston's secretary, Washington Miller, the "rascal" was a perfect little replica of Old Sam. According to Old Sam, Master Sam was as "robust and hearty as a Berkshire pig."

Soon after, Sam and Margaret began a new house at Grand Cane, twenty-two miles north of Liberty, on property Houston had owned for ten years. They were close by William and Antoinette Bledsoe's plantation and also that of another relative, Vernon Lea. Nancy Lea had moved in with Sam and Margaret the previous winter, and she came along with them to Grand Cane.

The year remaining in Houston's second term was perhaps the most important year of his presidency. The flame of annexation by the United States may have flickered from time to time, but it never really dimmed. All the arguments for and against annexation had gained added power with the growing call for abolition and the increasing sectionalism of the country. Texas became the vessel in which all the competing parties poured their hopes and fears.

From The Hermitage, Andrew Jackson led the fight. He said that he had always believed that Texas had been part of the Louisiana Purchase, and he adamantly denied that he had told Adams back in 1819 that the boundary at the Sabine was acceptable. "I again declare," said Jackson, "that Adams statement that I was consulted by him on the boundery of the Florida treaty [Adams-Onís] before it was made and that I agreed to the boundery proposed, the Sabine, is positively *false, false, false his diary to the contrary notwithstanding.*"

Adams had, of course, at President Monroe's order, consulted with

Jackson. They had gone over the boundaries with a map at Adams's house in Washington. Jackson also told Monroe that he should "be content with the Floridas." However, selective forgetting and elective denial have ever been the prerogative of politicians.

Although Houston himself had qualms about joining up with the United States—which was, in reality, he said, "two distinct nations," the North and the South—there was never any serious doubt about which way he wanted to lead Texas. "So far as I am concerned, or my hearty cooperation required," he wrote Jackson, "I am determined upon immediate annexation to the United States."

He was fearful that the instability caused by "wicked and ambitious men" who had flocked to Texas would eventually destroy the republic. "I wish to reside in a land where all will be subordinate to law," said Houston, "where none dare to defy its mandates." This February 16, 1844, letter to Jackson, was in many ways a manifesto.

> If there is any selfishness in my heart I do not know it. I have now lived for half a century, and thirty years of that time I have been chiefly engaged in active employment for, as I believed, the advancement of human happiness. How far I may have been useful is a question I never ask. How my actions are to be appreciated, so they are right, I never care. . . . Circumstances have thrown me into prominent and responsible situations, and like yourself, General, I have received a full share of abuse. But that has never deterred me from doing what I believe to be right, regardless of consequences.

Jackson replied on March 15. He had no doubt that the annexation treaty would be ratified and he defended the secrecy surrounding the negotiations and the wording of the treaty. Secrecy, he said, "prevents that arch fiend, J. Q. Adams, from writing memorials and circulating them for signatures in the opposition to the annexation of Texas." He predicted that "before this wretched old man can circulate his fire-brands, and memorials against the ratification of the treaty, it will be ratified by the Senate."

Great issues can often cause otherwise honorable men to bend the rules and to dissemble. Few issues in American history have caused such questionable behavior as the annexation of Texas. Houston was not exempt. He did not hesitate to play off the governments of England, France, Mexico, and the United States—often simply lying to gain his ends. He convinced Elliot that he was opposed to annexation and indeed wanted closer ties with England. The British chargé d'affaires dutifully relayed this good news back to Whitehall.

The British rightly viewed the United States as their most serious potential international rival and were anxious to prevent American expansion westward. The American government was equally alarmed by the apparent new friendliness toward England by Texas. The Tyler administration was not anxious for a powerful country to have hegemony over a weak and unstable republic on its southwestern border. The situation was further exacerbated by Anglo-American disputes over Oregon, the border between Maine and Canada, and the area around Lake Superior.

The old prejudices had not died. The British ambassador at Washington wrote to Palmerston after the 1830 elections, "The combinations of the lower Classes and their desire for influence at the Elections, are a cause of apprehension to the more respectable part of the Community." He no doubt had talked to Adams.

Palmerston had been secretary of war during the War of 1812 and he was still smarting over the defeat of British arms. Many in the British establishment, of both parties, never accepted American independence and certainly not the American form of government. In 1843, Lord Brougham ruminated aloud in the House of Lords that there was "a soreness of feeling on our side of the water" over the establishment of a powerful democratic government without a king, prelate, or nobility—especially since it had been "affected at the point of the sword after a series of defeat, disaster and disgrace to the British arms."

Successful diplomacy in any age demands long-range policies that serve the national interest, but in the nineteenth century this was especially so. The great time it took to send and receive messages necessitated that diplomats, even in the most remote outposts, could respond properly to a given crisis, confident that they were carrying out their government's policies.

American foreign policy has generally been quite the opposite, based more on expediency than on any grand plan. Indeed, the *Civilian and Galveston Gazette* in September 1843, complained that the United States government comprised politicians who were concerned only with electing successors of presidents. Great Britain, on the other hand, was held up as an example of a country that was governed by "policy."

This pro-Houston newspaper also counseled Texans to behave with style and flair. "Better fling your last dollar into the street, with an air," the editor advised, "than be suspected of poverty or shabbiness." This was, in effect, journalistic approbation of Sam Houston's own style of life, and Texans were quick to pick it up.

Diplomacy was something of a game, albeit with higher stakes than most sports, and neither Palmerston nor his successor in the foreign office, Lord Aberdeen, was happy to have another player. Aberdeen was of a different party but in total agreement about Texas and the United States. The republic must be kept apart from the United States.

The fear of English domination overcame any reluctance on the part of John Tyler to annex Texas. He moved quickly and Secretary of State Calhoun and the Texas emissaries, Isaac Van Zandt and James Pinckney Henderson, signed a treaty of annexation on April 12, 1844. Tyler sent it to the Senate for ratification on April 22.

Both Houston and Jackson were chagrined that their old enemy, Secretary of State John Calhoun, was now in charge. He had succeeded to the secretaryship when the more sympathetic Abel Upshur was killed when a gun exploded on board the U.S.S. *Princeton.*

But ratification was not to be. Party rivalry, petty jealousies, antislavery sentiment, and a genuine fear of a war with Mexico all combined to defeat the treaty of annexation overwhelmingly by a vote of 35–16 on June 8.

At The Hermitage, Andrew Jackson fulminated against the Senate, the English, and his old enemies Clay and Adams. Clay, who had resigned from the Senate and was running for president, had actively campaigned against the treaty, saying it was "not called for by any general expression of public opinion."

Jackson immediately wrote to Houston urging him not to become entangled with England. "All the skill of her diplomacy, all the energies at home and abroad, are directed therefore to undermine the prosperity of the U[nited] States and sow the seeds of dissension and dread among their people," wrote Jackson. "Great Britain is aiming at the overthrow of the Republican system. . . . But depend upon it she will deceive you. On whatever terms you make an alliance with her in less than three years you will find yourselves called on to give up not only your soil & negroes but your liberty."

It is hard to say which of Jackson's demons gave Old Hickory the most trouble, but the English probably had pride of place. He wrote to Pinckney Henderson not to trust Lord Aberdeen, in spite of the fact that Aberdeen had assured Texas that even though England was against slavery she would not interfere in the affairs of other countries. "Who can trust her abolition zeal, if its enthusiasm carries her beyond the limits she now prescribes for herself? Let the history of fanaticism, in all ages, answer," said Jackson.

The moguls and functionaries whose chief interest was party loyalty should have paid more attention to editorials such as the one that appeared in the *Bangor* (Maine) *Mercury*. They could have more accurately gauged the true sentiment of the majority of the American people in regard to annexation and the failure of the Senate to ratify the treaty.

> In future years when the people of this nation look back with mortification and chagrin upon this act of the most consummate folly, this moral and political treason to the best interests of the country, may the actors in the shameful transaction be remembered as we remember the opposers of our country in the last war, and may they become as immortal as that only traitor of our Revolution, Benedict Arnold, most deservedly "damned to everlasting shame."

Houston had only a few months remaining in office. He had believed that he would be the last president of Texas, but the U.S. Senate had denied him that honor. He now had to arrange for a successor. Secretary of State Anson Jones was Houston's choice, and elections were set for September.

In the meantime Sam had returned to Grand Cane, where in the early summer of 1844 he was again so ill that Margaret was fearful that he might die. He probably was suffering from a recurrence of malaria or he was felled by the dysentery that afflicted so many of the people on the edge of settlement. Perhaps the wound from the Horseshoe had reopened. Whatever the cause, for over a month he was completely bedridden. By mid-July, he had improved, but even then he was able to sit up for only an hour at a time.

His last days as president were not to be quiet ones, however. He had no sooner recovered from his illness when a problem that had been brewing for years finally got out of hand. Citizens in the area around Shelbyville in East Texas had always enforced the laws as they saw fit. They habitually ignored the central government and punished accused criminals without bothering with the courts. The obvious miscarriages of vigilante justice aside, the two factions—called Regulators and Moderators—were now competing between themselves to decide who should be the keepers of order.

Houston had had enough of the shootings, hangings, barn burnings, and general mayhem of the Regulator-Moderator War. He called out troops to restore order and enforce obedience to the government. The president spent the last two weeks of August personally supervising the suppression of the insurrection from his headquarters in San Augustine.

In "An Open Letter to My Countrymen," he exhibted an evenhandedness and fairness that defused the crisis. "It has not been in my power to possess myself with all the causes which led to this condition of things," he said. "Therefore, I abstain from making any decision as to the merits or demerits of the parties." As chief magistrate of the country, however, he was obliged to uphold the laws and he hoped not to have to resort to "such measures as would be as unpleasant to myself as they would be indispensable to arrest the unhappy condition of things."

His "mild and advisory course" worked. He even was careful to advise his troops not to feed their horses corn, but to graze them. Corn was in short supply in Shelby County, and such callousness could only offend the local people.

The leaders of both factions signed a peace treaty, with Houston looking on, and order was restored. The president left immediately for home and arrived at Grand Cane on election day, September 2, again seriously ill, with the most violent fever he had ever experienced.

Presumably, Houston voted for his candidate, illness or no, but even without his vote Anson Jones was easily elected the new president of Texas. The reticent and reserved New Englander had never cottoned to the crowd-pleasing and theatrical Houston, but they got along and Houston generally worked to ease the transition.

On September 24, however, Houston sent the secretary of state–president-elect an order that caused Jones consternation and created confusion among Houston's admirers. The English foreign minister, Lord Aberdeen, had offered what amounted to a protectorate over Texas. The Mexican threat would be eliminated permanently, but the trade-off was, of course, that Texas remain independent.

Houston told Jones to "Let our Representative (Dr. Smith or Col. Daingerfield) be instructed to complete the *proposed* arrangement for the settlement of our Mexican difficulties as soon as possible . . . adhering without abatement to the Rio Grande as a boundary *sine qua non.*"

On the back of the letter Jones wrote, "The within order cannot be obeyed for it would either defeat Annexation altogether or lead to a War between Europe and America." Furthermore, he said, "Gen. Houston has furnished no explanation of his motives for this course of policy," it would cause a war with the European powers, a revolution in Texas, and destroy his own administration.

Jones disobeyed the order, but he did seriously discuss the alternatives to annexation with the French and the English ministers, beginning in October, when Houston sent him to Galveston to confer with them and the American minister.

One possible explanation for Houston's strange behavior was his illness. He arrived in Washington on the Brazos a very sick man and he was taking large amounts of quinine for the malaria. Another possibility is that he was just playing the diplomatic game. He had no intention of abandoning annexation, even manipulating the incoming president if necessary. Four years later, however, Houston professed to be outraged when Jones bragged to the press that he had disobeyed him.

———

The Texas question became central to the national election of 1844. The annexationist James K. Polk of Tennessee, Little Hickory, narrowly defeated Henry Clay. Tyler was not in the least intimidated by the fact that he was an outgoing president with only three months left in his administration. He had put a new stratagem into the works designed to circumvent the two-thirds vote of the Senate that was required by the Constitution for the ratification of a treaty.

A congressional resolution would require only a simple majority.

Tyler began to push the Congress, many of whom shared his lame duck status, to pass an annexation resolution. Some fourteen different versions of annexation bills were introduced.

Tyler also appointed Andrew Jackson Donelson as chargé d'affaires to Texas. (It was assumed that, aside from sending Old Hickory himself, the best thing would be to send his nephew.) Houston was delighted to see his friend. It is some measure of the closeness of the two men that they slept in adjoining rooms and left the door open so that they could talk well into the night. Houston reassured Donelson of his continuing desire for Texas to be annexed to the United States.

Meanwhile Houston prepared his last message to the Congress. He presented it on December 4. He could point with pride to his achievements. There had been no incursions from Mexico in over two years. The receipts and expenditures of government were nearly equal. There was peace with the Indians.

His concern with the inequitable system of levying taxes is as relevant today as it was then. "It is plainly unjust that the law abiding citizen and faithful officer, should be charged with the burthens of government, and the dishonest and unpatriotic be permitted, by the defects of our statutes, to be relieved from the contribution of their fair proportion."

Houston also felt compelled to repeat in this last message a theme that he had sounded over and over again throughout his entire career. "It is not denied that there are among the Indians, as among our own people, individuals who will disregard all law and commit excesses of the most flagrant character," he said, "but it is unjust to attribute to a tribe or body of men disposed to obey the laws, what is properly chargeable to a few renegades and desperadoes."

As for France and England, "That they should evince anxiety for our separate existence and permanent independence as a nation is not only natural but entirely commendable," said Houston.

Five days later Houston delivered his valedictory. His farewell was uncharacteristically brief but he went right to the heart of the matter. Texas had been spurned twice by the United States. His countrymen should no longer petition but should wait until they were asked to join "the land of the broad stripes and bright stars" and not risk further degradation.

"One great nation is inviting us to a full participancy in all its privileges, and to a full community of laws and interests," he said. "Others desire our separate and independent national existence, and are ready to throw into our lap the richest gifts and favors." These last remarks were clearly intended not for Washington on the Brazos but for Washington on the Potomac. John Tyler could not have been sent a clearer message.

Before leaving the little town on the Brazos where he had signed the Declaration of Independence, helped to write the Constitution, been appointed commander in chief of the Texas Army, and served as president of the republic, Houston wrote to the two men whose actions had most influenced his life.

He assured Andrew Jackson that "Texas is free from all involvements and pledges," and while he felt "she should maintain her present position" if the United States "opens the door and removes all impediments, it might be well for Texas to accept the invitation."

And in a moving letter to Antonio López de Santa Anna, Houston asked him to free the only remaining Texan prisoner being held by Mexico, his old friend José Antonio Navarro. The great Tejano patriot had signed the Declaration of Independence and worked with Houston on the Constitution. As a member of the Santa Fe Expedition, he had been captured and sentenced to death on the direct orders of the dictator. The death sentence had been commuted to life imprisonment, but Sam now made one final effort to gain for Navarro his freedom.

———

Private citizen Houston reached his home at Grand Cane and a joyful reunion with Margaret and little Sam on December 19. No one was more pleased at his new status than his wife. In their four and a half years of marriage, they had been separated for weeks and months at a time by business, illness, and the all-consuming politics. Perhaps now they could have a more settled life. Margaret welcomed him home with a poem.

TO MY HUSBAND

Dearest, the cloud hath left thy brow,
The shade of thoughtfulness, of care,
And deep anxiety; and now
The sunshine of content is there.

Its sweet return with joy I hail;
And never may thy country's woes
Again that hallowed light dispel
And mar thy bosom's calm repose.

God hath crowned thy years of toil
With full fruition; and I pray,
That on the harvest still His smile
May shed its gladning ray.

Thy task is done; another eye
Than thine, must guard thy country's weal;
And Oh! may wisdom from high
To him the one true path reveal.

When erst was spread the mighty waste
Of water fathoms wide and far
And darkness rested there, unchased
By ray of sun or moon or star.

God bade the gloomy deep recede
And so young earth rose on His view,
Swift at His word the waters fled
And darkness spread his wings and flew.

The same strong arm hath put to flight
Our Country's foes—the ruthless band
That swept in splendid pomp and might
Across our fair and fertile land.

The same almighty hand hath raised
On these wild plains a structure fair
And well may wondering nations gaze
At aught so marvelous and fair.

Thy task is done. The holy shade
Of calm retirement waits thee now,
The lamp of hope relit hath shed
Its sweet refulgence o'er thy brow.

Far from the haunts of men
Oh may thy soul each fleeting hour
Upon the breath of prayer ascend
To him who rules with love and power.

13

Our Union—
It Must Be
Preserved

THE HOUSTONS—Sam, Margaret, and Sam, Jr.—greeted the New Year of 1845 at Grand Cane, on the Trinity River in Liberty County. For the first time in almost five years of marriage—indeed in his whole life—Sam seemed to have settled down. "I find my mind falling back into a channel," he wrote to Anson Jones, "where the current flows in domestic peace and quiet, without one care about the affairs of Government, and only intent upon domestic happiness and prosperity."

He opened a law office in Liberty, he continued his land speculation, and he had a good business providing firewood from Cedar Point for Galveston across the bay. And, of course, he continued his interest in breeding and trading horses.

Houston's interest in farming was still as an onlooker, however. The overseer ran the place and the slaves worked it. In the off season the usual custom was to lease out the slaves, and that autumn Houston rented a boy named William to Anson Jones for six months for seventy-five dollars. By all accounts, Houston was a kind master, once buying a slave so that a family would not be broken up, but two of his slaves did run away to Mexico. One of them, named Esau, may have been the same Esau who was Houston's body servant. If so it is just another instance of how shallow slave-master love actually was in the antebellum South, no matter how kindly the master.

Sam had also sobered up—at least he practiced what passed for abstinence. He drank only bitters and orange peel. This favorite drink, which he disingenuously assured Margaret was harmless, registered eighty proof, 40 percent pure alcohol—the same as bourbon, Tennessee whiskey, or gin.

He did backslide from time to time. One famous slide occurred at the house of some friends in Houston. During the night, in an alcoholic delirium, he ordered his manservant to get an ax and chop off one of the posts of the four-poster bed in which he was sleeping. He claimed it spoiled the view. Fortunately, Margaret was not present.

And late one evening in Liberty, a passerby heard moaning and cursing coming from the bushes alongside the dark street. He was shocked to discover that the hero of San Jacinto, the ex-president of Texas, had fallen down drunk and was unable to get up. Houston's Samaritan helped him back to the small office on Main Street where Sam often spent the night.

Margaret and her mother, true to their religion, organized the First Baptist Church at Concord, a few miles up the road from the Grand Cane plantation. The family rode to Sunday services in a strange vehicle, which was neither wagon nor coach but a combination of the two. Houston had it painted a brilliant yellow. When he attended church, which was not often, he traveled on horseback, riding alongside the family coach.

Meanwhile in Washington, Tyler was determined on an annexation bill before he left office. At his prodding, the House passed the measure by a large majority, 120 to 98, but the Senate still balked. The resolution, somewhat slightly amended, was finally approved by the upper house by a single vote, 27 to 25, on the night of February 27, 1845. The next day the House overwhelmingly passed the Senate version of the bill by a vote of 132 to 76.

John Tyler wished to have credit for this bold expansion of American territory, which he deserved, and he did not want to leave it to the incoming administration. On March 3, 1845, he ordered Chargé d'Affaires Andrew Jackson Donelson, who was in New Orleans, to return to Texas immediately and offer the republic annexation and statehood.

John Tyler's last official act strikingly paralleled that of Andrew Jackson eight years earlier. Just hours before he left office, Jackson had secured the recognition of Texas. Now, in the final hours of his presidency, Tyler secured its annexation.

It was left to Tyler's successor, James K. Polk, to complete the process of annexation, and he is generally credited, however unfairly, with acquiring Texas for the United States. A few days after assuming office, Polk instructed Donelson to await further orders before proceeding to Texas.

Polk's final instructions were basically the same as Tyler's, but they delayed Donelson's departure for Texas until March 24. By that time the British and French ministers had convinced Anson Jones to hold off on annexation while they worked for Mexican recognition of Texas and French and English guarantees of Texan independence.

For too long Sam had wished to visit Old Hickory at The Hermitage. The Old Chief was in his eightieth year and in frail health. It had been almost six years since Sam had seen Jackson and he very much wanted to show off his wife and his "hearty brat."

Despite his age and his health, Jackson had continued to lobby for annexation. Indeed, realizing that he did not have much time left he had worked even harder. Now the goal seemed near. The United States had made the offer, now it was up to the Texans to ratify it. But Jackson had no reason to worry. His brilliant nephew was the perfect man to be in Texas and Polk kept him there. The Tennessee circle—Polk, Houston, Donelson—commanded center stage, with Old Hickory directing from The Hermitage.

While the joint resolution set the terms of annexation, it also provided that the president could, if necessary, hold further negotiations over the terms of annexation if Texas so insisted. Here is where Houston could play a crucial role. He was still the key to annexation and the people would follow his lead.

At least outwardly, Sam Houston enjoyed his respite from official life, but his addiction to politics and fame was far stronger than any reliance on liquor. His period of remission did not last out the year. After all, he had been in politics at the highest levels for over twenty-five years. He began a lengthy correspondence with Donelson, who was now in Texas with the American offer. Any direct meetings between the two old friends had to be very discreet. Neither wished to embarrass Anson Jones or compromise Donelson's mission.

Houston believed that further negotiations, as provided in the third article of the joint congressional resolution, were indeed necessary. In particular he wanted guarantees that the boundary be set at the Rio Grande. His advocacy of new negotiations between equal parties rather than Texas accepting the dictates of Washington was used by detractors and enemies as proof that he opposed annexation. It is clear, however, that there was no truth in such charges.

As usual he was looking out for what was best for Texas and holding out for the best possible deal. Houston's usual prescience only deserted him when he predicted flatly to Donelson that "negotiation thro' commissioners will be the only means by which the desired object can be attained and that all other means must fail."

Houston was never above exaggerating the importance of what he had done, even though delivering a state into the Union needed no embellishment. However, he wanted to make sure everyone understood just how important Texas was in the world. Donelson had been at the very center of power for years and was not taken in by anybody's rhetoric. He surely raised an eyebrow when he read that "the salvation and future growth, prosperity, and safety of the States depend, upon the annexation of Texas to the Union." Donelson put the letters away and prepared to make the case for annexation to the president of Texas. Anson Jones received him on April 12.

———

The Houstons arrived in New Orleans at the end of May on their way to Tennessee. William Christy rejoiced that his old and dear friend was sober, married, and a father. On May 28 Sam spoke at a large public gathering and the next day he and his family boarded the steamboat for the trip up the Mississippi, the Ohio, and the Cumberland to Nashville.

The few days spent in New Orleans and the usual delays in ascending the Mississippi contributed to the most bitter disappointment in Houston's life. He arrived in Nashville on Sunday, June 8, at six-thirty in the evening. As soon as the boat was tied up at the landing on the Cumberland, Houston was informed that Andrew Jackson was near death.

He disembarked and quickly hired a carriage to take him and his family immediately to The Hermitage. A few miles out of Nashville, they met Jackson's physician returning to the city. The Old Chief had died at six o'clock.

Within the hour they entered the drive leading up to the great house. A weeping servant opened the door. Sam took his two-year-old son by the hand and led him down the hall and directly into the downstairs bedroom where Old Hickory was laid out. The frightened and confused little boy looked up at the tall man weeping beside him and then at the pale figure with the great shock of white hair lying on the bed. "My son," said Sam Houston, "try to remember that you have looked upon the face of Andrew Jackson."

At midnight Houston sat in an upstairs bedroom at The Hermitage and wrote to President Polk in Washington to give him the sorrowful news that their great friend and mentor was dead.

Andrew Jackson was buried two days later, Tuesday, June 10, at eleven o'clock in the morning. As he had on that sorrowful Christmas Eve in 1828, Houston led the funeral cortege from the house. Old Hickory was laid to rest beside his beloved Rachel in the marble tomb he had built for her in her garden.

Sam and his family remained in Tennessee for the rest of the summer as guests at the Donelson plantation, Tulip Grove, which adjoins The Hermitage. The second Mrs. Donelson, Elizabeth Martin Randolph, whom Donelson married five years after his wife Emily died, welcomed the third Mrs. Houston.

Sam at least could divert himself in the world of Tennessee politics and horses, but Margaret's movements were more circumscribed. The Hermitage and Tulip Grove were in mourning. Margaret dutifully observed all the rituals of grief, but she was not well herself and she had a rambunctious two-year-old on her hands. It was not a pleasant summer.

Donelson was still in Texas, quietly but indefatigably shepherding the cause of annexation while warily watching President Jones and the French and British ministers, who were still working to thwart annexation and keep Texas independent. Jones was honoring his promise not to act on annexation until word came from Mexico, but he was finally obliged to call the Texas Congress into session to debate the issue.

Jones's announcement of the special session was not greeted with joy, however, and his reputation was further damaged. Congress would not meet for two months. Why, the people, wondered, did they have to delay joining the United States? And not a few wanted to know the whereabouts of the Hero of San Jacinto and two-term president of the republic. If Houston believed so strongly in annexation why was he not in Texas lending his support to those who were for immediate action? Houston's absence created considerable suspicion as to his real motives and rightly so. Fortunately his presence at the deathbed of the almost godlike Old Hickory was a circumstance only the most cynical could continue to interpret as evidence of Houston's abandonment of a cause he believed in as fervently as anything in his life.

When it was announced that a treaty guaranteeing peace and Texan independence—on the condition that Texas not be annexed to any other country—arrived from Mexico City, Jones's ruin was complete. Sentiment for annexation had become almost unanimous, and the president was denounced. He was even accused of being in the employ of the British and burned in effigy.

Congress convened upstairs in Hatfield's Grocery in Washington on the Brazos on June 16 to decide between annexation or independence. Jones basically asked the Congress to reject annexation until he could strike a better deal with the United States, using the threat of a treaty with Mexico as a bargaining tool.

A hero like Houston might have been able to pull off this balancing act, but even that is doubtful given the mood of the Congress, which for once reflected the mood of the people of Texas. They had waited for ten years and would not be denied. The vote for immediate annexation was unanimous in both houses. The people had spoken, but Jones did not trust them. "The Senate are so much afraid of the people, they dare not do right," he said.

The last Congress of the Republic of Texas adjourned at Washington on the Brazos on June 28. Six days later on July 4, the Convention of 1845 opened at the old capitol in Austin. Thomas Rusk was president. Houston had been elected a delegate from Mongomery County, but he was still in Tennessee. His place was filled by Charles B. Stewart. One delegate in particular was received with great warmth and honor—José

Antonio Navarro. He had escaped from Mexico and made his way back to Texas. He was there as the delegate from Bexar and was the only Mexican in the room.

The convention almost echoed the unanimous vote of the Congress for annexation—there was one vote against—and then set about drafting a constitution for the new State of Texas. Until August 28, the delegates argued, fought, and threatened each other. There was also a strong movement to impeach President Anson Jones, who did not bother to appear in Austin until August 16.

The movement for impeachment failed but Jones's duties were much reduced. He announced October 13 as the date for submitting the Constitution to the people. The convention over and his duties completed, Rusk went on a two-day binge.

Houston, in the meantime, was making his way leisurely back to Texas. He and Margaret were at her brother's house in Marion, Alabama, when the convention ended. On Saturday, September 13, at Marion, and on Wednesday, September 17, at Greensboro, Alabama, he spoke to large and enthusiastic crowds on the annexation of Texas. Like everyone else, the reporter for the *Alabama State Review* was impressed by Houston's appearance. "He appears to be about fifty years of age," he said, "but moves with the firm elastic tread and erect carriage of the young Indian chief."

Margaret decided to stay behind with her Alabama relatives and Sam continued on to Texas for the October 13 referendum on the Constitution. Perhaps because there was no opposition, only about 6,000 people bothered to go to the polls, out of a population of about 125,000. Even allowing for the fact that half the population was female and another quarter were slaves, and thus not allowed to vote, the turnout was abysmal.

President Jones continued the sad job of closing down his government and retiring himself. He ordered the first elections to choose a state legislature and a governor. On December 15, in another pitifully small exercise of the franchise by the Texas electorate, James Pinckney Henderson was elected the first governor of the new state along with sixty-six representatives and twenty senators.

All the requirements for statehood had now been met—approval of annexation by Texas, a ratified state constitution, and a working government—and on December 29, 1845, the state of Texas was officially recognized by the United States Congress. The death of Jones's republic was dragged out, however. It breathed on for another two months before power was transferred officially to the state.

———

Margaret and little Sam had returned from Alabama in late November and Sam met them in Galveston. They were obliged to remain on the island for over a month because of the terrible weather. Further travel by boat was too risky. Weather aside, the only thing that marred the family reunion in that lovely island city was the news that Houston now gave Margaret.

He had decided to permit his name to be put forth when the newly formed state legislature met in February to choose the two United States senators from Texas. His election would be pro forma. The only issue was who would occupy the other Senate seat. He wanted Margaret and his son to go with him, of course, though they would have to leave for Washington in less than three months.

Before that, however, the Houstons would move once more. For the past year Houston had been developing a property of several hundred acres about thirteen miles east of Huntsville. The house itself was another rough Texas-style home, with two rooms and a dog trot on the first floor and with one large room above. He named it Raven Hill and it soon became the official home of the Raven, Margaret, and Sam, Jr.

Raven Hill was a large plantation, but it was no rival to the great showplaces of the tobacco and cotton barons of the South. Even the grandeur associated with such famous Texas plantations as Pecan Point and Eagle Island is illusory. In the 1830s and 1840s they were more nearly like the Peach Point described by Stephen Austin. That plantation was "still in the primitive log cabbins and wild shrubbery of the forest," he said.

On February 16, 1846, the first Texas state legislature convened in Austin, which had been constitutionally designated the capital—at least until 1850. Three days later, on Thursday, February 19, Anson Jones retired as president of the Republic of Texas and J. Pinckney Henderson was sworn in as governor of the State of Texas. As the flag of the Republic of Texas was slowly lowered, the old wooden flagpole broke in two.

On Saturday, February 21, with the Stars and Stripes of the United States now flying over the Capitol, the legislature convened to elect the state's first senators. Sam Houston received seventy votes and Thomas J. Rusk sixty-nine.

Senator Sam Houston of Texas celebrated the fifty-third anniversary of his birth and the tenth anniversary of the birth of Texas on March 2. Ten days later he left for Washington, alone. He was to have returned to the nation's capital sober, famous, and with a family. However, just after his election to the Senate, he and Margaret had discovered that their idyllic reunion at Galveston had produced more than just pleasant memories. Margaret was pregnant with her second child. She would remain in Texas.

Houston traveled via Galveston and New Orleans, where he caught the steamer up the Mississippi and then the Ohio. At Cincinnati, which had practically run him out of town in 1832 over the Stanbery affair, it was reported that the "quondam savage was distinguished from his *suite* by being enveloped in a huge Mexican blanket."

He arrived in Washington on Saturday, March 28, and once again set up a bachelor establishment at his old stomping ground, Brown's Hotel. The next day, early in the evening, Sam went to the White House to call on his Tennessee friend James K. Polk. There never existed two more opposite personalities: the tall, robust, ebullient, outgoing, warm, and expressive Houston and the short, cold, reclusive, humorless, deadly serious Polk.

As Houston entered the mansion and was greeted by the president each of them must have reflected on the vagaries of power. If it had not been for his disastrous first marriage, Houston could very well have been receiving Polk.

The charming Sarah Childress Polk, her husband's bridge to society, greeted Sam with her usual warmth. She was delighted at the news that there would be another Houston, but she regretted that Washington was to be deprived of Margaret's presence.

Given Houston's fabled independence, there had been some discussion, even fear, that Houston would go his own way in Washington in spite of his being so closely associated with Jackson and the Democrats. Polk was an even stronger party man than Jackson. He brooked no departure from party discipline. He was reassured to learn that he had nothing to worry about from Houston.

The next morning, there was a stir as Houston entered the Senate chamber to take his senatorial oath. He had dressed with care for the occasion, but there was none of the usual flamboyance—except for a new addition to his wardrobe. He wore a vest made of the spotted fur of a Mexican jaguar.

The giants Clay, Webster, Calhoun, Benton, and Van Buren warily regarded the new arrival. They barely noticed his fellow Texan. Rusk was neither intellectually nor socially equal to the task and admitted this was so. Houston, on the other hand, examined his senatorial friends and rivals with perfect equanimity. His achievements and his renown made him the match of anyone in the room.

He therefore felt no qualms about breaking a Senate rule straight off. It was not customary for freshman senators to address the Senate, but only two weeks later Houston rose to speak on the Oregon question.

Since 1818, England and the United States had pursued a policy of "joint occupation" of the disputed territory in the Pacific Northwest. It was agreed by treaty that citizens of either country were free to occupy land in the territory. However, the treaty could be abrogated by either power by giving a year's notice. In his annual message to Congress, Polk had proposed doing just that.

Along with annexation of Texas, further expansion into the Oregon Territory had become an issue in the 1844 elections. The great national argument over Texas was settled, but the editor of the New York–based *United States Magazine and Democratic Review,* John L. O'Sullivan, gave the expansionists a new lease on life and a compelling argument for even further expansion. He also added a term to the nation's vocabulary that, for better or worse, came to symbolize for Americans their distinct role among nations.

In the July–August 1845 issue, O'Sullivan proclaimed it was "our manifest destiny to overspread the continent allotted by Providence." In other words, American expansion was ordained by God himself, and the expansionist Democrats, led by their president, used the doctrine to justify extending the boundary west to the Pacific Ocean and north to 54° 40'—even though it meant that war with England was a distinct possibility. "Fifty four forty or fight," they cried, although not one American in ten, if the percentages were even that high, had any notion of how far north fifty-four degrees, forty minutes was or how much territory England was being asked to give up. It was almost all of present-day western Canada.

Polk was more conciliatory than he publicly let on. He was willing to set the boundary as far south as the forty-ninth parallel, and he instructed Secretary of State James Buchanan to so inform the British ambassador Pakenham. The British envoy refused to forward the offer to London.

Pakenham no doubt was strictly conforming to overall British policy. Houston was therefore correct when he said in his maiden speech, "No minister to a foreign court would assume so important a decision, unless well aware that it was in harmony and keeping with the policy and opinions of those who had delegated a trust to him."

This first speech, which went on much too long in spite of the senator's being "quite unwell," also revealed much about Houston's view of diplomacy. "Honorable senators have spoken of 'compromise.' I abhor the term," he said. "It implies that something unreasonable is demanded by one of the parties, and that the other, through over anxiety, is prepared or required to make a sacrifice of rights." As for *temporize*, "it implies that insincerity and duplicity are to pass current for open professions, when it is nothing more than the concealment of that candor which it would be honorable to express. These terms should be expunged from the political as well as social vocabularies of the world." Houston preferred the term "adjustment."

Semantics aside, most important for Houston was the president's right to negotiate the new adjustment. The Senate would have time later to approve it or disapprove it. Houston himself accepted the forty-ninth parallel as the new boundary but not if England were also given the navigation of the Columbia River. In fact, he said he would resign rather than vote for such a measure. Privately, however, he wrote to his friend Ashbel Smith, "I sustain the President in his course, and expect to do so, out & out."

On April 27, Congress passed the resolution authorizing Polk to abrogate the treaty. Meanwhile Lord Aberdeen and the Foreign Office had had time to reflect on the matter, and they changed their policy. American settlers by the thousands were already flocking to the Northwest over the Oregon Trail, and the issue threatened to become as volatile as Texas. A new treaty was drafted in London and transmitted to Washington well before news of the abrogation of the old treaty was received.

Pakenham was instructed to accept the forty-ninth parallel, but only if the western end of the new line were adjusted to the south so that Vancouver Island would remain British. The Columbia River lay in the American territory, but the British were to be allowed right of navigation. The Senate approved the treaty on June 15. There had been no more compromising, no more temporizing, only a very satisfactory "adjustment." Houston voted with his president and his party and, of course, remained in the Senate.

———

"The Times are big with Events!" Houston wrote Dr. Smith, and how right he was. The Senate was asked to make peace with England and war with Mexico in the space of less than a month.

Polk had satisfied two of his territorial obsessions, Texas and Oregon. The other great obsession, California, remained to be dealt with, but he hoped to acquire it by purchase from Mexico. Millions of dollars in damage claims were owed by Mexico, but Polk was willing to assume them and in addition pay Mexico $5 million dollars for New Mexico and $24 million dollars for California.

He dispatched John Slidell to Mexico City to reiterate that the Texas boundary was the Rio Grande and to make the offer for the territory between Texas and the Pacific. But Mexico had broken off diplomatic relations with the United States over annexation of Texas and refused to receive Slidell. An angry Polk began to talk of war.

American troops under Zachary Taylor had been in Texas for months to secure the new state. Taylor's crossing of the Nueces and setting up camp on the Rio Grande predictably was seen as a provocative act by General Mariano Arista. A Mexican force crossed the Rio Grande and skirmished with the Americans near Brownsville on April 25, 1846. Some Americans were killed and the others taken prisoner.

Two weeks later two serious battles took place between the Mexicans and the Americans—at Palo Alto on May 8 and at Resaca de la Palma on May 9. The Americans were victorious in both engagements, the last of the war fought on American soil.

News of the Brownsville skirmish reached Washington on May 11.

Polk's mind was made up. However, he sent a message to Congress asking not for a declaration of war with Mexico but for Congress to recognize that a state of war existed. Houston twice lectured his colleagues on Mexico, "a Government of brigands and despots, ruling with a rod of iron, and keeping faith with no other nation, and heaping indignities upon the American flag."

Calhoun was not persuaded that there was a state of war and urged delay. But next day the war bill was passed by a vote of 40 to 2. Houston briefly considered where his duty lay—with Taylor and his army on the Rio Grande or in Washington with the Senate. His age was not a factor. General Taylor was, after all, nine years older than he.

Polk offered Houston a commission as major general, but he wisely declined. The only proper role for the conqueror of the Mexicans at San Jacinto was commander in chief and that was impossible. He felt a twinge of reget—but was not at all surprised—when he learned that the newly commissioned Lieutenant Colonel Mirabeau Buonaparte Lamar was with Taylor's command at Matamoros.

Houston consulted regularly with the president on the war and the internal affairs of Mexico, and he was undoubtedly a party to the strange intrigues of that summer of 1846. Antonio López de Santa Anna was in exile in Havana, and the president of the United States arranged to have him smuggled back into Mexico. The hope was that Santa Anna would manage to regain control of the government—and arrange for the transfer of territory to the United States. All this, presumably, in exchange for his restoration to power.

The resourceful and ever duplicitous Mexican again displayed that cunning that seems to be the special preserve of the truly self-serving. On the direct orders of President Polk, the ship carrying Santa Anna was allowed to pass through the American blockade. He landed at Vera Cruz to general rejoicing and, as was expected, reassumed power almost at once. But any true understanding of the man stopped right there.

Polk and his advisers, including Houston, were outfoxed by this prince of foxes. Through the connivance of the United States, Santa Anna was home, was absolute ruler of Mexico, and was in command of the army. He then turned on his benefactors and went to war against them.

The dictator was also busy on the diplomatic front. In an attempt to prevent the inevitable loss of California to the United States, he proposed to cede the entire area to England. The offer must have appealed to that great old imperialist Lord Palmerston, who was back in power, but he had to reject it.

Palmerston knew he could not embrace such a scheme. He detested everything about the United States, but he did respect its power. Any such arrangement would lead directly to war with the former colonies. Besides, he also knew that by the time Santa Anna's offer had reached him in London the Americans would already have sent troops into New Mexico and California. He was right. Santa Fe was occupied by mid-August and Los Angeles was in American hands by the following January.

The summer of 1846 dragged on, with the Congress remaining in session until late August. Although Houston had no seniority in the Senate, he was nevertheless made chairman of the Military Affairs Committee. And even though Polk distrusted Houston's presidential ambitions he relied on him heavily.

As chairman he issued a report that is a perfect illustration of how quickly politicians line up at the public trough. On July 22, he recommended extensive improvements and additions to the harbors and fortifications along the Texas coast. He called for developing Galveston into a deep water port and opening up an inland waterway between Louisiana and the Rio Grande.

These were worthy goals but there is no question that the senator from Texas also would benefit personally by an unobstructed waterway from the Sabine River to the bay at Corpus Christi. He later endorsed the opening of a United States customs station on the Sabine.

Houston was finally able to escape the blazing heat of a Washington summer and head for Texas and Raven Hill on August 10. Margaret had written to him of their reunion. "I shall be sitting, as in bygone days, on your lap, with my arms around your neck, the happiest, the most blest of wives."

He probably arrived in time for the birth of his second child, Nancy Elizabeth—there was adequate time barring no major delays—but it is possible that he was still on the road on September 6.

Houston clearly loved his children, but his older child did present him with some problems. He was stubborn and willful, two traits that the father could recognize immediately since he shared them with his namesake. In letters to friends he delighted in quoting his son's childish babble, but when he wrote to the boy his words were so proscriptive that one doubts that his adoring mother ever read them to the toddler. His father was now at home, and the spoiled three-year-old could only wonder who this stern and rather forbidding individual could be.

Margaret, recovering from childbirth, spent much of the time in bed. She was happy that her husband was home, but her happiness was clouded because she knew that he must leave again in less than three months. The new congressional session was scheduled to begin on December 7. The pattern of separation that came to define Sam and Margaret's life together had been set years before in the fall of 1840 when he went to serve in the Texas Congress. However, then he was only a few days' travel from her. Now he was two thousand miles and two to three weeks away. She turned to her children and to God for company.

Although he had been gone since March and he would be home only briefly, Houston even now spent a good deal of time away from Raven Hill. The United States Constitution provides that one-third of the United States Senate be elected every two years. Therefore either Rusk or Houston was obliged to serve a shorter term to comply with the law. After they were sworn in, each drew from among three lots to determine the length of their terms—two years, four years, or six years. Houston drew the shortest lot, and therefore his term had to end when the Congress adjourned in 1847.

The Texas Legislature would probably reelect him to a full six-year term, but his old enemies had never rested and they were now hopeful that one of their own would be elected to the Senate. Therefore Houston had to politic while he was home. He had political fences to mend, constituents to satisfy, and, of course, speeches to make.

The Mexican War was popular but it did not have universal support. The Whigs had gone along with the president since they did not want their party to go the way of the antiwar Federalists in 1812, but now many of them had joined the opposition. The antiexpansionists had never believed in enlarging the United States much beyond the Atlantic seaboard. As for the abolitionists, in their zealotry they often were able to transmute any issue into a plot to extend slavery.

In August 1846, just a few days before adjournment, Representative David Wilmot, Democrat of Pennsylvania, attached an amendment to a bill appropriating funds for peace negotiations with Mexico. This "Wilmot Proviso" stated categorically that "neither slavery nor involuntary servitude shall ever exist in any part" of territory that should be acquired from Mexico. The bill passed the House, but the Senate adjourned without taking it up.

A new appropriations bill, with the proviso attached, was introduced in the next session. Again it passed the House, but the Senate drafted its own version of the bill, without the proviso. The House then went along with the Senate version, but the damage was done. Or rather the bandages were ripped off the old wounds. The Wilmot Proviso firmly attached the slavery issue to expansionism and refocused attention on abolition and sectionalism. The great issue that had been slumbering, fitfully, since 1820 now began to stir.

Houston saw the Mexican War in very simple terms. Mexico had sworn to go to war if Texas were annexed and had kept its vow. In a speech that ran for hours and was significant more for verbosity than for thought or philosophy, he held forth on behalf of President Polk's war and the Senate appropriations bill.

Houston had reversed his position on British navigation of the Columbia River in the first session. During the second session he also changed his mind on an important issue. He had been adamantly opposed to volunteer soldiers and elected officers who had nearly destroyed the Texas Revolution. Now, in another long and not very edifying speech, he now came out in favor of volunteer forces.

It is not possible for every elected official to distinguish himself in every session of the Congress, but Sam Houston was not just any elected official. The uncharitable might have said his performance on the floor of the Senate during this session was designed only to keep his name before the public. Indeed, the Texas papers generally praised him for being in the news and calling attention to Texas.

Houston was very much aware that no matter how famous and acclaimed a senator might be, he was still just one of fifty-two senators. However, in March 1847, when he returned home, he was no longer even one of many. His term had ended, and while the Texas legislature had not elected a replacement, neither had they reelected him.

———

Houston had personal concerns that winter of 1846–47. Margaret was seriously ill, and it was not one of her usual maladies. As soon as he had left for Washington, she had taken the children and gone to her mother's at Grand Cane. There a terrible soreness developed in her right breast and she discovered a lump.

Houston wrote to Margaret to have Ashbel Smith examine her, but his wife did nothing until February, when the pain became almost intolerable. A doctor was brought from nearby Liberty, but Margaret was too modest to allow a stranger to examine her. In a few more days she had become desperate and finally asked Ashbel Smith to come to Grand Cane.

Dr. Smith examined her and decided to remove the tumor at once. Unfortunately, the only painkiller Smith could get his hands on was whiskey, which the teetotaling Margaret had never tasted and certainly was not going to do now. She refused to drink it. Smith operated on a sober Margaret, who supposedly did bite down on a silver coin while he worked. The tumor was either benign or Margaret was very lucky. She lived for another thirty years.

Despite his worries over Margaret's illness, Sam put his senatorial duties first. He did not return to Grand Cane until April. She was physically somewhat better but still frantic that the tumor would reoccur. Houston, although he understood the possible gravity of the situation, never lost his sense of humor. In a letter to his friend Dr. Smith he could discuss his wife's fears and make jokes. While he was sympathetic, he clearly was not a great deal of support. In fact, he spent much of the time at his law office in Liberty, twenty miles from his wife, his children, and his in-laws.

Houston protested to Smith that he wanted only "home & peaceful retirement, with competency, and social quiet." If so, he should not have subscribed to the eastern newspapers. He had a very public spat over slurs he allegedly made against Zachary Taylor and there was an acrimonious exchange with former president John Tyler over what Houston called Tyler's "misappropriation of truth."

While Houston was willing to give Tyler some of the credit for annexation, he reserved the lion's share for Andrew Jackson. As for his "flirtation" with foreign governments, Houston said that if there had been no fear of "Texas forming connections with European powers, and especially with England, I doubt much whether, even at this day, Texas would have formed part of the American Union."

Baiting his enemies was one of Houston's greatest joys. "Occasionally to pester these rascals," he said, "I will let something be published, or about the time that they are ready to enjoy a triumph, I write a letter, or make a speech, or publish some letter, or 'secret message,' to throw them all back!!! In this way I amuse myself and harrass those who love me not!"

During his 1847 respite from government, Houston gave in to Margaret's entreaties to move from Raven Hill. She had been brought up in a proper town and much of her nervousness had to do with the oppressive loneliness of her life in an isolated house in the woods of East Texas.

They moved into Huntsville. The little town was already the home of other prominent Texans, such as Henderson Yoakum, and there was a small academy, which played a role in the Houstons' move. They had to think about educating their children.

Perhaps most important of all to Margaret, there was a Baptist church. Houston retained his cynicism toward organized religion and he only occasionally attended church with his wife. No matter. Margaret maintained the composure of the true believer. She could wait. She had sobered him up. She would deliver his soul to God.

Their small Huntsville house, which they named The Woodland Home, was almost a copy of the one they had just left. A wide, open hallway—a dog trot—ran completely through the house from front to back. On one side of this piazza, there was a bedroom for Sam and Margaret and on the other side a parlor with the good furniture, which included Margaret's rosewood piano. There was a large room upstairs for the children.

The house was unusually plain for someone of Houston's prominence—Houston always called it his log cabin—but it was all that he could afford. The truth was as plain as the house. The Houstons had no money. Fortunately they still owned a large amount of land. They could grow everything they needed for food, and they could sell timber and firewood for some cash but not much.

For most of his adult life, except for the famous and even less-profitable interlude with the Cherokees, Sam had been in public service. While others had been looking after their business affairs, he had been looking after the common good. Even if he had done otherwise, there is no evidence that he ever could have been as good a businessman as he was a politician.

———

In Mexico, American troops were as successful as they had been in the battles they had fought in Texas. General Winfield Scott advanced steadily across the country from Vera Cruz, and by the end of the summer he was before the capital. There was a brief armistice to allow peace negotiations, but they came to nothing and he resumed his march. Mexico City fell on September 14, 1847. Santa Anna resigned the presidency, but, true to form, he tried one last unsuccessful military adventure at Pueblo. He then again fled the country.

The Texas Legislature, thwarted by those opposed to Houston, still delayed electing a second senator. Thomas Rusk had to travel alone to Washington for the opening of Congress on December 6. Finally, the legislature bestirred itself and on December 18 the vote was taken. Houston was at The Woodland Home when an express rider from Austin rode up to the gate at four o'clock in the afternoon on December 20. His enemies' power had turned out to be only the power to delay his reelection. He received sixty-nine votes, one vote less than he received in 1846.

He traveled to Washington by way of Nachitoches, where he took the steamboat down the Red River to the Mississippi, and then north. "I cannot bear the Gulf route," said the old landlubber, referring to his trip with the Indians back in 1831. He finally took his seat in the Senate on January 24.

The final version of a peace treaty with Mexico was being worked out at Guadalupe Hidalgo. Polk wisely did not go beyond the stated aims of the war, which were humiliating enough for Mexico. Besides the cessation of hostilities, the boundary was firmly set at the Rio Grande and the United States acquired New Mexico and Upper California. There was a payment to Mexico of $15 million. Polk received the treaty on February 19, and the Senate ratified it on March 10, 1848. The United States now stretched from sea to shining sea.

———

President Polk was correct about Senator Houston's presidential aspirations. He had a growing constituency throughout the country and some support in the Congress itself, where he chaired the Democratic caucus. Some have charged that by 1848 it was too late for Houston, that he was too much the product of an earlier time. In fact, he was younger than either Zachary Taylor, Martin Van Buren, James Buchanan, or Lewis Cass, all of whom were being discussed as candidates.

Houston's popularity was especially strong in the Northeast. He was invited to speak in Boston, Hartford, Norwich, and several times in New York. Before the Democratic convention opened in Baltimore on May 26, he also traveled to North Carolina. His large audiences came to hear and see a larger-than-life hero and they were not disappointed. The hats, boots, jaguarskin vest, brilliantly colored Mexican serapes, silver spurs, and flowing scarves, all helped create a portrait of an individualist giant.

When he talked of war, the people knew that he had fought in great battles—Horse Shoe Bend, San Jacinto. When he talked of their hero Andrew Jackson, the people knew that he had been Old Hickory's close friend and ally. When he talked of the almost mystical sanctity of the Union and the particular destiny of the United States, Sam Houston echoed their own beliefs.

Being a popular public figure inevitably increased the daily irritations caused by the incessant petitioning of people from all over the country. Houston's mail was a constant and continuing problem. Many of the requests were valid and demanded his attention, in particular old claims of the widows and families of men killed in the Texas Revolution.

However, most of the mail was from strangers, hangers-on, and sycophants. They wrote for autographs, copies of the Constitution, appointments to judgeships or to West Point, military promotions, and federal jobs or raises. One correspondent demanded the removal of a postmaster who was demanding fifty cents for overdue postage.

Charles Campbell of Wyandotte, Ohio, wrote that since Houston was a public man he was "of course public property, & subject to be used as such." He then went on to ask that the senator send him information on Texas, steamer service on the Pacific Coast, the fare for both cabin and deck passage from Washington to Astoria, and the distance across the Isthmus of Panama.

Houston chafed at these intrusions, which were so time-consuming. His correspondence, however, took much more time than it need have because he was from the old school of preaching and writing. He had never learned to use one word when two would do. Even when he experimented with brevity he only got himself into trouble. Margaret complained that in his last letter he had forgotten to say "I love you."

Polk declined, as he said he would, to seek a second term, but the 1848 Democratic Convention did not turn to Houston but to another old Jacksonian, Lewis Cass. Houston campaigned actively for Cass all that summer even though in a speech to the Senate he had castigated those senators who "so far forget themselves as to huckster in a Presidential canvass." Speeches were one thing, party loyalty was another.

W. W. Ricky of Zanesville, Ohio, invited Houston to stop and speak there on his way home to Texas after Congress adjourned. The invitation released a flood of old memories and associations. "This district, I am inclined to think, is somewhat familiar from past occurrences," wrote Ricky. "We have still to combat an influence which you put down somewhat summarily, I will admit, nevertheless effectually years ago. I saw the old gentleman a few days ago, he is very bitter in his feelings, is a strong Taylor man. I allude to Wm. Stanbury."

When Sam had left Texas back in January, Margaret was six months pregnant. On April 13, she gave birth to a second daughter. He had expected and hoped for another son, but he came to idolize Margaret Lea, or Maggie as he called her. He did not let the birth of another child interfere with his public duties, however. He did not rush to back to be with his wife or to see his new daughter. Indeed, it was the middle of September before he arrived at The Woodland Home.

———

The Whig war hero Zachary Taylor narrowly defeated Cass for the presidency. The difference was the spoiler, former President Martin Van Buren. Antislavery Democrats, Conscience Whigs, and independents, who were clearly more concerned with voting their conscience than winning an election, founded the Free Soil party.

Van Buren was chosen to head the noble suicide mission, and in a further thumbing of the nose at the South, Charles Francis Adams, John Quincy's son, was named Van Buren's running mate. Van Buren attracted enough votes to split the party and elect Taylor, who had 163 electoral votes to Cass's 127.

On the Senate floor, Houston reflected on what Andrew Jackson would have thought of Van Buren's perfidy, his betrayal of the party that had rewarded him with the presidency in 1836. "But if the vision of the stern old warrior could break upon him as that old man would have looked, if living, on his traitorous course, the glance of the warrior's eye would exterminate him where he stands, and leave not a spot to mark the place."

Conscience was not the special province of either the Conscience Whigs or the Free Soil Democrats. There were men of good will in both the major parties who still hoped that the nation's problems could be solved amicably and the Union preserved. These men were tested throughout the election year of 1848 and especially by the bill to establish territorial government in Oregon—a major step on the road to statehood.

With the admission into the Union of Iowa in 1846 and Wisconsin in 1848, the balance of slave states versus free states became exactly even in the United States Senate. A three-way struggle now began. There were those who wanted to maintain the delicate balance through compromise and then there were the proslavery and antislavery forces who were determined to have the upper hand.

On June 2, Houston and Calhoun clashed over an amendment that Houston had added to the Oregon Bill in the hopes of ending the acrimonious debate. He proposed that the Oregon Territory be organized along the same lines as the Iowa Territory—which would, in effect, thwart the extension of slavery. Iowa had been governed by the Ordinance of 1787, which expressly forbade the extension of slavery into the Northwest Territories.

"I would be very glad," said Calhoun, "if the honorable Senator would inform us whether, under the provision as it now stands, the people of the South emigrating to that Territory would be permitted the enjoyment of their property as in the States where they now reside."

Houston disdained the euphemistic "property" in responding to his old adversary. The issue of "slavery" was not for the Congress to decide he said. That issue had long ago been settled by the Missouri Compromise, which disallowed slavery north of 36° 30'. Houston fully endorsed the compromise. Any changes should be left to the judiciary.

Clearly, Houston was trying to effect a compromise of his own by appealing to his southern constituency to respect history and not look for enemies where none existed. "I would be the last man to wish to do anything to prejudice the interests of the South, but I do not think that on all occasions we are justified in agitating this mooted question," he said.

On August 12, the Oregon Bill was reintroduced in the Senate, and Houston appealed to his southern friends to support the Union, not "to sow discord, and to stir up the passions of the country, and kindle them up to war." His remarks were directed chiefly at Calhoun and his states' rights protégé from South Carolina, Andrew Pickens Butler.

Talk of a convention of slaveholding states was already in the air, and Houston denounced it in advance. When Butler asked Houston if he thought it was treason for the South to have a convention, Sam sarcastically replied that of course they should meet and then "raise a puny war against the women and children who get up abolition papers." As for himself, he would never attend a southern convention or "aid in any scheme to bring about a dissolution of the Union."

Houston at first misjudged the breadth and depth of the antislavery movement. It was not, of course, limited to women and children. He never misjudged the breadth and depth of secessionism, however, and as he said, "The crisis so much spoken of had come."

Was there any man capable of saving the Union? Where was the politician with the courage of Jackson, who had threatened to hang the nullifiers from the nearest tree? Houston saw himself as that man, but how to effect his own elevation to the presidency?

The Oregon Bill, which essentially banned slavery in the territory, passed by a small majority on August 14. Houston's and Benton's votes were crucial to the victory. Calhoun returned home "to stir up the passions of the country." His call to boycott the presidential election and for southerners to consider secession indicated how far his zealotry might carry him. Benton and Houston were excoriated for betraying the South.

John C. Calhoun was in every way the intellectual and philosophical equal of his great contemporaries. Unfortunately, his penetrating intelligence and brilliant mind were put to the service of two indefensible institutions, states' rights and the perpetuation of slavery. He provided what he saw as philosophical foundations for both, and they became inextricably bound together.

Houston's stay in Texas between sessions was the briefest of visits. In less than sixty days he was headed back for Washington. No Texas political crisis and certainly no domestic problems were allowed to arrest his flight. He arrived in the capital on Saturday, December 2. The next day he wrote to Margaret, complaining that there was no letter from her awaiting him at his hotel.

The new session of Congress opened on December 4. The Oregon Bill had done nothing to calm the agitation. The question of slavery in the new territories continued to dominate the debate. In January 1849, Calhoun called a caucus of all the Southern members of the House and Senate. The meeting produced the so-called Southern Address, a threat that the South was prepared to secede from the Union rather than suffer the imagined wrongs inflicted by its antislavery, Northern tormenters. Neither Houston nor Rusk signed the Address.

Houston reestablished his friendships with several New Yorkers, most especially James Auchincloss, and he was even in touch with the embezzler Samuel Swartwout, who had been living very quietly after his return from England.

Auchincloss sent him a clipping from the *Boston Courier*. "As long as South-Carolina is South-Carolina we shall expect to be told that nothing grows in the United States but cotton, that political economy, good morals, the ten commandments, the catechism, are all developments of cotton."

The capital had never seen anything like the acrimony in the Congress, which peaked during the debate on the bill concerning territorial government in California and New Mexico. Calhoun had one of his henchmen insert an amendment that would extend the laws of the United States over the new territories acquired from Mexico. This seemed harmless enough and the bill passed. The eagle-eyed Daniel Webster, however, realized what Calhoun had engineered. The amended bill would override the old Mexican antislavery laws in those areas and slavery could thus be introduced.

All hell broke loose on the Senate floor. Houston appealed for calm as the legislators, in a riotous session that lasted most of the night, attacked each other verbally and physically. The scene was chaotic. Houston said that the United States Senate had "exhibited a spectacle to the civilized world at which we should cover our heads with shame."

He denounced Calhoun's trickery and the bill, which he said could only inflame passions further and threaten the Union itself. He asked to change his vote. "Sir," he said, "without California the States can exist; but, without the States of this Union, California is less than nothing. Let us preserve the Union."

Order was restored, but the bill passed the Senate. It became stalled in the House, however, and Congress adjourned without further action. New Mexico and California were left in a territorial limbo. But the Congress and the country had had a glimpse of how fragile the system was and how rational men could suddenly become irrational over the issue of slavery.

The next day, March 4, Houston was already on his way to Texas when Zachary Taylor and his vice-president, Millard Fillmore, took their oaths of office at noon at the Capitol. Before leaving Washington, however, he had issued one of the great broadsides of his career. His target was John Calhoun and he chose March 2, Texas Independence Day, for the attack, which was disguised as an address to his constituents.

Houston was responding to Calhoun's charge that he and Benton had betrayed their states and the South by their support of the Oregon Bill. According to Calhoun, theirs were the deciding votes in the passage of the bill and they should be punished.

"But upon what authority does Mr. Calhoun assume the character of guardian of the whole South?" asked Houston. "What apostolic mission warrants the extension of his infallibility beyond South Carolina, and the visitation of the excommunicating power upon the representatives of other States?" He accused Calhoun of betraying every president since James Madison and of having no principle in politics except the satisfaction of his own "morbid ambition."

"He has ever continued to smite the rock of agitation with the rod of all his influence," said Houston, "not, as did the ancient man of God, that the nourishing waters of health and conciliation might flow out, but to cause the bitter and poisonous water of sectional jealousy and disunion to overflow the land.

"Verily," he warned Calhoun, "the people of this great confederacy have retributive rewards in store for all statesmen, sooner or later, who thus minister in their affairs."

14

The North,
the South,
and Texas

T HE DEBATE over Oregon had raised issues that threatened the Union, but Oregon was still only a territory. Statehood was still years away and territories, after all, had no votes in Congress. A more immediate threat to the slave states was California. The discovery of gold had led to massive emigration, and the territory already had more than the sixty thousand people required for statehood.

During the next session of the Congress, California would petition for admission to the Union—almost certainly as a free state. From his home in Clemson, South Carolina, John Calhoun exhorted his fellow Southerners to stand together in defense of states' rights, and he began a movement to call a convention of the slave states.

Another South Carolinian joined Calhoun and Butler in attacking Houston. Sam and James Gadsden had served under Andrew Jackson in the Creek War. They first met at Fort Strother, Alabama, in 1814. Later, they were both at The Hermitage headquarters of Old Hickory. Gadsden, however, had long since fallen under the thrall of Calhoun, whom he had known since they were at Yale. During the nullification controversy he became anathema to Old Hickory.

Gadsden was one of the few people ever to address Houston by his first name—"My Dear Sam"—which may have contributed to their break. All others were careful to use whatever title Houston happened to have at the time.

In July 1849, Gadsden sent Houston the report of the South Carolina convention and in an accompanying letter he attacked Houston's hypocrisy, his "common school education," and his "coalescing with the enemies of the South." Further, Gadsden threatened Houston with publication of more personal material—a diary and a history—which he said would expose Houston and set the record straight.

Houston immediately published Gadsden's mean-spirited but private letter in the *Texas Banner*—along with his own vitriolic response, which he had crafted carefully and with much pleasure. "You are pleased to taunt me with a defective education," countered Sam. "While admitting the truth of this charge, I must say that I have long since learned to regard it as an incidental misfortune, arising from my circumstances in early life."

As for Gadsden's own education, to what use had he put it? "When the question arises, which of us has rendered the most efficient service to the nation, I will refer to your own 'Diary' and to your *forthcoming history* for the answer," said Sam.

For most Southerners the defense of slavery was based on protection of property rights. Calhoun and his followers, however, were not content with the argument that they were constitutionally entitled to their property. They argued that slavery was a positive good—particularly for the enslaved. "Never before," said Calhoun, "has the black race of Central Africa, from the dawn of history to the present day, attained a condition so civilized and so improved, not only physically but morally and intellectually."

Houston admitted that slavery was a doomed institution, but it must be allowed to die out gradually, over time. "Slave labor must be rendered unprofitable in the territory where it is now advantageously employed, before it is abandoned," he said. Congress could not abolish slavery without being "guilty of a great usurpation of power." The judiciary was therefore the proper forum. Any other policy ran the risk of destroying the Union.

Calhoun and the abolitionists were co-workers and confederates, and the result of their agitation would be the same, he said. "Could their designs be accomplished the end would be the destruction of the Union, and the degradation of the country from its present elevated position, to the control of reckless demagogues; from the enjoyment of liberal institutions, and the government of the free people to a condition of anarchy, weakness, and civil commotion."

Although the popular view is that slavery would have collapsed because it was unprofitable, in reality, for most owners, slavery was profitable. This argument against the collapse-of-its-own-weight theory is supported by the fact that in spite of the increasing number of slaves the prices for them continued to rise. The invention of the cotton gin led to the great expansion of an economically healthy institution rather than the revival of a dying one.

Eli Whitney's machine processed cotton quickly and cheaply, and the demand for the fiber soared. But cotton still had to be tilled and picked by hand, and the planters had to rely more than ever on slaves—the only large, cheap work force available. The demand soared, but when the foreign slave trade was banned, other ways had to be found to increase the supply.

It is estimated that the slave population increased about 30 percent each decade, but not all the increase came from natural population growth. There were still enormous profits to be made in the slave trade and, of course, there were men willing to take the risk. James Fannin, William Barrett Travis, and James Bowie all smuggled slaves into the United States and Texas from Cuba.

In only fifty years, the Cotton Kingdom was established, King Cotton was crowned, and an aristocracy was established in the American South. By 1849, cotton production had grown to two million bales. In 1793 it had been three thousand bales. The Gadsdens, the Calhouns, and the Butlers of the South were not going to give up their kingdom willingly. The foundation of the kingdom was, of course, the toil of almost four million slaves.

While Houston questioned the institution of slavery, as the owner of a dozen slaves he was content to let the institution die a natural death. His great and abiding concern was the preservation of the Union, and he was right that both the abolitionists and the secessionists, if allowed to proceed unchecked, could destroy the United States. The abolitionists, however, had the advantage of the moral high ground. The American South was the only part of the civilized world, besides Brazil, where slavery was legal.

In mid-November 1849, Sam left Huntsville for Washington. He carried with him a bouquet of roses and chrysanthemums that Sam, Nannie, and Maggie had picked for him at The Woodland Home. Margaret was in tears when she said good-bye. She was four months pregnant and had every reason to believe that Sam, as before, would not be home for the birth of his fourth child.

Congress opened on Monday, December 3. The Senate has seldom comprised such a celebrated, some might say notorious, group of men. Houston was joined by John Calhoun, Thomas Hart Benton, Stephen A. Douglas, Daniel Webster, Lewis Cass, John Bell, Jefferson Davis, Charles Sumner, and William H. Seward.

However, it was a returning member, a legendary figure who had been absent for seven years, who dominated the session. Everyone came to attention and the visitors in the gallery leaned forward as seventy-three-year-old Henry Clay of Kentucky came down the aisle and took his seat.

The Great Compromiser had lived quietly in Kentucky since his defeat by Polk in 1844. He had initially opposed the war with Mexico but finally came around to supporting it. Then, to his abiding sorrow and anger, his favorite son, Henry, was killed at the Battle of Buena Vista. Clay was rejected by his party in 1848. The Whigs turned instead to the war hero Zachary Taylor, whose ascendance Clay viewed as disastrous to the country as that of Jackson in 1828.

He had returned to the Senate to try and save the Union, and Houston found himself aligned with a man whom he had fought since 1825. He agreed with Clay about Taylor. While "Tyler had some intelligence and mind," he said, Taylor "would not rank high in any class of business men." Sam's assessment of his old nemesis was just as pointed. "Clay, you know, is elegantly vindictive, and never forgives or spares an enemy," he wrote to Henderson Yoakum.

In California the people were clamoring for immediate statehood. A convention had met at Monterey in September and, as expected, drafted a constitution that forbade slavery. It was approved unanimously, with even the Southern-born delegates at Monterey voting for it.

Congressional sessions were becoming increasingly acrimonious, and the previous Congress had been the most fractious in history. Now rabid Whig abolitionists, equally rabid Southern Whig secessionists, pro-Union Whigs, Free Soilers, Southern Pro-Union Democrats, Southern secessionist Democrats, and Northern Democrats squared off in the Capitol. Little wonder that it took three weeks to select a Speaker of the House of Representatives. Secession had never seemed such a real possibility.

The catalyst was the issue of statehood for California. Zachary Taylor advocated immediate and unconditional admittance as a free state. The president was willing to sacrifice the sacred senatorial balance between free and slave states. The Southerners rose to the attack, and Clay now set out to accomplish what he had come to Washington to do.

He conferred, as only he could, with other leaders in the Senate, in particular Daniel Webster, and on January 29, 1850, he submitted to the Senate the proposals that collectively became known as the Compromise of 1850. Clay was at first rebuffed, but his measures were reborn as five separate bills that took months to work out, debate, shepherd through both houses, and be signed by the president. Senator Stephen A. Douglas of Illinois was the chief architect of the plan.

One bill provided for the admission of California as a free state. Another set up territorial governments for Utah and New Mexico. The issue of slavery in the new territories was deferred. A third bill prohibited the slave trade in the District of Columbia. A fourth bill finally settled the northern and western boundaries of Texas. The fifth bill, designed to pacify the radical Southerners and gain their support, strengthened the Fugitive Slave Law.

Houston rose to voice his unequivocal support of the compromise. He called upon the "friends of the Union from every quarter, to come forward like men, and to sacrifice their differences upon the common altar of their country's good, and to form a bulwark around the Constitution that cannot be shaken. . . . They must stand firm to the Union, regardless of all personal consequences."

To great applause he said, "For a nation divided against itself cannot stand. I wish, if this Union must be dissolved, that its ruins may be the monument of my grave, and the graves of my family. I wish no epitaph to be written to tell that I survive the ruins of this glorious Union."

The process of ensuring the passage of a compromise was much simplified by the death of Calhoun on March 31. Houston remarked, somewhat ambiguously, "He has now finished his work and gone to another world." In response to a Southerner who felt that Sam had demeaned the great man, Houston replied, "But, sir, though death may have consecrated his memory, his acts, his writings, and his opinions are subject to criticism."

The final obstacle to the compromise was removed by providence. On July 9, Zachary Taylor died of typhoid. A more tractable Whig, Millard Fillmore, became the thirteenth president of the United States.

There was something for everyone in the Compromise of 1850—or at least enough to delay the crisis facing the Union. There was also enough in its provisions to anger almost everyone. The Fugitive Slave Law demonstrated how irreconcilable the differences were. The Northern states were never willingly going to return those unfortunates who had escaped bondage, and they practiced their own versions of nullification by refusing to enforce the law.

Benton was opposed to Clay's solution because he saw it as too much of a compromise. Indeed, he pronounced it a fraud. He in turn was attacked by another Unionist Southerner, Senator Henry S. Foote of Mississippi, who, alone of his delegation, favored the compromise. Foote so enraged Benton that it looked as if he were going to attack Foote physically.

As Benton moved toward him, the senator from Mississippi became so alarmed that he drew a pistol from his coat. As Benton threw open his own coat, shouting that he dared Foote to assassinate him on the floor of the Senate, their colleagues rushed to restrain them. It was another terrifying glimpse of the forces that were being set loose in the country.

———

In mid-February, Houston made an emergency trip to Huntsville. It was an unfortunate time for a politician who had just had a brilliant success with a major speech to leave Washington. Margaret, however, persuaded him that his presence was necessary.

Their properties were not being managed properly and although Houston's Senate salary made her less anxious about their finances the land was still vital to their support. There was also a social and moral scandal. Margaret's troublesome fourteen-year-old ward, Virginia Thorne, had run off and married the overseer, Thomas Gott, a man in his mid-twenties. Houston, no doubt, was passingly amused that his religious wife and even more religious mother-in-law were troubled by a man named Gott, but the scandal was real enough.

Margaret, as it turned out, had not limited her discipline of Virginia to pious remarks and biblical quotations. She took a rawhide strap and lashed the girl twenty times. The next night, as the girl sat on the porch with Mr. Gott, Margaret called to her to behave or she would get another whipping. Within a few days Virginia and the overseer fled to Ohio.

Houston quieted his wife's anxieties, did what he could to set the farms in order, and then returned to Washington. He had been gone just a few days when Margaret gave birth, on April 9, to his fourth child, a daughter, Mary Willie. Indeed, he had got only as far as Vicksburg. He had been away from Washington for six weeks and a few more days would have made little difference, but perhaps he had lost patience with domestic problems.

Houston's defense of the Union and condemnation of secession clearly had made him popular in the North, but to many Texans he appeared to be the devil himself. Pinckney Henderson, Memucan Hunt, and Anson Jones now despised him. His old enemy David G. Burnet more or less agreed with Houston on the question of secession but he disliked him for so many other reasons that this one point of agreement made no difference in the relationship between the two men. Mirabeau Buonaparte Lamar was, of course, fervently proslavery and prosecessionist.

Millard Fillmore signed all five compromise bills into law by the middle of September 1850. The country took a deep breath, and optimists looked to a season or two of calm. Realists knew that it was a crisis deferred not eliminated.

———

Thomas J. Rusk, who had worried so about his qualifications for the job, turned out to be the working member of the pair of Texas senators. Houston was now speaking from podiums all around the country. He was mentioned everywhere as a presidential candidate, and his incessant travel and lectures gave the impression that he was trying to build up support, especially in the North.

Friends were urging him to run, editorials were written favoring his candidacy, and his enemies attributed his every action to currying favor with the voters. But the object of all this attention remained not just noncommittal. He was totally silent. Not once during all this did Sam Houston mention running for president. There are no letters or documents in which he alludes to any such ambition. That he was in pursuit of the presidency seems clear but the proof is as elusive as proof of the goal of his retreat toward San Jacinto. In peace, as in war, he consulted no one and held no councils of war.

Sam Houston did hunger for the presidency, but he would not "compromise" or "temporize." He would not even make an "adjustment." At every opportunity he threw down the gauntlet in front of the Southern senators, who in less "high party times" would have served as his natural power base. The representatives and senators from the Deep South cannot have been happy to hear Houston say on the floor of the Senate, "The man who would conspire against this Union is more culpable, in my eye, than Benedict Arnold."

If Jackson had lived, there is little doubt that he would have supported Houston as the successor to Polk in 1848. Many Texans cynically believed that Houston's journey to The Hermitage in 1845 was undertaken with the purpose of planning such a move with the Old Chief.

When Lewis Cass was nominated in 1848, Houston's almost frantic touring on behalf of the ticket was seen as a move to position himself to run in 1852. His diligent colleague Senator Rusk, who supported his candidacy because it would be good for Texas, remarked somewhat wearily, "Gen'l Houston is off upon another visit to New York. I expect my best policy is to stick to my post."

Houston, however, did arouse himself in the Senate whenever anything concerned Texas directly. In the summer of 1850, he was actively lobbying his fellow senators on behalf of the Texas boundary bill. He wrote to Daniel Webster on August 11 that if "the Texas question is kept open, it gives food to disaffection, and ultraism."

As Houston prepared to return home to Huntsville in September, he received a troubling message from his wife. Mr. and Mrs. Gott had returned to Huntsville and filed charges of assault and battery against her.

Margaret's plight inspired Houston to write another moralizing letter to his eight-year-old son. "I suppose you go to the office for the mails and you will be happy, now & then, to get a letter for yourself," he said. This ingratiating and understanding opening—what might today pass for good child psychology—then gave way to rather preachy prose on sin and bad people. The lecture, a demonstration of his religious sincerity, seemed more appropriate for Margaret and perhaps was indeed intended for her prying eyes.

Margaret was pleased to hear any sort of sermon on evil, especially from her husband, who was slowly but inevitably being bent to her beliefs. She had weaned him from liquor. He assured her that he attended church every Sunday in the capital. And she was pleased to reflect that he had given up another of his grand passions. He swore to her that he had not once gone to the theater.

Houston arrived in Huntsville the first week in November, in the midst of the rancorous debate over the boundary settlement dictated by the Compromise of 1850. However, two thirds of the Texas Legislature accepted the new northern and western boundaries, and after years of turmoil Texas was complete. There were dissenters to be sure. The partisans of Southern radicalism were convinced that the legislature had bowed to Northern abolitionists. And the old-line followers of the Lamar school still believed that Texas should extend to the Pacific Ocean.

This latest visit home necessarily had to be even briefer than usual since Congress was to reconvene on December 2. The new session promised to be a model of orderliness compared to the previous one. Houston, however, knew that both of the extreme groups had to be watched with as much vigilance as ever. His suspicions were soon borne out when a movement began to call a convention in Richmond to draft a constitutional amendment guaranteeing Southern rights. The agitators in South Carolina were already at work to undermine the compromise. Houston was equally determined that the compromise be given every chance.

"It is impossible to close our eyes to the conspicuous figure South

Carolina is endeavoring to cut in this emergency," said Houston. "She coquetted with Mississippi, and produced that unlucky nondescript, the Nashville Convention. She courted Georgia, and offered the lead in the great enterprise to her, but that noble State contemptuously rejected it. She is now coaxing the Old Dominion to join her mad scheme, and offering, as an inducement to place in her giant hands the oriflamme of disunion. Will Virginia accept or refuse the proffered ensign of treason? I believe she will spurn it with disdain."

Houston's highest example was Andrew Jackson—"the pilot who weathered the first storm"—in his condemnation of those firebrands who still did not accept the Compromise of 1850, "Let us give up to croakers and prophets of ill the task of trampling on the constitution, ruining the country, and blasting its prosperity," he said. "The employment is congenial to their feelings, and affords them the only chance they have to attract public attention."

———

Sam had become one of the most popular speakers in America and he appeared at events that ranged from frankly political meetings to benefits for rebuilding a Philadelphia church destroyed by a tornado.

He had now been sober for years and was increasingly involved in lending his name to the temperance movement, which had become a favorite cause. This was not without its political hazards. The zealots of temperance were viewed by the drinking part of society in much the same way that a plantation owner with a hundred slaves viewed the abolitionists.

Maine had totally prohibited the sale of alcohol, and he had strong support for the presidency there, but his support in New York, which had unsuccessfully experimented with prohibition from 1845 to 1847, could disappear overnight. The New York Democratic leadership would be quick to scuttle any candidate who proposed going back to prohibition.

There was no doubt of Sam's sincerity on the temperance issue, even though it embarrassed his friends who knew him when. At Huntsville, after he made a speech to the Sons of Temperance at "a temperance blowout," his friend and house guest Ashbel Smith witnessed an extraordinary ceremony. A coffin was carried into the hall by some Huntsville saloon-keepers. After a macabre funeral service, "Drink" was buried in the nearby cemetery. At another time, Houston spoke in favor of allowing the Rev. Theobald Mathew, the charismatic Irish temperance leader, to be seated in the Senate chamber itself instead of the gallery. Father Mathew was at the beginning of a two-year American crusade in which a reported half-million American Catholics took the temperance pledge.

In Huntsville, Margaret's troubles with the Gotts were finally settled in 1851. Henderson Yoakum acted as her attorney, and Houston wrote to him in March to try to delay the trial until he could get home. He said he would not miss it "for millions," but miss it he did. The court was unable to reach a decision and the charges were dropped. However, the Baptist church, no doubt egged on by Houston's enemies, was prevailed on to investigate Margaret on charges that she had fostered immorality. There it was no contest. What Baptist church in Texas, or anywhere else for that matter, could possibly find anything wrong with the moral behavior of Margaret Lea Houston? Her fellow Baptists agreed that if she did, indeed, whip Virginia Thorne Gott, she must have had a good reason.

Margaret Houston, however, had other, happier things on her mind early in 1851. She had finally decided to join her husband in Washington for the next congressional session. Sam's eight- or ten-month absences had become intolerable. She said, "I am consoled by the reflection, that but a few weeks of our painful separation remain, and if I could get your letters regularly, I would be comparatively cheerful, but whenever a disappointment occurs I am completely unnerved." The "disappointment" was not receiving a letter from her husband in each post.

She was willing, even anxious, to move north, but she did not want to live in the city. She asked Sam to find a pleasant boarding house eight or ten miles from the capital. It would discourage callers and she would have him to herself at night. "Many other arguments will suggest themselves to your mind," she added forthrightly.

Houston began to plan for this new and happier domestic arrangement. He had moved into Willard's Hotel and his only steady company were the six canaries he kept in a cage in his rooms. He also placed small cards around the sitting room with the warning to guests that the senator went to bed precisely at 9:00 P.M.

Margaret Houston was serious about having Sam to herself when she came north to Washington. Sam asked Nicholas Dean and James Auchincloss in New York to help him find a suitable immigrant to act as nurse for the four children, who were to remain behind in Texas.

Dean and Auchincloss procured a Scotch Covenanter from the north of England named Isabella Murray. She was, said Dean, "So old—though still in the prime of usefulnes, as not to be sought after as a wife—and clean and neat."

Isabella Murray sailed on the steamship *Austin* from New York to Galveston on March 19, 1851. With her on board were also two bedsteads equipped for fixtures for mosquito netting, total cost forty-seven dollars. The Houston family was delighted with Isabella. The children, in particular the little girls, took to her immediately. Sam was pleased as well and wrote to Dean thanking him for his efforts and inviting him to visit his "rustic habitation," his "log cabin."

Houston was also clearly looking to the nominating conventions of 1852 when he said to his old New York friend, without directly mentioning the presidency, that if he wished to serve he could open a correspondence with several "suitable" gentlemen in Texas, among them Henderson Yoakum. Houston himself would stick to his policy of not writing any letter on politics "unless I intend it for the public eye, and I do not expect to write any for that purpose!!!"

Houston's reluctance to campaign actively for the nomination was the despair of his friends who pleaded that he could not hold off forever. Indeed, many Americans already thought he was too old—he was fifty-eight. This was Houston's time if there was to be one. His presidential star was at its zenith in 1851.

By mid-summer, Margaret Houston realized that she would not be going to Washington after all. She was pregnant again. Even if women of the time had traveled during pregnancies, which they did not, the trip would take place only weeks away from delivery.

At least Sam's long hiatus in Huntsville was happy. Margaret may have been disappointed in her plans, but she rejoiced in her children and was glad that another was on the way. Besides, she now had a nurse to help out. There was a continuous but welcome interruption of visitors to The Woodland Home; sometimes there were as many as twenty people for each meal. It seems no one came through East Texas without stopping to see Old Sam, but Margaret smiled and bade them welcome.

She did have deep misgivings about another group of visitors, however. As many as a hundred or more Indians might be camped out at the Houstons' at any given time. The children were entranced by their exotic visitors, and their father, The Raven, joined his Indian brothers for meals and talks that lasted for hours around the campfires. Their mother tried to ignore them, even though the smoke from their fires invaded her house and aggravated her asthma.

Meanwhile Dean, Yoakum, and others were going about their task, encouraged by Houston who still, however, limited his presidential utterances to his private correspondence. He wrote his cousin John, "I will not lay down my platform until I can do so before the nation, and when it will be fit, and 'nice.' " He had been elected to the Tammany Society in New York and he was going up there in January and "make 'old Tammany' ring!! . . . Foote, Douglas and others have had their day, and mine is to come!" On January 8, 1852, the Texas Democratic State Convention submitted Houston's name as someone "worthy to be the standard bearer of the party in the approaching canvass for the Presidency."

Houston was now back in Congress, which was quiet except for his own run-in with the cantankerous Senator Foote. The Mississippian had introduced a mischievous resolution whose only purpose was to force everyone to admit that the Compromise of 1850 was a "final settlement." Houston and others preferred not to rouse the sleeping dog of states' rights.

On January 20, Margaret gave birth to her fifth child, yet another daughter, whom she named Antoinette Power Houston. Her husband was lecturing in the Northeast. Twice he traveled to New York City, once in January for his induction into the Tammany Society, member 3322, and again in February when he received the gold medal from the Temperance Alliance.

Sam was the featured speaker at the Grand Temperance Banquet of the Alliance. The others on the program were Henry Ward Beecher, P. T. Barnum, Horace Mann, and Horace Greely. There was lighter entertainment as well. A quartet sang "Uncle Sam Is Rich Enough to Give Us All a Farm," and a Miss Godenow sang "The Bird's Temperance Song."

Finally, at the end of February he managed to return to Huntsville to see his fourth daughter. He stayed only until April 6, when he headed back to Washington and presidential politics.

Although their party was splintered, about the only way the Democrats could have lost the election of 1852 was by default. The Whigs were in even worse shape. The slavery issue threatened to destroy them as a party.

On June 1, the Democratic Convention opened in Baltimore. Lewis Cass, who had been defeated by Zachary Taylor in 1848, was the early favorite, followed by James Buchanan. In spite of his popularity with the rank and file, Houston's backers were able to deliver only eight votes of the party leaders for him on the first ballot—four of them from Texas. And he never received more than fourteen votes during any of the forty-nine ballots it took for the Convention to nominate a dark horse, Franklin Pierce of New Hampshire.

Even if Houston had pursued the nomination more aggressively it is doubtful that the Democrats would have risked running a Southerner, even though many felt he could be elected. But Sam Houston thought it was unseemly to pursue in a public and vulgar manner the great office once held by Washington, Jefferson, and Jackson. He was too proud to do the necessary politicking and compromising with the party bosses.

Even if he had done everything that was politically necessary to win the nomination, he could never have overcome the hostility, even hatred, stirred up by his votes on the Oregon Bill and the Compromise of 1850. He had lost the support of many of the Southern Democrats. Houston was, quite simply, no longer one of them.

The Southern radicals would not have been surprised to learn what their archenemy, the abolitionist Senator Charles Sumner, thought of Houston. "I was very much won by Houston's conversation," said Sumner. "He is really against slavery, and has no prejudice against Free Soilers. . . . I have been astonished to find myself so much of his leaning."

Three weeks after the Democratic Convention, the country lost the great champion of compromise. Henry Clay died in Washington on June 29. Houston was chosen to be part of the senatorial honor guard to accompany Clay's body back to Lexington, Kentucky. The funeral train traveled to Baltimore, Philadelphia, New York, Albany, Buffalo, Cleveland, and Cincinnati. The entire nation mourned the man who it was said had more ardent supporters and more bitter enemies than any other American.

Houston was as bereft as any of Clay's lifetime supporters. They had been bitter enemies for years, but he and Clay had come together over the compromise in their shared love of the Union. "Henry Clay deserved a monument of bronze, of marble, or of gold, to be placed in the rotunda of the Capitol," said Houston, "for men in aftertimes of great excitement to contemplate, and look upon as a man who blessed his country."

If Houston was angry or disappointed by the vote at the convention, he never let on. He campaigned vigorously for the ticket and Franklin Pierce was elected. His majority in the electoral college was 254 to 42. Even though the Whigs were finished as a national party, their candidate, Winfield Scott, nevertheless received 46 percent of the vote. Pierce's popular margin was less than sixty thousand votes, an ominous sign for the Democratic party.

At few other moments in the country's history has America needed a strong leader more than in 1852. The Democrats, however, were more interested in winning the election than in calming the storm or preserving the Union. They therefore delivered an amiable, smiling mediocrity to the White House.

The storm was not long in coming and once again, predictably, it blew in out of the territories. Also, predictably, it grew out of the Missouri Compromise. Senator Stephen A. Douglas of Illinois, another failed candidate for the Democratic nomination in 1852, was now actively promoting a northerly route for the proposed transcontinental railroad. In particular, he was insisting on Chicago as the eastern terminus.

During the waning days of the Fillmore administration, Douglas, chairman of the Committee on Territories, had introduced a bill to organize a Nebraska Territory and to build a string of settlements stretching from the Mississippi to the Pacific. These new settlements would, of course, be of great assistance in the construction of the northern route.

Douglas needed the support of Southern Whigs and Democrats to pass the bill, but they, naturally, were lobbying for a southern route for the railroad, which would pass through already settled territory. Of more importance to them, however, was the maintenance of slavery and its extension into the new territories. A bargain was possible.

Houston's political fences in 1853 were in perfect order. The Texas Legislature had reelected him to another six-year term, which would not end until 1859. He too advocated a transcontinental railroad, but he was vehemently opposed to Douglas's Nebraska bill—but not because Douglas's proposed railroad would not cross Texas. He swore to "prevent its passage if every bill in this body should be lost. . . . there is not one foot of land in the proposed Territory that does not belong to some band of Indians."

The bill was withdrawn and sent back to the committee. A new bill to organize two new territories out of the western lands—Kansas and Nebraska—was drafted and introduced in January 1854. This was the infamous Kansas-Nebraska Bill.

Not only had Houston's objections that the proposed territories included land that belonged to the Indians not been addressed, but the new bill contained a clause that would destroy the fragile sectional truce that had been worked out by the Compromise of 1850.

Residents in the new territories were to decide among themselves the question of slavery. This was directly counter to the terms of the Missouri Compromise, which forbade slavery north of 36° 30'. All of the area in question lay north of this line. But the drafters of the Kansas-Nebraska Bill easily surmounted the obstacle. They inserted a clause repealing the Missouri Compromise.

Franklin Pierce, who was nominated because he was a Northerner with Southern sympathies, backed Douglas's bill and passage by the Senate was certain. But Houston cared not at all that the supporters of the bill had the votes. He insisted on being heard as a member of the minority.

To the end of his life, Houston remained convinced that the bill was "concocted" by a "caucus of seven," led by Douglas and endorsed by the president. "Now all this I know," he said years later, "the calculation was to reëlect Mr. Pierce, so as to *make the South a Unit* and with it to carry Illinois, Indiana, and Pennsylvania." In that way, "Mr. Pierce would come in without New York."

Houston's speech against the Kansas-Nebraska Bill took up the better part of two days in the Senate. Even though he was ill, he was never as eloquent in defense of basic principles. He began his attack on February 14 with a defense of the Indians in their struggle against this new expropriation of their lands.

"I am aware," said Houston, "that in presenting myself as the advocate of the Indians and their rights, I shall claim but little sympathy from the community at large, and that I shall stand very much alone." How right he was. Augustus Caesar Dodge of Iowa, the author of the original Nebraska bill, accused him of "sickly sentimentality."

"It seems to be a foregone conclusion," Houston went on, "that the Indians must yield to the progress of the white man—that they must surrender their country—that they must go from place to place, and that there is to be no rest for them"—in spite of the guarantees that if they moved to the West they would be left alone.

He then quoted directly from the Indian treaties, which clearly declared "that said lands shall never be within the bounds of any State or Territory, nor subject to the laws thereof." But who was to protect the Indians and ensure this guarantee? "A Redeemer was given to the world, but the Indians have as yet found no Saviour. They have no salvation to look to but in the justice of this Government," Houston reminded his colleagues.

"Sir, these people are friendless," Houston cried. "They have no political influence; they have no hopes; no expectations to present to the ambitious and aspiring. They have no wealth with which to recompense their advocates and friends. They have not the blandishments and the refinement of civilization with which to win or to court public favor."

His description of the American Indians could serve as a portrait of any number of groups of the dispossessed, the disfranchised, or the hopeless of society. Houston, in the great populist tradition, picked up their banner and carried it into the Senate during the debate on the Kansas-Nebraska Bill.

The supporters of the bill were understandably outraged when he charged that anybody who would allow himself to be connected to these betrayals of the Indians "should have his name erased from the records of the country; it would disgrace the archives of the nation."

"If the Indians are to be driven off—if they have no rights to be respected—do not make a mockery of solemn treaties; do not destroy and disgrace this form of negotiation, but march your men with bayonets, and tell them 'you must go.' There is something manly in that—

something which I could smile upon. I should think it would be a glorious manifestation of villainy, but it is more manly than to steal. I despise a man who steals in the dark."

Houston fought on for his noble but lost cause. On February 15, he rose in the Senate to attack the second objectionable part of the bill—the repeal of the Missouri Compromise. He reaffirmed his loyalty to the Democratic party and the party platform, but his listeners knew they were in for more hard words when he said, "I have always thought that for any well constituted party, the Constitution of the United States was, perhaps, the best platform that we could get, and upon that I plant myself. There is precisely where I stand."

The Missouri Compromise was as binding as any treaty could have been between the North and the South. Indeed, it had preserved the peace between the two regions for thirty-four years. Houston called it "our wall of fire."

"But Sir," he said, "if it were opposing the whole world, with the conviction of my mind and heart, I would oppose to the last by all means of rational resistance the repeal of the Missouri compromise, because I deem it essential to the preservation of this Union, and to the very existence of the South."

Although he was careful to deny being a sectionalist, he pleaded for the Missouri Compromise as a Southerner. "But, Sir, my all is in the South. My identity is there," he proclaimed. "I claim the Missouri compromise, as it now stands, in behalf of the South."

Sam Houston had been in public life for almost four decades and for him the Kansas-Nebraska Bill was the most harmful piece of legislation introduced in all that time. From a twentieth-century perspective, it was also perhaps the most shameful piece of legislation. However, it was to be expected and it was inevitable. The sad drama of the destruction of the native Americans and the continued enslavement of the African-Americans had to play itself out in the mid-nineteenth century.

Houston was joined in his opposition to the Kansas-Nebraska Bill by John Bell of Tennessee. They were both members of the Committee on Territories, and they should have been able to tie up the bill in committee. Unfortunately, they were both away from Washington when the bill was discussed. Edward Everett of Massachusetts always maintained that had Houston and Bell been present the bill would never have been reported out of committee and Douglas had admitted as much to him.

However deservedly Houston can be criticized for not attending to his committee work, his performance during the debate redeemed him. On March 3, the day after his sixty-first birthday, he again took the floor. The battle was ending and a vote could be taken at any time.

It was after midnight when Houston rose to make his last plea. The Senate gallery was packed and the hallways were filled with people hoping to gain admittance to the great debate. In spite of the hour, his speech was another long and detailed lecture to his colleagues on their folly. Houston needed no excuse to speak for hours, but he went on at length that night to delay the vote.

Since his speech of two weeks before, he had been denounced throughout the South and, probably an even greater sin to his constituents, praised in the North. He was unimpressed by the storm he had stirred up in the South.

"This is an eminently perilous measure, and do you expect me to remain here silent, or to shrink from the discharge of my duty in admonishing the South of what I conceive the results will be?" he asked.

"I will do it in spite of all the intimidations, or threats, or discountenances that may be thrown upon me. Sir, the charge that I am going with the Abolitionists or Free Soilers affects not me," he belligerently cried in answer to his critics. He then warned them that if the bill passed its repercussions "will convulse the country from Maine to the Rio Grande."

"I adjure you to regard the contract once made to harmonize and preserve the Union. *Maintain the Missouri Compromise! Stir not up agitation!* Give us Peace!" he cried. He ended with the solemn warning that "in my opinion, upon the decision, which we make upon this question, must depend *union* or *disunion*."

Houston finished in the early hours of the next day. A vote was immediately taken and the bill passed the Senate 37 to 14. The only other Southern senator to vote against the bill was Bell. Thomas Hart Benton, who was then in the House, joined them in opposition when the House voted on the bill on May 22. This time the bill barely survived, but it passed 113 to 110.

Houston had one final round with the Kansas-Nebraska Bill and his enemies before he left Washington for home. Over three thousand New England ministers had signed a petition condemning the bill and forwarded it to Everett for presentation to the Senate. Douglas and other supporters were deeply offended and criticized the ministers for using their religious positions to advance political causes.

On March 14, Houston defended the clergy on behalf of the opponents of the Kansas-Nebraska Bill. He took on the responsibility in order to refute the charges that it was the abolitionists who had instigated the petition. Charles Sumner wanted to respond to Douglas, but Houston dissuaded him, whispering, "Don't speak. Don't speak! Leave him to me."

Houston then forcefully reminded the Senate that he and others had warned them of the serious consequences that would result from the passage of the bill. This petition was but the first manifestation of a coming crisis that was the product of the actions of the United States Senate not the people, who no matter what their profession had the right to petition the government. "If we wish to avert calamitous effects," he said, "we should prevent pernicious causes."

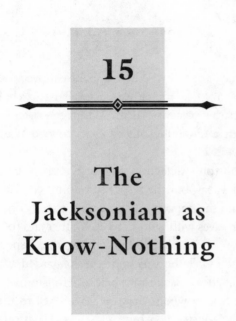

15

The Jacksonian as Know-Nothing

THE KANSAS-NEBRASKA ACT had as broad and as swift an impact on the American people as any legislation in the country's history. With its passage, a great chain of events was set in motion—the splintering of the Democrats, the birth of the Republicans, open warfare in "Bleeding Kansas," the election of Abraham Lincoln, the secession of the Southern states, and, finally, the Civil War.

Houston was worn out from his heroic but futile campaign against the bill, and he looked forward to getting back to Texas for a short spring visit to his family and friends. He had to look to some domestic chores before his journey home, however. Margaret had asked him to bring her a new dress and bonnet, and, of course, there always seemed to be more pairs of shoes to buy than there were children. Was it possible, he thought, that he could have five children? And now Margaret was expecting a sixth child.

Home was now the Baptist stronghold of Independence, Texas, a town of a few hundred people, about sixty miles west of Huntsville. They had moved there the previous autumn, supposedly because the town was the home of Baylor University and the Houstons were concerned about young Sam's education. In actuality, Margaret wanted to be near her relatives.

The Leas stuck together. When one Lea moved, other Leas soon tagged along. Nancy Lea, the rather fearsome matriarch, had gone ahead in 1852 to prepare a place for them. Margaret's sisters, Antoinette and Varilla, lived just a few miles out of town toward Washington on the Brazos.

Word of Houston's defection on the Kansas-Nebraska Bill had, of course, reached Texas, but the response was muted. The legislature was not in session and the opposition could not properly organize. They had to content themselves with writing to each other and to the newspapers. The reaction of the public, judging from the response to the few speeches he made while he was home, was guarded and polite.

As had happened so many times before, Houston was back in Washington and the Senate when Margaret gave birth to their second son, Andrew Jackson Houston, on June 21, 1854. Houston did not see the child until he returned to Independence in October.

The trip back home that autumn was by the most circuitous of routes—through Chicago. The presidency was calling again, and Sam was traveling and speaking throughout the northeast. In October, the Democratic party of New Hampshire announced that they "nominate and recommend for the office of President of the United States, Gen. Sam Houston, of Texas, to be supported by the people, independent of nominations which may be made by Conventions, State or National. We nominate him as the people's candidate."

Houston, notwithstanding the endorsement by the New Hampshire Democratic party, had already begun a flirtation with a new political party. The Republicans were not the only party that grew out of the Kansas-Nebraska Act. The American party, originally a secret society called the Order of the Star Spangled Banner, now became the home of many Americans who were repelled by both the Southern proslavery Democrats and the abolitionist Republicans. The slavery issue had destroyed the Whigs as a political force.

The American party had retained the initiation ceremony of the Order of the Star Spangled Banner, but members were enjoined not to speak of it. If anyone were asked about the oath, he was told to answer, "I know nothing." This response quickly and firmly fixed the party name in the American mind as the Know-Nothing party and so it has remained.

What also has remained in the American mind is the image of Know-

Nothings as xenophobic, anti-Catholic, anti-intellectual, and jingoistic, which they were. The term is still freely applied to anyone who displays any of these traits—and quite a few others.

Perhaps, like the boll weevil, Houston was "just lookin' for a home" when he joined the Know-Nothings in late 1854, but his alliance with the party has been a major obstacle to those who have tried to present his political career as a seamless defense of the Union and the under-privileged and oppressed, as exemplified by his opposition to the exten-sion of slavery and his advocacy of the American Indian.

Houston, however, could be neither a proslavery secessionist Demo-crat nor an antislavery, anti-Southern Republican. He needed a party that was pro-Union but not antislavery. It was for that reason that many prominent Southern Whigs joined the Know-Nothings, most notably John Bell of Tennessee.

It is human nature to want to be the last one in and then close the door. America has suffered from this from the very beginning. The settled colonials resented the great wave of Scotch-Irish immigrants in the eighteenth century, but their prejudice was tempered by the fact that the new arrivals were at least Protestant.

In the nineteenth century, immigration presented a new test for American tolerance. Between 1840 and 1860, two million Irish Catho-lics arrived in America—not just uneducated but for the most part illiterate. No matter. They were eligible for citizenship and the vote within seven years of their arrival. They were easily preyed upon and manipulated by unscrupulous politicians, and they were perceived by America's Protestant majority as threatening the political, social, and above all, the religious and moral structure of America.

The Irish were followed by a great influx of Germans, whose problem was not religion but language and—in the best Teutonic tradition—organization. German immigrants to Texas arrived with everything needed to set up a town and a viable society and they did not make any efforts to hide their scorn for their less efficient, indolent Anglo-Saxon neighbors.

Carl, Prince of Solms-Braunfels, was a leader in the German coloniza-tion of Texas. He landed at Galveston in July 1844, and his first colonists arrived in November. They lived in tents until a suitable site was selected for the new town and colony. One morning, while on a scouting expedition, the prince awoke to find snow in his tent. By noon it had melted, and he took this to be a sign that he had found the place for his settlement.

On Good Friday, 1845, the first wagonloads of German immigrants crossed the Guadalupe and began to build the town of New Braunfels. The fort and government building was christened the Sophienberg, after Carl's future wife, the Princess Sophie of Salm-Salm, whose picture was placed in the cornerstone. At sunrise and at sunset a cannon was fired from the fort to impress the Comanches who roamed the area.

Carl's description of the Texas landscape was rhapsodic. "To a traveler a stranger, there is no spectacle more fascinating than the prairies of the West during the months of April, May, and June. They spread themselves out before him like a costly carpet, richly green, with an embroidery of exquisite flowers of diverse colors. One cannot help but be apprehensive that the hoof of his horse does not trample these marvels of nature and disarrange their harmony."

He was less kind in his description of his American neighbors, who were "too lazy to raise vegetables, so also are they too lazy to dig wells on their homesteads. They therefore drink the stagnant water of some nearby creek." And, said the prince, "While the strong, healthy, and red-cheeked German immigrants become more active and lively whenever a fresh norther blows and the rain soaks them through the tent, the Americans, sensitive and pale-cheeked, huddle in the farthest corner of their homes around a stove."

The prince advised the Texans to give up their cornbread for properly baked wheat or rye, to drink only spring or cistern water, to eat fresh meat, and to replace poisonous whiskey with wine. They would then be as healthy as Germans.

Houston was unapologetic about his own nativism, and his speeches reflect his strong belief that everything American was better. Hence his ease and comfort with the American Indians were not just the products of an early indoctrination as the adopted son of a Cherokee chief. As the first Americans, the Indians fit easily into Houston's nativism.

Coupled with the anti-immigrant sentiment in the United States—many would say the cause of it—was the rise of a militant Protestantism, whose goal was the worldwide conversion of Catholics.

At this time, Houston completed his own tortuous and circuitous religious journey. Margaret and the president of Baylor, the Reverend Rufus C. Burleson, had chipped away until the last impediment was removed. On Sunday, November 19, 1854, in the cold waters of a creek about a mile west of Independence, Sam Houston was baptized. The ceremony had to be moved from the baptismal pool near the church because some mischievous local boys had filled the pool with brush and mud.

Margaret, Antoinette, Nancy Lea, the Houston children, and most of the town watched from the banks of Rock Creek as the sixty-one-year-old erstwhile Presbyterian, animist, Roman Catholic, and skeptic was lowered into the water in the arms of the Reverend Burleson.

Houston may have embraced religion, but he did not become the pietistic father superior portrayed by the Reverend William Carey Crane in his *Life and Select Literary Remains of Sam Houston*. Margaret asked Crane to undertake the task, and she insisted that there be a chapter on Houston's religious character. Crane, who at the time was president of Baylor University and as such was a sort of Baptist pope, happily obliged.

After his baptism, Houston returned to Washington, where he attended the E Street Baptist Church each Sunday. Back at Willard's Hotel, he then wrote his weekly letter to Margaret, giving her a précis of the sermon. He could also joke about religion—but, to be sure, not to Margaret. When a friend asked if all of his sins had been washed away in Rock Creek on that November day, Sam allowed as to how he felt sorry for the fish if they were.

Our Teutonic Tocqueville, Carl, Prince of Solms-Braunfels, had much to say on the subject of religion in nineteenth-century Texas—none of it favorable. "In the United States new sects are formed daily," he said, "any artisan, whose trade goes down hill because of business or negligence, picks a passage out of Holy Scripture and interprets it according to his own wish and peculiarity. He then proceeds with this new explanation to preach that 'the Holy Ghost has come over him' and solicits some old women, who form a small congregation around him. The Gospel having thus been preached to them and the crowd having been convinced of the correctness of his doctrine, they then proceed, as if the Holy Ghost had taken immediate possession of them, to influence their husbands. Soon the new prophet, surrounded by a nice congregation which assumes to support him, lives at their expense.

"It is a simple matter, a venture equal to many others," continued the prince, in his telling critique of American evangelicalism. "It is done according to the regular American style, and if the man is clever, he will not ask too great a salary. If he makes this mistake, the congregation will soon become disgusted, and his members will abandon him and his teachings and join another sect. In many instances they have changed so often that in the end they do not know what they believe or what they do not believe. Generally they end in complete paganism or mysticism.

"The American in Texas either belongs to the pietists with their hypocritical Puritanical customs, whereby he hopes to disguise his avarice, his greed for money, and his fraud, or he does not belong to any church at all, i.e., he doesn't believe anything. It is scandalous and shocking to hear the blasphemies such people utter. In spite of this they frequent the camp meeting held by traveling Methodist preachers."

Prince Carl also had strong opinions about slavery and the vile treatment of the Indians. "If by any chance a colored person happens to educate himself, it has been sufficiently proved that at times he can accomplish much more than the pallid Americans," he said.

As for the Indians, he sarcastically remarked that they enjoy "the protection of the 'law.' " Which means, he said, that when a drunken American mistreats or kills an Indian, "not even a rooster would bother to crow." The Germans had learned that the Indians could be trusted if they were treated justly. "Prudence, however, is the mother of wisdom," the Prince counseled—wisdom gained no doubt by the murder of two of his settlers by the Comanches.

The House of Representatives of the Thirty-fourth Congress had 104 Know-Nothings, or 44 percent of the total. The party seemed to be in the ascendant, but the issue of slavery was not an issue that allowed for half measures or further political compromise and the Know-Nothings would soon go the way of the Whigs. At mid-decade, the choices were rapidly being limited to two—proslavery or antislavery.

Houston continued his presidential quest as a Know-Nothing, and on February 22, 1855, he was invited to speak on slavery at Tremont Temple in Boston, the very center of antislavery sentiment in America. Indeed, William Lloyd Garrison, the most radical of the abolitionists, was in the hall. Garrison went so far as to advocate secession by the North—"No Union with Slaveholders"—and just seven months before, at an Independence Day celebration, he had burned a copy of the Constitution. Houston, who was ready to lay down his life in defense of the Constitution, now spoke to a man who had called it "a covenant with death and an agreement with hell."

From his speech at Tremont Temple, it is also clear that Houston did not hold blacks as equal to the American Indian and he argued that by no means were they ready for emancipation. Houston even questioned the biological equality of blacks. Here his position closely paralleled that of his other idol, Thomas Jefferson. If they were emancipated, "How would it be in the South?" he asked. "Turn them loose and they could not set up in business. Land could not be appropriated to them; and if it were they would not work it. They would be as they are in Bermuda and everywhere else where they are thrown upon their own resources. They are listless, inert, lazy, living on the fruits of the earth where they can be had, but never will be industrious."

There was renewed interest in the American Colonization Society and Houston joined some distinguished political forebears when he advocated sending emancipated slaves back to Africa. He envisioned a utopian ideal where all blacks would be returned "to the land of their origin," and from there they "may radiate science and religion throughout the continent of Africa." Resettlement, however, was as impractical in 1855 as it had been in 1825. Indeed, it was even more impractical. There were now four million slaves in America.

Houston's speech at Tremont Temple was a perfect demonstration of the inability of many Southerners to grasp the central, underlying objection to slavery of so much of the rest of the world. Slavery was not simply an economic issue. Slavery was not simply an issue of one section of the country telling the other what to do with its private property.

Slavery was immoral. It was wrong to hold people in bondage. The pro-Unionists could work out any number of compromises to pacify the North or to pacify the South, but their plans could not succeed as long as the "peculiar institution" existed.

While Houston was universally praised for having the courage to appear and defend the South—Senator Butler of South Carolina had declined the invitation—certainly no one was converted to his beliefs. However, some of the newspapers continued to endorse his political ambitions. The *Evening Gazette* said that "Sam is the coming man." Others disagreed, such as *The Congregationalist*, which stated that "a long life of immorality—of open and persistent trampling under foot of almost the entire decalogue—should incapacitate a man forever for our highest national honors, even though late repentance intervene."

Garrison, who followed Houston on the same stage the following week, used the speech for more practical purposes. He ran the entire text in *The Liberator* in order to facilitate his "dissection" of Houston.

———

In 1855, C. E. Lester published his *Life of Sam Houston: The Only Authentic Memoir of Him Ever Published*. Lester had first collaborated with Sam on a brief work called *Sam Houston and His Republic* back in 1846. Of that volume David G. Burnet said to Thomas J. Rusk, "I entertain no doubt that Houston is himself, the real author of that volume of lies—It is in strict consonance with his whole character and his course in life and the book bears internal evidence of the fact." He called the little book an "infamous production of an infamous *impostor*."

Burnet and Mirabeau Lamar hoped to settle some old scores, and they collaborated on a joint critique of Lester's idolatrous new work. Their remarks are a fair example of the kinds of passion that Houston could stir up, particularly among his enemies.

Lamar's influence is unmistakable from the mode of expression in the pamphlet. "We divine, with Plutarch, to take from Fable, her extravagance, and make her yield to and accept the form of history," they said.

Burnet and Lamar were vitriolic, relentless, and not unamusing—at least to students of political invective. They described the hero as an "eminent adept in the black arts" whose "indiscriminate familiarity" and storytelling abilities were "calculated to render him popular in camp and to attach an army of volunteers to his person."

"Gen. Houston is a demagogue," they said. "His mind, heart, manners; all conspire to fit him for distinction in that odious character." While they did admit he could be "flippant and witty in small talk" and had a "*physique* somewhat imposing" and could be "polite in his social intercourse and seemingly warm in his professions of regard to all," in reality he was "an isolated, heartless egotist, incapable of one abiding feeling of attachment."

Houston's early life and sojourn among the Indians were dismissed as "mythical nonsense." The "abandonment of a respectable position," the flight from the "salutary restraints of civilization," his "domestication with the Cherokees, even to marriage according to their heathen ritual," and his "adoption of the Indian costume and all their habits, in the most degraded phases" were the "workings of a guilty conscience, acting on an unstable, irresolute and depraved mind," they observed. "The genius of poetry has garnished the Indian life with much of the simplicity and innocence of man in his primeval state. . . . But experience teaches a different and more melancholy lesson."

They did not limit themselves to attacking Houston's personal life. The army's "besotted chief was sitting in the grog shops" of Washington on the Brazos or was on "a rogue's errand to the Cherokees" while "Travis and his co-victims" were defending the Alamo, they said. Even Houston's Cherokee name was derided. Burnet and Lamar claimed that the proper translation of *kalanu* was not "raven" but "turkey buzzard."

At San Jacinto, Houston supposedly passed out corn to his troops to plant when they got home. There was no such thing as San Jacinto corn, Lamar and Burnet scoffed. There was only "a large and noxious crop of Houston lies." As for his wound, it was slight and "would not have disturbed the presence of mind of a brave man." But, they allowed, at least it was evidence that Houston had actually been at the battle.

Displaying a stunning lack of prescience, they predicted that Sam Houston's "character when known and appreciated, will forever preclude his approach to the dignity of fame—His name is now in the transition state; and will as the light of truth dawns with increasing force upon it, pass from the dim famous to the notoriously infamous; where it will rest until covered by the dust of oblivion."

Burnet and Lamar's slanders were the beginning of a barrage of criticism from old enemies. If Sam had thought he was home free, that his constituents had forgiven his vote against the Kansas-Nebraska Bill and overlooked his publicly consorting with the Northerners and abolitionists, he was soon disabused.

The old order was rapidly changing, and Houston could not count on the support he had always enjoyed. Newcomers were pouring into the state. The population tripled between 1850 and 1860—from 200,000 to 600,000—and the slave population kept pace. From one fourth to one third of the population were slaves. Over half a million acres of land were given over to the growing of cotton.

Finally, Houston fired a few broadsides of the Old Sam at Burnet and company when he spoke at the San Jacinto battlefield in June. He had a few recollections himself to get off his chest. There had been abuse and slander going around and since he was afraid that the new settlers in Texas might believe it he decided to tell them what really happened in 1836.

Houston naturally made himself the hero of the story and Burnet and the cabinet a crowd of craven fools dashing toward Galveston to save their wretched skins. He accused Burnet of being so anxious to board the *Flash*—to "*Flash* out of the country"—that he shoved a woman out of the way.

He ended with a blistering indictment of his detractors. "I am willing," Houston said, "that my enemies may fester in the putrescence of their own malignity. They cannot hurt or disturb me."

Houston continued traversing the state, defending the Know-Nothings or, as he preferred to call the party, the American Order. One listener referred to him as the "chief priest" of the "new rite" who addressed his arguments to the "little miserable prejudices, of the ignorant." There were major speeches at Independence on July 24, at Washington on the Brazos on August 2, at Brenham on October 20, and at a Know-Nothing mass barbecue at Austin on November 23.

The message was the same each time. He was against the "policy of European potentates and statesmen, to throw upon our shores their refused population of convicts and paupers to pervert our ballot boxes and populate our poorhouses.

"The design of the American order," he said, "is not to put down the Catholics, but to prevent Catholics putting down Protestants." Americans, he insisted, should not place power in the hands of people whose allegiance is to the Pope.

"I am in favor of excluding from our shores persons who cannot come to the country with a certificate from our consular agents in the country which they leave, representing them as persons of good character." Such a policy, of course, would effectively end large-scale immigration.

With the exception of Lafayette, he denounced the foreign-born heroes of the American Revolution—Pulaski, Steuben, Kosciuszko, and even Alexander Hamilton. He agreed with the Know-Nothings that all immigrants should have to wait twenty-one years to vote. After all, America's own children had to wait that long for the franchise.

No matter what the message, Houston could hold an audience. "We have never before seen an audience so completely electrified, so thoroughly controlled by a speaker," said a reporter. "The transition from tears to side-bursting laughter, was sudden and frequent." They loved it when he told them that his opponent had "all the qualities of a dog save one—fidelity" or that he was "so cold that he could freeze a lizard's blood."

But when Houston mentioned his vote on the Kansas-Nebraska Bill, he encountered an "ominous silence." He was not deterred, however. And he would remind the crowd that the passage of the bill upset the delicate balance that had been maintained by the compromises and could only lead to dismemberment of the Union—always Houston's greatest fear.

Sam also took on the women's rights advocates. Many abolitionists were naturally involved in this cause as well, although many others steered clear of it because it took too much attention away from the slavery issue. Willim Lloyd Garrison, of course, was the exception. He embraced all radical causes and once refused to take part in a conference in London because there were no women present.

Houston's allegiance to the Know-Nothings was absolutely clear. "I believe the salvation of my country is only to be secured by adherence to the principles of the American Order," he told an audience at Independence. But Texans rejected the Know-Nothings in the August 1855 elections. They cast their votes for the Democrats and the maintenance of slavery. They were joined by most of the foreign born who had been attacked during the campaign, in particular the Germans and the Mexicans. Houston's active campaigning for the Know-Nothing party damaged him, but it was the residual anger over the Kansas-Nebraska vote that did him in when the legislature convened in November.

The county conventions had already censured Houston and called for his ouster from the Senate. On November 26, by a vote of 77 to 3, the legislature also condemned him. At the same time the lawmakers, to underscore their censure of Houston, unanimously reelected Rusk to another term—a year ahead of time.

Even though he had been rejected by the Texas Legislature, Houston's Senate term still had more than three years to run—until March 4, 1859—and he was determined to serve out the time. Many papers across the state called for his immediate resignation, but he ignored them and returned to Washington.

———

The American party, or the Know-Nothings, met in Philadelphia in February 1856 to choose a presidential candidate. Houston did not attend. Millard Fillmore and Andrew Jackson Donelson were chosen to head the ticket. Houston seemed not in the least perturbed at being passed over for the nomination, but he was surprised at Fillmore's being chosen since the ex-president had never been associated in any way with the Know-Nothings. In fact, Fillmore was traveling in Europe when he was nominated.

Privately, Houston had disavowed the party platform in advance—it endorsed the Kansas-Nebraska Act—and after the convention he told Donelson that he would not speak in behalf of the ticket. Donelson pleaded with his friend not to do anything against the party, and Houston agreed. Later he confided to a friend, "I could have added that dead Ducks need no killing!"

As for the presidency, Houston said, he would not exchange "one soul-thrilling kiss" of Margaret's "for all the Sceptres and nominations in the world. And just think of the Addendas, no less than six little Houstons to dandle on my knees, & kiss them and call them dear children."

Houston longed to return to Texas, but he remained in Washington, tending to his Senate duties, until late spring. He rarely socialized in the capital, but in April he was persuaded to attend a party at the home of House Speaker Nathaniel P. Banks. He stayed only long enough to eat an ice cream and stare at the most famous, or notorious, woman in America. "She is certainly a hard subject to look on," Sam wrote to Margaret of Harriet Beecher Stowe.

———

As Houston had predicted, Kansas became a battleground between the abolitionists and the proslavery forces. The New England Emigrant Aid Company sponsored two thousand antislavery settlers in an attempt to secure Kansas as a free territory. While their numbers were small, their impact was very large indeed.

In response, proslavery squatters and adventurers, particularly from Missouri, flooded into the territory to ensure that Kansas, when the time came, would vote in favor of slavery. The Texas Legislature appropriated fifty thousand dollars to send proslavery emigrants to Kansas.

On May 21, a proslavery mob sacked Lawrence and burned the hotel-headquarters of the New England Emigrant Aid Company and destroyed the offices of the proslavery newspapers. The "Sack of Lawrence" inflamed the North, and the massacre of five proslavery settlers at Pottawatomie Creek three days later by the fanatic John Brown stirred up the South. The Border War, or Bleeding Kansas, had begun and each of the opposing sides had a bloody shirt to wave.

The day before the sack of Lawrence, Charles Sumner finished a two-day philippic called "The Crime Against Kansas" in the U.S. Senate. The Massachusetts abolitionist spared no one who sympathized with slavery or the Kansas-Nebraska Act. In particular he singled out the state of South Carolina with "its shameful imbecility from Slavery" and Senator Andrew F. Butler, whose mistress was the "harlot, Slavery."

Two days later, Representative Preston Brooks of South Carolina, Butler's cousin, attacked Sumner at his desk in the Senate chamber, beating him so brutally with a walking stick that he was absent from the Senate for over three years.

The Democratic party was assembling for its national convention at Cincinnati when the news from Kansas arrived. Whatever chances Pierce had of being renominated, now disappeared. He had helped engineer the Kansas-Nebraska Bill and was seen as responsible for the disaster in Kansas. The convention turned to James Buchanan.

Houston's attitude toward the Know-Nothings during the 1856 campaign was a strange mixture of ambivalence, rejection, and enthusiasm. The canny politician in him said that the party was finished. However, he could not support the Democrats, and he most assuredly was opposed to the Republican candidate, John Charles Frémont, whose victory could only mean secession by the South.

Frémont was a general, explorer, adventurer, and millionaire whose exploits had long captivated the American public. He was also married to Jessie Benton, the daughter of the staunch Unionist Thomas Hart Benton.

In the presidential election of 1856, Sam Houston had no party, but he bit the bullet and bowed to his "sense of duty" and supported Fillmore and Donelson, who were adrift in the leaking boat of a third party. His "dead Ducks" comment was offset by a letter to Robert Irion in which he predicted that Fillmore would carry New York!

In August, in the midst of the campaign, he rose in the Senate to denounce the acrimony and hostility that had been set loose in the land. No doubt there were a few eyebrows raised by those who recalled Houston's own beating of Representative William Stanbery on Pennsylvania Avenue in 1832. However, Houston also warned "that an institution is sought to be fixed upon this country by every insidious and operative art which is calculated to put down Protestantism and establish Popery."

He clearly had not given up on the Know-Nothings, but in the general election his misgivings proved more accurate than his predictions. Fillmore and Donelson carried only Maryland. They had a total of eight electoral votes, and their popular vote was just 22 percent of the total.

Houston had stood apart from the most frenzied campaign since Old Hickory overwhelmed John Quincy Adams in 1828. The Democrats skillfully exploited the fear that a Republican victory would bring disunion and black equality. Even Benton, ever fearful of a breakup of the United States, supported Buchanan, who received 174 electoral votes to Benton's son-in-law Frémont's 114. The Republicans were not downcast, however. Their new party had carried eleven states.

Houston returned to the Senate to finish his term. His duties were the ordinary legislative tasks but his discharge of them revealed once again the side of Houston that had become obscured by his affair with the Know-Nothings.

He defended the government program for the distribution of free seeds to farmers. He objected to the proposal for enlarging and beautifying the grounds of the Capitol because dozens of people would be evicted from their homes and businesses with no right of appeal. He also was against the United States Government accepting the gift of The Hermitage, not because he was opposed to preserving Old Hickory's home but because the bequest specified that it was to be used as a military academy.

On March 4, 1857, the Democrat James Buchanan was sworn in as the fifteenth president of the United States. Houston ruefully reflected on the fact that he had lived through the administrations of Buchanan's fourteen predecessors and he had known twelve of them.

Two days after the inauguration, the Supreme Court handed down the Dred Scott Decision. Chief Justice Roger Taney and his four proslavery Southern colleagues on the court hoped to lay to rest the issue of whether Congress had the right to prohibit slavery in the territories, and not so incidentally strike a blow at Black Republicanism and the abolitionists. They proceeded to stand the Constitution on its head.

The case involved a Missouri slave named Dred Scott, who had lived with his master, an army surgeon, in Illinois and Minnesota. At the instigation of some white friends, Scott brought suit in 1846, arguing that since he had lived in a free state and a free territory he should be considered a free man. His suit eventually wound up in the Supreme Court.

In a sweeping decision, the court ruled that Congress had no power to prohibit slavery in the territories, that the Missouri Compromise was unconstitutional, and that a Negro whose ancestors were sold as slaves had no rights of citizenship and therefore no standing in court.

Far from annihilating the abolitionists and the Black Republicans and settling the issue, the North was even further agitated by the Dred Scott decision. Like the Fugitive Slave Law, the decision only strengthened the resolve of the antislavery forces. The *New York Tribune* succinctly stated their position. The decision was "entitled to as much moral weight as would be the judgment of a majority of those congregated in any Washington bar-room," said the paper.

During the closing days of the Senate session in the spring of 1857, Houston's thoughts turned seriously toward home. In a loving letter to his wife he talked of his "exile" and being "interdicted from all that is dear to me on earth." He clearly wanted to return home to Texas permanently, which was now an even more attractive prospect since they had moved again, back to Huntsville and The Woodland Home.

While his yearning for his family was genuine, his position in the

Senate was exceedingly uncomfortable for a man who was used to power. He could stay on until March 1859, but how much good could he do for his state in his present role? Besides, there was another plan afoot. The wily old fox was not about to retire to his lair just yet.

Back in Huntsville, on May 12, he wrote to his colleague Rusk, with some startling news. "Today I have declared myself a Candidate for Governor," he said. "So now the whip cracks, & the longest pole will bring down the persimmon. The people want excitement, and I had as well give it as any one."

The Democrats had met in Waco on May 4 and nominated Lieutenant Governor Hardin R. Runnels, a states' righter, for governor. Runnels was a poor speaker and he wisely declined to face Houston personally during the campaign. Sam, as only he could, made twenty-four speeches in East Texas between May 27 and July 3. Then, on July 7, he set off again for another round of appearances in the western counties, traveling as far as San Antonio. He spoke in fifty towns altogether. "The riders are all up and the Drum tapped," he wrote to his friend Ashbel Smith.

The riders may indeed have been up, but Houston traveled the campaign trail in a much more exotic fashion. On May 12, an intinerant plow salesman named Ed Sharp called on the senator in Huntsville. Houston had planned to leave for Houston the next day, but there was no room on the stagecoach. Sharp invited Sam to ride along with him.

The next morning, the sixty-four-year-old candidate climbed up into a brilliant red buggy with "Warwick's Patent Plow" emblazoned on the sides in enormous gold letters. For the next sixty-seven days Houston traversed Texas in the flamboyant gold-lettered red buggy.

They traveled in the morning or in the early evenings to avoid the oppressive heat—in Belton on July 19 it was 104 degrees—and for the most part slept outdoors. Houston protected himself with a light-colored linen duster and he carried his giant turkey-feather fan to cool himself and to beat away the flies.

Most of the press was anti-Houston, but the *Austin Gazette* was the most vitriolic, calling him "a melancholy picture of imbecility, vindictiveness and hate in old age." Much of the criticism had to do with Houston's platform manner. He was unremittingly scornful of his opponents, and if any of them showed up he would look down on them from the stage like an Old Testament prophet regarding the Sodomites. When he referred to the Waco Convention he invariably called it the "Wacko Convention."

The candidate was at Victoria on August 1 and from there he headed home. At Columbus he received the terrible news that Senator Rusk had committed suicide at his home in Nacogdoches. Houston had spent the night with his old friend when he campaigned there on May 30. The fifty-four-year-old Rusk had been despondent since his wife's death the year before, but Houston laid much of the blame for his death on Rusk's political opponents.

The election was held on August 3. Although it took weeks for the final vote to be tallied, the outcome soon became clear to the veteran campaigner as county after county delivered majorities to his opponent. Houston lost by about 4,000 votes out of 61,000 cast. He was in good spirits, however. "The fuss is over, and the sun yet shines as ever. What next?" he wrote to Ashbel Smith on August 22. "Will the spoils be equal to the wants of the spoil seekers? I fear not. Will the late victoy be equivalent to the State, & the country, for the murder of Genl. Rusk? I should say not." He longed to see his old friend Smith and "talk grave as well as laugh."

On November 7, the Texas Legislature elected J. Pinckney Henderson as Rusk's replacement, and while they were about it they elected Houston's successor as well. John Hemphill could not take office until Houston's term ended, but the legislators hoped to put pressure on Houston to resign early.

The news from Austin angered and insulted the old hero, but he would not give in. He left Huntsville in mid-December for Washington, where on January 19, 1858, he delivered a eulogy to Thomas J. Rusk in the Senate. He then asked for a thirty-day mourning period for his former colleague.

The two sessions of the Thirty-fifth Congress would be Sam Houston's farewell to Washington. He returned to the capital strangely rejuvenated by the Texas governor's race and the attacks of his old enemies. The death of Rusk also helped him cast off the lame duck lethargy of the last session.

Unfortunately for his posterity, his renewed energy was directed at instituting policies as reprehensible as his affair with the Know-Nothings. In February he introduced the following in the Senate.

> *Resolved,* That the Committee on Foreign Relations be instructed to inquire into and report to the Senate upon the expediency of the Government of the United States declaring and maintaining an efficient protectorate over the States of Mexico, Nicaragua, Costa Rica, Guatemala, Honduras, and San Salvador, in such form and to such extent as shall be necessary to secure to the people of said States the blessings of good and stable republican government.

"The facilities of communication with our Pacific possessions being through these regions, must necessarily be protected by this Government at all hazards, until we have a direct transit within our own territory," he said. In further defense of American hegemony and expansion, he executed a stunning departure from the Know-Nothing condemnation of the immigrant races of Europe. Indeed, he now seemed to be embracing them.

"We are an increasing people," said Houston. "We have continual accessions from other nations, and they become imbued with our spirit, and commingle with us and our enterprises. This mixture of races causes an irresistible impetus, that must overshadow and overrule that whole region."

Houston's protectorate scheme played to such filibustering hotheads as William Walker, the "grey-eyed man of destiny," who sought to extend Southern institutions—read slavery—into Central America, by force if necessary. Houston's plan was less overt. "This resolution," he insisted, "is not offered with a view to extending our dominion, but with a view of improving our neighborhood."

While Houston was promoting a protectorate, Walker was being tried in New Orleans for violating the neutrality laws. He was acquited and a hysterical and admiring Southern public continued to support his armed invasions until he was executed by a firing squad in Honduras.

Houston's protectorate resolution came to an end as well, but it was less noisy and much less sanguinary. On June 2, the Senate killed the resolution by a vote of 32 to 16.

Houston continued to be more attentive to the large issues of the day, but he did not neglect his constituents, nor did he overlook government matters. He voted against a retroactive pay raise for senators, and he was highly critical of the new sculptures to be installed on the Capitol, much to the disgust of the more artistically knowledgeable Jefferson Davis of Mississippi.

He also spoke against a new plan to remove the Great Raft—a centuries-old accumulation of logs that blocked the Red River. He suggested that the most expeditious way to clear the Great Raft would be to throw the $110,000 appropriation on the logs and let the people scramble for it. The raft would be removed very quickly as they searched for the money. This last can only have angered the residents of northeast Texas, who would benefit directly from clearing the river. But Houston was still an old Jacksonian when it came to government-supported internal improvements, particularly if they looked like pork. He was wrong about the raft, of course. Its permanent removal was possible, and the navigation of the Red River was a great boon to the entire area.

Sam Houston turned sixty-five during this session of the Congress. He was too stubborn to resign early and thus give in to his enemies—which, of course, was most of the Texas Legislature. He was determined to stay on in the Senate until his term ended naturally, but in his letters to Margaret there is no question that he was tired and wanted to go home to her and the children—even if he sometimes forgot their names.

"If I could only be with my Dear Wife and children," he said, "I feel that I would be happy, even if Andrew should tell me, 'I must learn them.' Poor little fellow, I can realize my love for him."

His concern for appearance was not limited to himself. He extended it to his wife and daughters, and he picked out dress patterns, fabrics, hoops, and hats and sent them by express to Texas. Although he protested that he knew little about fashion and dress, he made all his choices for them with great care and a discerning eye. And Sam would have another "brat" or "addendum" to "learn" when he finally got home that summer. Margaret gave birth to their seventh child, another son, on May 25, 1858, Sam, Jr.'s fifteenth birthday. She named him William Rogers Houston, after William P. Rogers, a good friend of the family.

Houston's new Senate colleague and old enemy, J. Pinckney Henderson, died in early June in Washington and was buried in the Congressional Cemetery. The two had never reconciled, and many in Texas felt that Houston was the wrong man to deliver a tribute to Henderson in the Senate. He spoke glowingly of Henderson, but his ending, a famous line from Gray's "Elegy," gave the game away. "The paths of glory lead but to the grave," said Sam.

Henderson's death led Houston to think that the Texas Legislature might now begin to reconsider its vote and ask him to stay on in Washington. To that end he began to court the Buchanan administration and attempt to make peace with the Democrats. He also went on another speaking tour of Texas after he returned home at the end of June.

The speeches, however, turned into a justification of all his previous behavior and served as a reminder to his constituents only of how good a speaker he was. He recanted nothing. On the contrary, he again attacked the idea of secession, stood up for the Union, defended his vote against the Kansas-Nebraska Bill, and called its sponsor, Stephen A. Douglas, the "prince of humbugs."

He derided the idea of a Southern League and its object of reopening the slave trade, though he still advocated a protectorate over Mexico as essential to preserving Southern institutions—in particular in being able to extend slavery to the south.

Houston has been credited with great consistency in his political philosophy. If this were so, then the protectorate was the exception that proved the rule. Such a scheme could only fire up agitation in the North and lead to the very split in the Union that he so feared.

Houston's final Senate recess did not revive his political fortunes in Texas, and he returned to Washington in December 1858 to face the fact that he truly would be leaving the Senate at the end of the second session of the Thirty-fifth Congress. Nevertheless he worked diligently up until the very end of his senatorial career, speaking out on a wide variety of issues and favorite causes.

He spoke in favor of the southern route for the transcontinental railroad, which not only benefited his home state but also was an eminently practicable route. His fight to have the corrupt Texas judge John Charles Watrous removed from office received high praise from all over the country, even from his worst enemies in Texas. The nine-lived rascal Watrous had survived all previous assaults, and he survived this one—remaining on the bench until 1869, when he was finally removed by a stroke.

But one paramount concern still preyed on Houston's mind. He did not want to leave the great national forum of the United States Senate without setting before the entire country his "Refutation of Calumnies Produced and Circulated Against His Character as Commander-in-Chief of the Army of Texas." On February 28, he rose to do just that—to relate in detail his version of the events of 1836. Sam intended this speech to be his farewell, and he ended, to great applause from the galleries, by saying that he prayed that "the nation will be blessed, the people happy, and the perpetuity of the Union secured to the latest posterity."

Unfortunately these were not his last words to the Senate. He was forced to sacrifice theater to duty. The next day he was compelled to defend on the floor the El Paso–San Diego mail route, which was in danger of being closed down.

Then, on March 3, the day after his sixty-sixth birthday, the old lion briefly addressed his colleagues one last time, to object to a proposed adjournment. He knew he would not be back the next day, and he was hesitant to let go.

"My opinion is, that if we leave the Senate Chamber we shall not meet again," he said. "Members are exhausted, and have been for several nights; and if they once retire to repose, they will not wake up again."

16

The End of
the Battle

FOR TWENTY-FIVE YEARS Sam Houston had kept the name of Texas
before the American public. Indeed, the man was synonymous with
the province of Tejas in revolt, the independent Republic of Texas, and,
finally, the state of Texas. For most Americans, he was the embodiment
of everything Texan. He was also the remaining link with an era that had
assumed mythological, even religious significance in American life.

Sam Houston was the last of an extraordinary band of men who, for
better or worse, had guided the country for most of the century. Clay,
Calhoun, Webster, and Benton were gone. Of those great public figures
who had been alive during Washington's presidency and had known
Jefferson, Madison, Monroe, and Jackson only Houston still lived.
Many of those Texas constituents who had forsworn him had already
begun to see the error of their ways.

Houston had represented Texas in the Senate for thirteen years. He
would be missed in Washington, and for days before his departure on
March 10, 1859, his lodgings at Willard's Hotel were crowded with
congressmen, senators, government figures, and the plain citizens who
came to bid him good-bye.

Houston assured Margaret that all he wanted was to be with her and
the children and raise sheep on the Cedar Point property. To that end,

he wrote Ashbel Smith and offered to buy his flock, which were already "on the Bay, and are used to salt water." Smith's acclimated sheep were to serve as the nucleus for the great flocks Houston planned to put on his nearby property.

"Now, my Dear Friend, don't you get provoked at me, for disparaging you in the way of sheep-husbandry," chided Sam. "I admit your universal intelligence, and ability in general matters, but you would not do, *personally,* as a sheep man!"

Houston had correctly characterized Smith. Furthermore, the peripatetic fifty-four-year-old bachelor physician was away from his Evergreen Plantation much of the time, in the east speaking at his alma mater, Yale, or visiting London, Paris, or Venice. Dr. Smith, nevertheless, declined to sell his flock and the would-be shepherd had to make other arrangements.

In January, Sam had written to Margaret a tantalizingly mysterious letter. He referred "In confidence" to the "Protectorate" and he was clearly hinting at some dramatic move when he said, "And I am sure that you would not be willing, tho' you might consent to it, to separate from any of the children, tho' you might have Sam, Nannie, & Willie with you." These were the three oldest children, ages sixteen, thirteen, and eleven, who conceivably could accompany their parents to some new place.

Houston was speaking of Mexico, but he was less guarded when he wrote to Ashbel Smith about his future plans. "I have none, and will have none," he said, "unless I go to Mexico, to take a look at the interior of the 'Halls of the Montezumas.' "

The Texas Democrats met at Houston at the beginning of May and renominated Runnels for governor. But the party was by no means united, and the acrimony at the convention was a preview of what the Democrats could expect throughout the country in the coming year—increasingly bitter fights over disunion, states' rights, secession, and slavery.

Once again the old political bugle began to sound, this time accompanied by the unmistakable drumbeat of popular support for Sam Houston for governor. On June 2 he answered the call and announced that he would run. But for the next month he said nothing else. Finally, he consented to speak at Nacogdoches on July 9, 1859. The man who had made fifty speeches in his pursuit of the governorship in 1857 made only this one speech during the entire campaign. Both his friends and his enemies were flabbergasted.

"My career is not disconnected with history," Houston began modestly. He then went on to recount some of the high points and some of the reasons for his actions. "The Nebraska bill has had its day," he reminded them, "and the results are to be seen. I was the only extreme Southern Senator who voted against it, and for that you whipped me like a cur dog. If I was wrong, I own it and take it all back, and if you were wrong I forgive you. So we will start even again. It is past."

At one point, as he was denouncing party platforms—"they are used to blind the people to the designs of men"—the platform on which part of the audience was seated collapsed. "There," he cried, "did I not tell you platforms were dangerous."

Houston's speech contained contradictions (he said he had never supported a protective tariff), evasions (he accepted without comment the Dred Scott decision as the law of the land), anti-intellectualism (he encouraged "home colleges" instead of "a great State institution"), and expansionism (under a protectorate, Mexico "would become Americanized and prepared for incorporation into our Union").

It was also an exceptionally effective campaign speech, in which he set forth his principles in no uncertain terms. He was opposed to banks, internal improvements by the federal government, distribution of the public lands to the states, a protective tariff, "latitudinous construction of the Constitution," and slavery agitation and disunion.

He restricted his opposition to reopening the slave trade to his fear of depressing the price of slaves and glutting both the labor market and the cotton market. "I will not discuss its morality," he said.

Houston had long since come to view any major issue in the context of whether it might cause the breakup of the United States. His abiding concern—which amounted almost to an obsession—was that the work of almost a century, however imperfect, could be destroyed by hotheads of both sections, defending, or imposing on others, what they perceived to be their rights. "You may take these men in their protean shapes, Nullificationists, Secessionists, African Slave Trade men, but they all mean disunion," he declared.

"Mark me, the day that produces a dissolution of this Confederacy will be written in history in the blood of humanity. All that is horrible in war will characterize the future of this people. Preserve Union and you preserve liberty. They are one and the same, indivisible and perfect."

Houston's cry that "I am a Democrat of the Old School. In politics I am an old Fogy" resonated with 36,227 voters on election day— almost 60 percent of the total. Texans had voted for the man, yes, but they had also become frightened at the prospect of disunion. Houston won because he was the more likely candidate to prevent such a calamity.

After his victory, Sam wrote to his private secretary of almost twenty years before, Washington D. Miller. "My Dear Miller, The report is that I am elected by 8. or 10. thousand votes. Will you be my private secretary?" Miller was now coeditor of the *Texas Democrat* in Austin, but that did not deter Sam. No friend was too exalted to escape being summoned to serve at court.

When Houston arrived in Austin in December 1859, he found a much different town from the place he had abandoned permanently as president of the republic in early February 1842. Back then he had called it "the most miserable place on the face of the earth."

A recent traveler through Texas—and one cognizant of both man-made and natural beauty—had pronounced Austin "the pleasantest place we had seen in Texas." Frederick Law Olmstead particularly praised the new Capitol, "a really imposing building of soft cream limestone."

The governor-elect was also taken with the new building on the hill at the end of Congress Avenue. He realized immediately the effect of delivering his inaugural address from the terrace at the top of the long flight of steps leading up to the second floor.

Governor Runnels was equally insistent that the ceremony and his valedictory be held indoors in the House chamber. They both had their way. Runnels delivered his farewell and then the entire crowd trouped outside to stare up at Sam.

The inaugural was uncharacteristically brief. Houston spoke for less than fifteen minutes. He called for construction of railroads, improved river navigation, and the "improvement and perfection of the common schools" so that education would be "disseminated throughout the whole community." As for higher learning, "when the foundation is firmly laid, it will be easy to erect thereon materials for a University, if the voice of the State should, at some future day, require the establishment."

He confronted head-on the secessionists and sectionalists, warning everyone to try to distinguish "between the wild ravings of fanatics and that public sentiment which truly represents the masses of the people." Freedom of expression was sacred, but "when thought becomes treason, the traitor is as much the enemy of one section as of the other." As for Texas, "She entered not into the North, nor into the South, but into the Union."

He allotted only about a quarter of his brief inaugural address to the problems presented by Mexico. Once in office, however, he began to devote an inordinate amount of his attention to his southern neighbor. As commander in chief of the Texan armies and then as both legislator and president of the republic, Houston had roundly condemned the many schemes and plots for expeditions into Mexico. Now, in the twilight of his career, Sam Houston himself began to dream of a much grander expedition, backed up by the might of the United States Army.

Houston's proposed protectorate over Mexico had by no means died on the floor of the United States Senate. It was very much alive, and Houston actively promoted his plan throughout the early part of 1860. He would first need an army, and he called for the organization of the Texas militia, even though he acknowledged that federal troops would have to be used in any international undertaking.

Juan Nepomuceno Cortina, a Texas-Mexican warlord, provided an excuse for renewed filibustering when he went beyond his assumed role of protector of those poor Mexicans who were being abused by the Anglos. Cortina invaded Brownsville twice and was de facto ruler of the entire southeast border area.

The week after Houston's inauguration, federal troops, under Major S. P. Heintzelman, routed Cortina and drove him across the Rio Grande. At the end of December, Houston issued a proclamation calling on all armed bands to disperse and sent a copy by express directly to Cortina. The bandit ignored it and there was another engagement on February 4. Defeated again, Cortina fled to the Burgos Mountains in Mexico.

In his message to the legislature in January 1860, Houston reaffirmed his support for a system of common schools and some aid to institutions "supported by private enterprise." However, he again gave the proposed state university the back of his hand. The previous legislature had passed a bill giving the school $100,000 from the funds paid to Texas as part of the Compromise of 1850 boundary settlement and also turning over the lands that had been set aside for a university back in 1839.

Under Houston, this act was repealed and the money allotted for defense of the frontier. It was thus another generation before the University of Texas was fully in operation. Although Houston's observation that the lands set aside for the university "will be greatly increased" in value was a sop to keep the legislature quiet, he was right. The lands turned out to lie on top of a vast pool of oil.

President James Buchanan kept a wary eye on Houston's Mexican intrigues, but Washington was more concerned with domestic problems, which loomed larger than any that could be contrived by would-be filibusterers. On October 16, 1859, the rabid, some would say crazed, abolitionist John Brown and a force of twenty-one men attacked the United States arsenal at Harpers Ferry, Virginia. Brown planned to seize weapons to equip an army of slaves and stir up a full-scale slave rebellion, invade the South, and wipe out slavery by force.

Lieutenant Colonel Robert E. Lee was home on leave in Virginia from the 2nd Cavalry, which was stationed in West Texas. He was dispatched to Harpers Ferry to end the rebellion. Two days later, Lee and his troops stormed the firehouse where Brown and his ragtag mob had taken refuge.

John Brown was hanged in December and in the North the antislavery movement had a hero and a martyr. To Southerners, however, he became a hated symbol of abolition and Black Republicanism. There would be no more periods of peace between the two regions.

Houston, meanwhile, was continuing his efforts to build up what would amount to a personal army. His friend Ben McCulloch, a hero both in the Texas Revolution and the Mexican War, was in Washington to sound out opinion and enlist support. "There will be stirring times on the Rio Grande ere long," Houston wrote. "What are you doing? See the President and the Secretary of War."

Robert E. Lee returned to Texas in February. He and Houston had first met when Lee was a cadet at West Point and Congressman Sam Houston of Tennessee was on the Board of Overseers. Lee cannot have cared for Houston very much. As a senator, Houston had condemned the system of military education at West Point, where Lee was superintendent from 1852 to 1855. Further, while speaking against a bill to increase the size of the regular army, Houston had derisively attacked the cavalry training on the Texas frontier—Lee's own regiment.

Soon after his return, Lee received two emissaries from the governor. Would the colonel be willing, they asked, to help pacify Mexico? Predictably, Robert E. Lee rejected any such scheme out of hand. "I have no doubt," he stiffly replied, "that arrangements will be made to maintain the rights and peace of Texas, and I hope in conformity to the Constitution and laws of the country."

About the same time he was attempting to suborn Robert E. Lee, Houston wrote to Secretary of War John B. Floyd and to President Buchanan about the problems with Mexico and the frontier Indians. The letter to Floyd was a bellicose and not even thinly disguised threat to invade Mexico. His letter to the president was more sensible—a plan to pacify the Indians on the frontier by treaties and annuities.

Governor Houston's dreams of military and political glory south of the Rio Grande were finally curtailed not so much by argument and opposition as by finances. The state was broke again. He had been seduced by promises of money and volunteers to further the scheme, but nothing was forthcoming.

Inexplicably, however, he still refused to recognize that he was violating a position of his own devising. This so-called protectorate was just another name for a revival of the Matamoros, Santa Fe, and Mier expeditions, which he had so condemned in the 1830s and 1840s.

John Brown's raid brought forth every conspiracy theory that could inflame an already frightened South. Hardly anyone believed that it was the work of a few zealots, and Brown's canonization by the North fed the suspicion. No slaveholder ever looked at his people again in quite the same way.

As was to be expected, Calhoun's South Carolina progeny led the reaction. The master would have been proud. In early January the state legislature met at Columbia and unanimously passed resolutions asserting the right of a state to secede from the Union. Governor William Henry Gist forwarded the resolutions to the other Southern governors.

On January 21, Sam Houston submitted the South Carolina resolutions and Governor Gist's accompanying letter to the Texas Legislature. Houston may have been diverted by the schemes of filibusterers and the nativist preachings of the Know-Nothings, but this new threat from the South Carolina secessionists called him back to his real work. His message to the Texas Legislature was a familiar one, but he had fresh and ingenious ways of restating it.

"I am happy to find my opinions on this subject have the sanction of all those illustrious names which we and future generations will cherish so long as liberty is a thing possessed or hoped for," he began.

Then, like the lawyer he was, he marshalled statements on unity and secession from George Washington, Thomas Jefferson, James Madison, and Andrew Jackson to build a case against South Carolina.

If a Southern Confederacy were established, could South Carolina guarantee its duration? "Grant her assumption of the right of secession and it must be adopted as a general principle," he pointed out. "I have been no indifferent spectator of the agitations which have distracted our councils, and caused many patriots to despair of the Republic," said the old warrior. "But I am yet hopeful, and have an abiding confidence in the masses of the people. I can not believe that they will suffer scheming, designing, and misguided politicians to endanger the palladium of our liberties.

"If there is a morbid and dangerous sentiment abroad in the land, let us endeavor to allay it by teaching and cultivating a more fraternal feeling," he advised the legislators. He recommended the adoption of resolutions dissenting from the right of secession.

Houston's enemies confronted him at once, led by the newly elected Texas Senator Louis T. Wigfall. A South Carolinian who had learned his secessionist rhetoric at Calhoun's knee, Wigfall despised Houston and his pro-Union principles. Papers throughout the state endorsed Wigfall's denunciations of the governor.

———

No election in American history has been anticipated with such dread as the presidential election of 1860. The Democratic convention opened at Charleston, South Carolina, on April 23, and in a matter of days the party split over the slavery issue. Fifty of the Southern delegates walked out. The convention continued, but the front-runner, Stephen A. Douglas, could not gather the two thirds necessary to win the nomination. But neither could anyone else, and after fifty-seven ballots the delegates gave up and adjourned until June, when they would try again in Baltimore.

The second time around, the bolters had returned to the fold but rival delegations also showed up, setting off a credentials fight and a second walkout. The regular Democrats who stayed behind nominated Douglas. The bolters nominated John C. Breckinridge of Kentucky.

In March, a group of Houston's friends had asked him if he would be willing to have his name placed before the Charleston convention. Houston replied that he thought political conventions were subversive of the will of the people. "If my name should be used in connection with the Presidency," he said, "the movement must originate with the people themselves, as well as end with them. I would not consent to have my name submitted to any Convention."

On April 21, at the anniversary celebration of the Battle of San Jacinto, his supporters took him at his word and adopted a resolution calling on the country to elect him president.

The new Constitutional Union party, which included old-time Whigs and Know-Nothings, among others, met in Baltimore on May 9. The party's position on the slavery issue was that it had no place on the agenda and was not even to be mentioned. Thus the Union was to be saved. The reporter of the *New York Herald* sarcastically observed that the "delegates may sleep with the nigger, eat with the nigger, but don't allow his wooly head to come into the convention."

On the first ballot, Sam Houston received 57 votes and John Bell 68½. After much politicking and campaigning by Bell, he eventually received the nomination 138 to 69. Houston did nothing to promote his nomination, although there were agents working on his behalf. Had he deigned to appear in person the results would have been far different.

The Republicans gathered in Chicago a week later and on the third ballot nominated Abraham Lincoln. William Seward, who had been the favorite going into the convention, was more than a little disappointed at his being passed over for a man whose experience included only one term in the U.S. House of Representatives and two failed attempts to represent Illinois in the Senate.

Seward and his followers nevertheless rallied behind Lincoln, and the Republican party went into the campaign united. With the other parties so fractured, Lincoln was assured of election if he held the North together.

The Republicans wrote off the South immediately. Not only did they not bother to campaign there, the party was not even on the ticket in ten states. Any "Black Republican" who showed his face in the slave states risked a fate worse than John Brown's.

The only contest in the South was between Bell and Breckinridge, although the Northern Democrat Douglas courageously campaigned there. Taking a leaf from Andrew Jackson's book, he declared in North Carolina that he would hang any secessionists from the tallest tree.

Throughout 1860 rumors of plots and rebellions swept Texas. Stories of abolitionists, provocateurs, and rebellious slaves poisoning the water supply and setting fires were everywhere. Great fires did occur in Dallas, Denton, Pilot Point, and Belknap, but the violence was one-sided. The so-called Committees of Public Safety were often no more than officially sanctioned gangs of thugs who did not hesitate to lynch either blacks or suspected abolitionists.

Houston remained even-handed and he caused an uproar in June when he pardoned a slave named George who was sentenced to hang for striking a white man. In the pardon, the governor cited "peculiar and aggravated Circumstances." Earlier he had stopped the continued whipping of a black slave boy named Abe who was sentenced to receive a total of 750 lashes for burglary.

The crisis forced Houston to spend the summer in Austin, although he yearned to be at Cedar Point. He asked Ashbel Smith to check on his property, but Smith was too slow in responding. "You did promise to visit the Point—and see the mill, and write to me. Do you recollect the promise?" he complained to Smith. "You have nothing to do, and could write often, and you know that your letters always interest me. I, now and then, snatch a moment from my duties to salute a *friend*, and I am sure that you out of your abundance could give me a part of your time."

He followed the national election campaign very closely. "I am with poltics as Falstaff was with strong Potations," he remarked to Smith. However, he had come to a "sage conclusion—if the people can do without my services, I am sure that I can do without their suffrages."

Houston was still being promoted for the presidency by a few die-hards, and he finally decided that an end must be put to it. In a letter to a supporter in Houston, he said, "As to my having any wish to be President, I can say before high heaven, I have not a single wish or desire to be placed in that office."

He also declined to support any of the candidates—in particular anyone connected with the Kansas-Nebraska Bill and the repeal of the Missouri Compromise, to which he attributed all the troubles in the Democratic party. Both Douglas and Breckinridge had helped draft the infamous measure.

In a message addressed to "Friends in the United States, he said, "I call upon my countrymen to forget me." They should remember instead, *"The Federal Union, it must be preserved."* Houston was well into his sixty-eighth year, and Margaret had given birth on August 12 to another son, Temple Lea Houston. Perhaps the strong potation of politics was at last losing its taste, or else he had become addicted to an even stronger potation—foreign adventure.

The idea of a Mexican protectorate had continued to simmer since the spring, and Houston occasionally stirred the pot by requesting the U.S. War Department to supply arms to Texas. There also were overtures from British holders of Mexican bonds who were anxious to get their money back. Reportedly the British were prepared to pay Houston a huge amount of money to lead an expedition across the border and they would settle an annuity on Margaret.

Houston had obliquely referred to the scheme in letters to his oldest son, Sam, Jr., but in late August he became more bold. "We look on it as a mission of mercy and humanity," he wrote to Ben McCulloch, "and it must not sink into the character of spoil and robbery. It must be to elevate and exalt Mexico to a position among the nations of the world."

Houston cautioned McCulloch to keep the plans quiet, else "it might create a thousand foolish or silly rumors." As, indeed, it would have—especially if it became known that Houston had asked McCulloch to look into the cost of eight to ten thousand Morse rifles.

———

On September 22, the Unionists held a mass meeting at Austin. The governor was in his element before the large and sympathetic crowd. Texas should not desert the Union no matter how the November 6 election went, he said. Thus far, no rights guaranteed by the Constitution had been taken away, nor would they be.

"If Mr. Lincoln administers the Government in accordance with the Constitution, our rights must be respected. If he does not, the Constitution has provided a remedy." Besides, even with a Republican in the White House, there would still be Democratic majorites in both houses of Congress.

While Houston hoped for Lincoln's defeat, with the opposition split three ways the election went as any astute observer knew it would. The North refused to be intimidated, as it had been in 1856, by Southern secessionist rhetoric and voted for Lincoln. He received 180 electoral votes, Breckinridge 72, Bell 39, and poor Douglas just 12. The popular vote told another, more ominous story. Only 40 percent of the electorate had decided for Abraham Lincoln and the Republicans.

Governor Houston called for calm and in late November he sent a joint resolution of the Texas Legislature to all the Southern governors. Texas hoped that it was still possible for "statesmen" to sit down and resolve their differences amicably.

The resolution aside, there was tremendous pressure on Houston to call the legislature to debate secession. All the other Southern states were already meeting or planned to do so. Houston procrastinated, hoping that the crisis would somehow play itself out. As a pretext, he feigned a budget crisis and the need for reapportionment. The state could not afford a special legislative session, and besides, the present makeup of the legislature did not accurately reflect the new legislative boundaries drawn the previous April.

His nemesis, Senator Wigfall, whom Houston called one of those "transplants from the South Carolina nursery of disunion," charged the governor should be tarred and feathered for his capitulation to the North. In Georgia, Alfred Iverson hoped that "some Texas Brutus may arise to rid his country of this old, hoary-headed traitor."

There were Brutuses aplenty in Texas, and while they were reluctant to wield a dagger, they did organize themselves into an effective opposition. In early December, they called for a secession convention to meet in Austin on January 28, 1861.

Houston could no longer thwart what appeared to be inevitable. On December 17, he himself announced a special session of the legislature to open January 21. And ten days later, he ordered an election to be held on February 4 to select delegates to the Convention of the Southern States.

South Carolina seceded from the Union on December 20, and by the time the Texas Legislature convened, Mississippi, Florida, Alabama, and Georgia had followed. Louisiana left the Union on January 26. In the southernmost tier of states Texas was alone.

The day before the beginning of the special session of the Legislature, Houston wrote to Major General D. E. Twiggs, the commander of the Texas department. He wanted to know, confidentially, what would happen to the federal arms and armament on Texas soil in the event of secession. Would the general turn them over to the governor? Houston warned that a mob might attempt to appropriate the arms. Twiggs answered that he had no orders and was awaiting instructions. He had, of course, already decided what to do. In the event of secession he would surrender arms, stores, and government properties to the Texas secessionists.

The legislature met on January 21 to consider first and foremost the question of secession from the United States, but Houston would still not be hurried. He began his message with a long report on the Indian incursions on the frontier.

As the legislators impatiently wondered if he was ever going to get to the subject at hand, Houston finally acknowledged the purpose of the gathering. Once again he reiterated the arguments for maintaining the precious link with the Union. "Ere the work of centuries is undone, and freedom, shorn of her victorious garments, is started out once again on her weary pilgrimage, hoping to find, after centuries have passed away, another dwelling place, it is not unmanly to pause and at least endeavor to avert the calamity," he said, pleading what now seemed a lost cause.

He then addressed what he saw as practicalities. The situation of Texas was unique. No other state in the South bordered on a foreign country. No other Southern state was at that very moment the object of attacks by wild Indians. The federal government annually spent millions to defend the frontier and Texas commerce and to support the postal service. Where was the money to come from if Texas were independent? "The people in many sections are already calling for relief," he said. "We cannot afford under these circumstances to plunge madly into revolution."

He insisted that the legislature let the people decide the issue. Surprisingly, the members agreed and Texas thus would be the only state where the people voted directly on secession. The Texas Secession Convention opened a week later, on January 28, and the next day the delegates voted 171 to 6 that "Texas should separately secede from the Union" and appointed a committee to draft an ordinance of secession that would be submitted to the people. It was read to the convention on January 30. The 1845 annexation by the United States is "hereby repealed and annulled," it read.

It was a dagger in Houston's heart. But the assassins were not finished. The referendum on the ordinance was scheduled for February 23. If the people accepted the ordinance of secession, it would be implemented on March 2, 1861—the twenty-fifth anniversary of Texan independence and, of course, Houston's own birthday.

But Houston had the last word that day. Late in the afternoon on January 30, Lieutenant Governor Clark, president of the Texas Senate, received a short note and some documents. "Sir: Enclosed, I have the honor to submit the report of the Superintendent of the State Lunatic Asylum, and commend the same to the consideration of your honorable body. Sam Houston."

The final convention vote on the Ordinance of Secession came on February 1. Houston attended but said not a word, impassively watching and listening as the delegates were polled. The chairman called the name of J. W. Throckmorton.

"Mr. President, in view of the responsibility, in the presence of God and my country—and unawed by the wild spirit of revolution around me, I vote no," said Throckmorton. In the gallery, someone hissed. Throckmorton was back on his feet in an instant. "When the rabble hiss," he cried, "well may patriots tremble."

The ordinance passed 166 to 8. It was now up to the people of Texas, and on February 4 the convention confidently adjourned until March 2. Their confidence was justified. The people voted three to one in favor of secession, and on March 4 the governor officially announced that secession was accomplished.

The next day the Secession Convention voted to join Texas with the Confederate States of America. Houston refused to recognize this action, maintaining that the convention had legally ended with the referendum on secession. It had no other authority.

The legislature was scheduled to reassemble on March 18 and he intended to bring before it all important issues arising out of the severance of ties with the government of the United States. He was also determined to go directly to the people and ask for a constitutional convention.

In the meantime, seven Texas delegates had already taken their seats in the First Confederate Congress at Montgomery, Alabama, and Texas troops, under Ben McCulloch, had forced the surrender of the federal garrison at San Antonio. Confederate president Jefferson Davis now moved to assert control over all military installations in the state.

Houston's response was swift and unambiguous. He informed the Confederacy that Texas was by no means a member state. Texans "have just resumed their nationality" and will not be annexed "to a new Government without their knowledge and consent."

The governor's rejection of the Confederacy enraged the convention, which was now for all practical purposes the legislature of the state of Texas. They struck back with an ordinance requiring all state officials to swear allegiance to the Confederate States of America.

On Friday evening, March 15, at eight o'clock, George W. Chilton, of the Committee of Public Safety, came to the governor's mansion. Houston receive him politely and calmly listened to his message. The governor was summoned to appear before the convention the next day at twelve noon and take the oath of allegiance.

Sam bade good night to Margaret and the children and retired to his upstairs bedroom. Throughout the night his family could hear him pacing the floor in his stockinged feet, occasionally leaving the room and walking up and down the long hall.

He remained awake the entire night, praying, searching his conscience, and writing a letter to the people of Texas. In the morning a tired but determined Houston descended the stairs. "Margaret," he said, "I can never do it."

Late in the morning, Houston left the mansion and walked over to the Capitol. The great crowd assembled outside the building parted to let him pass. He went directly to his office and laid the letter, addressed "To the People of Texas," on the desk. He then sat down in a rocking chair and began to whittle some small pieces of wood with his pocket knife.

In the House chamber, the convention began summoning the remaining government officials to declare their allegiance to the Confederacy. At precisely twelve o'clock the secretary called out, "Sam Houston!" Once again. "Sam Houston!" Then a third time. "Sam Houston!" The governor did not respond. He sat in the rocking chair and continued to whittle, the wood shavings falling silently at his feet.

————

Houston's silence was reserved for the usurpers of the government. He could not, however, abandon the people who were being led down this destructive path. "I am determined that those who would overthrow the law shall not learn the lesson from me," he said. Houston now went directly to the people with a memorable message, "To the People of Texas."

He refused, he said, to recognize the convention because it had not derived its powers from either the legislature or the people. In fact, it had usurped the powers of both and was functioning independent of the Constitution of Texas. The convention had effectively taken over all departments and powers of government and put them under the control of one body. "I am ready to lay down the office rather than yield to usurpation and degradation."

As for secession, "I have declared my determination to stand by Texas in whatever position she assumes," he reminded them. "I went back into the Union with the people of Texas. I go out from the Union with them; and though I see only gloom before me, I shall follow the 'Lone

Star' with the same devotion as of yore." He warned the people against aligning themselves with the Confederacy. It could only lead to the complete sacrifice of their independence in order "to pay tribute to King Cotton."

"Fellow-Citizens, in the name of your rights and liberties, which I believe have been trampled upon, I refuse to take this oath. In the name of the nationality of Texas, which has been betrayed by the Convention, I refuse to take this oath. In the name of the Constitution of Texas, which has been trampled upon, I refuse to take this oath. In the name of my own conscience and manhood, which this Convention would degrade by dragging me before it, to pander to the malice of my enemies, when by the Constitution the privilege is accorded me, which belongs to the humblest officer, to take my oath of office before any competent authority, I refuse to take this oath.

"I am ready to be ostracized," he declared, "sooner than submit to usurpation. Office has no charm for me, that it must be purchased at the sacrifice of my conscience, and the loss of my self-respect.

"I love Texas too well to bring civil strife and bloodshed upon her. To avert this calamity, I shall make no endeavor to maintain my authority as Chief Executive of this State, except by the peaceful exercise of my functions. When I can no longer do this, I shall calmly withdraw from the scene, leaving the Government in the hands of those who have usurped its authority; but still claiming that I am its Chief Executive.

"It is perhaps but meet that my career should close thus," said Houston. "I have seen the patriots and statesmen of my youth, one by one, gathered to their fathers, and the Government which they created, rent in twain; and none like them are left to unite it once again. I stand the last almost of a race, who learned from their lips the lessons of human freedom. I am stricken down now, because I will not yield those principles, which I have fought for and struggled to maintain. The severest pang is that the blow comes in the name of Texas."

When Houston did not appear before the convention, the governorship was declared vacant and Lieutenant Governor Clark was immediately sworn in. The following week Houston and his family were asked to vacate the Governor's Mansion.

Margaret dutifully but sadly began to arrange for the move back to East Texas. These fifteen months in Austin had been the longest unbroken amount of time that she and Sam had spent together since their marriage. She had watched with love and pride as Houston had become a proper father to his children, in particular to young Sam. He had taken a keen interest in the boy's development, advising him on everything from hats to penmanship. The governor had even walked over to Lavenburg's store and picked out himself the white Mexican hat that Sam, Jr., wanted and then instructed him how to break it in properly.

Young Sam was at the Bastrop Military Institute and Houston wrote to him regularly. He sent him a copy of Robert Burns's poem "Epistle to a Young Friend," which in terms of good advice "has but one Superior, and that is the Scriptures," said his father.

"Now is the seed time of life, and the harvest must follow. If the seed is well planted, the harvest will be in porportion to it," Sam told his son. He wanted a good education for the young man and lamented his own poor preparation. "Oh, if I had only enjoyed an education of one year, I would have been happy."

————

Since his election, Abraham Lincoln had watched the Texas situation closely and after his inauguration on March 4 he saw that he might exploit an opportunity that did not exist in the other Deep South states. Texas was run by a staunch Unionist who could perhaps be aided directly in his battle against secession.

It was probably during the short period between Houston's deposition from the governorship and his departure from the capital that an agent from President Lincoln arrived in Austin. Colonel Frederick West Lander delivered the president's offer to help Houston keep Texas in the Union. Lincoln proposed sending fifty thousand federal troops to reinforce those already in the state.

Houston had to refuse. It would have meant civil war in Texas. On March 29 he wrote to the federal commander, C. A. Waite, "Allow me to most respectfully decline any such assistance of the United States Government," said Houston. Further, he asked that all federal troops be removed from the state at the earliest practicable date.

There is some evidence that Abraham Lincoln also sent another messenger, George H. Giddings, a Texas mail contractor, to Texas with an offer of military aid. Houston called in J. W. Throckmorton, George W. Paschal, Ben Epperson, and D. B. Culberson—all Unionists—for advice. They assembled in the downstairs library of the mansion and Houston read them the Lincoln letter.

Only Epperson was in favor of the offer of troops, and Houston went along with the majority. However, he allowed as to how if he were twenty years younger he would not, that he would fight to keep Texas in the Union. He then burned the letter in the fireplace.

———

By the end of March, the large household was ready to leave Austin. Sam had decided that they would settle permanently at Cedar Point, but, in deference to Margaret, who wanted to be with her mother and sisters, they would spend some time at Independence. The yellow coach left town on the road toward Brenham, where they stopped for the night on Sunday, March 31.

Friends and admirers welcomed Sam to Brenham and asked him to speak that evening at the courthouse. He declined, and even though some of his old San Jacinto comrades continued to press him he held firm. Then word reached him that the secessionists in Brenham had said that they would not allow him to speak. Houston immediately changed his mind.

The secessionists had indeed stirred up the town against the "traitor" and a great crowd awaited him at the courthouse. As he entered, someone shouted, "Put him out!" Another cried, "Don't let him speak. Kill him!" Hugh McIntyre, a local planter, stilled the crowd by jumping up on the table and drawing his Colt revolver.

McIntyre was a secessionist and he disagreed with the governor, but he defended his right to speak. "There is no other man alive who has more right to be heard by the people of Texas," he shouted. "Now, fellow-citizens, give him your close attention; and you ruffians, keep quiet, or I will kill you." The sixty-eight-year-old statesman, the wounded hero of two great wars, then began to picture for a small Texas town the calamity that secession and disunion would visit upon the South.

"I declare that Civil War is inevitable and is near at hand," said

Houston. "When it comes the descendants of the heroes of Lexington and Bunker Hill will be found equal in patriotism, courage and heroic endurance with descendants of the heroes of Cowpens and Yorktown. For this reason I predict that the civil war which is now near at hand will be stubborn and of long duration.

"When the tug of war comes, it will indeed be the Greek meeting Greek. Then, oh my fellow countrymen, the fearful conflict will fill our fair land with untold suffering, misfortune and disaster. The soil of our beloved South will drink deep the precious blood of our sons and brethren.

"I cannot, nor will I close my eyes against the light and voice of reason. The die has been cast by your secession leaders, whom you have permitted to sow and broadcast the seeds of secession, and you must ere long reap the fearful harvest of conspiracy and revolution."

In less than two weeks, on April 12, the federal fort at the mouth of the harbor in Charleston, South Carolina—Fort Sumter—was fired on by Confederate forces. The Civil War had begun.

Houston and Margaret and the children were settling in at Ben Lomond when the news came of the first action of the war. The old house was still much as it was when Houston built it twenty years before. It was not a proper home for such a large family, and Margaret would have preferred to stay in Independence. But she was happy that at least her husband and the children were away from the poisonous atmosphere of Austin.

Eighteen-year-old Sam arrived home from Bastrop and immediately began to talk of going off to join the war. Instead, he was drafted into the tedium of living in isolation and running a farm. Had Old Sam forgotten that half a century before he had revolted against the same sort of life and fled—first to the Indians and then to the United States Army?

However, young Sam was needed at home far more than his father had ever been back in Tennessee. The family's livelihood now depended on Cedar Point. Their always difficult financial situation was now desperate, and they were obliged to live off the farm.

Sam Junior was a dutiful son, until July when he went off to drill with Ashbel Smith's newly formed Bayland Guards. This first taste of military life was enough to convince him to go to war. He returned home only long enough to tell his parents that he would be moving to Galveston for full-time training.

While Houston warned his son that "Houston is not, nor will be a favorite name in the Confederacy!" he was pleased that he would be with his old friend Dr. Smith. "Esculapius is transformed to Mars," he wryly remarked. His gift to young Sam was a new Confederate uniform. The boy's mother gave him a Bible.

The old general regularly crossed the bay to Galveston to watch the training of his son's regiment. The short training period was soon over, and instead of accepting a promotion if he would remain behind and aid in the defense of Texas, Sam Houston, Jr., chose to stay with Colonel Smith and the 2nd Texas Infantry and go to war.

On April 3, 1862, he was with the fifty thousand Confederates who moved north from Corinth, Mississippi, to attack the fifty-five-thousand-man Union Army in Tennessee. At Shiloh Church, near Pittsburgh Landing, on the Tennessee River, on April 6, the two armies met. Shiloh was the first of the great battles that came to characterize the war—massive armies thrown against each other with little regard for the number of casualties.

The next day, young Sam became just one of the twenty thousand men wounded or killed at Shiloh. The bullet that would have killed him was deflected by the small Bible that he carried in his breast pocket—his mother's parting gift. A Northern chaplain found him still alive on the field and when he saw his name in the Bible he asked if he were related to the great General Houston.

The Yankee chaplain had been one of the three thousand signers of the petition to the Senate protesting the Kansas-Nebraska Act in 1854. He now repaid the elder Houston's kindness to the petitioners by caring for his wounded son.

———

Sam Houston could not settle down. At age sixty-nine, he continued his restless wanderings around the eastern part of the state. After a few days, he would return to Cedar Point, but then he would be off again in his black buggy.

In May the Confederate military commander in Texas, General Paul Hébert, placed the state under martial law. Sam was not deterred in the least and continued his ramblings. Outside Houston, however, he was stopped by a military sentry who demanded to see his permit. "Go to

San Jacinto and learn my right to travel in Texas," he growled at the young solder, and drove on.

Constantly in trouble with the Confederate military authorities, Houston complained bitterly to Governor Francis R. Lubbock that martial law was not only unnecessary but it was also unconstitutional. The zealous provost marshal of Harris County was clearly keeping an eye on the old Unionist, and even interviewed his friends and neighbors. They "are especial in their inquisitions about matters which may transpire at my house, or what my children may say in their prattlings," said Houston to his friend S. M Swenson.

"It is not sufficient that we have given our son, and our means to defend and support the cause of Southern Independence," he said. "The reasons which I gave against secession and the predictions which I made are still brought up in the minds of my enemies and they cannot believe in my hearty support of the cause which is now of life and death to us all.

"If it were the will of my Heavenly Father that I should enjoy a tranquil evening and close of life, I would be thankful—but His will be done!" he said to Swenson. Houston did not really depend on the will of anyone, however, except his own. He wrote directly to the provost marshal and demanded that the harassment cease. Swenson was not as protected as Houston, however. His life was in serious danger because of his Unionist views and he had to flee to Mexico.

It was five months before Sam and Margaret learned that their son had been wounded at Shiloh but that he was alive. He was in a prison camp at St. Louis, but he was to be exchanged. In a few weeks and without any warning he came home to Cedar Point. He surprised his mother while she was working in her garden.

Soon the war came closer to home. On October 4, 1862, Union gunboats entered Galveston Harbor and the island was cut off from the mainland. The enemy was now just across the bay. Overnight Cedar Point became a dangerous place to live. By the first week in November the family was back in Independence, where Margaret wanted to settle. Sam, however, had set his mind on returning to Huntsville and The Woodland Home.

Alas, the house was not for sale, or at least not on terms that Houston could afford, and he decided to rent a house instead. He soon found a house that was large enough for his family and also satisfied his own eccentric nature—the Steamboat House, which sat on a slight rise overlooking Oakwood Cemetery. Not far away was the Texas State Penitentiary, which was now full of Union prisoners.

Margaret and four of the children arrived in Huntsville in December 1862. The older children stayed behind with Nancy Lea in Independence to attend school at Baylor.

The Steamboat House—with its long, narrow shape and the galleries along each side—did indeed resemble a Mississippi riverboat. The front was surmounted by twin, vaguely gothic towers with a steep stairway between them rising to the upper floor. Houston took the rather dark bedroom underneath the great outside front staircase. He could not comfortably climb up to the second floor.

His health had deteriorated markedly in the past few months. He had developed a serious and persistent cough and the old wounds had become even more painful as he aged. The wound in his right shoulder still drained from time to time, as it had since 1814.

Houston was able to walk over and chat with the Union prisoners of war, and through his influence some of them were allowed to go into the town. This fraternization with the enemy did not sit well with many of the townspeople but Houston characteristically ignored their disapproval.

Politics played a smaller part in his life, but not by choice. As he wrote to his friend E. W. Cave, who had also refused to swear allegiance to the Confederacy, "I need not write to you about politics as you wrote to me on a former occasion that you had eschewed them. For my own part I cannot for the life of me keep from thinking about them; though without any design of ever mingling in them again."

Such remarks as these kept alive the rumors that Houston plotted a return to office, and a speech in Houston two weeks past his seventieth birthday caused further speculation. Despite his predictions of Southern success, he still seemed to yearn for an independent Texas with additional territory. "A people whose expansive energies have carried our institutions thus far Southward, cannot be restrained if destiny points the way," he said. The Halls of the Montezumas beckoned one last time.

Houston predicted the eventual triumph of Southern arms and singled out such generals as Lee and Jackson. But he could not resist a swipe at generals "whose sole claim to position is West Point." While books helped, "God makes the general," said Sam.

Houston, however, wrote to the editor of the *Huntsville Item* forswearing all political ambition. But he also used his letter to point out what happens when citizens cast aside or trample on the Constitution. Habeas corpus and trial by jury give way to military tribunals, "as they have been in Texas," he pointedly remarked.

He ended this last political broadside by saying, "A man of three score years and ten, as I am, ought, at least, be exempt from the charge of ambition, even if he should be charged with having loved his country too well."

In early April, Houston summoned his friends James R. Cox, Joab Banton, W. H. Randolph, and W. T. Robinson to the Steamboat House to witness a new will. None of the children had reached their majority, and with the exception of one item, the entire estate was left to Margaret.

"To my eldest son, Sam Houston, Jr., I bequeath my sword worn in the Battle of San Jacinto, it never to be drawn only in defence of the Constitution, the Laws, and the Liberties of his Country. If any attempt should ever be made to assail one of these, I wish it to be used in its vindication."

There is no mention of educating his daughters, but he was explicit in how Margaret was to oversee the education of their sons. They were to acquire a thorough knowledge of English, Latin, geography, history, and the Scriptures. They were to spend no time in the study of abstract science. And they were "to be early taught an utter contempt for novels and light reading."

One of the enduring legends about Sam Houston is that he freed all his slaves before he died. A former slave even recalled Old Sam reading the Emancipation Proclamation from the porch of the Steamboat House and then telling them they were free. However, the first clause of Houston's last will flatly states, "I will that all my just debts be paid out of my personal affects as I think them sufficient without disposing of any of my family servants." So as late as April 2, 1863, the slaves were still personal property to be left to his wife, and when the will was probated on December 2, 1863, the inventory listed twelve slaves with a total value of $10,530.20.

In June, Margaret persuaded her husband to go to the mineral springs at Sour Lake, about a hundred miles from Huntsville, for a rest and for the mud baths. Without telling Margaret, he detoured through Houston and Galveston on his way to the resort. "I was delighted to learn from the Telegraph," she wrote, "that you had arrived in Houston and were looking so well."

He did not return to Huntsville for almost a month. His health had improved slightly and he continued his regimen of walking over to the penitentiary to chat with the Yankee prisoners or sitting quietly in his rocking chair in the yard of the Steamboat House.

The news of the war was disastrous. Ironically, two great military calamities had befallen the Confederacy on the same day—July Fourth, the birthday of the Union. Robert E. Lee had been defeated at Gettysburg and was retreating back into the South. A thousand miles away, on the Mississippi, Vicksburg had fallen to Ulysses S. Grant. Sam Houston was vindicated, but there was no joy in it. He knew the worst for the South was still ahead. The sufferings of his people had just begun.

One particularly hot July afternoon, Houston returned home from his walk with a severe chill. Margaret put him to bed in the quiet downstairs room. A servant stayed with him at all times to fan him and watch for any sudden changes.

Ashbel Smith came to minister to his great friend. He was now a brevet brigadier general and he delighted his patient by appearing in his uniform. After four days, however, Smith had to say his farewell and return to the army on the Gulf Coast.

At sunset on Sunday, July 26, Margaret sat beside her husband's bed reading from the Psalms. Houston had developed pneumonia, and his breathing was labored and erratic. Suddenly he seemed restless and his wife went and knelt by the bed and took his hand.

"Texas. Texas. Margaret," said the old soldier, and with these last words he was gone.

————

The Union prisoners, overseen by a ship's carpenter, fashioned a coffin for their newfound friend, and in the early morning they carried it up the hill to the Steamboat House. Houston's body, dressed in a black suit and a Masonic apron, was placed inside.

A few mourners gathered at four in the afternoon in the upstairs parlor of the Steamboat House. A heavy rain was falling. Margaret's Baptist pastor was away, so Houston was buried by a minister from the

denomination of his childhood. The pastor of the Huntsville Presbyterian Church, J. M. Cochran, conducted the service, which included the
reading of a poem by Margaret.

The small cortege left the house and followed the Masonic pallbearers
down the steep flight of steps and through the mud to the neighboring
cemetery. The Masonic graveside service was brief, and Margaret and
the children returned to the Steamboat House.

That evening, Margaret Lea Houston sat alone in the upstairs parlor
where her husband's body had lain that afternoon, reading her Bible,
which now bore this inscription.

Died on the 26th of July 1863 Genl Sam Houston, the beloved
and affectionate Husband and father, the devoted patriot, the
fearless soldier—the meek and lowly Christian.

Notes

6 Spotswood and his train: Rouse, *Planters and Pioneers.*

7 Next came the Scotch-Irish: Cowper, *History of the Shenandoah Valley.*

8 As one historian observed: Morton, *A History of Rockbridge County,* pp. 17–18.

10 In November 1753: Morton, *A History of Rockbridge County,* p. 32

11 Henry Adams observed: Adams, *History of the United States.*

12 His principal beneficiary: The will of John Houston, April 24, 1748. Augusta County Courthouse, Staunton, Va.

13 An impressive house still sits: There is a small roadside park with commemmorative markers near the site, which is at the juncture of Interstate 81 and U.S. 11, seven miles north of Lexington.

13 Robert put together impressive holdings: The will of Robert Houston, September 11, 1760. Augusta County Courthouse, Staunton, Va.

13 Each daughter wound up with goods: Inventory of Robert Houston's estate, November 18, 1761. Augusta County Courthouse, Staunton, Va.

14 Perhaps the young commander: Flexner, *Washington: The Indispensable Man.*

15 "Cousin America has run off": Rouse, *Planters and Pioneers.*

18 The path had once been part: Present-day U. S. 11 and Interstate 81 either follow or parallel the Great Warrior and Trading Path.

19 "You involuntarily fall": Jefferson, *Writings: Notes on the State of Virginia.*

20 "The first manifestation of grief": Sam Houston, *Writings,* vol. 6, p. 438.

20 He owned slaves: Inventory in James, *The Raven,* p. 11.

21 Samuel Houston's will: The will of Samuel Houston, September 22, 1806. Rockbridge County Courthouse, Lexington, Va.

26 But Sam "devoted all the time he could spare": *Life of General Sam Houston: A Short Autobiography,* p. 1.

27 The leader of the Hiwassee Cherokee: Lewis and Kneberg, *Hiwassee Island.* Much of the island and its archaeological treasures are now buried under the waters of Chickamauga Lake.

28 In the Cherokee cosmogony: Moony, *Myths of the Cherokee,* p. 239.

28 The great naturalist and traveler William Bartram: *Travels,* part 3, chs. 3–4.

30 In 1799 two Moravian missionaries: Steiner and Schweinitz, *Early Travels in Tennessee,* p. 464.

31 When his brothers finally found him: Lester, *The Life of Sam Houston: The Only Authentic Memoir,* p. 22.

32 No doubt fueled by whiskey: James, *The Raven,* p. 20.

33 Our old friend Bartram: *Travels,* loc cit.

34 Two prominent early settlers of Maryville: Ash and Bergeron, *The Sam Houston Schoolhouse.* The rebuilt schoolhouse and a small museum occupy the old site today.

34 Kennedy needed a teacher: Research by Sam Houston Schoolhouse personnel.

35 He therefore attempted to pick up: Sam Houston, *Life of General Sam Houston: A Short Autobiography,* p. 1.

37 These are thin majorities: Horsman, *The War of 1812.*

38 "And what have your craven souls. . . ." "There, my son": Lester, *The Life of Sam Houston: The Only Authentic Memoir,* p. 27.

38 The church refused: Records, New Providence Church, Brownsburg, Va.

38 He signed the letter: Sam Houston, *Writings,* vol. 1, p. 1.

38 Houston's appointment: *Complete Army Register.*

39 "Why not sell the air": Josephy, ed., *The American Heritage Book of Indians,* p. 206.

44 "The carnage was dreadfull": Hickey, *The War of 1812: A Forgotten Conflict.*

46 Jefferson wrote to Lafayette: Jefferson to Lafayette, February 14, 1815. Jefferson, *Writings.*

49 He dispatched all three letters. Sam Houston, *Writings,* vol. 1, pp. 1–3.

49 He knew he had to make a living: Sam Houston, *Writings,* vol. 1, p. 4.

49 Sam took along: Sam Houston, *Life of General Sam Houston: A Short Autobiography,* p. 3.

57 Houston was ordered: Meigs to Houston, October 9, 1817. Andrew Jackson Houston Collection, Texas State Archives, Austin.

58 As soon as Houston reported in: Houston to Jackson, December 18, 1817. Andrew Jackson Houston Collection. Texas State Archives, Austin.

58 He appealed for more blankets: Houston to Calhoun, December 28, 1817. *Calhoun Papers,* vol. 2, p. 180.

59 Governor McMinn ordered Houston: McMinn to Houston, January 16, 1818. Andrew Jackson Houston Collection. Texas State Archives, Austin.

60 He sent a one-sentence letter: Sam Houston, *Writings,* vol. 1, p. 8.

63 The judge's course was designed: Sam Houston, *Life of General Sam Houston: A Short Autobiography,* p. 3

63 Ludlow said that Sam: Ludlow, *Dramatic Life As I Found It,* p. 166.

68 "His passions are": Remini, *Andrew Jackson and the Course of American Empire,* *1767–1821,* p. 109.

69 "I will not pretend": Houston to Abram Maury, December 13, 1823. *Writings,* vol. 1, pp. 19–20.

71 The slavery issue. See Cohen, "Thomas Jefferson and the Problem of Slavery," for a discussion of Jefferson and slavery.

72 He later denied. Remini, *Andrew Jackson and the Course of American Empire, 1767–1821,* p. 390

73 "The distance of the people": Sam Houston, *Writings,* vol. 1, p. 21.

74 Sam had met a young woman: The account of this courtship is derived from a series of letters to John Houston, in Sam Houston, *Writings,* vol. 1, and from information supplied by Sarah Spruill of Cheraw, South Carolina.

75 "Clay is an eloquent man": Adams, *The Diary of John Quincy Adams,* March 9, 1821, p. 263

77 "It would be a source": Andrew Jackson Houston Collection. Texas State Archives

79 On February 2, 1826: Sam Houston, *Writings,* vol. 1, p. 28.

80 He heaped fire and brimstone: Sam Houston, *Writings,* vol. 1, p. 40

83 Ironically, he could have been arrested: "Some Episodes in the Life of Gen. Sam Houston," in *Bowling Green* (Ky.) *Messenger,* March 30, 1911. Also J. Marvin Hunter, Jr., "Sam Houston's Duel on Kentucky Soil," in *Frontier Times.*

84 "My firm and undeviating attachment": Sam Houston, *Writings,* vol. 1, p. 63

86 "Like the wounded serpent": Sam Houston, *Writings,* vol. 1, p. 69

86 "But, then, Sir": Sam Houston, *Writings,* vol. 1, p. 77.

86 Of Jackson, Houston said. Sam Houston, *Writings,* vol. 1, p. 88.

87 Houston then added. Sam Houston, *Writings,* vol. 4, p. 9.

90 In 1856, Houston said: Schlesinger, *The Age of Jackson,* p. 489.

90 Given his reputation: Sam Houston, *Writings,* vol. 4, p. 9.

91 The speech was a practical blueprint: Sam Houston, *Writings,* vol. 1, p. 115

92 Addressing her as "Mrs. Colonel Morse": Sam Houston, *Writings,* vol. 6, p. 1.

94 The people in this state: Polk, *Correspondence,* vol. 1, p. 130

96 The boat had arrived. Remini, *Andrew Jackson and the Course of American Freedom,* *1822–1832,* p. 157

98 "It has discharged every day": Lester, *Life of Sam Houston: The Only Authentic Memoir,* pp. 261–262.

98 "Looking seriously at me": Crook, "Sam Houston and Eliza Allen." *Southwestern Historical Quarterly.* July 1990. The most exhaustive research to date on the subject of Houston's first marriage.

100 Houston sat in the cheerless rooms. Sam Houston, *Writings,* vol. 1, p. 130.

103 "In dissolving the political connexion": Sam Houston, *Writings,* vol. 1, p. 131.

105 "The fact is very different": David Gouverneur Burnet Papers. Personal Correspondence, 1829–1861. Eugene C. Barker Texas History Center, Austin.

107 Noland, however, had no doubt: Friend, *Sam Houston: The Great Designer,* pp. 23–24.

107 Sam swore to the Old Chief: Sam Houston, *Writings,* vol. 1, p. 133.

109 "I care not what dreamers": Lester, *Life of Sam Houston. The Only Authentic Memoir*, pp. 54–55.

110 Houston fanned the flames: Sam Houston, *Writings*, vol. 1, p. 134.

111 The western Cherokee. Gregory and Strickland, *Sam Houston with the Cherokees*, 1829–1833, p. 14.

112 "To become a missionary": Sam Houston, *Writings*, vol. 1, p. 141.

112 "We do . . . Solemnly": Andrew Jackson Houston Collection. Texas State Archives, Austin.

115 While in Washington: Burnet to Houston, March 8, 1830. David Gouverneur Burnet Papers. Personal Correspondence, 1829–1861. Eugene C. Barker Texas History Center, Austin.

116 At the door: Remini, *Andrew Jackson and the Course of American Freedom, 1822–1832*, pp. 236–237.

117 "The affections of the people": Sam Houston, *Writings*, vol. 1, p. 149.

120 There were five of them. Andrew Jackson Houston Collection. Texas State Archives, Austin.

120 "In future when you shall": Andrew Jackson Houston Collection. Texas State Archives, Austin.

121 In the letter: Houston to Van Fossen, April 4, 1830; August 22, 1830. Sam Houston, *Writings*, vol. 1, pp. 147, 187.

124 Houston responded by running an announcement: Andrew Jackson Houston Collection. Texas State Archives, Austin.

126 Alexis de Tocqueville had originally planned: Jardin, *Tocqueville: A Biography.*

129 The day began calmly enough: For coverage of the case and the trial see *United States Congress Register of Debates for the 22nd Congress. December 5, 1831–May 9, 1832* and *Niles' Weekly Register,* April–May 1832.

131 At precisely twelve noon: Sam Houston, *Writings*, vol. 1, pp. 207–224.

133 "Nothing but the blackest malignity": Sam Houston, *Writings*, vol. 1, p. 257.

134 "I was dying out": Friend, *Sam Houston: The Great Designer*, p. 35.

134 The Stanbery affair: Sam Houston, *Writings*, vol. 7, p. 3.

135 He was unanimously elected: *Santa Anna, The Eagle: The Autobiography of Santa Anna*, p. 46.

138 The passport does supply: Andrew Jackson Houston Collection. Texas State Archives, Austin.

139 Irving rightly attributed: Irving, *A Tour on the Prairies*, p. 135.

140 Some friends in Tennessee. Lester, *Life of Sam Houston: The Only Authentic Memoir*, p. 64.

140 He wrote to his cousin John: Sam Houston, *Writings*, vol. 6, p. 1.

140 On December 1, Houston sent: Sam Houston, *Writings*, vol. 1, pp. 267–271.

143 Duwali and his band: The story that Duwali, or The Bowl, and his band fled west in 1794 after killing several whites who were traveling down the Tennessee River is a myth. Everett, *The Texas Cherokees*, p. 127.

145 "We have weddings": Stephen F. Austin Correspondence. Eugene C. Barker Texas History Center, Austin.

146 Jackson no doubt: Sam Houston, *Writings*, vol. 1, 274–276.

147 Events in the United States: Stephen F. Austin Correspondence. Eugene C. Barker Texas History Center, Austin.

149 Although he had agreed: Letter to Samuel M. Williams, January 12, 1834. Quoted in Barker, *The Life of Stephen F. Austin*, pp. 358–359.

149 "*You* must be elected": Stephen F. Austin Correspondence. Eugene C. Barker Texas History Center, Austin.

151 "All new States": Lester, *Life of Sam Houston: The Only Authentic Memoir*, p. 69.

151 In a usual burst: Sam Houston, *Writings*, vol. 5, pp. 5–6.

154 The divorce petition: Sam Houston, *Writings*, vol. 1, pp. 277–279.

155 Only three years before: Crook, "Sam Houston and Eliza Allen." *Southwestern Historical Quarterly*, 94 (July 1990): 26.

156 Houston was thought to be: Sam Houston, *Writings*, vol. 1, p. 294.

157 Sam then asked. Sam Houston, *Writings*, vol. 1, p. 285.

158 "He prays that the *fine*": Sam Houston, *Writings*, vol. 1, pp. 287–288.

159 Adams declined to attend: Adams, *The Diary of John Quincy Adams*.

160 "I was not desirous": G. W. Featherstonhaugh, *An Excursion Through the Slave States*. Quoted in Friend, *Sam Houston: The Great Designer*, pp. 60–61.

165 "Samuel Pablo Houston": Nacogdoches Archives, vol. 77, p. 43.

165 James Auchincloss wrote: Andrew Jackson Houston Collection. Texas State Archives, Austin.

168 "No more doubts": Barker, *Life of Stephen F. Austin*, p. 414.

168 "The morning of glory": Sam Houston, *Writings*, vol. 1, pp. 304–305.

171 "If I have claims": Sam Houston, *Writings*, vol. 4, p. 1.

173 "Permit me," he said: Andrew Jackson Houston Collection. Texas State Archives, Austin.

173 "His influence in the army": Sam Houston, *Writings*, vol. 1, p. 335

174 "I would be proud": Sublett to Houston, December 18, 1835. Andrew Jackson Houston Collection. Texas State Archives, Austin.

175 More important to Houston: Inventory dated January 14, 1836. Andrew Jackson Houston Collection. Texas State Archives, Austin.

176 But "I do not come": McLeod to Houston, December 31, 1835. Andrew Jackson Houston Collection. Texas State Archives, Austin.

176 Houston's control: Houston to Smith. Sam Houston, *Writings*, vol. 1, p. 321.

176 "No language can express": Sam Houston, *Writings*, vol. 1, p. 333.

177 "Colonel Bowie will leave": Sam Houston, *Writings*, vol. 1, p. 339.

180 The Indian treaty: For the text of the treaty see Sam Houston, *Writings*, vol. 1, pp. 358–360.

181 "Fellow citizens and compatriots". Proctor, *Battle of the Alamo*, pp. 25–26.

182 At 9 o'clock: Sam Houston, *Writings*, vol. 1, p. 361.

183 After listening to their story: Andrew Jackson Houston Collection. Texas State Archives, Austin.

184 The "enclosed order": Sam Houston, *Writings*, vol. 1, p. 365.

186 "Our forces must not": Sam Houston, *Writings*, vol. 1, p. 375.

188 "I intend desertion": Sam Houston, *Writings*, vol. 1, p. 372.

189 In a moving letter: *Telegraph and Texas Register*, February 20, 1836.

189 Attention, Volunteers! *Telegraph and Texas Register*, January 9, 1836.

191 "All foreigners who may land": Andrew Jackson Houston Collection. Texas State Archives, Austin.

192 "He is an ill-fated man": Sam Houston, *Writings*, vol. 1, p. 381.

192 "The desolation of the country": Smithwick, *The Evolution of a State*, p. 90.

193 "I consulted none": Sam Houston, *Writings*, vol. 1, p. 385.

193 "For Heaven's sake": Sam Houston, *Writings*, vol. 1, p. 385.

194 One such letter: Perry to Potter. April 9, 1836. Andrew Jackson Houston Collection. Texas State Archives, Austin.

197 He even had "a list": John Dor to Houston, 30 November 1835. Andrew Jackson Houston Collection. Texas State Archives, Austin.

199 "Your particular friend": Stuart to Houston, March 15, 1836. Andrew Jackson Houston Collection. Texas State Archives, Austin.

200 "After a satisfactory": Andrew Jackson Houston Collection. Texas State Archives, Austin.

200 "The enemy have crossed": Sam Houston, *Writings*, vol. 1, p. 409.

201 "Sir, The enemy are laughing": *Texas Sentinel*, May 17, 1841.

201 "When I assured": Sam Houston, *Writings*, vol. 1, p. 411.

201 "Few in the camp": Peña, *With Santa Anna in Texas*, p. 105.

203 "Sir: This morning": Sam Houston, *Writings*, vol. 1, pp. 413–414.

204 "A few hours more. . . . We view ourselves. Sam Houston, *Writings*, vol. 1, pp. 415–416.

206 "There would be no": Sam Houston, *Writings*, vol. 2, p. 24.

211 "Wishing to satisfy": Castañeda, *The Mexican Side of the Texan Revolution*, pp. 127–128.

212 "That man may consider": Lester, *Life of Sam Houston. The Only Authentic Memoir*, pp. 147–148.

214 "To Miss Raguet": Sam Houston, *Writings*, vol. 1, p. 415.

215 "To the *devil*": Linn, *Reminiscences of Fifty Years in Texas*, p. 264.

217 When liberty is firmly established: Sam Houston, *Writings*, vol. 1, p. 427.

218 Mason reported: June 4, 1836. Friend, *Sam Houston. The Great Designer*, p. 72.

221 During one meal: This is probably the most famous of the Houston anecdotes. In some versions, Houston spews out hot coffee.

222 "The exaltation that caused": Castañeda, *The Mexican Side of the Texan Revolution*, p. 89.

222 "Santa Anna living": Sam Houston, *Writings*, vol. 1, p. 435.

224 "At a former period": Sam Houston, *Writings*, vol. 1, p. 437

224 As one biographer: *Dictionary of American Biography*, vol. 2.

225 "I shall advise her": Barker, *The Life of Stephen Austin*, p. 432.

225 "You will learn": Sam Houston, *Writings*, vol. 1, p. 446.

226 Speaking more or less: Sam Houston, Inaugural Address, October 22, 1836. *Writings*, vol. 1, pp. 448–452.

229 "Nothing *now* could tarnish": Remini, *Andrew Jackson and the Course of American Democracy, 1833–1845*, p. 361.

229 They arrived in the capital: Hockley to Houston, January 1836. Andrew Jackson Houston Collection. Texas State Archives, Austin.

230 "The distinction, and character": Sam Houston, *Writings*, vol. 1, p. 487.

231 "But," he asked: Santa Anna, *The Eagle: The Autobiography of Santa Anna*, p. 58.

231 "My great desire": Sam Houston, *Writings*, vol. 1, p.487.

233 On Friday evening: Lewis to Houston, March 25, 1837. Andrew Jackson Houston Collection. Texas State Archives, Austin.

236 Houston for some time: Sam Houston, *Writings*, vol. 2, p. 153.

238 "March, Chieftain": Sam Houston, *Writings*, vol. 2, pp. 31–32.

239 "I on yesterday": Thruston to Houston, March 26, 1837. Andrew Jackson Houston Collection. Texas State Archives, Austin.

240 "We have not one". Henry Teal to War Department, May 5, 1837. Andrew Jackson Houston Collection. Texas State Archives, Austin.

240 "It is past midnight": Sam Houston, *Writings*, vol. 2, p. 99.

241 "We will never": Sam Houston, *Writings*, vol. 3, p. 8

241 "Economy is the mother": May 19, 1837. Andrew Jackson Houston Collection. Texas State Archives, Austin.

243 "I have ascertained": Ricord to Houston, January 26, 1837. Andrew Jackson Collection. Texas State Archives, Austin.

246 In June 1838: Sam Houston, *Writings*, vol. 2, p. 251.

248 "The question was solemnly": Sam Houston, *Writings*, vol. 2, p. 245.

249 "I have placed": Crawford to Houston, June 7, 1837. Andrew Jackson Houston Collection. Texas State Archives, Austin.

251 "I knew him to be deranged": Gambrell, *Anson Jones: The Last President of Texas*, p. 134.

252 "You may be assured": Sam Houston, *Writings*, vol. 2, pp. 280–281.

253 "No man living": Sam Houston, *Writings*, vol. 2, p. 270–272.

256 In this final message: Sam Houston, *Writings*, vol. 2, pp. 299–304.

258 Sam Houston was out: Sam Houston, *Writings*, vol. 2, p. 308.

262 "A thousand thanks": Sam Houston, *Writings*, vol. 6, p. 4.

269 He called it: Sam Houston, *Writings*, vol. 2, pp. 315–322.

270 "Vain hope!": Sam Houston, *Writings*, vol. 2, p. 264.

271 "I send by Lieutenant Moran": *Texas Sentinel*, January 15, 1840.

275 The huge herds: Sterne, *Hurrah for Texas: The Diary of Adolphus Sterne*, p. 74.

277 "Beneath the shade": *Texas Sentinel*, March 11, 1841.

280 Houston's "own fertile brain": *Texas Sentinel*, April 29, 1840.

281 As for the Indians: *Texas Sentinel*, January 22, 1840.

281 "You political brawler": Sam Houston, *Writings*, vol. 2, p. 386.

282 "G-r-e-a-t G-o-d!!": *Texas Sentinel*, June 17, 1841.

283 "I have no wish": Sam Houston, *Writings*, vol. 2, p. 387.

283 "For the want": *Weekly Texian*, December 29, 1841.

286 The fastidious Adolphus Sterne. Sterne, *Hurrah for Texas: The Diary of Adolphus Sterne*, p. 75.

288 "It seems that": Sam Houston, *Writings*, vol. 2, pp. 399–408.

292 His veto message: Sam Houston, *Writings*, vol. 2, p. 458.

295 "You are right!": Sam Houston, *Writings*, vol. 3, p. 14.

296 Houston responded directly: Sam Houston, *Writings*, vol. 2, pp. 513–527.

297 "I can never sanction": Sam Houston, *Writings*, vol. 3, p. 124.

297 Indeed, Hockley resigned: Sam Houston, *Writings*, vol. 4, p. 137.

298 All saloons: J.K. Holland, "Reminiscences of Austin and Old Washington." *Quarterly of the Texas State Historical Association*, vol. 1, no. 2 (October 1897); 92–95.

301 According to Old Sam: Sam Houston, *Writings*, vol.4, p. 233.

301 Soon after: The site is on Texas route 146, about eight miles from Moss Hill.

301 "I again declare." Remeni, *Andrew Jackson and the Course of American Empire, 1767–1821*, pp. 389–390.

302 "I am determined": Houston to Jackson, February 16, 1844. Andrew Jackson Houston Collection. Texas State Archives, Austin.

302 Jackson replied: Jackson to Houston, March 15, 1844. Andrew Jackson Houston Collection. Texas State Archives, Austin.

304 "All the skill": Jackson to Houston, July 19, 1844. Andrew Jackson Houston Collection. Texas State Archives, Austin.

305 "Who can trust": Jackson to Henderson, May 11, 1844. Andrew Jackson Houston Collection. Texas State Archives, Austin.

305 "In future years": Reprinted in *Civilian and Galveston Gazette*, July 6, 1844.

307 Houston told Jones: Sam Houston, *Writings*, vol. 4, pp. 371–372.

308 Meanwhile Houston prepared: Sam Houston, *Writings*, vol. 4, pp. 392–398.

308 "One great nation": Sam Houston, *Writings*, vol. 4, p. 403.

311 "I find my mind": Sam Houston, *Writings*, vol. 4, p. 408.

314 Houston's usual prescience: Sam Houston, *Writings*, vol. 7, p. 11.

315 "My son": James, *The Life of Andrew Jackson*, p. 786.

316 "The Senate are so much afraid": Gambrell, *Anson Jones, the Last President of Texas*, p. 404.

319 At Cincinnati: Friend, *Sam Houston: The Great Designer*, p. 168.

321 "No minister": Sam Houston, *Writings*, vol. 4, pp. 451–471.

321 In fact, he said: Sam Houston, *Writings*, vol. 4, p. 465.

328 As for his "flirtation": Sam Houston, *Writings*, vol.5, p. 21.

328 "Occasionally to pester": Sam Houston, *Writings*, vol. 7, p. 16.

331 "We have still to combat": Ricky to Houston, July 25, 1848. Andrew Jackson Houston Collection. Texas State Archives, Austin.

332 "But if the vision": Sam Houston, *Writings*, vol. 5, pp. 59–60.

334 "As long as South-Carolina": Auchincloss to Houston, January 11, 1849. Andrew Jackson Houston Collection. Texas State Archives, Austin.

335 His target was John Calhoun: Sam Houston, *Writings*, vol. 5, p. 82.

337 The Gadsden-Houston correspondence, July-September 1849, is in the Andrew Jackson Houston Collection, Texas State Archives, Austin.

338 "Never before": Calhoun to James H. Hammond. *Calhoun Papers*, 1837, p. 443.

338 "Slave labor must": Sam Houston, *Writings*, vol. 5, p. 106.

338 "Could their designs": Sam Houston, *Writings,* vol. 5, p. 99.
340 "Tyler had some intelligence": Sam Houston, *Writings,* vol. 5, p. 153.
341 "For a nation divided": Sam Houston, *Writings,* vol. 5, p. 144.
344 "The man who would conspire": Sam Houston, *Writings,* vol. 5, p.251.
344 He wrote to Daniel Webster: Houston to Webster, August 11, 1850. Andrew Jackson Houston Collection. Texas State Archives, Austin.
345 "It is impossible": Sam Houston, *Writings,* vol. 5, p. 265.
347 "I am consoled": Margaret Lea Houston to Sam Houston February 8, 1851. Andrew Jackson Houston Collection. Texas State Archives, Austin.
348 She was, said Dean: Dean to Houston, February 21, 1851. Andrew Jackson Houston Collection. Texas State Archives, Austin.
349 "I will not": Sam Houston, *Writings,* vol. 5, p. 316.
351 "Henry Clay deserved": Sam Houston, *Writings,* vol. 5, p. 517.
352 "Mr. Pierce would": Sam Houston, *Writings,* vol. 8, p. 118.
353 "I am aware": For the text of the speech see Sam Houston. *Writings,* vol. 5, pp. 469–499.
356 "Don't speak": Friend, *Sam Houston: The Great Designer,* p. 231.
356 If we wish: Sam Houston, *Writings,* vol. 5, p. 530.
358 "Nominate and recommend": Lester, *Life of Sam Houston: The Only Authentic Memoir,* p. 396.
360 "To a traveler": Carl, Prince of Solms-Braunfels, *Texas, 1844–1845.*
362 Houston continued: Sam Houston, *Writings,* vol. 6, pp. 167–177.
363 "Sam is the coming man": *The Evening Gazette,* February 24, 1855.
363 "Others disagreed, such as": *The Congregationalist,* March 2, 1855.
364 He ran the entire text: *The Liberator,* March 2, 1855
364 "I entertain no doubt": Burnet to Rusk, January 10, 1847. Burnet Papers, Barker Texas History Center, Austin.
364 "We divine, with Plutarch": Burnet Papers, Barker Texas History Center, Austin.
368 Later he confided: Sam Houston, *Writings,* vol. 6, p. 300.
370 However, Houston also warned: Sam Houston, *Writings,* vol. 6, p. 387.
372 "So now the whip cracks": Sam Houston, *Writings,* vol. 6, p. 444.
374 "In February he introduced": Sam Houston, *Writings,* vol. 6, pp. 508–512
377 My opinion is: *Congressional Globe,* 35th Congress, 2nd session, 1858–1859, p. 1651.
378 To that end: Sam Houston, *Writings,* vol. 7, p. 189.
379 He referred "In confidence." Sam Houston, *Writings,* vol. 7, p. 225.
380 "My career is not": Sam Houston, *Writings,* vol. 7, pp. 343–367.
381 A recent traveler: Olmstead, *A Journey Through Texas,* p. 110.
383 Under Houston: Sam Houston, *Writings,* vol. 8, p. 71.
384 "There will be stirring times": Sam Houston, *Writings,* vol. 7, p. 473.
384 "I have no doubt": Friend, *Sam Houston: The Great Designer,* p. 303.
385 His message to the Texas Legislature: Sam Houston, *Writings,* vol. 7, pp 429–441.
386 If my name should be used. Sam Houston, *Writings,* vol. 7, p. 554
386 The reporter: Parks, *John Bell,* p. 353.
388 "You did promise": Sam Houston, *Writings,* vol. 8, p. 109.

393 Houston's silence: Sam Houston, *Writings,* vol. 8, p. 264.

393 "To the People of Texas": Sam Houston, *Writings,* vol. 8, pp. 271–278

395 "Epistle to a Young Friend": The young friend was Andrew Hunter Aiken, and Burns's poem is a typical eighteenth-century catalogue of do's and don't's from an older mentor. Sam Houston, *Writings,* vol. 7, pp. 33–34.

396 Only Epperson: Westwood, "President Lincoln's Overture to Sam Houston," *Southwestern Historical Quarterly,* vol. 89, October 1984, pp. 125–144.

396 "I declare that Civil War": Sam Houston, *Writings,* vol. 8, pp. 295–299.

400 "I need not write": Sam Houston, *Writings,* vol. 8, p. 327.

401 One of the enduring legends: Sam Houston, *Writings,* vol. 8, pp. 339–340. The total value of Houston's estate was $89,288.

403 "Died on the 26th": Bible of Margaret Lea Houston. Sam Houston Memorial Museum, Huntsville.

Bibliography

Acheson, Sam. "Sam Houston." *American Mercury* 11 (1927): 487–95.

Adams, Henry. *History of the United States of America During the Administrations of James Madison.* The Library of America. New York, 1986.

Adams, John Quincy. *The Diary of John Quincy Adams.* Edited by Allan Nevins, New York, 1951.

Agnew, Brad. *Fort Gibson. Terminal on the Trail of Tears.* Norman, Okla., 1980.

Alden, John R. *Pioneer America.* New York, 1966.

Ambler, Charles Henry. *Sectionalism in Virginia from 1776 to 1861.* Reprint, New York, 1964.

Ash, Stephen V., and Bergeron, Paul H. *The Sam Houston Schoolhouse.* Maryville, Tenn., 1976.

Austin, Stephen F. *Correspondence.* Barker Texas History Center. Austin.

Barbee, David Rankin. "Sam Houston—The Last Phase." *Tennessee Historical Quarterly* 13 (March 1954): 12–64.

Barker, Eugene C. "The San Jacinto Campaign." *Quarterly of the Texas State Historical Association* 4 (April 1901): 237–72.

Barnard, J. H. *Dr. J. H. Barnard's Journal, from December 1835 to March 27th, 1836. Giving an Account of the FANNIN MASSACRE.* Goliad, Texas, 1912.

415

Bartram, William. *The Travels of William Bartram: Naturalist's Edition*. Edited by Francis Harper. New Haven, Conn., 1958.

Biographical Directory of the Texan Conventions and Congresses 1832–1845. Austin, 1941. Reprint, San Augustine, 1986.

Boyd, Bob. *The Texas Revolution: A Day-by-Day Account*. San Angelo, 1986.

Braman, D.E.E. *Information About Texas*. Philadelphia, 1857.

Brice, Donaly E. *The Great Comanche Raid*. Austin, 1987.

Bruce, Henry. *Life of General Houston*. New York, 1891.

Bryan, George Sands. *Sam Houston*. New York, 1917.

Bugbee, Lester G. "The Old Three Hundred." *Quarterly of the Texas State Historical Association* 1 (October 1897): 108–17.

Burnet, David Gouverneur. Papers. Personal Correspondence, 1829–1861. Eugene C. Barker Texas History Center, Austin.

Busfield, Roger M. "The Hermitage Walking Stick: First Challenge to Congressional Immunity." *Tennessee Historical Quarterly* 21 (June 1962): 122–30.

Calhoun, John C. *Papers*. 16 vols. Edited by Robert L. Meriwether. Columbia, S.C., 1959.

Campbell, Leslie Lyle. *The Houston Family in Virginia*. Lexington, Ky., 1956.

Cantrell, Greg. "Sam Houston and the Know Nothings: A Reappraisal." *Southwestern Historical Quarterly*. January 1993.

Carl, Prince of Solms-Braunfels. *Texas, 1844–1845*. Houston, 1936.

Castañeda, C. E. *The Mexican Side of the Texan Revolution*. Austin, 1928.

Catton, Bruce. *The Coming Fury*. New York, 1961.

Chalkley, Lyman, ed. *Chronicles of the Scotch-Irish Settlement in Virginia: Extracted from the Orginal Court Records of Augusta County 1745–1800*. 3 vols. Baltimore, 1989.

Clay, Henry. *The Papers of Henry Clay*. Edited by James F. Hopkins et al. 10 vols. Lexington, 1959–91.

Clayton, W. Woodford. *History of Davidson County, Tennessee*. Philadelphia, 1880.

Cohen, William. "Thomas Jefferson and the Problem of Slavery." *Journal of American History*. December 1969.

"Compendium of the History of Texas." *Texas Almanac*. 1860.

Cowper, William. *History of the Shenandoah Valley*. 2 vols. New York, 1952.

Crane, William Carey. *Life and Select Literary Remains of Sam Houston, of Texas*. Philadelphia, 1884.

Creel, George. *Sam Houston: Colossus in Buckskin.* New York, 1928.

Crockett, G. L. *Two Centuries in East Texas.* San Augustine, 1932.

Crook, Elizabeth. "Sam Houston and Eliza Allen: The Marriage and the Mystery." *Southwestern Historical Quarterly* 94 (July 1990): 1–36.

Davidson, Donald. *The Tennessee.* Vol. 1. *The Old River.* New York-Toronto, 1946.

Davis, Claude Brion. *The Arkansas.* New York-Toronto, 1959.

Day, Donald, and Ullom, Harry Herbert. *The Autobiography of Sam Houston.* Norman, Okla., 1954.

Delgado, Pedro. *Mexican Account of the Battle of San Jacinto.* Austin, 1878.

Diehl, George West. *The Rev. Samuel Houston, V.D.M.* Verona, Va., 1970.

Domenech, Abbé Emmanuel. *Missionary Adventures in Texas and Mexico.* London, 1958.

Dowdey, Clifford. *The Golden Age: A Climate for Greatness, Virginia, 1732–1775.* Boston, 1970.

———. *The Virginia Dynasties: The Emergence of "King" Carter and the Golden Age.* Boston, 1969.

Dunaway, Wayland F. *The Scotch-Irish of Colonial Pennsylvania.* Baltimore, 1979.

Duval, John Crittenden. *Early Times in Texas.* Austin, 1892.

Dykeman, Wilma. *The French Broad.* New York, 1955.

Edwards. C. Edwards. *Sam Houston and His Republic.* New York, 1846.

Ehle, John. *Trail of Tears: The Rise and Fall of the Cherokee Nation.* New York, 1988.

Ehrenberg, Herman. *With Milam and Fannin. Adventures of a German Boy in the Texas Revolution.* Edited by Henry Smith. Dallas, 1935.

Eisenhower, John S. D. *So Far from God: The U.S. War With Mexico 1846–1848.* New York, 1989.

Elliott, Sarah Barnwell. *Sam Houston.* Boston, 1915.

Ellis, Joseph Henry Harrison. *Sam Houston and Related Spiritual Forces.* Houston, 1945.

Everett, Dianna. *The Texas Cherokees: A People Between Two Fires, 1819–1840.* Norman, Okla., 1990.

Faris, John T. *Old Churches and Meeting Houses in and Around Philadelphia.* Philadelphia, 1916.

Flanagan, Sue. *Sam Houston's Texas.* Austin, 1964.

Flexner, James Thomas. *Washington: The Indispensable Man.* New York, 1974.

Folmsbee, Stanley J., et al. *Tennessee: A Short History.* Knoxville, 1969.

Foreman, Grant. *Pioneer Days in the Early Southwest.* Cleveland, 1926.

————. "River Navigation in the Early Southwest." *Mississippi Valley Historical Review* 15 (June 1928):

————. "Some New Light on Houston's Life Among the Cherokee Indians." *Chronicles of Oklahoma* 9 (June 1931): 139–52.

————. *Fort Gibson. A Brief History.* Muskogee, Okla., n.d.

Foster, William Omer. "The Career of Montfort Stokes in Oklahoma." *Chronicles of Oklahoma* 18 (1940): 35–52.

Franklin, Benjamin. *The Autobiography of Benjamin Franklin.* Private ed. Chicago, 1915.

Frantz, Joe B. *Texas: A History.* New York, 1976.

Friend, B. Llerena. *Sam Houston: The Great Designer.* Austin, 1954.

Frome, Michael. *Strangers in High Places.* Garden City, N.Y., 1966; Knoxville, Tenn., 1980.

Gambrell, Herbert. *Anson Jones, the Last President of Texas.* Austin, 1947.

Godfrey, William. "Campbell Family Historical Subject." *Cheraw Chronicle,* 1939.

Gregory, Jack, and Strickland, Rennard. *Sam Houston with the Cherokees 1829–1833.* Austin, 1967.

Guild, Josephus Conn. *Old Times in Tennessee. With Historical, Personal and Political Scraps and Sketches.* Nashville, Tenn., 1878.

Hamilton, Jeff. *My Master.* Dallas, 1940.

Heritage of Wilkes County. North Wilkesboro, 1982.

Herrera, Rafael Trujillo. *Olvidate de "El Alamo."* Mexico City, 1965.

Hickey, Donald R. *The War of 1812: A Forgotten Conflict.* Urbana-Chicago, 1989.

History of Tennessee. Chicago-Nashville, 1887.

Hodges, Lee. "Mexican Notes and Personalities of the Struggle for Texas." *Rice Institute Pamphlet,* 40 (October 1953): 25–49.

Hofstadter, Richard. *The American Political Tradition.* New York, 1948.

Hogan, William Ransom. "Amusements in the Republic of Texas." *Journal of Southern History* 3 (1937):

Hogan, William Ransom. *The Texas Republic. A Social and Economic History.* Norman, Okla., 1946; reprint, Austin, 1990.

Holland, J. K. "Reminiscences of Austin and Old Washington." *Quarterly of the Texas State Historical Association* 1, no. 2 (October 1897): 92–95.

Hooton, Charles. *St. Louis' Isle or Texiana*. London, 1847.

Hopewell, Clifford. *Sam Houston: Man of Destiny*. Austin, 1987.

Hopkins, Kenneth. *English Poetry: A Short History*. Philadelphia-New York, 1962.

Horsman, Reginald. *The War of 1812*. New York, 1969.

Houston, Sam. *Life of General Sam Houston: A Short Autobiography*. Reprint, Austin, 1964.

———. Papers. Personal Correspondence. Andrew Jackson Houston Collection. Texas State Archives. Austin.

———. *Writings (1813–1863)*. Edited by Amelia W. Williams and Eugene C. Barker. 8 vols. Austin-New York, 1970.

Houston, Rev. Samuel R. *Brief Biographical Accounts of Many Members of the Houston Family*. Cincinatti, 1882.

Hunter, J. Marvin, Jr. "Sam Houston's Duel on Kentucky Soil." *Frontier Times* 28, no. 2 (November 1950): 57–59.

Irving, Washington. *The Journals of Washington Irving*. Edited by William P. Trent and George S. Hellman. New York, 1970.

———. *A Tour on the Prairies*. New York, 1835.

James, Marquis. *The Life of Andrew Jackson*. Indianapolis-New York, 1938.

———. *The Raven*. Indianapolis, 1929. New edition, Austin, 1988.

Jardin, André. *Tocqueville: A Biography*. Translated by Lydia Davis, with Robert Hemenway. New York, 1988.

Jefferson, Thomas. *Writings*. Edited by Merrill D. Peterson. The Library of America. New York, 1984.

Johnston, R. B. "The Stokes Family of 'Mourne Rouge.' "

Jones, Maldwyn F. "Immigration." *Encyclopedia of American Economic History*. Edited by Glenn Porter. New York, 1980.

Josephy, Alvin M., Jr., ed. *The American Heritage Book of Indians*. New York, 1961.

Kemper, James Lawson. "The Mexican War Diary of James Lawson Kemper." *The Virginia Magazine of History and Biography*. 74 (1966):

Kennedy, John F. *Profiles in Courage*. New York, 1955.

Ketcham, Ralph. *James Madison: A Biography*. New York, 1971.

Key, Francis Scott. *Speech of Francis S. Key, Esq., Counsel for Gen. Samuel Houston . . . on His Trial Before the House of Representatives for a Breach of Privilege*. Washington, D.C., 1832.

Kinnear, Duncan Lyle. *Some Events in the History of the Timber Ridge Presbyterian Church and Its Community.* Blacksburg, W. Va., 1958.

Kinsley, James. *The Poems and Songs of Robert Burns.* 3 vols. Oxford, 1968.

Lanman, Charles. *Biographical Annals of the Civil Government of the United States, During Its First Century.* Washington, 1876; reprint, Detroit, 1976.

Lester, C. Edwards. *Life and Achievements of Sam Houston: Hero and Statesman.* New York, 1883.

————. *The Life of Sam Houston: The Hunter, Patriot, and Statesman of Texas. The Only Authentic Memoir of Him Ever Published.* Philadelphia, 1867.

Lewis, Thomas M. N., and Kneberg, Madeline. *Hiwassee Island: An Archaeological Account of Four Tennessee Indian Peoples.* Knoxville, Tenn., 1946.

Linn, John J. *Reminiscences of Fifty Years in Texas.* Austin, 1986.

Long, Jeff. *Duel of Eagles.* New York, 1990.

Love, Thomas B. "Houston, Lincoln and Texas Secession." *Frontier Times* 18 (May 1941): 363–67.

Ludlow, Noah M. *Dramatic Life As I Found It.* St. Louis, 1880.

MacMillan, Dougald; and Jones, Howard Mumford. *Plays of the Restoration and Eighteenth Century.* New York, 1931, 1962.

Magill, Frank N., ed. *Critical Survey of Drama, Foreign Language Series.* 6 vols. Englewood Cliffs, N.J., 1986.

Malone, Dumas. *Jefferson and His Time.* Vol. 1: *Jefferson the Virginian.* Boston, 1948.

McCall, Edith. *Conquering the Rivers. Henry Miller Shreve and the Navigation of America's Inland Waterways.* Baton Rouge, La., 1984.

McPherson, James M. *Battle Cry of Freedom: The Civil War Era.* New York, 1988.

Merk, Frederick. *History of the Westward Movement.* New York, 1978.

Meserve, John Bartlett. "Governor Montfort Stokes." *Chronicles of Oklahoma* 13 (March 1935): 338–40.

Michener, James A. *The Eagle and the Raven.* Austin, 1990.

Middleton, John W. *History of the Regulators and the Moderators.* Fort Worth, 1883; reprint, San Augustine, 1987.

Miller, John Chester. *The Wolf by the Ears: Thomas Jefferson and Slavery.* Charlottesville, Va., 1991

Mooney, James. *Historical Sketch of the Cherokee.* Reprint, Chicago, 1975.

————. *Myths of the Cherokee and Sacred Formulas of the Cherokee.* Reprint, Nashville, Tenn. 1982.

Moore, Michael Rugely. "Houston, Lamar, Bowles and the Removal of the Cherokee Indian." *Touchstone* 2 (1983): 19–21.

Morton, Oren F. *A History of Rockbridge County, Virginia.* Staunton, Va., 1918.

Muir, Andrew Forest, ed. *Texas in 1837: An Anonymous Contemporary Narrative.* Austin, 1958.

Nixon, Pat Ireland. *The Medical Story of Early Texas.* 1946.

Nuttall, Thomas. *A Journal of Travels into the Arkansas Territory During the Year 1819.* Philadelphia, 1821.

O'Connor, Kathryn Stoner. *The Presidio La Bahia.* Austin, 1966.

Olmstead, Frederick Law. *A Journey Through Texas.* Reprint, Austin, 1978.

Ordinances and Resolutions of the Convention. Held in the City of Austin, 28th of January, 1861, February 24th, 1861. Austin, 1861.

Overdyke, W. Darrell. *The Know-Nothing Party in the South.* Baton Rouge, La., 1950.

Parks, Joseph Howard. *John Bell of Tennessee.* Baton Rouge, La., 1950.

Partlow, Miriam. "General Sam Houston in Liberty County." *Liberty, Liberty County, and the Atascosito District.* Austin, 1974.

Peña, José Enrique de la. *With Santa in Texas. A Personal Narrative of the Revolution.* Translated and edited by Carmen Perry. College Station, Texas, 1975

Pessen, Edward. "Social Mobility." *Encyclopedia of American Economic History.* Edited by Glenn Porter. New York, 1980.

Pohl, James W. *The Battle of San Jacinto.* Austin, 1989.

Polk, James K. *Correspondence of James K. Polk.* 3 vols. Edited by Herbert Weaver et al. Nashville, Tenn., 1969–75.

Pope, Alexander. *The Iliad of Homer.* New ed. New York, 1943.

Proctor, Ben H. *The Battle of the Alamo.* Austin, 1986.

Prucha, Francis Paul. "Andrew Jackson's Indian Policy: A Reassessment." *Journal of American History* (December 1969):

Quiller-Couch, Sir Arthur. *The Oxford Book of English Verse: 1250–1918.* New ed. Oxford, 1966.

Reid, John; and Eaton, John Henry. *The Life of Andrew Jackson.* Philadelphia, 1817. Bicentennial ed. Tuscaloosa, Ala., 1974.

Reid, Mary. "Fashions of the Republic." *Quarterly of the Texas State Historical Association* 45 (January 1942): 244–54.

Remini, Robert V. *Andrew Jackson and the Course of American Democracy, 1833–1845.* New York, 1984.

———. *Andrew Jackson and the Course of American Empire, 1767–1821.* New York, 1977.

———. *Andrew Jackson and the Course of American Freedom, 1822–1832.* New York, 1981.

———. *The Legacy of Andrew Jackson. Essays on Democracy, Indian Removal, and Slavery.* Baton Rouge, 1988.

Ridley, Jasper. *Lord Palmerston.* New York, 1970.

Roberts, Octavia. *With Lafayette in America.* Boston-New York, 1919.

Roosevelt, Theodore. *Thomas Hart Benton.* Boston-New York, 1886. Reprint, 1914.

Rouse, Parke, Jr. *Planters and Pioneers: Life in Colonial Virginia.* New York, 1968.

———. *The Great Road From Philadelphia to the South.* New York, 1973.

Sanchez Lamego, General Miguel A. *The Siege and Taking of the Alamo.* Translated by Consuelo Velasco. Santa Fe, N. Mex., 1968.

Sandbo, Anna Irene. "Beginnings of the Secession Movement in Texas." *Southwestern Historical Quarterly* 18 (July 1914): 41–73.

———. "The First Session of the Secession Convention in Texas." *Southwestern Historical Quarterly* 18 (July 1914): 162–94.

Santa Anna, Antonio Lopez de. *The Eagle: The Autobiography of Santa Anna.* Edited by Ann Fears Crawford. Austin, 1967.

Schlesinger, Arthur M., Jr. *The Age of Jackson.* Boston, 1945; reprint, New York, 1989.

Seale, William. *Sam Houston's Wife.* Norman, Okla., 1970.

Shearer, Ernest C. "Sam Houston and Religion." *Tennessee Historical Quarterly*" 20 (March 1961): 38–50.

Shirley, Glenn. *Temple Houston, Lawyer with a Gun.* Norman, Okla., 1980.

Shuffler, Ralph Henderson. *The Houstons at Independence.* Waco, Tex., 1966.

Smithwick, Noah. *The Evolution of a State or Recollections of Old Texas Days.* Austin, 1983.

"Some Episodes in the Life of Gen. Sam Houston." *Bowling Green Messenger.* March 30, 1911.

Sondley, F. A. *A History of Buncombe County, North Carolina.* Asheville, N.C., 1930; reprint, Spartanburg, S.C., 1977.

Spotswood, Alexander. *The Official Letters of Alexander Spotswood*. 2 vols. Richmond, Va., 1882–85.

Starkey, Marion L. *The Cherokee Nation*. New York, 1946; reprint, 1972.

Sterne, Adolphus. *Hurrah for Texas: The Diary of Adolphus Sterne*. Edited by Archied P. McDonald. Austin, 1986.

Terrell, A. W. "Recollections of General Sam Houston." *Southwestern Historical Quarterly* 16 (October 1912): 113–36.

Tompkins, E. P., M.D., and Davis, J. Lee. *The Natural Bridge and Its Surroundings*. Natural Bridge, 1939.

Turner, Martha Anna. *Sam Houston and His Twelve Women*. Austin, 1966.

United States Congress. *Register of Debates*. 22nd Congress. December 5, 1831–May 9, 1832.

Van Deusen, Glyndon G. *The Life of Henry Clay*. Boston, 1937.

Waggoner, Leland T. "Sam Houston's School." *Chattanooga Sunday Times Magazine*. December 15, 1935.

Wall, Bernhardt, and Williams, Amelia. *Following General Sam Houston: From 1793 to 1863*. Austin, 1935.

Wallace, Ernest, and Vigness, David M. *Documents of Texas History*. Austin, 1963.

War of the Rebellion: A Compilation of the Official Records of the Union and Confederate Armies. Washington, D.C., 1890.

Warren, Robert Penn. *How Texas Won Her Freedom: The Story of Sam Houston and the Battle of San Jacinto*. San Jacinto, Tex., 1959.

Washington, George. *The Writings of George Washington*. Washington, D.C., 1940.

Webb, Walter Prescott, and Branda, Eldon Stephen, eds. *The Handbook of Texas*. Austin, 1952–76.

Westwood, Howard C. "President Lincoln's Overture to Sam Houston." *Southwestern Historical Quarterly* 89 (October 1984): 125–44.

Weyland, Leonie Rummel; and Wade, Houston. *An Early History of Fayette County*. Lagrange, 1936.

Whitley, Edith Rucke. *Membership Roster and Soldiers: The Tennessee Society of the Daughters of the American Revolution*. Nashville, Tenn., 1961

Wilbarger, J. W. *Indian Depredations in Texas*. Austin, 1889.

Williams, Alfred Mason. *Sam Houston and the War of Independence in Texas*. Boston-New York, 1893.

Williams, Samuel Cole. *Early Travels in the Tennessee Country 1540–1800.* Johnson City, Tenn., 1928.

Wisehart, M. K. *Sam Houston: American Giant.* New York, 1962.

Wooten, Dudley G., ed. *A Comprehensive History of Texas, 1685–1897.* 2 vols. Dallas, 1898; reprint, Austin, 1986.

Worth, S. Ray. *Tennessee Cousins: A History of Tennessee People.* Austin, 1950.

Wright, Muriel H. "Early Navigation Along the Arkansas and Red Rivers in Oklahoma." *Chronicles of Oklahoma,* March 1930, pp. 65–88.

Yoakum, Henderson. *History of Texas.* Reprinted in Vol. I, Dudley G. Wooten, ed. *A Comprehensive History of Texas, 1685–1687.* Dallas, 1898; reprint, Austin, 1986.

PHOTOGRAPHIC CREDITS

Archives Division—Texas State Library: photos 1, 6, 7, 13, 20, 21, 31, 35, 36

The Center for American History, the University of Texas at Austin: photos, 17, 18, 29

From the Collection of the Dallas Historical Society: photo 16

Daughters of the Republic of Texas Library at the Alamo: photo 4

Houston Public Library: photo 14

Sam Houston Memorial Museum: photos 15, 19, 27, 28, 32, 33

C. E. Lester, *The Life of Sam Houston* (Philadelphia: C. G. Evans, 1860): photos 8, 9

Library of Congress: photos 3, 22, 37

The National Archives, U.S. Signal Corps: photo 2

Punch, December 4, 1847: photo 24

The San Jacinto Museum of History, Houston, Texas: photos 5, 10

Alex E. Sweet and J. Amory Knox, *On a Mexican Mustang Through Texas,* 1883/The University of Texas, Institute of Texan Cultures: photo 11

Tennessee Historical Society, Tennessee State Library and Archives: photos 25, 26

Tennessee State Library and Archives: photo 23

Vanity Fair, April 6, 1861: photo 34

Vanity Fair/The Center for American History, The University of Texas at Austin: photo 30

Yale Collection of Western Americana, Beinecke Rare Book and Manuscript Library: photo 12

Index

ABOUT THE AUTHOR

MARSHALL DE BRUHL has edited and contributed to many works of history and biography, including the *Dictionary of American Biography* and the *Dictionary of American History.* He lives in New York City and Asheville, North Carolina.

ABOUT THE TYPE

This book was set in Galliard, a typeface designed by Matthew Carter for the Mergenthaler Linotype Company in 1978. Galliard is based on the sixteenth-century typefaces of Robert Granjon, which give it classic lines yet interject a contemporary look.